Thomas G. Bonney

The Alpine Regions of Switzerland and the Neighbouring Countries

A pedestrian's notes on their physical features, scenery, and natural history

Thomas G. Bonney

The Alpine Regions of Switzerland and the Neighbouring Countries
A pedestrian's notes on their physical features, scenery, and natural history

ISBN/EAN: 9783337085063

Printed in Europe, USA, Canada, Australia, Japan

Cover: Foto ©Andreas Hilbeck / pixelio.de

More available books at **www.hansebooks.com**

THE ALPINE REGIONS

OF SWITZERLAND

AND THE NEIGHBOURING COUNTRIES.

Cambridge:
PRINTED BY C. J. CLAY, M.A.
AT THE UNIVERSITY PRESS.

THE MATTERHORN FROM THE VAL TOURNANCHE.

THE ALPINE REGIONS

OF SWITZERLAND

AND THE NEIGHBOURING COUNTRIES;

A PEDESTRIAN'S NOTES

ON THEIR PHYSICAL FEATURES, SCENERY, AND
NATURAL HISTORY.

BY

T. G. BONNEY, M.A., F.G.S., &c.

FELLOW OF ST JOHN'S COLLEGE, CAMBRIDGE;
MEMBER OF THE ALPINE CLUB.

WITH ILLUSTRATIONS BY E. WHYMPER.

Cambridge:
DEIGHTON, BELL, AND CO.
LONDON: BELL AND DALDY.
1868

THIS VOLUME IS DEDICATED

TO

WILLIAM MATHEWS, M.A.,

JOHN CLARKE HAWKSHAW, M.A.,

AND MY OTHER TRAVELLING COMPANIONS,

IN REMEMBRANCE OF

OUR PLEASANT ALPINE WANDERINGS.

PREFACE

So many works upon the Alps have appeared during the last ten years, that an apology is almost required for adding to their number. Still, the majority of these are monographs, devoted, either to special topics —as the books of Forbes and Tyndall, or to particular districts—such as Dauphiné, the Oberland, and the Bernina, rather than works attempting to give a general view of the very diverse subjects of interest connected with the Alpine Chain. I have therefore in the present volume endeavoured to put together a few notes, which may serve not only to give those who cannot travel a general idea of the Alpine Regions, but also, at the same time, be useful as a kind of handy-book to those who are purposing to visit them.

I must not, however, be supposed to have attempted anything of the nature of a formal guide-book, scientific or topographical. Had I endeavoured the one, it must have been a mere compilation; for I cannot pretend to more than a general acquaintance with such subjects; while the other has been made needless by *The Alpine Guide*,—so admirably edited by my friend Mr Ball,—and by many more, designed rather for the ordinary tourist, such as the Guides of Murray, Baedeker, &c., and (in French) the valuable *Itinéraires* of M. Joanne.

The two points, then, that I have kept before me in writing this book are :—(1) That it should not be confined to any single district or country, but should endeavour to deal with the Alps as a whole; restricting myself only, where I could, to the properly *mountain* regions; (2) that it should as far as possible touch upon all the principal points of interest connected with them, and aim to be popular and general, rather than exhaustive. I felt that I could the better attempt the former, because I happen to have a tolerably general acquaintance with the whole chain, having in the course of ten journeys wandered, usually on foot, over every Alpine district included between lines drawn, one through Genoa westward, and the other through Venice northward; during which I have crossed about eighty mountain passes, explored a good deal of rarely visited country, and had, I believe, a fair view of every important peak in the Alps, from the Viso to the Terglou. With regard to the second purpose, I have endeavoured to be accurate, but at the same time have avoided, as far as possible, scientific nomenclature; except where—as in the chapters on natural history—it seemed better to give the Latin appellations of a few animals and plants, the trivial names being often so very uncertain and variable.

In the hope of rendering the work more readable, I have cast it as much as possible into a narrative form; this must excuse the rather frequent occurrence of the first personal pronoun. If one has seen a thing, it seems simpler to say 'I have seen,' than to use a periphrasis which, to me at least, often seems to savour of the 'pride that apes humility.' The same form has been used even in statements which now may be regarded as common matter, describing things as I saw them; although they may already have been seen and described by many others, and I may, in some cases, have used their accounts to refresh my own memory. My endeavour has been to record, to the best of my power, the various things which strike and impress persons who, like myself, have received an ordinary English education, feel a general interest in scientific subjects, and have a sincere love for the beauties of Nature.

The books to which I have chiefly referred are *The Alpine Guide*, which I have generally followed for nomenclature and the altitude of mountains; the delightful volumes of Forbes and Tyndall, for the theories of Glacier Motion; and Tschudi's *Les Alpes* (the authorised translation of the original work *Thierleben der Alpenwelt*) for the natural history; aided occasionally in this last by the kind suggestions of my more scientific friends, chief among whom I may thank Professor Newton. Other works, which have been more sparingly used, are noted from time to time in the text. I did not see Mr Morell's *Scientific Guide to Switzerland*, which appears a very careful and laborious compilation, until my own book was written, and the greater part of it in print. I have also to thank my friend, the Rev. G. F. Browne, for some useful hints.

I cannot hope to have wholly escaped error; still I trust that no very serious mistakes or omissions will be found; and if this little volume help any travellers to enjoy their Alpine journey more, on the principle involved in the old story, 'Eyes and No-eyes,' the trouble which I have taken with it, and that has really been considerable, will be amply repaid.

T. G. B.

TABLE OF CONTENTS.

CHAPTER I.

PAGE

General configuration of the Alps.—Signs of pressure and **elevation**.—Effects of denudation; water, frost, and ice.—Example of the **Col de la Lauze**.—Beds and plains of gravel and detritus.—Cause of elevation of mountains.—Scenery affected by the nature of rocks.—Rocks divided into Crystallines and Coherents.—Compact crystallines.—Slaty crystallines.—Cleavage and foliation.—Compact **and slaty coherents.—Effects of weather** upon these rocks.—Scenery of compact crystallines; their distribution, and that of slaty crystallines.—Distribution of **compact and slaty coherents**.—Mountain forms.—Effects of weather on cleavage, stratification, and joints.—Formation of precipices.—Gneiss and Dolomite.—Pyramidal peaks.—Forms of summits.—Sketch of the Alpine Districts.—Cottian Alps.—High Alps of Dauphiné.—Savoy Alps.—Graian Alps.—Pennine Range.—Oberland.—Lepontine Alps.—Rhætian Alps.—Lombard Alps.—Noric Alps.—Italian Tyrol.—Carnic and Julian Alps 1

CHAPTER II.

Formation of valleys.—Cracks.—Gorges of erosion.—Gorge of the Trient. Cirques.—Valleys of outcrop.—Valleys of depression.—The Alpine Lakes.—**Lac de** Bourget.—Lac d'Annecy.—Lac Léman.—The Lowland Lakes.—Lake of Zurich.—Lake of Constance.—Lakes of Thun, Brienz, Lucerne, and Wallenstadt.—Lakes of the Eastern Alps.—The **Italian** Lakes, **Orta,** Maggiore, Lugano, Como, Iseo, and Garda.—Alpine Waterfalls . 36

CHAPTER III.

Glaciers.—Expedition on the Gorner Glacier.—Terminal ice-cave.—Moraine.—Crevasses; cause of their formation.—Surface of a **glacier.—Glacier** tables.—Channels.—Moulins.—Veined structure in glacier ice.—Halt at Auf der Platte.—Ascent towards the Lys-joch.—Séracs.—Formation of a glacier.—Crevasses in névé.—Summit of the Pass.—A rapid descent.— Cause of glacier motion.—Dilatation theory.—Viscous theory.—Dr Tyndall's objections.—His explanation.—Marks of past glacier-action.—Moraines.— Perched blocks.—Explanation of their presence.—The erratics of Monthey and the Jura.—Rounded, polished, and scratched rocks.—Erosive power of glaciers.—Epoch of their greatest extension.—Oscillations of glaciers in historic times 55

CHAPTER IV.

Glacières.—Expedition to some near Annecy.—How to get breakfast.— Ascent to the Glacière du Grand Anu.—Its entrance.—Description of interior.—Prismatic structure of the ice.—Glacière de l'Enfer.—A subglacial reservoir.—Glacière de Chappet-sur-Villaz.—Hidden tunnel in the ice.— Return to Aviernoz.—Cause of Glacières.—Caverns.—The Beaume des Vaudois.—Wind-lochs.—Perforated rocks.—Legend of St Martin.—Springs. —Salt Springs of Moutiers Tarentaise and Bex.—Baths.—The Springs of Pfäfers and gorge of the Tamina.—Mines 88

CHAPTER V.

Avalanches.—Ice avalanches.—The avalanches of the Jungfrau.—Fall of the Bies Glacier.—Dust avalanches.—Ground avalanches.—Accidents from avalanches on higher peaks.—Accident of the Col du Géant.—Slip on the Piz Mortaratsch.—Avalanche on the Haut-de-Cry.—Other avalanches. —Effect of noise.—Bergfalls.—Falls of the Diablerets.—Fall of the Rossberg. —Destruction of Pleurs.—Fall of Monte Antelao.—Land-slip at Cortina.— Floods.—Bursting of the lake formed by the Gétroz Glacier.—Storms.— Earthquakes.—Tourmentes.—Tourmente on the Grimsel.—Wind on Mont Blanc.—The Föhn.—Thunder storms.—In a thunder cloud.—Colour of the snow.—Luminous snow.—Red snow.—Colours of the sky.—Sunset on Mont Blanc.—Causes of the after-glow 113

CHAPTER VI.

Alpine Mammalia.—The Brown Bear.—Varieties.—Its habits.—Fight with a bear.—'A pleasant vulgar tale.'—Bears of Berne.—The wolf, its habits.—The chase.—Anecdote.—The fox, its habits.—The lynx.—The wild cat.—The badger.—Other mammalia.—The beaver.—Rabbits and hares.— The marmot, its habits.—The chamois, its habits and agility.—Chamois' horns.—Its food.—Bezoar.—Sense of hearing and smell.—An unexpected meeting.—Adventure of a chamois hunter, 'vestigia nulla retrorsum.'—End of a chamois hunter.—Poaching feuds.—The bouquetin, its horns.—Habits. —Legends.—Other quadrupeds 160

CHAPTER VII.

The Alpine Birds.—The lämmergeier.—Its appetite.—Cases of carrying off children.—The golden eagle.—Other birds of prey.—The raven.—Its thievish habits.—Choughs.—Nutcrackers.—Other birds.—Game birds.—Water birds.—Fish.—Reptiles.—Frogs and toads.—Salamanders.—Lizards. Snakes.—Mollusca.—Lepidoptera.—Beetles, &c.—**Fleas.**—**Glacier fleas.**   190

CHAPTER VIII.

Alpine Botany.—Deciduous **trees.—Coniferous trees.**—Larch, Spruce, Silver, and Scotch fir, Arolla.—Brushwood.—Dwarf pine.—Junipers.—Rhododendrons.—Fruit-bearing **shrubs.—Alpine flowers.—Alpine ferns, mosses, and lichens**   208

CHAPTER IX.

Agriculture.—Corn.—Vegetables.—Hay, **dangers** of the wild-hay cutter. —Vine.—Making wine.—Forests.—Wood-cutting.—Perils of that work.— Slide of Alpnach.—Châlet life.—Bread.—The châlets.—The different kinds of châlets.—A Bernese farmer's house.—Châlet villages.—Cow and sheep châlets.—Nights in châlets.—Châlet des bergers de Provence.—The management of the cows, and of the dairy.—Cheese making.—Ranz des vaches.— Sheep and shepherds.—Bergamesque sheep.—Goats.—St Bernard dogs.   227

CHAPTER X.

The Alpine Passes.—Mont Genèvre.—Col du Lautaret.—Mont Cenis. —Tunnel through the Alps.—Little St Bernard.—Simplon.—St Gothard. —The Bernardino and Splügen.—The Maloya.—The Julier.—The Albula.— The Bernina Pass.—Reschen-scheideck.—Toblach-plateau.—The Brenner. —The Furka.—The Oberalp Joch.—The Stelvio.—The Ampezzo Pass.— Convent of the Great St Bernard.—Mule and foot paths.—Glacier passes.— The Col Durand and the Trift Joch   261

CHAPTER XI.

Alpine legends.—Dragons.—**Various** species.—A winter in a dragon's den.—The dragon stone of Lucerne.—Legend of the Clariden Alps.—The **Lost Valley.**—Mont Pilatus.—Legend of Heiligenblut.—Witchcraft.—The **lunatics of** Morzine.—Local customs.—Burials.—Crucifixes.—Amusements. **Abbaye des Vignerons.**—Welcome to the sun.—Antiquities.—Celtic.—Lake settlements.—Architecture, Roman and mediæval.—Fortresses.—Old castles. —'Holy Mountains.'—History.—Persecutions of the **Vaudois**.—**La Rentrée glorieuse**.—The **story of Tell**, and the war for freedom.—Growth of the Swiss confederation.—The campaign of 1799.—Napoleon's passage of the **Great** St Bernard.—Macdonald's passage of the Splügen.—The Tyrolese rising.—**Hofer** 285

CHAPTER XII.

Season for travelling.—Alpine districts.—Companionship.—Baggage.—**Hints to** walkers.—Alpine dangers.—Falling stones, ice, or snow.—Insecure footing.—The Matterhorn accident.—Use of the rope.—Conclusion . 320

LIST OF ILLUSTRATIONS.

PLATE I.
The Matterhorn from the **Val Tournanche (south view)**.
(The route followed in the earlier attempted **ascents lies** for the most **part** along the left-hand ridge; the summit has now been reached from this side also.)

PLATE II.
The Pointe des Ecrins and Crête du Pelvoux **from the Col de la Lauze (Dauphiné)**.

PLATE III.
The Drei Zinnen from Landro (Ampezzo Pass).

PLATE IV.
Entrance to the Glacière du Grand **Anu**.

PLATE V.
Interior **of the Glacière du Grand Anu**.

FIGURE 1. (Page 5).
Diagram of broken and contorted Strata in a Cliff of the Oldenhorn.

FIGURE 2. (Page 16).
Diagram of joints and stratification in **Dolomite**.

FIGURE 3. (Page 19).
Effects **of weather on** joints and stratification. **Dolomite in decay**.

FIGURE 4. (Page 21).
Diagram of Peaks **formed of fragments of contorted strata**.

FIGURE 5. (Page 57).
Terminal ice-cave **of a glacier**.

FIGURE 6. (Page 60).
Crevasses on a glacier.

FIGURE 7. (Page 94).
Diagram of prismatic structure in ice.

FIGURE 8. (Page 109).
The Gorge of the Tamina, from near the springs.

FIGURE 9. (Page 176).
Chamois descending to feed.

FIGURE 10. (Page 187).
Bouquetin.

FIGURE 11. (Page 236).
Châlet Village, with the Sasso di Pelmo, from above Caprile (Italian Tyrol).

FIGURE 12. (Page 243).
Swiss Châlet.

FIGURE 13. (Page 276).
Swiss Carts, &c.

FIGURE 14. (Page 321).
View in the Graians. The Grivola from the Col de Chécruit.

FIGURE 15. (Page 333).
Geological Section across the Chain of Mont Blanc, from the Brévent to the Mont Chétif.

NOTE. Plates I.—III. and Figures 2—4, 11, 14, are selected with a view of illustrating some of the more characteristic mountain forms. Plates I., II., with Figure 14, representing the slaty crystallines; Plate III., with Figures 2—4, 11, the harder coherents. All the woodcuts, except Plates IV., V., and Figures 7, 15, are by Mr Whymper. For these two Plates, I have to thank the Publishers of *Good Words*, who have kindly permitted me to use blocks originally engraved for that periodical. All, except Figures 5, 6, 8—13, 15 are from my sketches; but it is only just that I should express my sense of how much some have gained in artistic effect, without the slightest loss in accuracy, by passing through Mr Whymper's hands. Figure 8 is from a photograph, one in a set of admirable views of the Tamina Gorge, taken by Mr England, who has most courteously allowed me to have it copied.

THE ALPINE REGIONS.

ERRATA.

Page 5, in explanation of Figure insert *E Dark limestone*
,, 24 line 24, for *easternmost* read *westernmost*
,, 44 ,, 23, for *Righi* read *Rigi*
,, 54 ,, 12, for *Chrysophrase* read *Chrysoprase*
,, 104 ,, 14, for *glacière* read *glacier*
,, 106 ,, 18, for *Lantaret* read *Lautaret*
,, 108 ,, 27, *seven hundred feet.* Perhaps this estimate is too great.
,, 110 ,, 21, for *latter* read *cliffs*
,, — ,, last line, for *right* read *left*
,, 141 ,, 28, for *lea* read *lee*
,, 202 ,, 8, *porthoptera; sic*, in the passage cited, probably *orthoptera*
,, 309 ,, 7, for *Faust* read *Furst*

with the Maritime Alps at the head of the Gulf of Genoa. It would be bounded on the east by a narrow land-locked strait, now the valley of the Rhone and Saone. A still narrower strait, through which the former river at present escapes from the mountains, would cut it off from the long ridges of the Jura; and all along its northern face, protected here and there by clusters of islets, and broken by fiords like the western coasts of Scotland or of Norway, would roll the broad waters of the German Ocean. Its eastern extremity would sink down into an

FIGURE 7. (Page 94).
Diagram of prismatic structure in ice.

FIGURE 8. (Page 109).
The Gorge of the Tamina, from near the springs.

FIGURE 9. (Page 176).
Chamois descending to feed.

FIGURE 10. (Page 187).
Bouquetin.

FIGURE 11. (Page 236).

...who have kindly permitted me to use blocks originally engraved for that periodical. All, except Figures 5, 6, 8—13, 15 are from my sketches; but it is only just that I should express my sense of how much some have gained in artistic effect, without **the slightest** loss in accuracy, by passing through Mr Whymper's hands. Figure 8 is from a photograph, **one in a set** of admirable **views** of the Tamina Gorge, **taken** by Mr England, **who has most** courteously **allowed me to** have it copied.

THE ALPINE REGIONS.

CHAPTER I.

If the whole surface of Europe were to be depressed vertically about 500 yards, it would be changed from a continent into several groups of mountainous islands. The loftiest and most conspicuous among these would lie in a general direction from E.N.E. to W.S.W., between the 43rd and 48th parallel of latitude; with the exception of one long narrow spur, which would extend for many miles to the S.E. This group would be composed of the mountain chains now classed together under the general title 'The Alps'; the spur being the Apennines, which at present form the backbone of central Italy and the southern boundary of the great Lombardo-Venetian plain, and are fused with the Maritime Alps at the head of the Gulf of Genoa. It would be bounded on the east by a narrow land-locked strait, now the valley of the Rhone and Saone. A still narrower strait, through which the former river at present escapes from the mountains, would cut it off from the long ridges of the Jura; and all along its northern face, protected here and there by clusters of islets, and broken by fiords like the western coasts of Scotland or of Norway, would roll the broad waters of the German Ocean. Its eastern extremity would sink down into an inland sea like that of Marmora; to which the narrower parts of the present Danube valley would be a Dardanelles and a Bosporus. This mass of mountains, the great highlands of Central Europe, is therefore of the utmost physical and geographical importance. Rising in places to a height of more than 15,000 feet above the sea, and covered for an extent of many thousand square miles with perpetual snow, it is the chief feeder of four of the principal rivers in Europe, the Po, the Rhone, the Rhine, and the Danube. But for those barren fields of ice high up among the silent crags, the seeming home of winter and death, these great arteries of life would every summer dwindle down to paltry streams, feebly wandering over stone strewn beds. Stand, for example, on some mountain spur and look down on the Lombard plain, all one rich carpet of wheat and maize, of rice and vine; the life of those myriad threads of green and gold is fed from these icy peaks which stand out against the northern sky in such strange and solemn contrast. As it is with the Po, so is it with the Rhine and the Rhone; both of which issue from the Alps as broad swelling streams; so too with the Danube, which although it does not rise in them, yet receives from the Inn and the Drave almost all the drainage of the Eastern districts.

Nor is this the only interest of these mountain chains. Since they rise to a height, which compensates for difference of latitude and gives them a temperature ranging from almost tropical heat to arctic cold, plants, relics of an old world flora, have retreated before the advancing wave of heat; and isolated families, clustering round the mountain summits in various parts of Europe, shew how districts now far apart were once united, when in the glacial epoch the climate of central Europe was very different from what it is at present. Here also birds and beasts elsewhere extinct have found a refuge, among the untrodden peaks, from the attacks of man; who himself has often, in like manner, sought in the same fastnesses protection against the assaults of a stronger brother. It is therefore to be expected that the Alps, at once the barrier between and the natural camp of refuge of northern and southern Europe, should offer many subjects of interest to the traveller, the naturalist, and the historian. To describe some of these will be the endeavour of the present volume.

So far as the writer's experience has gone, until, at any rate, very lately, there were few parts of the world about which untravelled folk entertained vaguer notions than the Alps; in fact he has often suspected some of his questioners of believing that Switzerland was a generally 'lumpy' country, with one great peak, Mont Blanc, in the middle of it. The efforts of the Alpine Club and the increased facilities of travelling have no doubt partly dispelled this error; but a good many maps, still in common use, depict the Alps as a single ridge encircling Italy; or, when compelled by the largeness of their scale into a little more detail, indulge in some suggestive scratchings between the rivers, and pepper the surface with a few names, often wrong, in which important and unimportant are mingled together in most admired confusion. A brief account of the general configuration of the Alpine region may therefore not be useless, in the course of which the most probable explanations of it will be slightly noticed.

A very slight examination of a good map, especially one in which the rivers are picked out in a different colour, will shew that over the greater part of the Alps the valleys may be divided into two classes; the one containing those which have a general direction from E.N.E. to W.S.W.; the other, those whose course is at right angles to this line; and the former will be found to be, as a rule, much more extensive than the latter. This configuration prevails almost universally throughout the Western and Central Alps[1]; in the Eastern

[1] The above division though without geographical significance is convenient for purposes of reference. The Western Alps include the mountains of France,

the longer valleys run nearly east and west, the shorter nearly north and south. However, it may be correctly stated that as a general rule the valleys in the Alps are divided into two classes at right angles to each other. This unity of plan naturally suggests the idea that the upheaval of the Alps was not produced by numerous isolated forces, acting independently of each other as to time, place, and direction, but by one or more systems, in obedience to some general law. A closer examination confirms this supposition, though it shews at the same time that there may have been oscillations and variations in the actions of the upheaving forces, and that they have rather operated with greatest intensity round a number of separate centres, than, as at first sight would appear most natural, along lines corresponding with the general direction of the principal chains. Hence, if we drew a line about each of these central districts we should find that, roughly speaking, the map was covered by a number of ovals of various sizes which were so arranged that their longer diameters corresponded generally with the direction of the principal chains.

Geologists are not yet agreed upon the causes which have played the principal part in giving to the Alps their present configuration. Most rocks, whatever their present condition may be, were once soft mud at the bottom of the Ocean. Assuming then that its level has not greatly altered, and there is no reason to suppose that this has been the case, many of the Alpine cliffs must have been raised through a vertical height of several thousand feet. It is also probable that these rocks were originally deposited in tolerably horizontal beds. Therefore where they are so no longer, they must have been tilted during the process of upheaval. In the Alps we very commonly

Savoy, Piedmont and the main chain as far as Monte Rosa; the Central take the west of Switzerland, and the adjoining parts of Lombardy and Tyrol; while the Eastern contain the remaining district.

find them thus tilted, often indeed only slightly, but occasionally at a very considerable angle; in some places they are even rolled and crumpled together, like the leaves of a pamphlet when it is doubled up again and again, or those of a book when it is crushed together at the two ends. Now, if instead of flexible paper, we were squeezing sideways some more solid

(Fig. 1.) Rough Sketch of cliff in one of the northern spurs of the Oldenhorn shewing crumpled and broken strata. From hills N.E. of Ormond dessus.
A. Limestone.   C. Limestone.
B. Clayey shale, darker and banded in upper part.   D. Banded shale.
S. Snow.   ×. Hill in foreground.   × ×. Glen.

substance, or pressing it upwards from below while its two ends were confined, it would obviously crack and split in places, and if we continued the pressure, the layers would often be forced far apart. As these signs of pressure are very evident in the Alpine rocks, this question naturally suggests itself,—Are the valleys which furrow the country cracks where the rising strata have yielded to the pressure below, or depressions produced by inequalities in its exertion; or are they to be explained, wholly or partially, by some other cause? The answer first returned was that they were in most cases cracks; in a few, folds in the superficial strata; and little note was taken of any other agency than pressure. There is no doubt that the general direction of the valleys does, in a very remarkable degree, coincide with what must have been the lines of greatest strain upon the strata; if we suppose, as the form of the crystalline masses appears to justify us in doing, that the greatest upheaving forces were exerted over a series of oval areas with a certain definite arrangement. Still, a careful examination will shew that, though the general course of the valleys may be due to pressure, resulting perhaps from subterranean heat, it is rather by sub-aerial and sub-aqueous agencies that we must seek to explain their form and consequently the contour of the mountains. Denudation, that is, the action of air and water, has been producing its effects both while the Alps were rising, and since they came to rest: it is still at work; the countless streams which, fed by the snows and rains, ceaselessly leap down each mountain side, furrow its cliffs with gorges and its slopes with glens, saw deep notches in the rocky barriers of lakes, and thus draining off their waters either leave the smooth floor of ooze, the accumulation of centuries, to become green meadows, or begin again to transfer it to some lower level. No doubt when first the hills began to rise above the sea, its waves wore each summit into cliffs and ridges, like those which we may now see around any rock-bound coast. Perhaps too some of the great rock amphitheatres may have been thus formed, at the head of inland fiords. The sea's marks are still, I think, plain upon many of our western Welsh hills, but time's carking tooth has made it difficult in the case of the Alps to assign to salt and fresh water their proper share in the work. The latter may be said to have had the advantage of the last word; and, like the finisher of a statue, it has obliterated the traces of the pointer's chisel. Some persons indeed dilate so largely upon the effects of erosion as to apparently forget that, even upon their own shewing, there must be a cliff before there can be a gorge, and a hill before a glen. Before ever the stream began to carve, there must have been some well-marked fold or crack; or else the valleys would follow a far more uncertain and eccentric course than they now do. It would be almost impossible that water finding its way out of an irregularly upheaved mass of land should have ploughed out over so great an extent of country systems of valleys which, as has been already said, obey this general law, that the shorter trenches lie from N.N.W. to S.S.E. and the longer from E.N.E. to W.S.W.

Still, although we may refuse to allow water to be the sole agent in the sculpture of the Alps, there can be no doubt that it has been a very important one; and that not only when in a liquid state, but also in a solid. Nature often employs the ice-wedge as well as the water-saw. Water in freezing expands with tremendous force. Many of us have had too much experience of this property from the burst pipes which make a thaw such an ill-omened word to a town householder, so painfully suggestive of slop and discomfort, followed by a long plumber's bill. The rock, then, being traversed in several directions by cracks, about which we shall presently have more to say, allows the water to permeate it; this by freezing splits off great blocks and sends them thundering down the cliffs. The snow also upon the higher summits descends towards the valleys in large masses of moving ice, called glaciers, which wear away the rock beneath. Some persons, indeed, struck by the force of these huge ice-ploughs, which were once far vaster than they now are, have assigned to them a very important share in scooping out the Alpine valleys and lakes. This question is too long a one for discussion here; but my own opinion, which has been formed after some study and a careful examination of many parts of the Alps, is that the erosive power of glaciers has been vastly over-estimated by their advocates; and that, though they may sometimes deepen a hollow or widen a valley which already exists, they in general do little more than wear away inequalities in the surface, and are to the other agents very much what the emery-paper is to the chisel.

We talk commonly of the eternal hills—they are as perishable as every other thing in this world. There is a spot, more than eleven thousand feet above the sea, in the Alps of Dauphiné[1]—it is only one instance among many—where there is a small island of dark shale upon a great plateau of hard crystalline rock. Stand upon it, and you may see some four miles to the north a long range of the same shale; then turn round to the south, and you may perhaps catch, through a battlement of jagged peaks, a glimpse of a dark rolling line to the south which marks the presence of the same deposit. This little island and one or two similar to it give us every reason to suppose that these shales once extended over all this intervening space, some twenty-five miles across, which is now occupied by the highest peaks of Dauphiné: all that mass, many hundred feet thick, has been removed by sea or by river and spread over the plains of south-eastern France. Stand by the Arve as it rushes through the valley of Chamouni; its waters are not that liquid crystal which poets couple with mountain streams, but as turbid as if nature had been having a heavy wash and was emptying away the suds. Take up a glass-full, and let the contents settle; the fluid will become transparent, and a fine mud cover the bottom. Examine this sediment under a microscope, or even with a pocket lens; you will find it consists of minute fragments of those minerals which compose the rocks in the neighbouring mountains. Not a year then passes without something being taken from the mass of Mont Blanc and borne away by the Rhone, how far we cannot say—perhaps to increase the ooze at the bottom of the Gulf of Lyons. The plains of south-eastern France, North-Italy and Bavaria, from which in many places the mountains rise as from a sea, are overspread with vast layers of sand and gravel, every pebble and every atom in which has been brought down from the Alps; nay, more, the beds of many of the larger valleys are level, often marshy, plains formed of similar deposits. So rapidly indeed do the mountains rise from them,

---

[1] The Col de la Lauze, leading from La Grave to St Christophe.

that in many places you may stand on turf, level as a bowling-green, and place your hand against a precipice. These valleys also seem to shew that there have been changes in the level of the Alps. It is scarcely possible that such smooth plains of gravel can have been deposited without that part of the country being under water. In some cases this may have been done when the Alpine lakes were more extensive than at present, but this explanation can hardly be applied to all, for the valleys have often been filled up by a considerable thickness of drift below the spots where barriers exist, which has again been cut through to a depth of many feet by the existing stream. Any one who mounts to some commanding spot on the side of a great valley, such, for example, as the upper Rhone, or Rhine, will see that almost without exception a sloping talus of earth forms a kind of glacis in front of the entrance to every lateral valley. Some would attribute this formation to the overflowings of the torrent in times of flood; but, seeing that its stream often passes through a ravine cut in the talus, the explanation, though no doubt sometimes a true one, does not appear sufficient. If, however, the main valley were under water, the diminished velocity of the torrent on entering it would cause the immediate deposit of a large quantity of the material with which it is charged, and so a bank of this kind would be formed. I am therefore inclined to think that when the Alps had assumed a contour corresponding roughly with the present, and were on the point of being finally raised above the sea, they appeared for a while as an island group pierced by long fiords, into whose calm, land-locked, recesses the glacier streams poured their turbid waters. This has probably happened, though on a smaller scale, in our Welsh hills, and Switzerland then would not have been very unlike the present condition of some parts of the north-west coast of Norway. The last traces of marine deposits appear (so far as I know) to be anterior to the epoch when the glaciers had their greatest extension[1]; and the occurrence of freshwater gravels, sand, and even limestones, in some of the lowlands abutting on the Alps, seems to shew that, since they rose for the last time above the waves, considerable denudation has taken place, during which probably the rivers were larger and the lakes and marshes much more extensive and numerous than now.

What the agent has been which has upraised these huge masses, it is hard to say. Probably in many cases it was the expansion of underlying beds which were being melted by subterranean heat; how this was generated we are yet hardly in a position to decide; one thing however is pretty clear, that large masses of rock have been, in familiar language, baked or stewed while subjected to enormous pressure, or have been fused in the vast crucible of nature till as great a change has been wrought as when glass is produced from nitre and sand, or porcelain from clay. It is however enough for our present purpose to know that heat and pressure have been called into play to raise on high the mountains which the atmospheric forces are as constantly endeavouring to lay low.

It is therefore very clear that the scenery of any part of the Alps will depend in a great measure upon the nature of the prevailing rock and its power of resisting the action of air and water. Now we may roughly, but sufficiently for our present purpose, divide rocks into crystallines and coherents[2]. The first of these divisions contains all rocks which either have once been in a molten state or, if originally stratified, have been subsequently much altered by heat and pressure. Of these the former have been called 'compact crystallines:' a class which includes the different varieties of granite, trap, and lava; the latter, or slaty crystallines, were no doubt once sedimentary

---

[1] See Chapter III.
[2] Used by Mr Ruskin in the fourth volume of *Modern Painters*, a book that no lover of the Alps should be without.

rocks, but the above causes have very often entirely effaced their original structure, while bestowing upon them a new one, which in some cases is called cleavage, in others foliation. A rock is said to shew 'cleavage' when it can be cleft or split in a direction different from that of the layers in which it was originally deposited; as is the case with Welsh or Cumberland roofing-slate, in which the 'bedding' can sometimes be seen inclined at an angle to the surface planes. This structure is generally supposed to be mainly due to great pressure, and to take place along planes at right angles to the direction of the pressure; it may be observed in a large number of slates of different mineral composition. A foliated rock is composed of various minerals, which are so arranged as to resemble tightly-pressed layers of leaves; sometimes the whole mass consists of these leafy plates, at others bands of some hard mineral are interposed; the layers too are not generally level for any great distance, as in the slaty rocks, but are waved or crumpled, or run irregularly one into another. It must, however, be remembered that, although in these cleaved or foliated rocks the original stratification may have been entirely obliterated, still the larger layers or beds may frequently be plainly distinguished, owing to differences in their constituent particles or mineral composition. The second division of rocks, the coherents, contains those which have not been materially altered since their deposition; they also may be divided into compact and slaty: the former including sandstones and limestones, the latter shales and slates which have not the property of cleavage.

Now of these four classes of rocks, the first—the compact crystallines—though often extremely hard, is, partly from its granular texture and still more from the minerals which it contains, very much more liable to be affected by the weather than one would at first sight suppose. Granite, though a proverb for hardness, often may be found rotting and crumbling away after a comparatively short exposure. It is therefore rather rare to find lofty precipices, and still more so bold peaks, in any region where this rock abounds; the fissures which traverse it, and admit the air and water within it, cause the masses exposed to break up into large boulders, which often bestrew the ground and crown the ridge with no bad imitation of cyclopean fortifications. A granite district therefore is generally marked by massive but rather low mountains, with somewhat rounded outlines, and has a waste and desolate aspect, which is produced by the frequent wildernesses of decaying boulders—such, for example, as the upper part of the St Gothard pass, or the hills above Baveno on the Lago Maggiore. Where this is not the case, the granite will generally be found to shew some traces of foliation, and it is remarkable how great a difference the slightest tendency to this structure produces in the durability of the rock. Thus, for example, the talcose granites of Dauphiné and of Mont Blanc rise into some of the wildest forms to be seen in the whole of the Alps[1]. It is, however, often very difficult to draw the line between the compact and slaty crystallines, and to say where granite ends and gneiss begins: most of the rock around the Pelvoux in Dauphiné, which is now generally referred to gneiss, is quite undistinguishable in small specimens from true granite; and, though it has been stated by the best authorities that granite does not occur in the neighbourhood of Monte Rosa, I should certainly be disposed to call by that name the rocks of Auf der Platte, at the head of the Gorner Glacier. The Bernina group offers on the whole the boldest granite scenery that I know; elevated plateaux, often with precipitous broken sides, rather than peaks, are commonly characteristic of this formation. The same remark applies to several of the more distinctly volcanic rocks, which, however, are rare in the Alps, only appearing in any

---

[1] Plate II.

THE POINTE DES ECRINS AND CRÊTE DU PELVOUX.

quantity in the Italian Tyrol, and to the various porphyries. Of this rock, also rather rare, there is one extensive bed in the neighbourhood of Botzen forming an irregular strip running from N. to S. some forty miles long by twelve wide, through which the outlet of the Adige has been cut. Here the great rounded walls of dull purplish-red rock, clothed in many places with brushwood and supporting large upland plateaux of the richest herbage, produce a scene of singular luxuriance and beauty, especially when their tints are heightened by the glow of the setting sun. Beautiful as they are at all times, there is then something almost unearthly in their splendour; and one who has not made an evening journey from Meran to Botzen, or from the latter place by the gorge of the Kuntersweg, hardly knows what treasures of colour the Alps can afford.

The slaty crystallines almost without exception are found to compose the highest Alpine districts, and form, as it were, the backbone of the Alps. The comparatively narrow strip, which makes its appearance below the unaltered sedimentary deposits to the north of Nice and Mentone in the Maritime Alps, rapidly widens out as this group turns northward, until, to the west of Turin, it occupies a large part of the district between the plain of Piedmont and the valleys of the Drac and Isère[1]. This great mass of crystalline slates, broken here and there by a narrow trough of sedimentary rock, curves gradually round to the north-east, forming the loftier peaks of Dauphiné, the Maurienne, and the Tarentaise—till it rises to a height of more than 15,000 feet in the peak of Mont Blanc. The mass, of which this is the summit, is a kind of island of crystalline rock, girdled by a band of more or less altered sedimentary deposits; which are the continuation of a narrow trough

[1] In certain parts, however, the rocks and shales, though considerably altered by heat and pressure hardly deserve the name of crystalline, and present features more characteristic of the coherents.

that takes its beginning on the northern face of the Dauphiné Alps. The crystalline rocks appear again in the watershed of the Pennine chain, and extend almost without interruption over it and the Graians. For several miles they are not found upon the right bank of the Rhone, but when, between Leuk and Visp, the course of the river is deflected from its usual south-westerly direction, they cross the valley and form the greater part of the higher Oberland. Thence, with occasional slight breaks, they occupy the whole Alpine district between the Italian Lakes, the Valtelline, and the Upper Rhine, and are extensively developed in the tangled knot of mountains in which rise the streams supplying the Hinter Rhein and the Inn. In the Tyrol they form the watershed between Germany and Italy; the great central ridge, between the valley of the Inn on one side and the valleys of the Rienz and Drave (the long trench of the Puster-thal) on the other, being wholly composed of them.

The compact coherents vary considerably in their power of resisting the action of weather; but as a rule, sandstones are much more easily disintegrated than limestones. The former however, though largely developed in the subalpine region of Savoy and Switzerland, about the lakes of Annecy, Geneva, Neuchatel, Zurich, and Constance, are very rare among the higher Alps, and have then been so much altered by the action of heat that they may rather be classed among the crystalline rocks, their grains being often fused together so as to form a compact mass. The limestones as a rule are tolerably hard, and in many cases have so far been altered by heat as to be more or less crystalline. They, interbedded with the slaty coherents, abound over a large portion of the Alps. In the western district they are almost wholly absent upon the eastern slopes of the watershed, but are developed extensively around the crystalline zone which extends, nearly without intermission, from the Pelvoux group to Mont Blanc; the Alps of southern and western Dauphiné, **and of Savoy,** consisting almost wholly of them. On the **eastern face of this zone** they form a comparatively narrow **band, which crosses the** watershed to the south of Mont Blanc and, after skirting the south-eastern face of that chain, recrosses between it and the Great St Bernard to the northern side. For some 70 miles to the east of this pass these deposits are almost wholly absent, appearing again on the eastern shore of the Lago Maggiore. From this point a broad band begins, which stretches away to the eastward, forming the elevated but interrupted zone of mountains in **which the** rivers of north Venetia take their **rise.** In the **central district,** the sedimentary deposits of Savoy **are continued on the** right bank of the Rhone, and **extend without interruption to the** E.N.E., forming several of **the higher** summits in the Oberland and the beautiful country about **the lakes of Thun,** Brienz, and (partly) Lucerne. Beyond the trench **through** which the Rhine flows into the Lake of **Constance** they extend **in** the same direction along the left bank of the Inn, and form the picturesque mountain district of North Tyrol and Bavaria[1].

These then being the components of the mountains, and this their general distribution, we may proceed **to** describe the forms which they most generally assume **under the erosive action to** which they are exposed. It has been **already stated that in all, a few** compact crystallines **excepted, there is more or less** tendency **to split in certain directions.** This is especially true of the slaty rocks, **whether crystalline or coherent; and the compact coherents,** though not fissile, generally occur in beds of no great **thickness, which are distinctly separated the one** from the other[2]. Hence these rocks can all be split in a direction parallel to some **fixed plane,** which, **if** they be coherents, **will in most** cases not be very steeply inclined to that of the horizon. It is therefore obvious that water will most easily make its way along these planes of separation, and, by acting

[1] See Appendix, **Note I.**   [2] **See fig. 2.**

as a wedge or as a saw, will split off pieces from the main mass. This, however, is not the only way by which the destroyer can penetrate. If you look at the face of a cliff in any mountain country, you will generally see that it is traversed by certain fissures, which are often more conspicuous from a distance than is the bedding or cleavage of the stone. These joints, as they are called, will commonly be found to traverse the mass in directions inclined at a considerable angle one to another, and often at right angles, roughly speaking, to the bedding or cleavage planes. At times they are of considerable width; at others it would be impossible to introduce even a thin sheet of paper into them; still large or small, there they are; and there are the weak points in the rock. Hence it is rather a collection of columns, like a group of irregular crystals (often four-sided), than a solid mass; the columns too are not monoliths, but piers of masonry; so the water finding a way down the joints breaks them up into their component stones or sends large fragments of them toppling down. A very few minutes

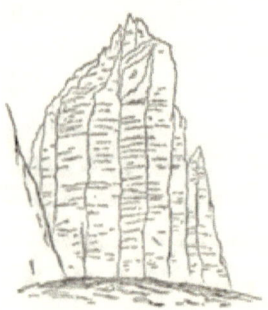

(Fig. 2.) Effect of joints and stratification in Dolomite; from one of the crags of the Drei Zinnen near Landro, Tyrol.

spent in examining the face of a cliff and the form of the fragments at its base will shew of what importance these joints are in the disintegration of the mountains[1].

[1] See figs. 2 and 3.

THE DREI ZINNEN FROM LANDRO.

CALLIOPE

From this it is clear that the form of a mountain, so far as it is due to erosion, will chiefly depend on three things; the direction of the planes of cleavage or bedding (or of both), the form of the joints, and the durability of the materials. When the strata (or cleavage planes) dip inwards it is clear that a fragment of stone may be detached from the face of a cliff and yet rest on a lower ledge. Hence the rate of ruin in a mountain so formed will be more gradual, and the precipices generally bold and lofty. If on the contrary the dip is outwards, every fragment as it is detached will roll down, and fresh surfaces being constantly exposed, the work of destruction will be more rapid and the cliff be more sloping. It does not however follow that such a one is easier to climb; for, though the inclination is less steep, the hold for hand and foot is not so good, and the readiness with which stones fall is often a considerable danger. This was remarkably exemplified in the ascents of the Matterhorn. The cleavage planes there dip from east to west. The earlier attempts, all unsuccessful, were by the less steep south-western ridge[1], and were rendered very dangerous by the uncertain hold and the frequent fall of stones. Remarking this Mr Whymper determined to attempt the unpromisingly precipitous eastern face, and found that, notwithstanding its steepness, there was comparatively little difficulty[2] and no danger from showers of stones.

It will also be obvious that when the columnar structure is well developed in rocks the scenery will generally be bolder; since it is favourable to the formation of precipices and crests. When there are no joints for the air and water to penetrate, the surface of course is removed uniformly, and the general

---

[1] See Plate I.

[2] The fearful accident during the return of the party did not happen upon this side of the mountain, but upon a portion of the northern face to which they were obliged to diverge near the summit; the ascent, however, has since been effected from the south-west.

tendency—as a little observation of sandstone rocks will shew —is to obliterate rather than to produce a cliff. Hence a stream, which in some cases will but increase the slope of a mountain, will in others carve its side into a precipice; and of course the harder the material the steeper will be the cliffs that are thus formed, although the time required for effecting the work will be much greater.

Crests cannot of course exist where the stone is soft or liable to crumble away uniformly, and therefore, as I have already stated, are rare in the true granitic districts; they are boldest and grandest where the stone is not only hard but well jointed. Then the destroying agents which, owing to a variety of causes, produce unequal effects upon these irregular columns, soon carve the ridges into jagged pinnacles, often bristling with spines like the back-fin of a fish. The precise outline of these of course depends considerably upon the rock. Perhaps the most singular forms occur almost at opposite ends of the Alpine chain, in the talcose gneiss of Dauphiné and in the dolomitic limestone of the Italian Tyrol. The former weathers into crystal-like blocks with smooth facets, whose edges are often as sharp as knives; the curving planes of foliation at times giving a flame-like appearance to the outlines of the crests. The latter rock, though extremely hard in hand specimens, has a considerable tendency to break up into small blocks, being stratified often in not very thick and nearly horizontal layers; and being also gashed by enormous vertical joints, it exhibits the grandest precipices and some of the wildest ridges that I have ever seen. Still, wild as these may be, their forms can never be confounded with those of the crystalline rocks; for, however sharp their pinnacles may appear at the first glance, careful examination will always shew that their outline is that of ruined masonry, and that, if one may so express it, the stones can be counted which still remain in every crumbling battlement and tottering turret.

True pyramidal or cone-shaped summits, whether of snow

(Fig. 3.) Effects of weather on joints and stratification. Dolomite in decay. 'Last scene of all in mountain history'; from near Cortina d'Ampezzo.

or rock, are rare. Perhaps the most striking examples, among the great mountains, are Monte Viso in the Cottian Alps, the Pointe des Ecrins in Dauphiné, the Pourri in the Tarentaise, the Grivola in the Graians, the Matterhorn and the Weisshorn in the Pennines; and of these only three would upon more careful examination be retained as presenting this structure; the summits of the Viso, the Grivola and the Matterhorn being really short and nearly level ridges. These six are all of slaty crystalline rock, which usually, as less liable to disintegration, offers the boldest summit forms. Peaks which at the first sight appear to be pyramidal are common enough, but a closer scrutiny will almost invariably shew that they are either only gable-ends, backed up from behind by a ridge whose slope is but slight compared with that of the others—such as the Ailefroide in Dauphiné, the Levanna in the Maurienne, the Grandes Jorasses in the Pennines, and the Shreckhorn in the Oberland, with many others—or else the culminating points of ridges which, though steep enough when regarded edgewise, appear from another point of view as rather obtuse-angled triangles. Very commonly the upper part of a great mountain consists of one or more broken and irregular ridges projecting from the snows for a height of a few hundred feet, so that, as in the case of Monte Rosa, there are two or three rival peaks[1] which do not differ greatly in height. In almost every mountain, as might be expected, there is one principal ridge, corresponding with the watershed of the chain, whose slope, at any rate on one side, is less than that of the others which coalesce near the peak. Not uncommonly the summit is a rounded dome of snow, such as that of Mont Blanc; which of course implies that the rocky mass beneath is tolerably level. In the limestone districts the upper parts of a mountain are very often gently-sloping plateaux of snow, through which perhaps a low ridge or tower crops out to form the summit: a fragment, which from some accidental cause has resisted the destroying agents better than the rest of the bed of which it has formed a part. Such mountains are common enough in the limestone district between the chain of Mont Blanc and the crystalline *massif* of the Oberland; they seldom much exceed a height of 11,000 feet.

Though, except in the dolomitic region, the limestone peaks do not generally equal the crystalline in the boldness of their outlines, they often surpass them in the grandeur of their precipices. The cirque of the Fer à Cheval, near Sixt, of the Creux de Champs, under the Diablerets, the southern face of the Gemmi Pass, the northern cliff of the Wetterhorn and Jungfrau, the Croda Malcora, with several of the other dolomitic mountains, are almost, if not wholly, without rivals in the crystalline districts. This superiority is mainly caused by the

---

[1] In Monte Rosa there is the Höchste Spitze, 15,217 ft., the Nord End, 15,132 ft., the Zumstein Spitze, 15,004 ft., the Signal Kuppe, 14,964 ft.; besides a tooth in the ridge of the first only a few feet lower than the summit.

structure of the limestone rocks, and by the fact that they are often interbedded with strata of softer shales. If the latter

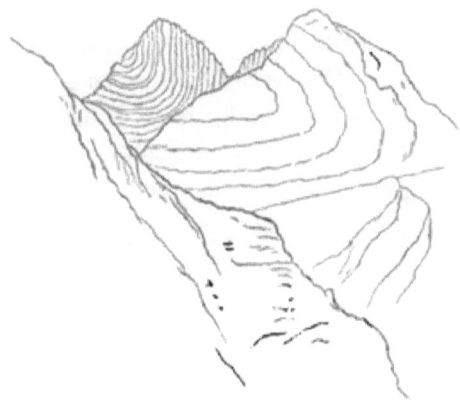

(Fig. 4.) Mountain Form. Peaks formed of fragments of contorted strata which perhaps on this account have resisted denudation. On the Sorapisse; seen in descending to Auronzo from the Tre Croci Pass.

deposits are **thick and dip** inwards, **the profile of the cliff** presents **the wall** and bank outline **so common** in the limestone regions; if, however, they are thin, nearly horizontal, **and more developed in the lower than in the upper part of the mountain, magnificent precipices will be produced. Hence, what has been happily termed the 'writing-desk formation' is very common in the limestone districts—the slope being the result of stratification, the precipice of jointing.**

Turning then to a map of the Alps and remembering what has been said of the distribution of the various rocks, we will attempt a brief sketch of the scenery in the principal Alpine districts. Passing by the Maritimes as being little more than a smaller edition of their neighbours, we come to the Cottians. These consist of wild craggy ranges whose splintered crests are usually between nine and ten thousand feet above the sea, the only important peak being the Viso (12,643), the central point of the district; from the immediate neighbourhood of which several valleys radiate. The form of the district and its southern position are unfavourable to the formation of glaciers, so that though its streams are comparatively small, their waters are beautifully pure and limpid. Chlorite slate is common, and serpentine is not unfrequent, hence the colours of the rocks are often very rich, deep greens and purples predominating. The vegetation is luxuriant, the scenery varied, the sternness of the barren crags being frequently relieved by distant glimpses of the sunny Piedmontese plain; and if only the accommodation were better, few places would be more popular with the lovers of Alpine beauty than the Viso valleys.

The High Alps of Dauphiné, a great mass of crystalline rock almost isolated from the principal chain by the valleys of the Romanche and the Durance, offer to the traveller some of the grandest scenery in Europe. The loftiest summit, called the Pointe des Ecrins, rises to a height of 13,462 feet; but there are twenty more which exceed 12,000 feet, and a considerable number not much lower, which for the most part are arranged on a horseshoe plan round about the river Venéon, a tributary of the Romanche. The glaciers are numerous, some being of considerable extent, and are often remarkable for their extreme steepness. The distinguishing features of the district are the bold outlines of the mountains, which are certainly unequalled by any in Savoy or Switzerland, and the abruptness with which they rise from the narrow valleys—often mere gorges—which surround them. It is very accessible, some of the finest scenery being within an easy day's journey from Grenoble; but it is hardly ever visited, for unfortunately the accommodation is at present so bad as to repel the majority of travellers; some however of the most characteristic views can be seen without moving from the excellent carriage road which, starting from Grenoble, skirts the northern face of the district, passing through the two most celebrated

'combes' or gorges, and, after crossing the isthmus of the Col
du Lautaret, descends to Briançon. Along this sufficiently good
quarters may be found at two or three places, and from
Briançon Turin may easily be reached by the Mont Genèvre.

The Savoy Alps also principally consist of a great and
nearly isolated spur, between the valleys of the Isère and
the Arc, which is united to the main chain at the Col
d'Iséran and contains the highest summits of the district, the
Grand Casse (12,780) and the Pourri (12,491); but several
peaks which range between eleven and twelve thousand feet,
and one or two which even surpass the latter elevation, stand
upon the watershed between France and Italy, and upon the
ridge separating the valleys of the Arc and Romanche. The
rocks here consist of crystalline slates and more or less altered
sedimentary rocks. Snow-fields and glaciers are numerous, but
not extensive; the scenery is very varied, and often on that
account not less attractive than in some of the grander regions.
As in Dauphiné, the bad accommodation is a great drawback;
and unfortunately but little of the best scenery is visible from
the two high roads, those of the Cénis and Petit St Bernard,
that traverse parts of the district.

In the Graian Alps are usually included the great spur
which runs out eastward to form the south side of the Val
d'Aoste and the shorter spurs at the head of the valley of Lanzo.
On the latter, just east of the watershed, are a couple of fine
peaks, the Levanna and the Pointe de Séa, about twelve thousand feet high; and the valleys of Lanzo and of the Orco are
at once grand and exquisitely luxuriant. Nearly as rich in
colour and vegetation as the Viso valleys, they are perhaps even
more varied in their scenery, and are certainly formidable rivals
The greater peaks of the Graians are grouped on or near the
ridge of the former spur. They are all of crystalline rock (two,
the Grand Paradis and the Grivola, exceeding 13,000 feet), very
bold in outline, having on their northern flanks several con-

siderable glaciers, and a number of beautiful valleys which descend into the broad trough of the sunny Val d'Aoste. The accommodation for travellers, not long ago very bad, is now improving; and before long one or two spots in the Graians, Cogne above all others, will be favourite places of resort.

To the north of the Graians we come to the Pennine range, which forms a part of what may be termed the backbone of Europe, and includes the highest summits in the Alps; every peak, save one, above 14,000 feet being in this district. Here also the law, already mentioned as prevailing throughout the Alps, of parallel troughs and ranges running from E.N.E. to W.S.W., is more clearly indicated than in any of the regions further south. Its limits are formed by the great valleys of the Rhone and Doire on the north and south respectively, and the shorter depressions of the Val de Montjoie and the Simplon Pass on the west and east. Hence a general sinking of the surface for about seven thousand feet would convert this district into a long and narrow mountainous island deeply indented by numerous fiords, from which in many parts the higher peaks would rise very precipitously. A geological map shews it to consist of five *massifs* of granitic rock, uplifting on their flanks a quantity of sedimentary slates, most of which have been much altered, so that the greater part of the district may be reckoned among the 'slaty crystallines.' The two westernmost of these *massifs*, those of Mont Blanc and of the Aiguilles Rouges (better known in connexion with a minor summit, the Brevent), may fairly be linked together, since they were probably upraised by forces, which acted simultaneously, though not quite uniformly, over the whole region between the Drac and the upper Rhone. A glance at the map also shews that a broad band of granitic rock extends over the whole of this region, the summits of which lie in two lines running from N.E. to S.W., separated in places by troughs of almost unaltered sedimentary rock of the Jurassic age. Indeed, the northern extremity, which belongs, as has just been said to the Pennine Alps, is entirely isolated by a narrow zone of these deposits, which occupies the depression of the Col de la Seigne, a pass leading from the valley of the Doire to that of the Isère, and is cut through by the valleys of the Arve and the Trient; so that a section from N.W. to S.E. across either of these valleys would show the compact and slaty coherents resting in a basin of the crystallines, which tower above them on either hand, and are often exposed in the beds of the torrents. The northern of these two ranges is a single ridge, the summits of which range from about eight to ten thousand feet; the southern contains the sharp peaks which are grouped around the monarch Mont Blanc. The ground-plan of the latter *massif* is one long ridge, which, except at the two extremities, preserves a very uniform direction and throws out a series of long spurs to the north-west. On this ridge—the watershed between Savoy and Piedmont—is situated Mont Blanc itself, with several other lofty peaks; but many important mountains, well known to English travellers as the Aiguilles of Chamouni, lie upon the spurs. Chief of them is the Aiguille Verte, rising to a height of 13,432 feet above the sea. Their distinguishing name—the Needles—is derived from the sharp splintered forms assumed by the rocks, talcose gneiss and mica slate, composing their crests. The above-mentioned ground-plan of this district renders its valley scenery at times rather monotonous, especially near the two great places of resort, Courmayeur and Chamouni; at the former, the precipitous southern face of the main range, though inexpressibly grand, is almost too wall-like for picturesque effect; while at the latter, the valley of the Arve is such a complete trough that the peaks are obscured and dwarfed by the uninteresting slopes of their shoulders, and even the grandeur of Mont Blanc is much diminished. To thoroughly appreciate the beauty of this district one must either wander up the glaciers which occupy the valleys between the northern spurs, and while standing on the icy floor of some secluded

amphitheatre take a near view of the surrounding crags; or
better still, climb some well-situated peak, on the opposite side
of the bounding valleys, such as the Brevent or the Cramont,
whence only the grandeur of the whole chain and the wonderful
outlines of its several peaks can be justly estimated. Indeed I
am inclined to think that they are best appreciated when seen
rising above one or two intervening ranges, especially if these
are formed of a different rock; as for example when viewed
from some of the Savoy hills, between Sixt and the Lake of
Geneva. Certainly I never so fully realised the enormous size
of Mont Blanc itself as when I saw it for the first time, from
the slopes of Monte Rosa, some fifty miles away, towering
against the sky far above all its attendant aiguilles.

At the north-eastern extremity of the *massif* the summits
become rapidly lower, and the crystalline rock disappears beneath the shales of the Col de Ferrex, the lowest depression
in the whole Pennine chain between Mont Blanc and Monte
Rosa. This trough of deposits (belonging to the Jurassic age)
is however scarcely more than five miles in width, and the slaty
crystallines reappear in the neighbourhood of the Great St
Bernard Pass, where they rise to a height of above 12,000 feet
in the summit of the Vélan, a mountain whose snowy dome
is well known to all who have followed that ancient route
from Martigny to Aosta. Somewhat to the east of this appears the third patch of granitic rock, breaking through the more
distinctly slaty beds and forming the axis of the main chain.
The tributary glens of one large valley, the Val Pelline, conduct
its waters to the Doire, but on the north, five (including that
of the Visp, which forms the eastern boundary of the *massif*) descend to the Rhone. The centre of this portion of the Pennines,
when viewed from any commanding point on the north or
the south, will be seen to consist for the most part of a lofty
glacier-covered mountain mass, most of the summits of which
do not rise very much above the general level. At the western

extremity is one magnificent giant, the Grand Combin, which reaches the height of 14,164 feet; and at the eastern are grouped some of the most striking peaks in the whole range of the Alps. These are the Dent Blanche, the Weisshorn, the Dent d'Hérens, and the Matterhorn. The former two with several fine, though to them subordinate, peaks lie upon a ridge which forms the eastern boundary of what might be called the central Pennine district, and look down into the valley of the Visp; the latter are on a ridge, between the Val Tournanche and the Val Pelline, which forms a kind of outlier of the main group. But few of these peaks can be seen with advantage from the Rhone valley; or indeed, with the exception of the Combin, from the valley of Aosta. Before they become visible, one must generally ascend the opposite slopes for several thousand feet; and it is only by exploring the various lateral valleys that any idea can be gained of the magnificence of this part of the Pennine chain. The inhabitants of several of these were not so long ago almost a proverb for squalid misery. Hence, though of course Mont Vélan was familiar to the tourists who streamed across the Great St Bernard, and Zermatt in the Visp valley has for some years been a formidable rival to Chamouni, all the rest of the region was a dozen years ago almost as rarely visited as the Caucasus or the Himalayas. Within this short period small inns have been built near the heads of the other valleys, in several of which the traveller can obtain all that is really needful—wholesome food and a clean bed. The most important crystalline *massif*, that of Monte Rosa, lies beyond the valley of the Visp, or, to speak more correctly, of the Gorner Visp; for the western branch is of the more importance orographically; seeing that it appears to correspond with a rather wide and well-marked gap in the line of the higher summits, connecting it with the Val Tournanche. It is not easy to divide this group from another *massif* of the same rock which lies on the east side of the

Saas-Visp and is continued beyond the depression occupied by the Simplon road, which, as we have already said, is usually considered to form the eastern boundary of the Pennines. The mountains forming the southern slopes of this group exhibit some peculiarities; for they mainly consist of slate containing a large proportion of hornblende, which is pierced by a long spur of crystalline rock, forming a kind of outlier of the Graian *massif;* and just where they sink into the plain of Piedmont are broken by considerable outcrops of granite and porphyry. The principal summits in the above group are ranged either on the watershed or on two spurs to the north of it: among the former is Monte Rosa, the second summit of the Alps, which is not as Mont Blanc, a great snow dome, but is a mountain mass crowned by a mural diadem of peaks, the highest of which, but little overtopping its neighbours, reaches 15,217 feet. On one spur also are the twin peaks of the Dom and Taschhorn, little under 15,000 feet; and the crest of the loop of mountains about the Gorner glacier, some twelve miles in length, scarcely ever sinks below 12,000 feet. The glaciers of this region, as may be supposed, are very extensive, but the forms of the mountains are hardly so striking as those of their neighbours in the last district.

To the north of the eastern half of the Pennines lies another celebrated range, forming the opposite bank of the great valley of the Rhone, and extending between that river and the Rhine. On its northern face are the vast deposits of sedimentary rock, shale and limestone, for the most part unaltered, which form the mid-Alpine region of Switzerland, and rise around many of the most beautiful lakes. The summits of the eastern and western extremities of this chain are all composed of the same rocks, which are also found upon some of the highest peaks on the northern verge of the central mass. The northern face is very precipitous, and the glaciers here are consequently much shorter and steeper than on the other. A good general view of this group from either the north or south shews that the western end consists of a row of table-shaped mountains—great blocks of shale and limestone—without any conspicuous peaks, no one of which quite attains a height of eleven thousand feet. These, with the similar district on the other side of the gorge through which the Rhone descends from Martigny to the Lake of Geneva, form a connecting link between the Mont Blanc and Oberland *massifs*, which are thus united by a kind of natural causeway. This is composed of the Buet, Pic de Tenneverges, Dent du Midi, and other less well known summits on the one side of the Rhone, and by the Diablerets, Wildhorn, and Wildstrubel on the other. Although the glaciers here are small, and the mountains rather blocks or ridges than peaks, this district affords in my opinion some of the most beautiful scenery in the Alps. The limestone precipices are often of extraordinary grandeur, the tints of the rock are rich and varied, shades of pale fawn colour predominating; and the fertility of the soil causes its green alps and immense fir woods to be almost without rivals. There is hardly a valley in the north Savoy Alps or in the Western Oberland which is not worth careful exploration; and is not equal, if not superior in beauty, to its better known neighbours in the central district. Still, upon the northern face of this, as all who have visited Switzerland know well, some beautiful limestone scenery is to be found, especially about the Lakes of Thun and Brienz, and the well-known valleys of Lauterbrunnen and Grindelwald.

In the Central Oberland the principal summits appear to be arranged along two lines, that on the north forming the watershed, between which the great mass of the Finster Aarhorn, the culminating peak of the whole district, makes a connecting link. The spaces thus enclosed are occupied by vast fields of snow and ice, and are divided by minor ridges into several glacier basins, most of which find their outlets through gaps in the southern line. Some of the higher peaks are composed of coherent rocks, which are here raised to a greater elevation than in any other part of the Alps. The variety of scenery thus produced has justly made the Oberland one of the most popular districts of the Alps. The valley of the Aar is surrounded by crystalline rocks, granite, gneiss, and mica slate, desolate yet wildly grand, with bold peaks connected by splintered ridges. Those of Grindelwald and Lauterbrunnen afford rich slopes of pasture and pine wood, broken as we approach their heads by magnificent limestone cliffs and terminating under the enormous wall of precipices, which is crowned by the craggy head of the Eiger and the snowy summits of the Mönch and Jungfrau. To the east of the Aar is an intricate mountain mass, lying between it and the valley of the Reuss, where, although the inner crystalline peaks do not reach so great an elevation as in the Oberland proper, there are several outlying summits in the coherent region to the north, which surpass ten thousand feet. East of the Reuss valley the crystalline axis disappears before long under the unaltered rocks, and the only important mountain mass, that of the Tödi, lies in the angle between the upper parts of the Reuss, the Rhine, and the Linth. The greater part of this district closely resembles the Western Oberland in structure and geology, and is hardly inferior to it in beauty of scenery.

The next region to be noticed is that of the Lepontine Alps, which may be considered as extending between the depressions crossed by the Simplon and Splügen passes in the one direction, and between the Lombard Plain, and the trough occupied by the heads of the Rhone, Reuss, and Vorder Rhein, on the other. The structure of this district is more intricate than that of those hitherto described, and can hardly be explained in the limits to which we must restrict ourselves. The mountains consist chiefly of crystalline or highly altered coherent rocks, and do not rise to so great an elevation as in the neighbouring chains. There is therefore comparatively little snow, and the main ridge when seen from a distance, appears rather monotonous and uninteresting; still the long irregular valleys which descend from **it towards** Italy afford some exquisitely varied and beautiful scenery, not so well known as it deserves, except in the immediate neighbourhood of the lakes of Maggiore, Lugano, and Como.

Proceeding further to the east we come next to the district called the Rhætian Alps, a name derived from the important tribe which long contended with Rome for the possession of **its** fastnesses. Here we must ask our readers to glance at some map which represents the Eastern Alps on a tolerably **large** scale. They will perceive that the plan **of long valleys extending** in a general direction from east **to west, with shorter ones** nearly at right angles to them, is **still preserved; and that there** are two principal parallel chains, **including between** them a long trough, called the Puster-thal, in the middle of which an upland plateau forms a watershed, **whence the** Rienz flows westward to seek the Adriatic by the channel of the Eisack and the Adige, and the Drave eastward to mingle its waters with the Danube. Moreover, just as the Rhone breaks through the Oberland ridge at Martigny, so does the Eisack escape from the Puster-thal at Botzen; the line of which is prolonged up the Vintschgau (the upper valley of the Adige) in a way that somewhat reminds u° **of** the correspondence between the valleys of the Upper Rhone and **Arve.** There **is,** however, **one point of** difference between these two districts, namely, the clear definition of the central chain—that forming the great watershed—by the huge trough of the Inn. In fact a few visits to commanding peaks in East Switzerland and the adjoining Tyrol and Lombard Alps will show that there are **in** this region three very distinctly-marked troughs; the southernmost occupied by the Val Telline and Val di Sole, the **next by** the Vintschgau and Puster-thal, and **the** northernmost and most extensive by the Inn. The chains between these troughs are intersected by nearly parallel depressions, the first of which is the Val di Non, which conveys the waters of the Val di Sole to the Adige; the next, the valley between Nauders and Mals, in which is the scarcely-marked watershed between the Inn and the Adige; the third, the valley of the Adige from Meran to Botzen; and, lastly, the gap in the main chain which is crossed by the Brenner Pass. It will be also observed that most of the lateral valleys preserve a general parallelism with these more important channels. The outbreak of porphyry in the neighbourhood of Botzen has a little obscured the relation of the valleys in that neighbourhood, and I do not yet feel certain whether we ought to look for the prolongation of the Val di Sole trough in the lower part of the Fassa-thal, or in the gorge through which the Eisack escapes from the Puster-thal to join the Adige at Botzen.

To return then to the Rhætian Alps, which form the westernmost district of this region. These consist of several masses of crystalline rocks, with frequent patches of almost unaltered coherents. The most important mountain districts are the long ridge between the Rhine and upper valley of the Inn, containing a number of fine peaks, about eleven thousand feet high, but without any extensive glaciers, and the Bernina *massif*, consisting of several lofty snow-clad summits, the highest (from which the district is named) being 13,294 feet above the sea. Here, and in the southern outlier of the Monte della Disgrazia (12,074 ft.), granite is extensively developed, and some of the most varied and beautiful scenery in the whole Alpine chain may be found. The best head-quarters for travellers are at Pontresina, a little village situated on a tributary torrent of the Inn, a few miles from the principal glaciers. Not many years ago this place was almost unknown to English travellers; it is now a favourite place of resort, and bids fair to become a formidable rival to Chamouni, Grindelwald, and Zermatt. It is unusually accessible; for no less than four excellent carriage-roads descend into the upper valley of the Inn, two coming from the Rhine valley, and the other two from different parts of North Italy.

To the east of this rises the Orteler group, a series of short but lofty spurs, several of whose peaks considerably overtop the central point from which they radiate. The greater part of this group consists of almost unaltered coherent rock, of which the highest summit, the Orteler Spitze (12,814 ft.), is composed. In the northern part of the Rhætian Alps the coherent rocks are also extensively developed; and the Voralberg and adjoining Bavarian Alps may be regarded as a continuation of the broad belt, which, as has been already said, runs along the north-western and northern face of the great mountain fortress encircling North Italy.

To the south of the Rhætian Alps, and separated from them by the trough of the Val Telline and Val di Sole, is a considerable group, mainly consisting of sedimentary rocks, which is commonly called the Lombard Alps. Its chief peculiarity is the central *massif* of the Adamello, a huge glacier-covered island of granite, the highest point of which, the Presanella, is 11,688 feet above the sea; and is nearly equalled by two neighbouring summits, the Adamello and the Carè Alto. There are also some fine dolomitic peaks in the eastern part of the group, the chief of which is the Brenta Alta (10,771 ft.), and the scenery generally is very luxuriant and beautiful. The great heat of many of the valleys renders the early summer or late autumn the best period for travelling here. This remark indeed applies to the greater part of the Tyrol, Austrian as well as Lombard; the heat in July and August being often such as to interfere much with the comfort and even health of the pedestrian.

We have next to describe the great Noric chain; and for this purpose may for one moment imagine ourselves standing upon one of the higher summits in the range which faces it on the south. Before us lies the deep trench of the Puster-thal, and far off on the left the valley of the Vintschgau is seen stretching away towards the Inn. Above this latter rises an extensive glacier-clad range—this is the Oetzthaler Alpen, the westernmost of the groups which compose the Noric chain. Its highest peak, the Weisskogel, is 12,620 feet above the sea; but the general elevation of the whole mass causes it and the adjoining summits to appear lower than they really are. Next, after a slight interval, rises another and somewhat similar group, except that it is evidently inferior in extent and height; these are the Stubayer Alps, the peaks of which are some two thousand feet below those of the Oetzthaler group. Then comes a wide and deep gap; through this the Brenner Pass gives easy access by road and rail from the Puster-thal to Innsbruck. Beyond this depression a dark ridge gradually rises up—these are the Ziller-thaler Alps; they are streaked with snow, but it is deeper on their northern slopes. Beyond them towers a chain of snowy peaks; and still to the right of this a yet loftier ridge, culminating in one sharp glittering cone, that instantly arrests the eye—these are the Venediger and Glockner *massifs*, which, with the Ziller-thaler Alps, are often classed together under the one name of the Tauern group. Their glaciers are of considerable size, and many of the peaks of great beauty and grandeur; the culminating point being the Gross Glockner, the Great Bell, the summit of which is 12,958 feet above the sea. Beyond this the mountains sink down again, only here and there rising much above the snow-line, the highest summit east of the Glockner *massif* being the Ankogel (10,664 ft.). As can be readily seen from their outlines, the peaks of this chain consist mainly of crystalline or highly-altered rock.

We must now turn to the group south of the Puster-thal, on which we have supposed ourselves to be standing, which forms what is commonly denominated the Italian Tyrol. Although its peaks do not rise to any very great elevation, only one exceeding eleven thousand feet, its scenery is of extraordinary grandeur, owing to the presence of vast deposits of dolomite. This, in the magnificence of its precipices and singularity of its outlines, surpasses even Dauphiné, but is inferior to it in the size of its glaciers, there being only one of any importance in the whole district. Very beautiful too are the colours of these limestone cliffs; the prevailing tint is a rich fawn colour, which is varied by shades of silvery or purplish grey, and sometimes streaked with deep red, as though streams of blood had dripped down the rock. When these ruined towers of dolomite stand out against a stormy sky or dimly loom through mist or rain, their appearance, so lifeless, so ghastly barren in comparison with the rich pine-woods and green alps which in many places clothe their feet, produces a strange sense of awe. Another peculiarity of the district is the presence of extensive beds of volcanic tuff and ash, which are almost, if not wholly, wanting in other parts of the Alps, and of great masses of trap and porphyry. In fact some of the valleys are supposed to have originated in the craters of ancient volcanoes. Their direction and forms are much more irregular here than further to the west; those on the southern slopes are considerably longer than the others, and most of the principal peaks stand upon spurs to the south of the watershed. The streams from nearly all these valleys do not enter the Adige, but are conveyed by two rivers, the Piave and the Tagliamento, to the Adriatic. Another noteworthy peculiarity is that the majority of the great peaks are grouped around a deep depression, through which runs the important Ampezzo road, leading from the watershed of the Puster-thal to Venice. To the east of this cluster the range bears the name of the Carnic Alps, but very few of the summits surpass nine thousand feet; still the presence of dolomite often renders the scenery quite as striking as in mountains of a much greater elevation: while in the Julian Alps, still further to the east, which in character and formation are very similar, the general level of the ranges has sunk so much that the Terglou *massif*, the highest point of which is 9,370 feet above the sea, stands out more grandly than many Swiss mountains which surpass it in elevation by two or three thousand feet.

CHAPTER II.

HAVING thus pointed out the general form of the Alpine valleys, and their connexion with the various forces which have determined the contours of the Alpine chains, it may be well to describe rather more fully one or two of their distinguishing features. There are three ways in which a valley may have had its origin, (1) as a crack in uplifted strata; (2) as a fold or depression in strata which have been unequally elevated; (3) as a channel or inlet worn by the action of tides or currents in shallow seas, in strata which have afterwards been raised above highwater mark. It is however probable that most of the larger valleys have had their beginning in one of the two first-named ways. In the first of these it is obvious that the strata exposed in the slopes on either side will dip away from the centre of the valley, though of course not necessarily to the same extent; and it is possible that if the fracture has occurred near the junction of two deposits of different strength, the beds on one side may be elevated much more than on the other, and the valley correspond with what is in geology termed a fault. In the second case, the beds will dip towards the centre of the valley; and in the third the valley will be excavated out of them; so that they will be exposed as in the sides of a railway cutting. In the Alps, however, there is no single valley which can be considered as an unaltered example of any one of these types. All, however they may have been originally formed, have been immensely modified by the action of denudation. Perhaps both sea and streams have been engaged on this work, but there can be little doubt, that, at any rate for thousands of years, only the subaerial agencies have operated. Every peak, every mountain slope, every glen, bears distinct traces of the action of air and water, of heat and frost. The contour of a valley therefore very much depends upon the materials of the hills through which it is cut. If these are soft and yielding, it will be wide and open, with gentle slopes on either side: if they are hard and tenacious, it will be narrow and deep, between steep hills or precipices.

Instances of both kinds are of course common enough in the Alps, and it would be an endless task to enumerate them, Some of the finest examples of the latter occur in Dauphiné, and in the Italian Tyrol. Wherever we find rocks which unite hardness and durability, such as gneiss or crystalline limestone, there we shall find the most magnificent precipices and the narrowest valleys. The most striking are those in which the original fissure appears to have been very narrow, and the stream to have done little more than deepen this. Such, for example, are the Combe de Queyras and the Combe de Malaval in Dauphiné, the gorge of the Reuss near the Devil's Bridge, the Via Mala on the Splügen Road, the Finstermünz on the Inn, and the Kuntersweg on the Eisack. In each of these the bottom of the defile is almost always the bed of the torrent, and the roads which traverse them are among the greatest feats that engineers have accomplished. Besides these, there are in many parts of the Alps smaller gorges, whose sides are as nearly as possible vertical, and whose depth is often two or three hundred feet, while their breadth is perhaps not generally more than from twenty to thirty. To descend into them is of course almost always impossible; but by cautiously approaching some projecting crag, or from the narrow arch which has often been thrown across them to bear some Alpine road, a view may be obtained of the torrent thundering below between walls of rock dappled with lichen stains, and draped with delicate ferns or sturdy tufts of mountain shrubs. There are hundreds, I had almost said thousands, of these in the Alps. For example, I remember three near Zermatt; and wherever the rock is hard and the streams are strong, there they are sure to be found. Generally a change in the strata from which a valley has been excavated, is marked by a corresponding alteration in its form. If, for instance, soft shales are resting on hard slate, the upper part of the valley is a gentle slope, but when the torrent has worked its way to the lower bed, the change is instantaneous: instead of a trench it cuts a groove, so that the cross section of the valley is like a Y. Not unfrequently the stream appears to have cleared away all the softer shale before it has had time to bury itself in the hard rock below. There are some curious instances of this on each side of the Romanche in Dauphiné. The grandest of these narrow gorges in the Alps are those of the Tamina and the Trient. Of the former we shall have to speak in describing some remarkable mineral springs that are discharged into it; the latter—which has only lately been rendered accessible—demands a brief notice before leaving this subject.

On the well-known route of the Tête Noire from Chamouni to Martigny, the stream of the Trient joins that of the Eau Noire, which has descended what orographically appears to be the main valley. Here both the valleys have become narrow and steep; still they are not impassable, and a rough track leads from the Tête Noire inn to the rivers, and up to the village of Finhaut on the left bank of the united streams. A little further down, the Trient is lost to sight in a narrow gorge, from which it does not emerge until it enters the valley of the Rhone.

A well-made mule-road on its left bank, passing through fine scenery, and winding down by a leaping stream under the shade of walnuts and Spanish chestnuts, brings the traveller to the level bed of the Rhone valley, within a few minutes' walk of the mouth of the gorge. On either side are vertical walls of rock, several hundred feet in height, separated by a narrow fissure often not twenty feet in width. The torrent roars below, and the precipices on either side would not afford footing to a goat, but a framework of wood has been skilfully secured by wire ropes to the cliffs, so as to form a slender but perfectly safe road, about three quarters of a mile in length, along the narrowest part. It is difficult to say whether this most extraordinary gorge is to be regarded as formed mainly by erosion, or by cracking of the rock. I examined it very carefully, but could not detect any clear traces of the action of water above a height of 30 or 40 feet from the present stream. The planes of foliation in the crystalline rock, a hard mica schist, slope steeply inwards, and there are many small fissures transverse to the main chasm. In one place there appears to have been originally a barrier of rock or break in the level of the torrent bed, which gave rise to a cascade; but the stream has long since cut clear through this. However, whether mainly formed by fracture of the mountains during upheaval, or by the slow sawing of the glacier torrent, it is the most magnificent gorge in the crystalline rock which I have ever seen; perhaps one of the most remarkable that exists in Europe.

There is yet another feature in the Alpine valleys which deserves notice; namely, the cirques. By this term, borrowed from the Pyrenees (where they are much more common than in the Alps) are denoted semicircular basins, at or near the heads of valleys, surrounded by precipitous walls of rock. The limestone districts appear the most favourable to formations of this kind, but I only know of three really grand examples in the Alps; these are the Fer à Cheval near Sixt, the Creux de Champs under the Diablerets, and the cirque in the Croda Malcora near the head of the Val Auronzo in the Italian Tyrol; the first two run one another hard for the prize of beauty. The Creux de Champs is, I believe, on the larger scale; but the greater height of unbroken limestone cliff and the number of small waterfalls, which descend from every cleft like threads of silver or scarves of gauze, perhaps give the palm to the Fer à Cheval. One of the most singular that I have ever seen is the Croda di Lagazoi, to the north-west of Monte Tofana (Italian Tyrol); which from the summit of that peak appears like an ancient amphitheatre with a breach at one end; a small glen being surrounded by an elongated oval or horse-shoe-shaped wall of rock; one of the most extraordinary among the strange mountain forms which distinguish that region.

Several valleys form what have been termed 'valleys of outcrop.' In this case the stream follows either the line of a fault, or the outcrop of some stratum which yields more readily to its action than the neighbouring beds. Its original course must have been determined by a fissure or depression, generally the former; and therefore it is really only a valley of fracture or depression, modified by circumstances. This kind is most commonly formed at the junction of crystalline and sedimentary (or little altered) rocks; and examples may be found in several of the important Alpine valleys, such as in the upper valley of the Romanche, in parts of the valley of the Rhone above Martigny, and of the Inn between Landeck and Innsbruck.

Valleys of depression do not very frequently occur on a large scale. One of the best instances which I have seen is the upper part of the Ampezzo Thal, where this structure is very conspicuous. Smaller examples, however, of this formation are common enough in the limestone districts. To mention two out of many, there is one near the Col de Pillon between the Oldenhorn and the Diablerets, and another among the mountains near Wesen on the left bank of the Linth.

In close connexion with the subject of Alpine valleys is that of the lakes, which are more abundant in Switzerland than in the neighbouring countries. Savoy has but two, the Lac de Bourget, and the Lac d'Annecy; these lie just at the border of the limestone district, and extend into the softer sandstones which fringe it on the west. The former lake is about 12 miles long and $1\frac{1}{2}$ broad; the greatest depth being 256 feet. Its waters traverse a marshy plain to join the Rhone; but no great increase of them would bring the lake once more up to that river, making it a miniature Albert Nyanza, and a slight further rise would cause them to overflow the low barrier, if it can be so called, which separates them from the Isère valley. The Lake of Annecy is 1450 feet above the sea, and about 100 feet deep: it is $9\frac{3}{4}$ miles long, and from 1 to 2 wide. There is much picturesque and interesting scenery around its banks.

Some 23 miles to the north of Annecy, and like it, partly in the limestone, partly in the sandstone district, lies the Lake of Geneva, which is also called Lac Léman, from its Roman name Lacus Lemanus. In shape it is a crescent, with the horns pointing S. and S.E. Its height above the sea-level is about 1230 feet, and the greatest depth is variously stated from 984 to 1200 feet. The northern shore is 56 miles long, the southern 44, and the greatest breadth of the lake is about 8 miles. The Rhone, turbid with glacier mud, pours its waters into the northern end. They soon deposit their burden and leave the lake of the clearest and brightest blue. Their purity, however, is not long maintained, for, about a mile below Geneva, the muddy Arve comes sweeping down from Mont Blanc. For a while the two streams run side by side without mingling their waters, but the Rhone yields at last to the contamination, and is not purified again till it is absorbed into the ocean. The sediment thrown down by the river as it enters the lake is rapidly filling up the eastern end, and there is evidence to shew that during the present era the marshy plain of the Rhone valley has been advanced westward about 1½ miles. There can indeed be no doubt that the lake once extended as far as the rocky barrier between Bex and St Maurice, some 11 miles beyond its present margin; the whole intervening tract being now a level alluvial plain obviously deposited by the river. The scenery of the lower end is somewhat tame, the northern shore consisting for many miles of gently sloping hills, which are covered with vines, and thickly peopled. The limestone mountains of Savoy gradually approach the southern shore, and the upper end of the lake lies in a kind of defile between them and the first ranges of the Oberland *massif*. In the severest winters ice forms round the edge and at the lower end of the lake, but its whole surface has never been known to be covered. Its waters are occasionally subject to sudden oscillations called *seiches* or *leidèces*; the greatest recorded being on the morning of the 16th September A.D. 1600, when they rose and fell four times through a space of five feet[1]. These *seiches* generally occur during unsettled weather, and are supposed to be caused by unequal atmospheric pressure on the surface of this great sheet of water. Sudden and violent squalls are not unfrequent, rendering the navigation dangerous for small boats; and as they are often accompanied by driving rain and thick mist, an accident may not be seen from the shore till help is unavailing. Nor is an upset the only thing to be dreaded, for the waves rise quickly, and run high enough to swamp a small boat, if it be not skilfully directed. I remember that one evening in the summer of 1856, the steamer was obliged to remain for the night in the port of Ouchy; because the lake was so rough that the passengers, many of whom were

---

[1] *Conservateur Suisse*, v. 21.

miserably sick, could not have landed at any station above that place. On another fine afternoon during the same summer we started in our boat from Ouchy to pick up a party of friends about a mile further down the lake. There was not a breath of air to ruffle its glassy surface, and we rowed the whole distance. Just as we embarked our passengers, a gentle breeze sprung up, so we hoisted a couple of sails. It freshened so much, that before long, we struck the mizen, and in a few minutes more, not without difficulty, lowered the mainsail. The waves were then running so high that we at once rowed back towards the shore, which was less than a mile distant. The squall however fell as rapidly as it had risen, and before we reached land, the lake was again quite calm.

The Dranse, a river draining a large tract of the limestone district of north Savoy, enters the lake about the middle of the southern shore, near the pretty watering place of Evian, which, with its neighbour Thonon, are the only towns on the left bank; and indeed the latter is hardly more than a village. On the opposite shore the principal places are Lausanne, Vevay, and Villeneuve, at the embouchure of the Rhone; and between the last two, amongst lovely scenery, are the villages of Clarens, immortalised by Byron, and Montreux, the favourite winter retreat of invalids, with the celebrated castle of Chillon.

The lakes of Neuchâtel and Bienne, though belonging to Switzerland, cannot be claimed for the Alps; their left bank being formed by the long ridges of the Jura, which descend to the water's edge. On their right is a range of undulating hills, the verge of the lowlands of central Switzerland, above which rise the noble outlines of the Bernese mountains. The Lake of Neuchâtel (the Lacus Eburodunensis of the Romans), named from the picturesque old town near its northern end, is about 24 miles long and from 4 to 6 broad. It is 1427 feet above the level of the sea and 488 in greatest depth. Most of the streams from the eastern face of the Jura are received by it, and all the water from the extensive northern slopes of the low hills, which, insignificant as they seem, form part of the watershed between the Rhine and the Rhone. In a small parallel valley to the east is the little Lake of Morat. Unimportant in other respects, its eastern shore is famous in history, as the scene of the crushing defeat of the Burgundians by the Swiss in 1476, when numbers of the fugitives perished in its waters. A marshy tract, the favourite haunt of herons and wildfowl, separates the lake of Neuchâtel from that of Bienne or Biel, named from the little town near the northern end. It is about $10\frac{1}{2}$ miles long, $2\frac{1}{4}$ wide, and 231 feet in greatest depth. Rather nearer to the southern extremity is the wooded St Peter's Isle, which was for some time the retreat of Rousseau in 1765; his room is still shewn to visitors. An unusually high flood, such as that of 1816, can still convert these three lakes into a single sheet of water.

In the same lowland district of middle tertiary sandstones and conglomerates, but in lines, roughly speaking, at right angles to the above lakes, lie (in a north-easterly direction) the Lakes of Sempach, Zug, Zurich, and Constance. Sempach is only interesting for the battle fought upon its shores between the Swiss and Austrians in 1386. The Lake of Zug is much more beautifully situated, and the views from its waters of the Righi and other mountains of a hard conglomerate, called nagelflue, are very picturesque. Its depth is remarkable, being about 1280 feet; nearly equal to its height above the sea, which is 1369 feet. Its waters flow into the Reuss.

The Lake of Zurich is little more than an extension of the valley of the Linth, or perhaps it would be more correct to say, of an ancient channel of the Rhine[1]. Though rarely more than 2 miles broad, it is 26 miles in length; the greatest depth being 640 feet, and the mean height above the sea 1341 feet. The interesting old town of Zurich stands at the western end,

[1] See page 48.

on the efflux of the **Limmat**. Its banks are undulating and richly cultivated; and in clear weather noble views of the snow-clad peaks of Glarus and Uri add greatly to its beauties. About 6 miles from the upper end a tongue of land **extends** from the south shore, more than half way across the **lake; and** the waters **of** the strait thus formed are so shallow that a bridge, supported on wooden piles, has been constructed across it. No part of **the** basin above this barrier is deep, hence it is not unfrequently frozen over in winter, a rare occurrence with most of the larger Swiss lakes.

The Lake of Constance or Boden See (the Lacus Brigantinus or Acronius of the Romans; **Bodamicus of the middle** ages) chiefly lies beyond the **Alpine district, properly so called.** It is to the Rhine what the **Lake of Geneva** is to the Rhone, and probably, like it, once **extended much further up** the valley. In shape it is an irregular oval, about 41 miles long, and from $4\frac{1}{2}$ to $9\frac{1}{2}$ wide; the mean height above the sea being 1306 feet, and **the greatest known** depth **1027.** Above 13 miles from the northern extremity the Rhine quits it at Constance, passing through a narrow straight into a second irregular lake, called the Unter See. The arm above Constance, which **bears the** name of the Ueberlinger See, is seldom more than about 2 miles wide. The scenery is generally tame compared **with that of** the other Swiss lakes; **but is bolder towards the southern end,** where fine **views of the Tyrolese and Appenzell mountains are** obtained. It forms the boundary of five countries, Switzerland, Baden, Wurtemberg, **Bavaria, and Austria; and** besides Constance there are other small **but busy towns on its** banks. Its waters often rise 2 or 3 yards during the melting of the snow, and *seiches* (here called *ruhs*), are observed **as** on the Lake of Geneva. The gales from the E. and **N.E. are** dangerous, but most of all the south wind (Föhn), which is said to raise waves six yards high. The southern end is being rapidly filled up by the sediment brought **down by** the **Rhine.**

In the limestone region of Switzerland we have the Lakes of Thun, Brienz, Lucerne, and Wallenstadt. The first two are closely connected together, and form a portion of the valley of the Aar. They are only separated by a low wide dam, which has evidently been formed by the detritus from the waters of the Lütschine and Lombach, and on which stands the fashionable town of Interlaken. The Lake of Brienz is about 9 miles long and 2 wide; its surface is 1946 feet above the sea, and its greatest depth more than 2000 feet. The turbid waters of the Aar flow into the lake, which has evidently once extended several miles further up the valley, where there is now a marshy flat. In consequence of the quantity of silt discharged into it by the Aar and the Lütschine, the water is of a much greener tinge than that in the Lake of Thun. This is 11 miles long and 2 broad, its greatest depth is 768 feet, and its mean level is 23 feet below that of the other lake. The Kander, soon after being joined by the Simme, enters it near the western extremity; and so makes it the receptacle of nearly all the drainage from the north face of the western Oberland. Formerly this river flowed through a depression parallel to the lake and joined the Aar some little distance to the west. The present channel was cut in 1714, and a considerable delta has already been formed about its embouchure[1]. The scenery of these two lakes is deservedly celebrated; the mountains rise steeply for some five thousand feet or more above the water, with bold and varied outlines. Their lower slopes are either richly cultivated or densely wooded; the upper, green pastures or pine forests. The cliffs of pale yellowish-grey limestone are often very striking, and the snowy forms of the Eiger, Mönch, and Jungfrau are well seen from several points. The view of the

[1] A strange story is told by Fredegarius, *Chronicon*, § XVIII. who states that the waters of the Lake of Thun became so hot that the fishes were boiled: this phenomenon is said to have happened A.D. 598-9. Some sulphureous and bituminous springs on the side of the lake may perhaps help to explain as much of the story as is true.

last from Interlaken up the valley of the Lütschine is the great—I had almost said the sole—attraction of that place. Besides this there is the beautiful waterfall of the Giessbach on the south shore of the lake of Brienz, and the picturesque old town of Thun, at the western end of the other lake.

The Lake of Lucerne or Vierwaldstätter See (Four-Forest-Canton-Lake)[1], one of the most irregular and beautiful in Switzerland, does not lie entirely in the limestone district; still, except in the neighbourhood of the town of Lucerne its scenery is generally bold, and at the eastern end very grand. Its outline is very remarkable; and as it has much bearing upon the moot question of the origin of lakes in mountain districts, I venture to quote the following extract from the Alpine Guide[2], as well expressing the opinions which I had independently formed: "To the orographer it appears to lie in four different valleys, all related to the conformation of the adjoining mountains. The central portion of the lake lies in two parallel valleys whose direction is from E. to W., the one lying N. the other S. of the ridge of the Bürgenstein. These are connected through a narrow strait scarcely ½ mile wide, between the two rocky promontories called respectively the Untere and Obere Nase. It is not unlikely that the southern of these two divisions of the lake—called Buochser See—formerly extended to the W. over the isthmus whereon stands the town of Stanz, thus forming an island of the Bürgenstein. The W. end of the main branch of the lake, whence a comparatively shallow bay extends to the town of Lucerne, is intersected obliquely by a deep trench whose S. W. end is occupied by the branch called Alpnacher See, while the N. E. branch forms the long Bay of Küssnacht or Küssnachter See. It will not escape notice that these both lie in the direct line of a valley that stretches with scarcely a break parallel to the chain of the Bernese Alps from

---

[1] Uri, Schwyz, Unterwalden, and Lucerne.
[2] Central Alps, § 26, *Route A*.

Interlaken to the Lake of Zug. At the E. end of the Buochser See, where the containing walls of the lake-valley are directed from E.N.E. to W.S.W., it is joined at an acute angle by the bay of Uri, or Urner See, lying in the N. prolongation of the deep cleft that gives a passage to the Reuss, between the Bernese chain and the Alps of North Switzerland. The breadth of these various sections of the lake is very variable, but it is usually between one and two miles. Its mean height above the sea is 1437 feet, and the greatest depth hitherto measured 1140 feet." Of the former extension of the lake to the S. of the Bürgenstein there can I think be no doubt. The strait has been gradually silted up by the sediment from the Engelberger Aa and other streams. The Alpnacher See has also once extended further to the S. in the direction of the little lake of Sarnen; and the flat district to the S. of the bay of Uri is only a delta of the Reuss. The story of Tell and the tale of Anne of Geierstein give an additional interest to the beautiful scenery of this lake and its picturesque old town; and those who have read the former will not forget the dangers of its waters when the Föhn is raging.

The Lake of Wallenstadt lies in a narrow valley between steep limestone mountains; of which the northern range— the Churfirsten—rises from the water side in precipitous terraces, crowned by bold craggy peaks. Beautiful in scenery, the position of the lake also makes it peculiarly rich in sunrise and sunset effects. The narrow, deep, and remarkable trench in which it is situated opens a communication between the valley of the Rhine at Sargans and the sandstone district of N. Switzerland; and appears to any one descending that river the natural prolongation of the valley, the opening on the right, by which the stream escapes to the Lake of Constance, being far less conspicuous. I have little doubt that formerly either the Rhine, or an arm of it, flowed along the channel now occupied by the Lakes of Wallenstadt and Zurich and by the river Limmat. These two lakes only differ in level by about 52 feet, and are separated by a swampy plain, which is nothing more than a delta, deposited chiefly by the turbid waters of the Linth, the formation of which in former days no doubt was accelerated by the rocky breakwaters of the Buchberger, two steep mounds which still rise conspicuously above the marshes. The whole of this delta was formerly almost uninhabitable, but the cutting of the Linth and Escher canals has done much to render it salubrious. To the east of the Lake of Wallenstadt, the valley is also very level, being a delta formed by the Seez and other torrents; and the highest point in it (near to Sargans) is said to be only 25 feet above the present level of the Rhine. The barrier which finally diverted the stream of that river appears to me to be a talus formed by the fall of some débris from a mountain to the north, just at the narrowest part of the valley; the immediate effect of this would be to lower slightly the level of the two lakes and expose a considerable portion of the deltas.

In the Austrian Tyrol are no lakes of any importance; and it is not till we reach the almost subalpine region of the Saltzkammergut that we again meet with them. In the beautiful valleys of this district there are several, the largest of which, the Atter See, is about 12 miles long and 2½ wide. There are also some small lakes in Carinthia, all narrow in proportion to their length, the most considerable, the Wörther See, being about 12 miles long. The Bavarian lakes can scarcely be said to belong to the Alpine region.

Returning to the Alps, we find, nestling among the long spurs which slope down to the plains of Piedmont and Lombardy, a group of four lakes, Orta, Maggiore, Lugano, and Como. Through two of these, Maggiore and Como, passes all the drainage which descends from the south side of the watershed of a great mountain quadrant, of which Monte Rosa and the southernmost peak of the Orteler group are the extreme points. The Lago d'Orta, though very small, is a gem of beauty; richly wooded mountains, becoming bolder towards the north, rise all around it, and its glassy surface is broken by one picturesque island. A low barrier of porphyry rock cuts it off from the Italian plain, so its waters are discharged from the northern end into the Lago Maggiore. This, the Lacus Verbanus of the Romans, occupies a part of the sinuous valley of the Ticino, about 42 miles in length, advancing to the verge of the plain. Its general width is from 2 to 3 miles, except where it receives (on the west bank about 15 miles from the S. end) the important affluent of the Tosa, up the valley of which it extends for about 2 miles, but the alluvial plains above it, here and at the embouchure of the Ticino, shew that its waters once covered a much larger space. The western coast-line appears to be continued across the above-named arm by a group of low rocky islets called the Borromean Islands, from an illustrious Italian family whose property they are. On one of them, the Isola Bella, is a large but unfinished palace, the summer residence of its owners, overlooking the water; and the slate rock behind has been converted at great expense into a series of terrace gardens, in which flourish several shrubs and trees rarely seen so far to the north of the equator. These render the place interesting; for the rest, what one may call the 'tea-garden style' of ornamentation is so prevalent that most visitors are inclined to dispute the propriety of the epithet Bella, and to prefer its more unassuming neighbour, the Isola Madre, where also are some fine tropical plants. The lake is chiefly surrounded by crystalline rocks, but the southern part of its east bank is limestone. There is granite near the embouchure of the Tosa, and a little porphyry near the southern end. Like the neighbouring lakes it is liable to periodic winds; the *tramontana* which blows from midnight to morning from the north; and the *inverna* which comes in the opposite direction from midday to evening. One of the most remarkable things about it is that, while its surface is only 646 feet above the sea level, its bed is generally far below; the depth of the water in some places being said to be as much as 2615 feet.

The Lake of Lugano is something like a small model of the Lake of Lucerne. Wilder than its neighbours on either side, it is not seldom preferred to them; and the bold though not very lofty mountains which surround its irregular bays, with the occasional richness of its shores, will always make it a favourite. It is 889 feet above the sea, and its depth, which is very variable, is in some places greater than that measurement.

The lake of Como, the Lacus Larius of the Romans, in form resembles an irregular Λ, and occupies a portion of the valley of the Mera. Near its upper end the stream of the Adda enters from the east, bearing down the drainage of the whole Valtelline; and the sediment deposited by its waters has formed a marshy plain, which has completely isolated the northern end of the lake, so that it now forms a separate sheet of water under the name of the Lago di Mezzola. Of the two southern arms, the eastern, from which the Mera issues, is termed the Lago di Lecco; the western, separated from the plain of Lombardy by a low barrier of hills, is called the Lago di Como.

The upper part of the lake occupies a valley in the crystalline rocks, the two lower arms, with a small space to the north of them, lie among the limestone strata. The length measured along either arm is about 37 miles, and the breadth generally varies from 1 to 2 miles; the greatest being $2\frac{1}{2}$ miles. Its height above the sea is 699 feet, and its depth, which is always considerable, is in some places more than 1900 feet. The mountains around it are varied and often bold, rising from five to eight thousand feet above the level of the water; notwithstanding this, the foreground scenery is thoroughly Italian; the vegetation is rich; the foliage, among which grey masses of olive are often seen, is luxuriant; the houses are massive and southern in character; villas with well-kept gardens in many places on the Como arm almost fringe the lake; and though some complain that its comparative narrowness gives it more the character of a river, this combination of wildness and luxuriance causes it to be generally considered the most beautiful of the Italian lakes. Sudden thunderstorms and squalls are not uncommon, and are at times rather dangerous to small boats. In settled weather there are periodic winds; the *breva* from the south, which, setting in a little before noon, often blows with considerable force during the hotter part of the afternoon and subsides in the evening; and the *tirano* from the north, which blows softly during the night and early morning. The shores of the Lecco arm are comparatively desolate, the mountains here rising precipitously from the water, but the rest are thickly peopled by a busy and industrious race.

Nearly 30 miles further to the east, among sloping hills which occasionally rise to a height of five or six thousand feet above the water, is the rarely visited Lago d' Iseo, occupying a sinuous valley that forms the channel of the river Oglio. It is 627 feet above the sea, and about 700 feet deep. Its length is about 17 miles and its general breadth about 2 miles; except in the middle, where the distance of the opposite shore is greater, but the surface here is broken by a large rocky island.

The last and easternmost of the Italian lakes is the Lago di Garda, the Lacus Benacus of the Romans, which occupies a valley parallel to the great trench of the Adige, and is separated from it by the ridge of Monte Baldo. The Mincio, draining the eastern face of the Adamello, enters the lake at the northern end and quits it at the southern, near the fortress of Peschiera; so well known of late years as one of the angles of the Austrian quadrilateral. Its length is about 48 miles; the upper part occupies a straight and regular trench, about two miles across, enclosed by bold mountains; the lower widens out into a number of rounded bays among the gentle slopes that fringe the Lombard plain. The vineyards and gardens, the groves of olives and citrons, varied by the white-walled and red-roofed houses and by the campaniles of numerous villages, the sparkling blue waters of the lake and the mountains beyond it, rising through a haze almost as blue, with glimpses of far distant snows, form a scene of luxuriant beauty that can never be forgotten. Its shores are classic ground in history and literature. Virgil, born near the reed-fringed Mincius, has celebrated the storms which still lash its waters into a sea-like fury[1]: and on the narrow peninsula of Sermione, the ruins of the villa are even now shewn where Catullus wrote many of his exquisite poems; the forces of Austria and France manœuvred and contended along its western shore in 1796, until the contest was closed by the decisive battle of Medola, in which Napoleon I. dealt a fatal blow to the Austrian supremacy in Lombardy and Venetia; Peschiera was besieged and taken by the Piedmontese in 1848, and it protected the Austrian right in the struggles of Solferino and Custozza.

With one word on the Alpine waterfalls, this chapter must be concluded. To give a list of them would be a formidable task, for there is hardly a valley in many districts, of which we may not say

> ......like a downward smoke, the slender stream
> Along the cliff to fall and pause and fall did seem,
> A land of streams! some, like a downward smoke,
> Slow-dropping veils of thinnest lawn, did go;
> And some thro' wavering lights and shadows broke,
> Rolling a slumbrous sheet of foam below[2].

Not only are they far more grand and beautiful than any— however much belauded by local guide-books—which we possess in our islands, but also most of them have this further advantage, that the traveller can enjoy them in peace, without the annoyance of mendicant brats, would-be *ciceroni*, and other varieties of the vampire tribe, who infest the neighbourhood

---

[1] *Georg.* II. 160.   [2] Tennyson, *The Lotos Eaters*.

of 'sights.' At a few indeed of the larger Alpine waterfalls, some favourite 'look-out' is within a gate to which a silver key must be applied; but usually there are hundreds of other points of view, at which after you have sacrificed to the Penates of the place, and been taken the orthodox round, you may lie down and gaze undisturbed. As the number is so great, and a waterfall even harder to depict with the pen than with the pencil, I shall only name a few of the finest, and leave the reader to find the others for himself in each Alpine valley that he may visit. There is the Rhine fall near Schaffhausen, where a whole river tumbles over a ledge of limestone rock, a wall of 'shattered chrysophrase,' with a roar that shakes the neighbouring crags; the Staubbach, one column of pendulous spray against three hundred yards of precipice; the Giessbach, leaping through the pine-woods from cliff to cliff to the Lake of Brienz; the Aar fall and Arlenbach, plunging with united waters into a misty abyss in the rifted gneiss-rock; and the Tosa sliding over granite domes in bell-like sheets of liquid glass. Scarce inferior to these is the triple fall of the Reichenbach, and the Sallenche[1] weaving an endless veil of foamy threads; with many another, named and unnamed, in the valleys near Lenk and Sixt, Kandersteg and Lauterbrunnen. They are also very abundant and beautiful in Dauphiné: the finest perhaps being the Torrent du Diable near St Christophe, and the Saute de la Pucelle near La Grave; and are by no means wanting in the Graian and Savoy Alps. In the German Alps are the magnificent cascades of the Kriml, but on the whole they are less frequent in the Tyrol (especially the Italian district) and in the Cottian Alps, owing no doubt to the comparative smallness of the snowfields; but even here a few very beautiful instances may be found, at all events in the spring, before the intense heat of summer has dried up the streams.

[1] Near Vernayaz on the left bank of the Rhone Valley, bearing locally a far less euphonious name.

CHAPTER III.

THERE was a time, how many centuries ago we know not, when every mountain-chain of any importance in Central Europe was covered with perpetual snow, and the head of every valley was occupied with one of those masses of ice which are called glaciers. Now, they have vanished from the Jura, the Vosges, and the Cevennes; they linger indeed clustered around a few of the highest Pyrenean peaks; but it is only in the Alps that we can see them in real grandeur, unless we choose to journey northwards toward the Scandinavian Mountains. A glacier is, I believe, a thing at once most difficult to describe to a person who has never seen it, and that which makes the strongest impression upon every visitor to the Alps. Perhaps the various subjects of interest connected with the ice region will be most easily delineated by interweaving them with an account of an expedition[1] upon one of the most important glaciers—the Gorner—which descends from the western face of Monte Rosa.

[1] The expedition, for convenience, is described as taking place during a single day. In reality it was performed in two journeys. It would be possible, though fatiguing, to go as described in the text; but it is usual to pass the night at the Riffel Hotel at a height of about 8000 feet, and gain from it the level part of the glacier on the following morning.

Let us suppose ourselves at Zermatt, at the head of a grand valley in the Pennine Alps. Before us rises a wall of cliffs crowned with a smooth drapery of snow, from which, as from a sea, the fatal Matterhorn towers up in a vast snow-streaked pyramid four thousand feet in vertical height. Down a ravine on the left descends a huge mass of ice, not smooth and glittering like the snows above, but torn with innumerable rents, and dull with scattered débris. Like the giant claw of some hidden monster it rests on the meadows and the pine-covered slopes, a fitting sign of the Titanic force which has played so large a part in the sculpture of the earth's surface.

Let us make our way towards it along the rough mountain path, through the meadows, purpling now with crocus flowers. Large blocks are scattered here and there over the pastures; and the out-cropping rocks are not as usual splintered and rough, but smoothed into domes. How these blocks came hither, and what was the force which has planed the slaty rock, we will presently enquire. We draw near to the ice, and stand on the brink of a ravine, down which the torrent rushes, and a cool breeze ever plays even on the hottest day. Mounting a little further by the side of the stream, we see the end of the glacier burying itself under piles of broken stone; before us is a cavern in the ice, from which the torrent leaps forth to the light of day; the dome-shaped vault closes down upon the water, its pure blue colour deepening in intensity as it approaches to contrast with the turbid stream. In this way are born many of the Alpine rivers, which are not as in our own country slowly gathered together from innumerable springs, but start into life with almost full-grown vigour. The beauty of the blue ice-vault tempts us to try to gain a footing on some of the rocks which seem so invitingly placed as stepping-stones beneath it; but there is treachery in its siren loveliness. Ever and anon, without the slightest warning, large masses detach themselves from the roof, and fall crashing into the stream below; and more than one accident has been the consequence of an incautious approach.

(Fig. 5.) Terminal ice-cave of a Glacier.

Turning away then from it, let us walk along the face of the ice, keeping a careful watch upon the stones poised upon the verge of its cliffs, which every now and then come hopping down with sufficient momentum to bring scientific observation, and perhaps life, to a close. Against it are piled here and there blocks of every size, from that of a cottage downwards; and in places the surface is quite hid under a coating of pulverised stone. This is called the terminal moraine, and these blocks have been slowly brought down by the glacier from the mountain peaks above. In some glaciers this moraine rises like a miniature chain of hills; here, however, it is comparatively small, and we infer from this that the glacier is advancing. A little further on, and this conjecture is proved, for, at the very foot of the sloping cliff of ice, we come upon a meadow, the green turf of which is crumpled up into a wall two or three feet in height, by the slow yet resistless onward pressure of this giant ice-plough. In passing we may also notice that here and there deep fissures run up into the ice. In this glacier, however, they are not so large, or so remarkable as in many others; as for example at Grindelwald or Rosenlaui, where they extend for a considerable distance into the glacier. In the latter the pure blue of its glassy walls has an almost unearthly beauty. The cause of these fissures we will presently explain; let us now mount upon the ice, choosing a place where the slope is as gentle as possible, and where there are no nicely poised blocks above, threatening a sudden fall. Cutting a step here and there with our axes, where the slope is steepest or where an inconvenient fissure obliges us to turn aside, we find ourselves in a few minutes on the surface of the great ice-stream. Making our way as best we can among these fissures, which for the future we will call crevasses (their local name), we gain a convenient spot, from which we can survey a good extent of the glacier; and seating ourselves on a fallen rock, let us look around.

Above, and on each side of us, is the ice, rent in all directions by crevasses, to thread whose intricate labyrinths will be no easy task. Fantastic enough are the forms of the broken ice cliffs; towers and pinnacles, strange shapes like weather-worn statues, here rise on high, there seem nodding to a fall; here a knife-like ridge divides two chasms, there a blue arch spans a yawning gulf; all around the blocks which are travelling downward lie poised on the slippery slopes. Of those that start on this journey comparatively few arrive at its end uninjured; the rest fall into these abysses, and are crushed to powder between the glacier and its rocky bed. What then is the cause of these crevasses? The glacier, as we said, is not at rest, but in constant motion. It is literally a great ice stream; though not a fluid, like water, nor a viscous mass, like honey, which can readily adapt itself to any inequality in its rocky bed. Hence it is rent and riven asunder under the constant strains to which it is subjected. Nor is this the only cause of fracture; though ice is a solid, yet a glacier resembles a river in these respects—that the top moves more quickly than the bottom, and the middle than the sides. The latter of these inequalities in motion causes one class of crevasses; for the sides being, as it were, held back by friction against the rocks, a strain is produced in the direction of a downward line crossing diagonally the direction of motion, by which the ice is rent asunder, and crevasses are formed along the sides, which extend some distance into the mass, and of course point upwards. Other crevasses are formed by rocks projecting into the glacier, and by many other causes. But does a crevasse thus formed always remain? a little examination will shew that it does not. When by a change in the level of the bed, or by a narrowing of the sides, the icy masses are pressed one against another, they freeze together, and the crevasse heals up. This is due to a property of ice called regelation, in virtue of which the surfaces of two blocks of ice, if wetted, freeze together when placed in contact. The rocks which are scattered about us are themselves not without interest; for among them may be found specimens of nearly every cliff in the great amphitheatre, from which the Gorner glacier takes its rise. Here lie mingled together quartz and felspar, mica and chlorite slate, mottled serpentines and fibrous asbestus, with black tourmalines from Monte Rosa. Hence the moraine of a glacier is often an excellent collecting ground for the mineralogist.

Let us now thread the icy maze that cuts us off from the upper plateau of the glacier. This will be a task of more than one hour; the axe will often come into play, and a steady head and foot be needed, as often as a narrow ridge is crossed with deep blue chasms on either hand.

At last we gain the comparatively level field of ice around which rise the snow-clad Pennine giants. In front of us is the

(Fig. 6.) Crevasses on the Glacier.

mass of Monte Rosa; to the right the ridge of the Lyskamm, with all the slaty beds that, like courses of masonry, build up its precipitous face, beautifully defined by fine lines of snow; then the twin peaks of the Jumeaux; next the snow cap of the Breithorn, with the hump of the little Mont Cervin; and in the back ground the Matterhorn itself, with many a lesser peak.

For a considerable distance the bed of the glacier is comparatively smooth; hence there are no more of those intricate crevasses, through which we have just had to thread our way; but here and there a long narrow fissure extends for a considerable distance across the ice. These however are generally not too wide to jump, and so are no hindrances. The surface of the ice is still rough and crisp from the night's frost, like a bed of coral, and affords an excellent footing. We can now understand how the moraines are formed, for we see that in this single glacier several ice streams are welded together, which descend from different parts of the enclosing wall of mountains. From the crags that border each of these, fragments, detached by the frost and the storm, fall down upon the ice below. Hence when two of these streams unite, their stone-covered sides form a dyke or mound, which often rises to a height of at least 30 feet above the level of the surrounding ice. It must not, however, be supposed that the elevation of this bank is wholly due to the stones which compose it, for they shelter the ice underneath them, and preserve it from being melted by the sun.

From this same cause are formed glacier tables, some of which can now be seen at no great distance. They consist of a flattish stone, often 8 or 10 feet square[1], supported upon a comparatively small stalk of ice, so as to roughly resemble a gigantic mushroom. Once, these stones were lying upon the surface of the glacier; by slow degrees the ice melted away all round them; now the slanting rays of the morning and evening sun are gradually hollowing out their pedestal, till at last it will fall from under them, and the process will begin anew. The smaller fragments of stone however produce a contrary effect; for, by becoming thoroughly warmed with the sun, they melt away the ice in contact with them, and thus form small pits in its surface.

Besides the crevasses, the glacier is also furrowed by smaller and shallower channels, which are mainly excavated by running water. No sooner do the first beams of the rising sun glance upon the ice, than they begin to disintegrate the crystalline structures, which the night frost has built up, and to destroy the tiny mirrors on which they glitter so brightly.

---

[1] M. De Charpentier, *Essai sur les Glaciers*, p. 63, gives the dimensions of one as about 19 feet long, 14 ft. wide, and 8½ ft. thick, with a stem of ice 7½ ft. high.

Thus streams are formed, which rush down the slope of the glaciers, working out a channel for themselves, till at last they are engulfed in a crevasse. From the depths of this, the plash of falling water comes up with a pleasant and occasionally almost musical note. At times, however, in the morning, when these streams burst the bonds in which the night's frost has imprisoned them, they are apt to startle unaccustomed travellers. I was walking one morning over a glacier in Dauphiné, when I heard a sharp crack close at hand; this was followed by a riving bursting sound, as though the glacier itself were going to open under my feet: then came a louder crash, and then a rush of falling water, which explained the mystery. The channel of one of these streams had been frozen up during the night in several places, and the noise was caused by the accumulating waters forcing their way along their wonted course.

As we walk up the glacier we shall probably get a sight of one or two *moulins*. These are deep well-like cavities into which a stream plunges with a loud roar. They are formed in the following way: if, owing to some inequality in the bed of a glacier, a small surface crack is opened, intercepting one of the channels of drainage, the stream of course plunges into it, and in falling scoops away the surrounding ice. The sides of the crack, as the glacier advances, will be pressed together again, and united by regelation; and the same motion forwards will tend to neutralise the effect of this water saw, and retain the moulin in nearly the same position on the glacier. One of the best proofs which I have ever seen of the correctness of this explanation was on the Roseg glacier near Pontresina. We were walking along one of the surface streams, and came to a place where its course was intersected by a long narrow crevasse, which extended for a considerable distance across the glacier, and engulfed all the water. At this point the chasm had been widened by the friction of the falling stream, so that its walls were about two feet apart. Here then was a moulin which had not long been in action; but about 8 feet in advance was a second deep shaft, connected with the first by a dry channel in the ice about two feet wide. This one was oval in form, about six feet by four, the longer axis corresponding with the direction of the channel, and on each side of it a crevasse parallel to the former, and nearly closed, could be traced for a considerable distance. By dropping stones into it, we estimated its depth to be about 60 feet. It was therefore evident that some inequality in the rock either beneath, or a little higher up than, the first crevasse, caused the glacier to break as it passed over. The waters of the stream were engulfed in the rent thus formed, and at once began to wear away its sides. For a while, as the glacier advanced, the crevasse moved down with it below the obstacle, while the stream day by day worked its way slowly backwards, enlarging the pit. At last the ice above could no longer bear the tension to which it was submitted, and a new crevasse opened in the old spot, by which the water was speedily cut off; the channel and shaft in front were thus left dry, and the walls of the crevasse on either side pressed together again[1]. The blue walls of these wells, polished by the falling water, are often very beautiful; but a near approach to their slippery brinks is sometimes hazardous, for a fall would be fatal, since their depth is usually very great.

In our examination of the crevasses we shall have been struck by a not unfrequent peculiarity in the appearance of the ice, which looks as though it were bedded; layers of blue and white ice succeeding one another with tolerable regularity. We can see traces of the same structure on the surface of the glacier, which is furrowed by the apparent lines of strike produced by the outcrop of these beds. These are

---

[1] Dr Tyndall has found as many as six forsaken shafts in advance of an active one. *Glaciers of the Alps*, p. 364.

very conspicuous when any one stands on the rocks a few hundred feet above the surface of the glacier, and looks down upon it.

Come now to the edge of a crevasse, and examine the blue and white bands. Take an axe, and cut away some of the icy wall in order to get a clear and vertical surface. The structure then becomes very distinct: the ice is evidently composed of two varieties, arranged with considerable regularity in parallel layers; one of which is much bluer and more transparent than the other. Now come a little further, and look at this projecting corner of an ice cliff. Here is the bedding again, only in this place it does not run vertically, but almost horizontally, dipping slightly inwards. In passing over some inequalities in the rock below, this part has been by some means twisted or wrenched from its original position. Examine the face of the ice more carefully; the top layer, a couple of inches or more in thickness, is white ice, crumbling and disintegrated. Take your alpenstock or ice axe, and you will find it breaks easily into small irregular fragments, like crushed sugar-candy, many of which are wet to the touch, and not much harder than a well-moulded snowball. Below this is a layer of blue ice, half an inch or so thick; then another white vein rather thicker; then a blue, and so on, each plate varying from about half an inch to an inch in thickness. Now stoop down, and look closely along the edge of the cliff. You will see that all the blue layers stick out beyond the white, just as the harder strata do in the face of a cliff of banded shale. Put your finger to one of the white bands; the ice is soft and 'slushy', so as to be easily scraped out for the depth of an inch or so. Being less solid, and containing more air than the blue veins, it yields more quickly to the sun's heat. Now you see how the little furrows are formed, which, by collecting dust in their hollows, render this structure visible from a distance. But we can learn something more if we observe how the work of destruction is carried on. Press against one of the blue layers; it is firm, and will not yield to your finger, so you must chop it out with an axe. Now hold up a fragment to the light; it is perfectly pure and transparent, but still not quite solid, for small bubbles may here and there be seen within; and besides these, it is perforated by a number of fine tubes. These bubbles contain air, which has been squeezed out of the surrounding ice, and instead of escaping has by some accident lodged here and there within the mass. If you place a fragment containing some of these chambers in water, the temperature of which is above the freezing point, you will see little bubbles of air rise to the surface as the ice melts, or by holding it in the sunlight and near your ear, may hear them break through their prisons with a snapping noise, like bursting gorse-seeds on a summer day. Now examine the tubes : they are all arranged nearly or quite vertically, and their diameter varies from the thickness of a horsehair to about one twelfth of an inch. Some pierce quite through the plate, others only extend a little distance into it. What then has formed them? It is the water which drains from the dissolving white ice above. This trickles down through the crevices in the softer bed, till it reaches, drop by drop, the harder layer below. Here it collects in any chance depression, and then slowly eats its way downward; each drop that trickles from above aiding in enlarging and deepening the hole once begun. Thus the plate of solid ice is honeycombed by these water drills, which will slowly enlarge their bore-holes, till at last it too will crumble away. Now return to where these beds crop out nearly vertically, and you will see fine cracks running with tolerable regularity along the surface of the glacier; these are not crevasses which are just beginning to open[1], for they are parallel to the veined

---

[1] A crevasse of any size does not open suddenly in a glacier. Sometimes, but very rarely, the ice may be heard and seen to crack; but even then the chink formed is very narrow and enlarges slowly. Though I have been dozens of times on glaciers, I have never yet witnessed this phenomenon.

structure, and the crevasses generally cross it at a considerable angle. At any rate that is the case here, where this structure has only just been produced by the ice from the wide snowfield above being squeezed through the narrow trough between the Gorner Grat and the base of the Jumeaux. These cracks also, I believe, are due to the unequal melting of the two kinds of ice; water collects in the miniature valley between the blue ridges, and works its way down in a thin film at the junction of the two layers, just as it does when a sand-bed rests on a clay. Then, if there comes a night cold enough to reconvert it into ice, by expanding in freezing it splits the layers asunder, and the cracks thus formed are sometimes enlarged by water which afterwards runs into them. But it may be asked, what proof is there that this veined structure is the result of pressure, and not of that bedding which we noticed up above? We are mainly indebted to Dr Tyndall for the answer[1]. First of all, he observed, that many substances under pressure do become laminated, as for example, piecrust, after it has been well rolled, or the surface of rails that have been in use for some time on a railroad. A block of Wenham-lake ice after being squeezed in a Bramah press exhibited a number of streaky layers at right angles to the direction of the force employed, an experiment which shewed that ice was one of the substances capable of lamination. He observed, that this veined structure is first clearly seen when the glacier has been subjected to considerable lateral pressure by being squeezed through some rocky gorge or 'structure mill,' and that the planes are then roughly parallel to the sides of this passage, that is, perpendicular to the direction of greatest pressure; that it does not exist upon glaciers which are not so squeezed, the ice of which is either wholly amorphous, or exhibits only the original bedding. And finally, he discovered an instance where in a kind of border land, at the entrance of one of these 'mills,' the

[1] *Glaciers of the Alps*, p. 376.

ice exhibited both structures. Examples of this are of course very rare, for in such a position the glacier is generally much broken up; and the sides of the clefts cannot be narrowly examined without great personal risk. I have looked for it several times, but have not yet been fortunate enough to find a good instance; others, however, have been more successful, and two or three are recorded; enough to confirm, if it were needed, that described by Dr Tyndall.

Passing onwards toward Monte Rosa, we begin to notice a thin coating of snow spread over the surface of the glacier. This gradually thickens, till at last the hard ice can only be seen in the walls of the crevasses. Caution is now needful; for sometimes the drifting snows freeze together, and form a covering over the narrower crevasses which is often too weak to bear a man's weight. Where the snow is whitest, there it is most dangerous; and when we see much of this around us, we must tie ourselves together with the rope. We now have completed the second stage of our journey, and arrived at the foot of one of the tributary streams which unite in the great basin which we have just crossed.

Let us here halt awhile on some rocks which are situated at the foot of Monte Rosa, and from their form are called Auf der Platte. This is a favourite resting-place for parties who are making the ascent of the mountain. The smooth granite slabs furnish convenient seats, and though snow and ice are all around, not a few flowers flourish on the thin soil which here and there has been formed by the disintegration of the rock. Here are patches of gentian so studded with the dark blue stars of its flowers, that the leaves cannot be seen; here is the purple of the saxifrage; there the pale pink of the moss-like androsace, with the pale glacier ranunculus opening its flowers on the very edge of the snow. The knapsacks are generally unpacked here, and full justice is done to their contents. Hard boiled eggs disappear rapidly; and the mutton, though tough, and perhaps not distantly related to goat, follows their example. A hole in the snow makes a cellar for the wine, and iced water may generally be found at no great distance.

From this point we have a good view of the tributary glacier, which we purpose to ascend. It lies in what, were the climate more tropical, would be a steep glen between the cliffs of Monte Rosa and of the Lyskamm. The slope of this glacier is far steeper than that of the main stream, which we have hitherto followed; consequently its surface is much more fissured, and its crevasses are more irregular than those below. Here and there are sudden breaks in the level, so that a wall of ice runs almost across the glacier, and threatens to be no slight obstacle to our upward progress. In many parts the surface of the glacier is broken by a series of intersecting crevasses, like the strands of a net, which divide the ice into blocks resembling huge towers, often rudely quadrangular in plan. These broken masses are strikingly different from the more irregular and fantastic blocks in the ice-fall below. From their resemblance to the cracked surface of a mass of curd they have received the patois name of séracs, which has now become universal. We shall however describe them more minutely when we are threading our way among them.

Quitting the rocks, we direct our steps towards the cliffs of the Lyskamm. Here most of the crevasses are bridged over with snow, and it is often needful to probe them with the alpenstock, before we can trust ourselves to their uncertain support. Often its point pierces the crust of snow, and reveals the blue walls of the concealed chasm, sinking down to an apparently unfathomable depth. There would be but little chance of escape for the unlucky wight who might be engulfed in it; but by tying ourselves together with a strong rope, all danger is avoided. On arriving near to the base of the Lyskamm, we emerge from this net-work of crevasses and commence the ascent of a kind of channel in the glacier, up which walking is comparatively easy. This, however, at last ends at the foot of a pile of séracs, which extend almost across the glacier. Pausing for a few moments to hunt for the clue to this labyrinth, we notice that the ice-fall appears most practicable in the neighbourhood of the Lyskamm, and bear away to the right of it. Our guide adroitly threads the maze, now hewing steps along a frozen slope, with a deep chasm yawning below; now cutting his way down a wall of ice to reach a fallen block or mass of snow that bridges some gulf otherwise impassable. At last we find ourselves upon the edge of a wide trough that for some distance runs like a canal across the glacier. Its steep banks are of unequal height; the one upon which we stand being perhaps 20 feet above its bed, while the other is nearly double as much. It is no doubt a great crevasse, that has been partly choked up by fallen ice and snow. We slide down the one side, walk across and commence ascending the other, which, though not actually vertical, is so steep that we can only mount it by clambering with hands and feet in the holes which our guide punches out as he advances hand over hand. A few feet below the top, the wall is rent by a narrow crevasse which slopes down into the ice; but the entrance at the part where we are climbing is masked with snow. My companions pass this without difficulty, but the snow begins to break away under the feet of the one who precedes me; consequently when I tread upon the step, it yields at once and leaves me for a few moments anchored by the hands, with my feet kicking about in free space. Those above, however, seeing my plight, terminate it by a haul at the rope, which brings me up like a bale of goods, and lands me at their feet. We are now upon a sort of terrace immediately under the Lyskamm, which is pleasant walking enough; though the scattered blocks of ice and the long furrows ploughed across the snow shew that our path is sometimes raked by volleys from the cliffs above. While we have been mounting, a change for the worse has come over the sky; a thick grey mist has settled down on the mountains round; a cold blast comes in fitful puffs across the ice; and falling snowflakes fill the air. Advance is for a time useless; we seek the shelter of a gully in the ice, and console ourselves with studying the fantastic forms of the wilderness of séracs below. While thus detained, let us beguile the time by saying something more about the nature and formation of a glacier.

From the snow, which is falling around in feathery clusters of delicate spiculæ or in fine six-petaled flowers[1] of exquisite beauty, have been built up the icy masses over which we were climbing; as the coral reef is raised by the polyp's star-like skeleton. Rain seldom falls at this elevation; for the vapours which thus descend on the green fields in the valleys below are here thrown down as snow or hail.

To explain more clearly the formation of a glacier, let us carry our thoughts back to the time when these mountains first reared their bare rocks on high beneath the heavens. We need not now inquire how nearly their then configuration resembled that which we at present behold; or what parts in their sculpture have been played by the riving force of hidden fires, or by the slow chiseling of water, air, and frost; but let us suppose them standing as yet unflecked by snow. As time passes on, either by change of climate or by their rising still higher, and so reaching a rarer and consequently colder atmosphere, their tops are sprinkled with the winter's snow. The summer's sun at first melts this away; but with the increasing cold, it lingers longer each year, till at last it remains unmelted in this sheltered glen between the two mountains. Year by year the mass accumulates; each summer melting

---

[1] These snow flowers or stars are not unfrequently seen falling in the higher Alps, especially if the day be still. I have not often observed them in England. I think only twice since the year 1860. Their forms under the microscope are of great variety and beauty.

somewhat away, but each winter adding more largely to the store. What then has transformed the powdery snow into solid ice, and changed the opaquely white feathers of the one into the transparent blue solid of the other? If we consider to what the whiteness of the snow is due, we shall see that this change is mainly the result of two causes. Why then is the snow opaque and ice transparent? Because the former contains more air than the latter. It is a law of nature that light cannot pass out from a denser into a rarer medium, unless it strike their common surface at a proper angle. If it does not do this, it is reflected back within the denser medium. Hence the light is often unable to pass through the many-faced little crystals of ice of which snow is composed, and thus that, which in the solid mass would be transparent, is in minute fragments opaque. Take, for example, a piece of the purest glass; pound it, and it becomes a dull white powder: or take a lump of clear rock salt; crush it, and you have the white grains ready for the table. The snow therefore has become transparent by the expulsion of the air which was among its tiny crystals. How then has this been done? Partly by alternate thawing and freezing, and partly by pressure. As the surface snow melts away under the rays of the sun, the water thus set free trickles down into the mass below, dissolving many of the finer particles of snow with which it comes in contact, until it is reconverted into ice by some fall in the temperature. By this means the mass of loose snow becomes a semi-solid cake. We may see the same process going on during a thaw in England, where heaps of snow have been piled up by the road side. As they melt away, they assume more and more the appearance of ice; and though rapidly diminishing in bulk become much more solid. If we look at the sides of some of the tower-like masses in the séracs below us, we shall see distinct traces of bedding; the faces of white ice being crossed by thin grey lines, like courses of masonry. Between the deposition of each one of these bands an interval of time has elapsed, during which the surface of the snow has become somewhat soiled by the dust blown upon it from the neighbouring rocks.

This process however of freezing and thawing from the changes of temperature is not so important an agent in the conversion of snow into glacier-ice as is the remaining one, the pressure exercised by the mass itself. Every school-boy knows that the more he squeezes a snow-ball the harder it becomes; and, were his muscles strong enough, he might render it solid ice. By the help of a Bramah-press snow may be converted into transparent ice; and anyone can perform the experiment for himself with an ordinary screw-press, though probably with only partial success. As the glacier descends towards the valley, the weight of the upper part presses heavily on the lower; especially when it meets with any obstacles to its progress. Hence the original bedding is gradually effaced, and is not unfrequently replaced by the veined structure which we have already described.

The storm having now blown over, we will proceed onwards; though the mists still shroud the peaks of Monte Rosa and hang low over the pass. The crevasses in the upper part of the glacier, or *névé* as it is usually called, are very different in shape from those lower down; being rather great pits than chasms in the ice. Let us turn slightly out of our course to visit one of them : it is a huge gulf, 80 or 90 feet in length and in places perhaps 30 across; the snow slopes gently away from beneath our feet towards its mouth, curling over its precipitous walls in a beautiful but treacherous cornice. This terminates in long pendent icicles of delicate blue, reaching down towards the bluer depth below. Near one end the gulf is bridged with a mass of snow, which is fringed underneath with a forest of icicles; some of which are almost as large as the stem of a fair sized pine tree. The overhanging cornices often render it no easy matter to approach near enough to obtain a good view of such crevasses; but their beauty will well repay the cost of some time and trouble.

A little longer walking through the fog brings us to the top of the pass, from which we ought to obtain an extensive view. No chance however is there of this to-day; the cold mist has long blotted out the distant mountains, and now not even the neighbouring peaks of Monte Rosa can be seen. Under these circumstances there is nothing left but to follow the example of the king of France, and having marched up the hill, to march down again.

When we come to the brink of the large crevasse, which gave us some little trouble in mounting, the best plan appears to descend by a glissade[1] so that our speed may carry us over the smaller crevasse in the side without breaking through. We accordingly start, just as we are, roped together; our guide first, my friend second, myself third. All goes well for a little while, but when about twelve feet from the bottom, the guide somehow loses his balance and falls. It does not seem worth while to try to anchor the party, so I slide on. Quicker than this has taken to tell, my friend is jerked off his legs; another moment, the rope tightens round me, and I feel myself flying through the air. This is followed by a promiscuous plunge into the soft snow beneath, whence we emerge looking like millers, but none the worse. We easily mount the other side, pick our way as best we can through the maze of crevasses below, where we find that the snow bridges have not improved in strength since the morning, and finally, after taking a somewhat different path, regain the rocks of Auf der Platte. While crossing over the level ice-field between these and the ridge of the Gorner Grat, it may be well to say a few words concerning the nature of that glacier motion to which allusion has already been made.

[1] This is done as follows; each person slides with the feet level and pretty close together, leaning back upon his alpenstock, and regulating his pace by pressing its point more or less deeply into the snow.

Although several theories have been advanced to explain the cause of glacier motion, three especially have attracted attention. The first of these, in point of time, was advanced by Scheuchzer in 1705, and developed by M. de Charpentier. The idea is as follows: that the whole mass of the glacier is traversed by a number of exceedingly minute fissures or veins; that these are filled from time to time with water, produced by the ice thawing under the influence of heat or pressure, which, owing to some change in the external circumstances, is again frozen. Water, it is well known, expands when it is converted into ice: hence the freezing of a quantity of water, dispersed throughout the body of the glacier, would, if it were unconstrained, cause expansion in all directions. In the case however of a glacier on a mountain side, motion takes place in the only unopposed direction, that is, downwards. To this theory there are many grave objections: it does not satisfactorily explain several of the peculiarities of glacier motion, such as its resemblance to that of a river, and the fact that it is continued even during the coldest winters, and is not liable to any marked change when there is a sudden alteration in the temperature of the surrounding air. The advocates, moreover, of this theory have failed to prove the existence of these fine veins or capillaries, as they are commonly called. No doubt, near the surface of a glacier, the ice is often ill compacted, and readily breaks asunder, but this is only because, like river ice, it has become 'rotten' through exposure to the air. In the body of the glacier no such tendency to separation can be detected. Dr Tyndall[1] and Mr Huxley made a number of experiments on the Mer de Glace and its tributaries, and were unable to find any proof of their existence in sound unweathered ice. Holes were bored carefully in the ice, and filled with coloured liquids, but these did not in any way diffuse themselves in the surrounding ice. Dr Tyndall says 'I have

[1] *Glaciers of the Alps*, p. 338.

myself seen the red liquid resting in an auger-hole, where it had lain for an hour without diffusing itself in any sensible degree. This cavity intersected both the white ice and the blue veins of the glacier; and Mr Huxley, in my presence, cut away the ice until the walls of the cavity became extremely thin, still no trace of liquid passed through them.' The above explanation of glacier motion generally goes by the name of Charpentier's or the Dilatation theory.

The next is called, from its eminent upholder, Forbes' or the Viscous theory. Principal J. D. Forbes, whose high qualities as a mountaineer, writer, and man of science, entitle him to the name of the British De Saussure, after a number of experiments on the motion of glaciers, and a close examination of their phenomena, came to the following conclusion with regard to them. 'A glacier is an imperfect fluid, or a viscous body, which is urged down slopes of a certain inclination by the mutual pressure of its parts[1]." The consistency to which reference is here made, is illustrated by the example of thick mortar, tar, or mixtures of plaster and glue. This theory undoubtedly accounts for most of the phenomena of glacier motion; it has however met with a strong opponent in Dr Tyndall, who refuses to admit that ice has all the properties which are essential to the idea of a viscous body. In order to make clear the dispute between these two eminent men of science, it will be necessary to enumerate the results of some of Dr Tyndall's experiments, which are described by him in the 'Glaciers of the Alps.' After a number of observations he came to the conclusion that a glacier could not stretch so much as seven-tenths of an inch in five hours, or be bent through an angle of 1° 50′ without breaking into numerous crevasses[2]. He also found that, although a mass of ice could be pressed into almost any shape whatsoever, the change of form was effected, not by its stretching, but by its shattering and

[1] *Travels through the Alps*, p. 365.   [2] Pages 314, 326.

reuniting: and that in a word, although ice when subjected to *pressure* presented analogies with a plastic body, it failed to do so under *tension*. He also observed that when a sunbeam was passed through a plate of ice, which had been formed regularly, star-like flowers appeared within the ice, lying in planes parallel to its surface; shewing thus that the crystals of which the mass was composed, the courses as it were of its masonry, could be detected in taking it to pieces by a process the reverse of that which had built it up. He applied the same test to glacier ice, and found that in it no such definite planes of freezing could be detected. Sometime before Dr Tyndall commenced his experiments, Dr Faraday had shewn that two pieces of ice, if placed in contact with their surfaces moistened, would always freeze together. This property, then, Dr Tyndall applies to explain the phenomena of glaciers; he considers that glacier ice cannot in any sense be called a viscous body or fluid; because it has not been proved that it can be stretched in even a slight degree without breaking. He maintains therefore that a glacier descends a slope by reason of its own weight, the pressure of the mass of snow above it, and perhaps the gradual melting of that part of its surface which is in contact with its bed; that during its descent it is continually being broken by tension, and being healed by regelation, when that tension is removed or replaced by pressure; consequently that, although many of its phenomena are suggestive of plasticity or viscosity, it cannot in strictness be said to be endued with any such property. The question at issue cannot perhaps as yet be regarded as wholly settled; still Dr Tyndall has certainly proved that ice, if plastic at all, is only so in a very slight degree, and that Professor Forbes was unfortunate in making use of the term viscous, as being very liable to misconception and standing in need of many limitations.

So much then for the phenomena of glaciers; and now as we

are close to the edge, let us choose a place where we can get on to the moraine, and after a short scramble over the loose stones gain the rough path which runs along to the cliffs of the Gorner Grat, and gradually leads us to the Alpine pastures, over which lies the way to the Riffel hotel, where we shall find a good supper and a comfortable bed.

But as the red glow has not yet begun to light up the snows of Monte Rosa, we may linger awhile about the base of the Riffelhorn, a dark peak of serpentine, now too well known as the closing scene of one most promising life[1]. We cannot fail to remark that the rocks here are in many places very smooth, and have a peculiar rounded contour; and if we have made good use of our eyes during the morning, we shall have already noticed similar forms down below by the side of the glacier. It is therefore evident that the ice once passed over this place, and a little observation will shew us that the glaciers in the Alps once extended far beyond their present limits. There are several marks by which we can follow up their trail, the principal of which, to use their customary titles, are moraines, perched blocks, and rounded, polished, and scratched rocks. You have already seen the great piles of stone at the end, by the sides, and sometimes in the middle of the glacier. Now it is evident that if the ice were to melt away, these huge ridges would be left stranded upon the bottom of the valley. This is exactly what has happened. Often in walking among the Alps, you find in some valley, miles below the glaciers, perhaps just at its mouth, one or more of these great stone banks. A little examination shews that they cannot have fallen from the cliffs above, supposing such to exist; their form and position render that impossible; very likely also they are composed of rocks which you know to be

[1] Mr K. Wilson, Fellow of Trinity College, Cambridge, was found lying dead beneath the crags of the Riffelhorn. It is supposed that he had climbed to the summit and missed his footing in descending. The accident happened in the evening of July 18, 1865.

only found near the head of the valley. Running water cannot have transported these heavy blocks so far, nor piled them up so nicely; therefore you are convinced that they must have been brought by a glacier, even though, as is not unfrequently the case, you know that there is no longer one in the valley. These piles of stones are generally terminal moraines; the lateral are less common, probably because, owing to the steep slope of the mountain sides, they do not preserve their form, but roll down as the glacier retreats, or are carried down by the effects of atmospheric denudation, and so cannot be distinguished from other débris. Still I have occasionally seen very clear examples, where a great causeway, now perhaps nearly covered with grass and alpine shrubs, extends along the hill-side for some distance. There is, however, hardly a valley among the crystalline districts, where traces of terminal moraines may not be detected. Of course their size depends partly on the nature of the rocks higher up, and partly on the length of time during which the glacier has remained nearly at the same limit. Sometimes the ice appears to have made two or three rapid retreats, with long halts intervening, so that the moraines are arranged one within the other in curving lines a few dozen yards apart. One of the best instances which I have seen of this is in the upper part of the Romanche valley, above Villard d'Arène, in Dauphiné, where there are four or five of these moraines clearly defined and separated by a short interval. Sometimes the glacier appears to have retreated more leisurely, and the ground is covered for a considerable distance with enormous irregular piles of rubbish; between these may be occasionally observed little green plots, which have evidently once been pools of muddy water, such as may still be seen by the side of many large glaciers. There is a very fine instance of this at the opening of the Val Viola near Bormio; indeed I do not think I ever saw a greater number of well-marked old moraines, than during a walk from the Bernina to the Stelvio road, by the Val di Campo and this valley; and yet there are now only a few stray patches of snow on the pass which connects them. Occasionally these old terminal moraines are of enormous size. There is one in the Val Roseg, which can hardly be less than five hundred feet high. It is now overgrown with trees, and the torrent has cut its way through one end, making an excellent section of it; but it appears to have once completely barred the valley, and formed a lake in the green basin above it. It is plainly visible from Pontresina, like a great causeway, though it must be some four miles away. In most of these cases the glacier appears to have retreated tolerably uniformly and quickly from its last position of rest to pretty nearly its present limits, and the nearest of the old moraines is generally a considerable distance from the present end of the ice.

Perched or erratic blocks, that is boulders resting in positions to which they could not have rolled, are also tolerably clear signs of former ice-action. If we find a block of granite, several tons in weight, in a limestone district, or resting on the top of a hill, we are sure that it cannot have rolled thither, and know of no force which could transport it from its original site without the aid of ice. Sometimes indeed these blocks may be the relics of moraines, the smaller stones of which have crumbled or been washed away; but I think that this is not often the case. They are not sufficient to prove that a glacier has once occupied the spot where they are found, because they may have been transported by icebergs when the surrounding country was under water.

For example, on the slopes near Monthey, a little village on the left bank of the Rhone, at the opening of the Val d'Illiez (some 11 miles from the head of the Lake of Geneva), lie a number of blocks, chiefly of grey granite[1], which have

---

[1] It would perhaps be more correct to say, 'used to lie'; for many I believe have been broken up since I saw them, to make a road.

evidently come from some part of the Pennine chain, probably the eastern end of the Mont Blanc range. They are thickly strewn over the slopes, a few minutes' walk above the village, both among the vineyards, and especially upon a kind of slight plateau or step on the hill-side, which is occupied by a wood of Spanish chestnuts. Among the gnarled old trunks of these, they lie—I had almost said in thousands,—great and small, from the size of a pumpkin to that of a cottage. Though generally they occur singly, in this wood they are occasionally piled one on another. The zone which they occupy is according to M. de Charpentier about three quarters of a league long, and from 500 to 800 feet wide. He also gives the dimensions of one of the largest, called the Pierre des Marmettes, as 63 feet long, 32 wide and 30 high, and the content as 60,480 feet cube[1]. Their height above the sea, roughly speaking, must be about sixteen or seventeen hundred feet.

Again, on the slopes of the Jura, some few hundred feet above Neuchâtel, lie more of these blocks, scattered over the cornfields and among the woods. They too were once more numerous than at present, for the road-makers have been at work among them; but a considerable quantity may still be found in the course of an hour's ramble. A few are of mica slate, but the majority are of the same granite as those of Monthey. The finest specimen (in a little wood of oak and fir, at a height of about 2300 feet above the sea) is said to be about 50 feet long, 20 wide, and 40 in greatest thickness; and to contain about 40,000 cubic feet[2]. It is called the Pierre-à-bot; from the curious resemblance which it bears to a squatting toad. It either rests upon the limestone rock, or is only separated by a thin soil. At a short distance are three or four smaller blocks, and many others may be found lower

---

[1] Probably these measurements are in French feet, 1000 French = 1065 English feet. *Essai sur les Glaciers*, p. 126.

[2] Perhaps too great. My estimate was about 12 yards long and 5 wide.

down the hill. In one place I noticed four lying close together; and in another a little heap of boulders, but no signs of moraine. They are chiefly scattered over a belt of ground, the vertical range of which must be at least two or three hundred feet, and are not confined to this part of the Jura.

Their presence here is commonly explained by supposing that in former ages the glacier of the Rhone, swelled by tributary streams from Mont Blanc and the Savoy Alps, not only occupied the bed of the Lake of Geneva, but also overflowed all the lowland basin between the Alps and Jura, and that the former limits of this monstrous ice-sea are marked by these stranded blocks. No doubt this is quite possible; and if certain mounds in the plain of Piedmont have been rightly identified with the terminal moraines of glaciers, which once occupied the southern valleys of the Alps and the Italian Lakes, the northern glaciers can hardly have had a less extension. Still, if these erratics on the Jura, and those above Monthey are the relics of moraines, either myriads of smaller blocks must have been removed by the aid of air and water, or else the moraine of the Rhone glacier must have differed very remarkably from every other that I have ever examined. The blocks at Monthey lie in a sort of bay under the lee of the Dent du Midi, into which, if the country were under water, icebergs would probably be often swept by the eddying current of the Rhone, as it rushed out of the narrow gorge at St Maurice, which was perhaps the limit of the glacier. There running aground, they would slowly melt away, and deposit their stony burdens. These blocks are certainly below those upon the Jura, probably three or four hundred feet, and must therefore have been stranded at a later period, when the glacier had shrunk considerably, and there was no tributary from the Val d'Illiez; they are however numerous enough to shew that the level of the ice must have been nearly stationary for a considerable period. What then has become of the enormous piles of débris, which in this case we might fairly expect to find still remaining along with them? There is nothing in the configuration of the Val d'Illiez to account for such a wholesale denudation: and as there is evidence in the drifts to the north of the Lake of Geneva to shew that this district was under water at a time when erratics (though of a smaller size) were being transported, I cannot yet consider the hypothesis, that these blocks were left on their *present* sites by the Rhone glacier, as proved, although it may seem presumptuous to say so when such weighty authority can be quoted in its favour.

The other great sign of the former presence of a glacier is the peculiar shape and appearance of the rocks over which it has passed. The blocks of stone which fall into the crevasses are crushed into pieces between the ice and the rock below, and the fragments becoming embedded in the glacier, convert it into a huge file, which rasps the mountain-side as it slowly slides along. Thus all inequalities are ground away, and a smooth surface formed. There is however one peculiarity which at once distinguishes rocks worn by a glacier from those which have been exposed to the action of running water. The stream, with its plunging currents and whirling eddies, has a power of engraving, which the glacier does not possess; it can but rub and scrape. The one is the chisel, the other the file of nature; the one ploughs, the other grinds. The bed of a stream therefore is full of concave hollows: that of a glacier is marked by convex surfaces and swelling domes of rock. These from their resemblance to the curving back of a sheep are called *roches moutonnées* by the French geologists, and the name is very commonly used by English writers. They may be found in almost every Alpine valley, where the rock is tolerably durable; and, even where the surface is much weathered, an experienced eye can often detect their contours on the mountain-side. Granite, and most kinds of limestone, do not retain these marks so well as the crystalline slates, among which sometimes, where the rock is hard and fine grained, the surface has been brought by the ice rubber to a high polish. Come for instance into this little glen, which runs parallel to the Gorner glacier; in which every rock is rounded like a rolling wave, and look carefully along the cliffs of chlorite-slate at the side. It is perhaps thousands of years since the glacier passed its icy burnisher over their surface, and yet here and there are bits of rock, the polish of which is brighter than the columns of many a building that has not weathered the storms of ten centuries. There are, however, generally signs that the emery powder used has been a little too coarse; for here and there are fine scratches on the surface, all pointing in one direction down the valley. Some fragment of quartz, fixed in the ice, has left its mark here, like the glazier's diamond on a pane of glass. Sometimes when a larger piece than usual has been embedded, a deep score or groove has been cut out; and these striations may be detected on the domes of rock, when all trace of their polished surface has weathered away. It is not easy to find good specimens of this handwriting on the wall so far from the glacier; generally if you want to see it, especially in the limestone district, you must scramble down by the side of the ice, and look for some spot over which it has passed at no distant period. There, indeed, you may sometimes find the stone chisel in the very act of engraving; and if you waited long enough might estimate the rate at which its work was done. Now and then, however, some lucky chance has preserved one of these natural Ogham inscriptions. I have, for instance, a fragment of smoothed and scratched black limestone, which I broke off a rock by the side of the Stelvio road near Bormio, now miles away from any glacier. It had been covered up by a thin layer of soil, probably when the ice retreated, which had remained until some chance alteration in the road exposed it to view.

Some geologists, among whom are several very eminent men of science, have attributed to glaciers a far greater share in the sculpture of the Alps than has been here indicated. They have supposed that not only have they rounded the surfaces of cliffs, and in some cases buried themselves more deeply in their rocky channels, but also have ploughed out many of the greater Alpine valleys, and of the depressions now occupied by important lakes. To discuss this difficult subject would be too long a task for a work like this; I must therefore be content with merely stating that, even admitting the great extent claimed for the ancient glaciers of the Alps, admitting also that all the Swiss and Italian lakes were once overflowed by them, I do not think that there is evidence enough to allow of our attributing to a glacier, however large, such powers of erosion as would be required for the purpose. No doubt under peculiar circumstances—as at the foot of steep descents—shallow basins and tarns may have been hollowed out by the ice, such as those on the upper part of the Bernina pass; but I think that generally the scooping power of a glacier is very slight. The Gorner glacier (as stated above) in advancing across a meadow, did but tear up a foot or two of the soil, which was crumpled up in front so as to form a wall a yard or so in height. Of course a glacier by sliding along a valley must somewhat deepen the bed, and in certain cases the moraines left by them act as dams to retain the waters; still I cannot but believe that the lake valleys, whatever may have formed them, existed before the time when the glaciers passed along them; and that the glacier was much more a consequence of the valley than the valley of the glacier. I should often prefer to account for a lake by supposing that some local upheaval has formed a barrier (like that which closes the Rhone valley at St Maurice), or that, in the case of some of the smaller lakes, a moraine or bergfall—as at the Lago d'Alleghe in the Italian Tyrol—has dammed up the waters of the river.

Such being the evidence in favour of a former extension of the existing glaciers, the question naturally arises, is there any to fix the period in the world's history at which this took place? There can be little doubt that the epoch of greatest extension corresponded with that which in geology bears the name 'glacial;' one, in which the climate of Northern Europe was arctic, when our coasts were often ice-bound, perhaps for months, like those of Greenland at the present time; when the mammoth, the rhinoceros, the urus, and the reindeer, with the hyæna and cave-lion, roamed over the frosty fields. Then, when the valleys of Wales and of the English Lakes were filled deep with ice, the tributary glaciers from each Alpine glen united to form those mighty streams which bore the erratics of Monthey and Neuchâtel, if not to their present sites, at least far away from their parent rocks. To this period also we should of course assign all the moraines found near or beyond the openings of the great Alpine valleys. How long it may have lasted we cannot tell, but at its close the retreat of the glaciers appears to have been tolerably uniform for a considerable space, after which interval two or three halts occurred before they reached their present limits. It is not easy to fix exactly the number of these, but I think there were not less than two distinct pauses; one, during which those enormous masses of moraine were deposited which are now often found, either at the mouth of a lateral valley, or at any rate a few miles below the present ends of the glaciers—such as, for example, that in the Romanche valley about an hour's walk above Villar d'Arêne, those between Frutigen and Kandersteg, that in the Val Roseg, those at the opening of the Val di Campo on the Bernina road, and of the Val Viola near Bormio on the Stelvio, with many more in similar situations. At these places the glaciers must have shrunk very slowly, with frequent halts. The other pause, if there was not more than one, is that to which belong the moraines now found within a mile or two of the ends, or a few hundred yards from the sides of the present glaciers, as, for example, those near the Rhone glacier. These, though very clearly defined, are generally smaller than the above-named; and the terminal moraines are often arranged concentrically, sometimes four or five in number, one near another, thus shewing as many periods of comparatively brief repose.

That the glaciers even now are not at rest is well known, and considerable oscillations have been recorded in the last fifty years. I have already mentioned one in the case of the Gorner glacier; a much more remarkable instance is that of the Brenva glacier[1], which in 1818 and the previous year rose so far above its former level as to destroy the little chapel by the path up to the Col de la Seigne, and since then has sunk down to a depth of 300 feet below it. But there is also some reason to think that a few centuries ago the glaciers were considerably less extensive than they now are. The evidence in favour of this has been collected with much care by M. Venetz[2], and it may be thus summed up:—(1) Traditions: in a great number of the higher Alpine valleys there are stories stating that passes, which now, from the extent of glacier to be traversed, are closed to all but mountaineers, were formerly comparatively easy. Now, although singly many of these traditions are of little value, and some obviously absurd, still, when taken collectively, like a bundle of sticks, they have a certain strength; for it is difficult to see how such traditions, reaching back to no very remote time, could exist in localities so widely separated as Dauphiné and the Tyrol without some basis in fact. (2) Fragments of paved roads which have been partly destroyed by the increase of snowfields and glaciers; such as those on the Monte Moro, on the Saas Pass, and on the Susten

---

[1] Forbes, *Travels in the Alps of Savoy*, p. 205.

[2] Venetz, 'Sur les variations de la température dans les Alpes de la Suisse' (*Denkschriften der Allgemeinen Schweizerischen Gesellschaft*. Band I. Abtheil. 2).

Pass, &c. (3) Recorded instances of the formation of small glaciers in the memory of persons living. (4) The remains of trunks and roots of trees and shrubs considerably above the height at which they now grow; and (5) Documents, imposing taxes upon fruits which can no longer be ripened in the places named, and regulating the rights of communes over passes which now are practically closed. M. Venetz mentions twenty-two instances belonging to one or other of these classes, and states that he could add largely to them, "Il nous auroit été facile d'en citer davantage. Si nous avions eu le temps de faire les recherches nécessaires, et si nous voulions adjouter foi à des traditions populaires, nous citerions une infinité de cas pareils." As I am aware of many that he has not mentioned, in other parts of the Alps, I am inclined to think that there is 'something in it.' He believes the period when this reflux of the glaciers began to have been early in the seventeenth century.

CHAPTER IV.

HAVING thus spoken of glaciers, let a few words be said of glacières or ice-caves. Modest, as beseemeth females, they lie hid underground; yet, though troglodyte in habits, are not without a certain weird beauty. They occur in the Jura, and in several parts of the mid-alpine district. In the former region are several: among which are La Genollière, near Arzier; S. George's, Pré de S. Livres, Grace-dieu, near Besançon; and Monthezy in the Val de Travers: in the latter, the Schaf-loch, near the lake of Thun, Fondeurle, near Die (Dauphiné), and, in the neighbourhood of Annecy, the Glacières du Grand Anu, de Chappet-sur-Villaz, and de l'Enfer. All these (except the last-named) are described, together with several others, by my friend, the Rev. G. F. Browne, in a very interesting book[1], and in his company I had the pleasure, in the summer of 1865, of visiting the three last-mentioned.

Having left Annecy by an early diligence, we were put down by the road-side after a few miles' drive, and made our way by

---

[1] 'Ice-caves in France and Switzerland.' There is a further description of the last three in *Good Words* for November, 1866.

a cross-country lane to Aviernoz. An amusing little adventure befel us *en route*. We had left Annecy fasting, in the expectation of finding an *auberge* at Les Olliers, a small hamlet just off the high road, through which our path lay. Much to our disgust we discovered that the answers to our queries became vaguer as we neared the supposed site of this very needful accommodation; and that the *auberge*, promised at one end of the winding lane, which did duty for a street, resolved itself at the other into a farm-house, where perhaps they would entertain us. However, we were much too hungry to dream of going further; so walking up to the door, after running the usual gauntlet of yelping curs, we accosted the owner, and explained our wants in the neatest and most appropriate speech that we could devise; hinting, though of course so delicately as not to offend his susceptibilities, that we were quite ready to pay for what he gave us. His reception, however, was at first not enthusiastic. As Browne remarked, "It was cold,—not to say supercilious." He was vague on the possibility of breakfast, until he had ascertained that we had nothing to sell in our knapsacks, and that my friend's axe was not for cutting wood. As, then, it became evident that we were neither colporteurs nor charcoal-burners, the barometer of our respectability obviously rose one degree; and he invited us within. Bread, milk, and cheese were produced; and while the table was being spread, another question or two was asked, which, seeing that he was amusingly puzzled about our social position, I answered, so as only to put him gradually on the right scent. There was obviously a rise of another degree; he severed a huge slice from a flat loaf of brown bread, as large as a grindstone, and bade us fall on. I took up this slice, and was going to cut a piece from the inside. "Stop, stop," said he, "don't take that, it will be hard, it will do for my little horse; cut from the loaf!" Another question or two was asked; from the answers to which he learned that we were not only travellers for our own pleasure, but also going to visit his distinguished friend M. Métrail, ex-Maire of Aviernoz (the owner of two of the glacières). The mercury at once went up to set fair; and it was remembered that there were eggs in the house. Just at this moment one of the farm labourers came in to get his breakfast, and, walking up to the table, took hold of the *loaf*: our host at once checked him, and bade him cut from the inside of the *slice*,—shewing that he held the man perhaps 'something better than his dog,' but only a very 'little dearer than his horse.'

So there are social distinctions even in Alpine Arcadias, and a 'below the salt' in a Savoyard homestead. A little more talk, and a laugh at his mistake about our professions, which he frankly confessed, led to his volunteering to join us for the day; during which he catechized us severely about England and the English Church, shewing by his questions that the popular notions of it among the Roman Catholics of the Alps are, that its doctrines are on a par with those of Renan, and its rites and ceremonies with those of the Quakers.

At Aviernoz we were enthusiastically welcomed by M. Métrail, and M. Rosset, the village schoolmaster. After a few minutes spent in necessary preparations, we set off for the glacières: these are all situated in a range of limestone mountains which rises steeply immediately behind the village to a height of about 6000 feet above the sea, and separates the basin of the Arve from the Lake of Annecy. Two belong, together with a considerable quantity of corn-land near the village and of rich pasturage on the mountains, to our friend, who nevertheless lives in a small cottage, which, for absence of furniture and presence of dirt, could not easily be matched in England. As the cattle were *à la montagne*, we had no need to carry much provision: bread, however, was essential, as that in the châlets only existed in the form of *pain noir*, which is as hard and dry as a pumice-stone, and about as digestible to an

ENTRANCE TO THE GLACIÈRE DU GRAND ANU.

unaccustomed stomach. A large cake of white bread, about eighteen inches in diameter, was accordingly fetched from the household stores, spitted on a sharp stick, and placed on a small boy's shoulder, our host's son-and-heir, who bore it manfully up the steep zig-zag path. A pleasant walk through the woods, with occasional fine views towards the lake of Geneva, brought us in about an hour-and-a-half to the châlets, simultaneously with a smart shower, so we went in to get some lunch. Here was comparative luxury, for besides the usual varieties of cheese, the larder contained a piece of ham. Seating ourselves on the native one-legged stools, we made good use of our time. My companions set to work at once on the ham; but, notwithstanding my Dauphiné education, I cannot say that I prefer it raw; especially now with the fear of *trichina* before my eyes. How to broil it without forks was rather a puzzle; a clasp-knife might have served, but it is very hot work for the fingers. Necessity, however, sharpens the invention. There were some billets of pine-wood in a corner: from one of these I cut a long splinter, pointed it, transfixed a slice of ham, and there was a toasting-fork complete. My cooking done, I had an unctuous feast: unmoved by the censure of Browne, who scorned me as 'Epicuri de grege porcus.'

By the time we had done ringing the changes upon goat-cheese and cow-cheese, fresh and salted 'séracs', the rain had nearly stopped; so we set off over a wild district, partly pasture and partly bare rock, for the Glacière du Grand Anu. The limestone hereabouts weathers into ridges, separated by narrow fissures, like the mountain limestone in many parts of England, the sides of which are richly clothed with holly-ferns and many Alpine plants.

After about half-an-hour's walk we came to the mouth of the glacière, which is situated on a bleak, rocky plateau, with here and there a few thin patches of larch or brushwood. It was certainly a wild looking place. We were standing at the end of a deep and comparatively narrow chasm[1]: at our feet a steep slope of crag and débris led down to the base of the opposite precipice; on either hand the cliffs descended in a series of walls of nearly vertical rock, with here and there a ledge on which luxuriant ferns had formed a leafy cornice, and pine-trees had fastened their roots and raised their green pinnacles. In front, in the face of the precipice, was a vast natural gateway, some seventy feet in height, which opened into a dark cavern, whose icy floor could barely be distinguished. Snow was lying at the bottom of the descent and on the threshold of the glacière, just beyond which it rose up in a large conical pile. After gazing for a little while on this singular scene, the more striking to me from its being so entirely unexpected, we descended into the chasm. The track was narrow, and in one or two places steep enough to require a little caution; the rocks, however, terminated in a slope of broken fragments, and these again in snow. When we reached the bottom, the effect of the great natural doorway of rock, rising seventy feet above us, was indescribably grand. We now saw the cause of the snow-cone, which from above had seemed a little puzzling. Immediately over it was a natural shaft or fissure in the rock, forming a kind of sky-light to the vestibule of the cavern; it is therefore evident that the snow which falls from above down the shaft raises this pile. As it is said to lie during the winter twelve feet deep on the plateau above, the size of the heap is not surprising. The cavern itself is circular in plan, about sixty feet in diameter; the floor is solid ice, and slopes gradually down towards the further end. Owing to the size of the doorway, a candle, though useful at times, is not absolutely necessary. The walls are covered with sheets of ice, transparent as the finest glass, which invest like a drapery each prominence of rock. The effect was as if a number of cas-

---

[1] Plate IV.

INTERIOR OF THE GLACIÈRE DU GRAND ANU.

cades had been instantly arrested on their downward course, and changed into ice. It reminded me most of a scene in the great cutting through the Lias rock on the London and North-Western Railway, during the severe frost at the close of 1860. The soft shales there, parted by bands of limestone, are saturated with water, which keeps constantly dripping down the sides of the cutting; the frost had gathered together these myriad drops into a series of frozen cascades, and fringed each ledge with streamers and stalactites of ice. So was it in the cave, except that in many parts the ice was so pure and so evenly distributed, that every crack in the rock below was visible. The most striking object was an icy buttress, on the left of the entrance;—flying buttress, it might almost be called, for it was partly separated from the wall of the cave,—whose glassy covering fell down to the floor in the most perfect and graceful curves[1].

Facing the entrance, at the further end of the cave, was a dark pit in the ice, about eight feet across. My companion had measured this the year before, and found it to be not less than fifty-one feet deep. On the right-hand side, close to the rock, was another pit, about five feet wide, just like a well. We had intended, if possible, to descend this, and had brought with us a strong rope and pulley for the purpose. After cautiously sounding the edges of the pit to try their strength (the walls are slightly hollowed out near the top), we crept on hands and knees to the mouth, and looked down. On lowering a lamp for a short distance, we saw, not without regret, that the walls were lined with huge icicles, and that the edges of the pit were in rather an unsafe condition. Hence it would have been difficult to fix the pulley and so arrange the rope, as to avoid chafing, and almost impossible to have kept it from striking against the pendent masses of ice, and bringing them

[1] Plate v.

down on the adventurer's head as he swung to and fro below. The risk therefore appeared too great to be justifiable, so we reluctantly abandoned the project. Fastening strips of magnesium wire to a pole, we burnt them over the mouth, and dropped blazing pieces of paper to illuminate the icy walls of the shaft; we next lowered our lamp by a long string into the abyss; it descended seventy feet vertically, and then reached a slope of ice, down which it slid until it disappeared beneath our feet. This may perhaps be the entrance to another cavern; it is at any rate, in all probability, the shaft by which, during the spring thaws, a stream of water is conveyed into the earth, so that for part of the year these shafts are real *moulins*.

These observations finished, we again illuminated the cave with magnesium wire, shedding an unearthly brilliancy over the glassy walls. I noticed that the surface of the ice on both walls and floor was slightly wet; and on the latter were a few small pools of water, the temperature of which was about $32\frac{1}{2}°$ (Fahrenheit), the temperature of the air being $34·2°$. The ice on the walls well exhibited the peculiar prismatic structure which had been previously noticed by my companion. The sides of

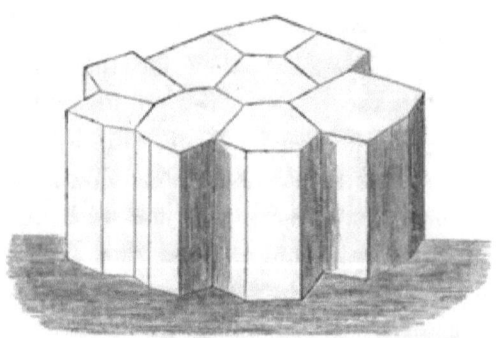

(Fig. 7.) Prismatic structure in ice; about half natural size.

these prisms, rendered visible by reflected light, traversed the mass perpendicularly to its surface, like the calcareous network in septaria-stones. A few blows with an ice-axe detached a piece, five or six inches square, which I then with little difficulty broke up into its component prisms: these resembled in shape miniature basaltic columns. The majority of them appeared to be hexagonal, but in some cases they were imperfectly formed. This done, we scrambled back up the steep slope, and, after completing a sketch of the entrance, set off to examine another of these caverns, the Glacière de l'Enfer, which had not hitherto been visited by foreigners.

The year before Browne, under the guidance of our friends, had failed in hitting off its inconspicuous entrance; this time in spite of the mists we found it without trouble; but it was in every way much less impressive than the one which we had just left. A steep slope of broken rock led down to a natural door-way in the face of a low cliff, composed of horizontal strata of limestone, in the chinks of which a few stunted fir-trees were growing. This portal opened immediately into a roughly circular hall about seventy-five feet in diameter and ten to twelve in height. The roof of both was formed by the flat surface of one of the beds of rock; the floor was a nearly level mass of ice, but the side nearest the entrance was covered with rubbish from the talus outside. The walls stained with damp, the absence of the ice-curtains, and the dirt-sprinkled floor, gave a dismal and dreary look to the cave. On the right-hand side of it we found a fissure, by means of which we climbed down between the ice and the rock. It led gradually under the icy mass towards the centre of the cave, and by dint of much pushing and struggling, gaining a plentiful coat of mud in the process, we managed to force our way along it for two or three yards, until it became too narrow to admit us further. Just at this point, a good sized stone, several of which were frozen into the icy roof, came down with a crash close to me; so not caring to run the risk of being preserved for future ages like a Siberian mammoth, I took the hint, and, passing the word to my companion, backed out again as fast as possible.

Continuing our examination of the cave, we found that opposite to the entrance there was a chink two or three feet wide between the rock and the ice. Taking the precaution to fasten a rope round my waist, I scrambled down for about twelve feet, and then found that I was close to the mouth of a hole, which sloped inwards and downwards through the solid ice, at an angle of about 30°. It was some two feet in diameter, and the further end was lost in the darkness. Scrambling back, I reported what I had seen, and Browne descended in his turn. He made many attempts to lower a lamp down the slope, but was unable to see how it ended, partly because the instrument, which he had imprudently purchased from a well-known tradesman in Cambridge, was literally a dark lantern, and partly because the tunnel curved slightly to one side[1]. Failing therefore to make discoveries with his eyes, he tried what could be accomplished by his ears, and threw down a large log of wood, which happened to be lying close at hand. Directly after this had slid out of sight, a loud crash was heard, followed by the splash of water. When the murmur of this died away, there commenced a strange gulping noise, almost as regular as the beats of a pulse, which was continued little altered, except that it was repeated at rather shorter intervals, until we left the cavern, at least a quarter of an hour after. It had an eerie unearthly sound, and gave one the idea of some monster watching for his prey below that treacherous slope of ice, at the bottom of the unguarded fissure. The tunnel obviously led to a subglacial reservoir, and this was probably covered by a thin crust of ice; the log in falling had broken this and disturbed the water below, which then commenced bubbling up and down through the

---

[1] Measurement with a string gave the length of the tunnel to this point as about 23 feet. Hence the icy floor of the cavern must have been at least 24 feet thick.

hole, and making a gulping noise, just as it sometimes does when oscillating up and down in a pipe.

After quitting this cavern we walked along the crest of the range for some distance, and then turned to the north, to visit the Glacière de Chappet-sur-Villaz, which is situated in the rocky face of a shoulder of Mont Parmelan, at the head of a glen descending to the west of Aviernoz. Although the day was still dull, we saw enough during this walk to shew that the views of the Lake of Annecy on the one side, and towards Geneva on the other, must in fine weather be very beautiful. A steep scramble up a narrow gully in the rock brought us to the glacière, which differed greatly from the other two. The entrance was a mere hole, a few feet wide, in the face of the cliff, giving access to a narrow fissure, the slope of which descended rather steeper than that of the gully outside; down this we scrambled in almost total darkness; for our lamp had now nearly abandoned its function of giving light and confined itself to greasing our fingers. To make the matter pleasanter we came occasionally upon masses of snow, wedged into the fissure and partly blocking it up; and the uncertainty of whether they were strong enough to bear us, or might not let us down for four or five feet with a run, gave a zest to the proceedings.

We first came to a small chamber into which some beams of light struggled from a little opening far above; it was floored with ice, and had some fine sheet ice on the walls. A rough descent then led us down to a place where the cavern branched out into two chambers: one of these, that on the left, was a lofty fissure, four or five feet wide; its floor was covered for a depth of two or three feet with the clearest water, beyond which the rocky walls faded away into the darkness. The other chamber was floored with ice, which descended from one corner like a frozen cascade, its graceful outlines and transparent purity being most beautiful. We were, however, obliged to mar it; for we knew that behind that flowing curtain was concealed the entrance of a tunnel, which we were anxious to explore. With some labour we hewed away a mass of ice about fifteen inches thick, and made an aperture just wide enough to admit a man's body. This led into a narrow tunnel, apparently running through the solid ice, which sloped gently downwards until it was lost in the darkness. Browne said that it had been much larger the year before, now it was barely two feet in diameter. We fastened a piece of magnesium wire to the end of a pole, and thrust it when lighted into the tunnel. Though it lit up beautifully the glassy walls and transparent curtain of ice, it did not enable us to see where the tunnel ended. Browne then determined to try whether he could force his way along it. Fastening the rope about his waist, he crept feet foremost through the hole, and so wriggled along for a yard or two: finding, however, that the narrowness of the passage prevented him from turning, or indeed from using his arms or legs to any purpose, he called to us to haul him back, and was accordingly drawn out like a cork from a bottle. One would not have thought that any living creature could have inhabited this subglacial cavern, but when he emerged from it, several flies about half an inch long were on his coat, and on looking into the hole we saw others running actively about the walls of their icy prison[1]. This increase of the ice was provoking, for the previous year the want of a rope alone had prevented my companion from following up the passage.

This done, we scrambled back to the light of day, and then descended to Aviernoz; arriving there just in time to escape a violent thunder-storm, which, had it come a few minutes earlier, would have speedily drenched us. During our absence the ex-lady-mayoress had concentrated her energies upon a dinner, to which we speedily were summoned. To those accustomed to civic hospitalities our *carte* may seem meagre; for

---

[1] Since determined to be *Stenophylax* (*Hieroglyphicus?*), Stephens, *S.* (*testaceus?*), Pictet, and a *Paniscus*, species unknown.

the feast mainly consisted of soup, omelette, fried beans, pudding, and cheese. We, however, were too hungry to quarrel with it; still less with the excellent cider which was served at table. The rain ceased during dinner; so after compensating our friends for their time and trouble, we walked in the twilight down to Thorens, a somewhat larger village, boasting of an inn. Here is a guest-chamber, containing two bedsteads, one wooden, the other iron. We tossed for choice; I won, and, to Browne's surprise, chose the apparently less comfortable iron one. The event justified the selection, for I slept undisturbed through the night; except once, when I wakened to a dim consciousness of his humbly apologizing for keeping the candle alight, and plaintively complaining that his bed was alive with bugs: soon after which the enemy, by concentrating their forces, compelled him to evacuate the position; and he encamped for the remainder of the night upon three chairs.

A few words may be said in conclusion on the probable cause of these glacières. Several theories have been proposed to account for their existence; most of which do not seem to me very satisfactory. I believe them to be simply caves, in which a quantity of snow has accumulated, and has been converted into ice; the principal agent in the change being probably water, which finds its way down through the crevices and partings of the rock; in a word, they are ice-houses, filled and replenished annually by nature instead of by man. The snows of each winter supply the summer's waste, and the very water, as it trickles down, is converted into ice. Probably the thermometer falls below the freezing-point every night, for in those which we visited the mercury only stood from $1°$ to $2°$ above it, when the outer air was about $48°$. There is then no reason why glacières should not be found in any part of the world, where the rock has a tendency to form pit-holes or caverns, provided these are in direct communication with the surface, and a sufficient quantity of snow falls during the winter to counterbalance the summer's loss. In the neighbourhood of the first glacière I noticed several deep, natural pits and chasms, considerably smaller than it, at the bottom of which snow was lying. My companion had always considered the glacière of Chappet-sur-Villaz an insuperable objection to this theory; because, on his first visit, the passage leading down into it was entirely free from snow, and the shape of it and the entrance, seemed to render it very improbable that snow could get in from the outside. We, however, as I have said, found a great quantity of snow in the passage, so that this difficulty was effectually removed. At what period these glacières were first formed, I cannot pretend to say; it may be that some of them are relics of the glacial epoch, the last fragments of the mighty ice-field which once covered so large a portion of the high lands of Europe; as, however, there have probably been oscillations in temperature since this time, it is more likely that they do not go back to such a remote antiquity. Be this as it may, they are well worth a visit; and, so far as I know them, will fully repay the small amount of trouble and discomfort which a journey to them at present entails.

Besides these caverns, occupied by masses of ice, there are many others in the Alps, as in every mountain region. They are more numerous in the limestone districts than in the harder crystalline rocks, but none are of sufficient magnitude to attract many visitors. Some of the best known, such as the Grotte aux Fées near Vallorbe, the Temple des Fées in the Val Travers, the source of the Lionne, and the Chaudière d'Enfer in the Vallée du Lac du Joux, are in the Jura; but there is no lack of them in the Alps; for instance, the Tannes de Corgeon near Chateaux d'Œx, the cave near the Nant d'Arpenaz (valley of the Arve), the Mondloch on Mount Pilatus, and many others.

In some of these have been found coins, Roman and mediæval, bones, fragments of pottery, pebbles of foreign rocks, weapons of stone and metal, shewing that they have in past time frequently served as a lair for wild beasts or a retreat for man. Not unfrequently the smaller grottoes are still occupied by the shepherds when tending their flocks on the higher pastures; and some, like the Faulberg by the Aletsch Glacier, often afford shelter to the mountain climber. These commonly go by the name *Balm* in German, and *Beaume* in French; and not unfrequently some legend is connected with them; this one was the abode of some holy hermit, that a place of refuge during a persecution or an invasion. In Appenzell, 4924 feet above the sea, are two caverns in the face of a cliff. One has for two hundred years been fitted up as a chapel in honour of St Michael; and here, every year on the day of the great archangel, mass is said, and the incense ascends from this natural high place; of the same kind is Notre Dame de Sex above St Maurice (Valais), near to which is a cavern called the Grotte aux Fées, containing fine stalactites. In the steep cliffs overhanging the Val Sapenière, at the base of the Pelvoux, is a cavern called the Beaume des Vaudois; this, according to history, was the scene of one of the most monstrous of those acts of cruelty which, under the show of a zeal for religion, have too often brought disgrace upon the cause of Christianity. In the fifteenth century the inhabitants of the Val Louise (of which the Val Sapenière is a tributary glen) were all disciples of Waldo. This crying sin was brought to the notice of Pope Innocent VIII.; and he issued a bull, authorising a crusade to be preached, in order "to root up and extirpate such a detestable set, and the foresaid execrable errors." Accordingly a considerable force, headed by the Pope's commissioner, Albert Cataneo and a certain captain named Palud, invaded the valley during the summer of 1488. The Waldenses, seeing that resistance was unavailing, abandoned their houses and retreated to this cavern, taking with them their wives and children, their flocks and herds, and provisions for two years. The narrow path leading to its mouth was blocked up with rocks, and they too hastily deemed themselves secure. La Palud, seeing that an attack from below was almost hopeless, led round a troop by a circuitous route over the rocks and upper pastures of the Pelvoux, and reached the brow of the cliff above the cave. Thence he let down a number of men by ropes to the entrance. A panic seems to have seized upon the Waldenses at this unexpected appearance of their persecutors; some threw themselves over the cliffs; a few were cut down on the spot, and the rest fled into the recesses of the cavern. La Palud feared to let his men follow them; so he piled up all the wood[1] that he could collect before the entrance, lighted it, and awaited the result. A few miserable wretches charged desperately through the flames, only to die by the weapons of their merciless foes; the rest remained within, and before long everything was quite quiet. It is said that when the smoke cleared away and the soldiers entered, they found the corpses of four hundred infants, and that altogether more than three thousand persons were massacred. Probably the numbers may be somewhat exaggerated, but I fear that there is no doubt that the details are substantially correct; and that this was the mode in which the Church of Rome of the fifteenth century interpreted her Master's injunction—"A new commandment I give unto you, that ye love one another[2]."

Cold draughts of air, of course, generally issue from these caverns in warm weather, and if the opening be small, the force of the current is often considerable. To these 'blow-holes' the name of *windloch* is given. The cause of their existence is obviously the difference of temperature between the air within

---

[1] It was probably juniper; for this is the only shrub that now grows there, the smoke of which is peculiarly pungent and suffocating, as I know from experience in this very neighbourhood.

[2] S. John xiii. 34.

and without; and **in accordance with this** it is observed, that in winter the direction of the blast is often reversed. Examples may be found near Seelisberg, on the Emmeten-alp, in the Isen and Schächen thals, in the Canton of Unterwalden, **on** Mount Pilatus, near Quarten on the Lake of Wallenstadt, in the Klönthal, &c.[1]

Sometimes also singular perforations may be observed in the face of a cliff, shewing the sky as through a window. These have generally been made by a stream which, in following up some chance fissure, has drilled the rock, and now perhaps, owing to a change of level or climate, has either sought another channel or ceased to flow. Good instances of these are in a buttress of the Geiselstein, visible from the Ampezzo road; on the Fedaia Pass, above Caprile; the Martinsloch, near the Segnes Pass, through which the sun shines for four days in the year on the village church of Elm; and the Heiterloch on the flank of the Eiger. The last two are accounted for in a far more satisfactory manner than by the prosaic reason given above. Each is connected with the history of the holy giant, St Martin. The former hole was made by the Devil when escaping from the Saint, or *vice versâ*. I really forget which the legend asserts. The other was certainly made by the Saint, and in the following manner. The Unter Grindelwald glacier issues from a gorge between the Eiger and the Mettenberg. In former days this opening was much narrower than it now is; and consequently sometimes became choked up with ice. The streams were by this means dammed back, and glacial lakes formed, which in due course burst, and did much mischief. So the peasants summoned the Saint to help them. Should he blast the rocks? Unfortunately gunpowder was not then invented. Should he follow Hannibal's example, and dissolve them with vinegar? *Vin ordinaire*, an excellent substitute, was no doubt abundant,

---

[1] Tschüdi, *Les Alpes*, p. 36.

but the process would have been slow. *Solvitur*, not exactly *ambulando*. The Saint stands on the glacier, puts his alpenstock against the Eiger, and his back against the Mettenberg, and gives one mighty shove. The mountains yield a freer passage to the ice, and the hole on the one mountain and a depression made by the Saint's back on the other, attest to this day the truth of the legend!

Somewhat akin to these apertures are the outlets of subterranean springs, not uncommon in the limestone districts, where the rock is often greatly fissured. One of the best known is the so-called **Sieben Brunnen** (Seven Fountains) at the head of the Simmen-thal, some two hours' walk from the village of An-der-Lenk. Just at the foot of a great cliff of the Wildstrubel, on which rests the Räzli glacière, is a slope of shale and débris, supported by a terrace wall of rock, some dozen feet in height. The streams (no doubt supplied from the glacier above) break out from the bottom of this slope, and at once form a pretty little cascade. When I saw them in 1865 the definite title Seven was wholly inappropriate; for they formed an almost continuous sheet of water some six or seven yards across, with one or two smaller jets, which issued along the same line a short distance on the left. From inaccessible apertures in the face of a great precipice of stratified rock and shale on the left bank of the Trafoi glacier, between the Orteler Spitze and the Stelvio Pass, three streams issue near to each other, two of which are of considerable size, and form grand waterfalls. They also are no doubt supplied from the glacier above, as the strata dip from it towards the openings. In the Badia-thal (Tyrol) a number of clear streams break out through the mossy turf and limestone blocks at the foot of a mass of moraine or débris, and in a few minutes form a brook, some four yards across and a foot deep. Other instances might without difficulty be found; all these I have myself seen.

Mineral springs abound in all parts of the Alps. Chief in

commercial value are the salt springs of Moutiers Tarentaise, and of Bex. In the former place the brine is very weak, only containing about 1·8 per cent. of saline matter. Hence, if evaporated in the ordinary way, the result would not repay the expense of the works. The process adopted is exceedingly simple and ingenious, and the cost very slight. Upright frames are filled with faggots of blackthorn, piled loosely one above the other so as to give free passage to the air: the brine is then allowed to flow along many small channels, from which it drips through a multitude of tiny holes upon the faggots; through these it trickles down, dropping from twig to twig, and losing a quantity of water by evaporation in its descent. On arriving at the bottom, it is collected in pans, whence it is pumped up again to the channels, and the process is repeated. The brine is treated in this way in two or three houses, until finally the amount of salt in solution is increased to about 22 per cent., 160 measures being reduced to about 11, when it is boiled in the usual manner[1]. Fine cords, stretched vertically on frames, are also employed with great success, instead of faggots, in the later processes, but the unconcentrated brine quickly causes them to rot. The springs, it should be mentioned, are tepid, having a temperature of about 98° (Fht.); they are supposed to issue from the point of junction of sedimentary and crystalline rock (limestone and dark schist). The mines of Bex furnish both brine (which however has of late years much decreased in quantity) and rock salt; a fine vein of the latter, of immense extent, was discovered in 1823. The excavations, consisting of extensive galleries with some large pits and chambers, are curious; but being wholly artificial have no beauties to recommend them to a visitor, and I am afraid my own impression was that 'le jeu ne valait pas la chandelle.'

It would be no easy task to enumerate all the Alpine

---

[1] See Bakewell, *Travels in the Tarentaise*, Vol. I. Ch. VI. for further details.

springs which possess medicinal virtues—for there is hardly a valley of any importance which does not boast of at least one. Switzerland alone is said to have two hundred and forty-six bathing establishments; many indeed only of local, but others of European reputation. Among them are hot springs and cold springs, with waters saline, sulphureous, alkaline and chalybeate; some nauseous and others very pleasant. Among the most noted in the Dauphiné Alps are those of Allevard, situated in the midst of very charming and varied scenery, and built on the banks of a rapid stream, called the Bréda; just where it issues from a narrow defile. The waters closely resemble those of Eaux-Bonnes in the Pyrenees; being charged with sulphydric acid and carbonic acid gases, and containing a considerable quantity of chloride of sodium. They are beneficial in disorders of the skin, stomach, and lungs, and in cases of rheumatism. The patients drink them as well as bathe in them, and also inhale the gas which is given off at the source. The Baths of Monêtier at the foot of the descent from the Col du Lantaret are less fashionable, but have been in use since at any rate very early in the middle ages. There are two springs; that on the north of the village is surrounded by a circular stone basin, from the bottom of which thin cloud-like streams of a milky hue, with frequent bubbles of gas, keep constantly rising to the surface of the water. This is tepid and slightly saline in taste, and the conduits through which it runs off are stained ochrous-red. The warm springs, at which is the primitive bathing establishment, are on the other side of the village. The hottest of them has a temperature of 107·6 Fahrenheit. These are considered very beneficial in gastric and paralytic disorders, also for bruises and fractures. The well-known springs of Uriage in the valley of the Isère are also tepid (temperature 81·1 Fht.), and are sulphureous. From the ruins which have been discovered in the neighbourhood, it is evident that they were frequented in the Roman times. All these springs issue from near the junction of **crystalline and** sedimentary rock, in accordance with a law (pointed out by Principal Forbes), which will be found to hold very generally **not only in** the Alpine but also in other districts of Europe.

There are besides, celebrated tepid springs at **Brides-les-Bains** in the Tarentaise, and at Aix-les-Bains near **the Lac de Bourget.** The **former** were rediscovered in 1819, after **having** been **buried for many years by an** inundation of **the river; the latter were known to the Romans.** The springs of Brides, which vary in **temperature from 93° to 97°** (Fht.), **contain sulphates of** magnesia **and lime, and muriate of soda; they are good for scurvy, rheumatism, and nervous debility;** those of **Aix** are partly sulphureous, and have a temperature of about 113° (Fht.). They are much frequented **by patients suffering from** disorders of the skin and **of the digestive organs.**

In the Graian Alps are the springs **of Courmayeur,** saline and chalybeate; **La Saxe,** warm **and sulphureous; Pré St Didier,** warm and **very** slightly saline; St Vincent, **similar to** the first named; all very beautifully situated and **much frequented;** and on the southern side of the chain those of **Ceresole, effervescent, tonic, and very delicious,** but **at present not much** visited.

In **Switzerland, perhaps the most remarkable are those of** Leuk, **Stachelberg, Pfäfers, and St Moritz.** The first are **situated near the foot of the magnificent limestone precipices down which winds the track from the Gemmi Pass, and about** eight **miles from the little town of the same name in the Rhone** valley. The **waters, which have a temperature of about 120°** (Fht.) are saline, **and are much esteemed in scorbutic and cutaneous** disorders. The patients **lead a kind of amphibious life, passing** sometimes **as** much as **eight hours in** the bath. **To prevent time** hanging **heavy on their hands,** floating tables **enable them to take refreshments, read books, and play games;** and, **as a complete costume is worn, both sexes assemble in the** same *piscine*, while friends lounge in the surrounding galleries. The Stachelberg springs are so strongly impregnated with sulphur that the water is quite yellow. The coffin-like troughs, used as baths, have or had a kind of lid, furnished with a hole, through which the patient's head and shoulders project, in order to save his nose as far as possible from the fumes, which, when I bathed there, were strong enough to discolour a gold ring in very short time, and make me smell like a walking box of brimstone matches for some hours after.

The most romantically situated springs are those of Pfäfers, which issue from the rock in a narrow gorge of the Tamina. Halting at the Ragatz station on the Sargans and Coire Railway, a hot and dusty road leads through this fashionable watering place—a Swiss Cheltenham—to the mouth of a narrow glen in the mountain range that rises immediately above it. Steep wooded slopes on the right, and steeper precipices of grey rock fringed with pines on the left, descend to the very brink of the rushing torrent, and a road, broad and easy now, but driven with no little labour, runs along the former side. After about half an hour's walking the walls of the glen approach still nearer, and at last appear to close together. Here, on the last spot that enjoys a brief daily visit from the sunbeams, is the bath-house, an irregular pile of buildings, containing spacious corridors and saloons, with numerous steamy cells for bathers. Passing through this, a foot-path leads into the gorge, a deep and narrow cleft in the rocks, which rise on either hand in nearly vertical walls, some seven hundred feet above the murky waters of the torrent. The pathway, a frame of planks, either notched in the rock or supported by iron bars, is about a dozen yards above the stream, and though often wet with the dripping of springs, is made quite safe by a stout hand-rail. Here and there the rocks appear to close over head, and you grope your way in a twilight gloom; then they part again and shew a glimpse of fringing trees and blades of grass glittering in the sunlight; while perhaps one stray beam struggles through the shade and for a moment gleams upon the gloomy torrent.

(Fig. 8.) The Gorge of Pfäfers.

Presently a dense mist is seen rising from the waters; it is the reek of the hot springs, wildly beautiful when lit up by the sunbeams. The spring-heads are protected by a vault of masonry, and approached by two short tunnels. Most of the water is conveyed in pipes to the bath-house below, and to those at Ragatz; the rest is discharged into the Tamina. The temperature is not quite the same in all the springs; that of the principal one is about 99° (Fht.). The waters are limpid and almost tasteless; containing hardly any minerals, except a very small quantity of soda and magnesia. They are valuable in various disorders of the stomach and bowels, and in certain rheumatic and nervous affections. These springs were known in the eleventh century, but the danger of access caused them to become unused and forgotten. More than a hundred years later, in 1240, a hunter, while scrambling about the rocks above, saw the steam rising from the chasm and spread the news of his discovery. For a long time the unfortunate patients could only approach them by being lowered with cords to the little ledge of rock close by the springs. Here they are said to have been left, with a supply of food, until they had gone through the appointed course; and it certainly speaks well for either their constitutions or the virtues of the waters that any of them escaped with life from such a dismal abyss. The gallery stops at the springs, and the rest of the gorge is inaccessible; but from a bridge hard by there is a fine view up it. At the first glance one would suppose that it was literally a rift in the rock, but a careful examination of its course and walls cannot fail to convince that it has been sawn out by the torrent, pot-holes and other water-marks being distinctly visible on the latter up to the very top. A little bridge gives access to a very fine example of the former, its mouth being about fifteen yards across. The closed parts, which seem to make so strongly for the rift theory, prove to be only places where the gorge has been choked by débris rolling into it from above; and the stream must have cut its way slowly down through the rock, along the planes of joints, from the floor of the valley above to the present level of the torrent-bed.

    The Baths of St Moritz in the Engadine, among the beautiful scenery of the Bernina region, are now becoming very fashionable. The bath-house, a huge building, stands nearly 6000 feet above the sea, on a level and rather marshy meadow, near a little lake, on the right bank of which is the village of St Moritz, occupying a slightly higher and far better situation. The water of the springs contains iron, alkaline salt, and carbonic acid gas, is beautifully pure, and very refreshing. Its effects are tonic, and it is prescribed in cases of scrofula and general debility. In the Alps further east may be mentioned the Baths of Le Prese (sulphur), Bormio (warm and alkaline), Sta Catharina (chalybeate), Bad Gastein (slightly alkaline), and Brags (alkaline?), with many others. The last-named, in a glen descending from the south to the Puster-thal, are not generally known, but enjoy an extraordinary local reputation for cures of rheumatic complaints.

A glance at the more solid mineral wealth of the Alps must suffice. Gold is found in several places in small quantities; chiefly in the neighbourhood of Monte Rosa. The principal mines are at Pestarena in the Val Anzasca, where they have been in operation ever since the days of the Romans, if not longer. The lodes occur in a compact gneiss rock; and the ore is generally contained in yellowish pyrites of iron, mixed with white quartz; and in none of the specimens which I have seen could it be discerned by the eye. The matrix is ground to a coarse sand, then mixed with quicklime, after which some mercury is added, and the whole is churned in water. By this means the gold is separated from the pyrites, quartz, and other impurities. The mines are described at length by De Saussure[1] and Mr King[2]. Silver also is found in several places, often mixed with lead. The mines of La Grave in Dauphiné are tolerably productive; and that near Auronzo (Italian Tyrol) is also valuable. Formerly those of Primiero, in the latter district, were very celebrated, but they have now been abandoned for many years. Remarkably rich deposits of nickel are worked at La Balma in the Val Sesia and at Migiandone near the Simplon road. Lead mines are not unfrequent; copper is obtained in the Val Pelline, Val d'Aoste, Val Sesia, and in many

[1] *Voyages*, § 2132. [2] *The Italian Valleys of the Alps*, p. 455.

other places, as well as iron;—perhaps the most noted mines of the latter mineral are at Cogne in the Graians. The ore is of a dark greenish-purple colour, and so exceedingly heavy that a specimen might be picked out in the dark from a heap of other stones. Anthracite is found occasionally; an important bed being worked near La Mure in Dauphiné. As for building-stones, granites, serpentines, and marbles, there is of course almost any quantity, but many valuable beds of these are very little worked, owing to difficulties of access and transport.

The granite quarries of Fariolo on the Lago Maggiore are much used, and supply a large part of northern Italy. The great columns of the new basilica of S. Paolo at Rome were hewn here. The felspar in it is a pale red, of a slight rosy tint that blends beautifully with the grey quartz and dark mica-spots; very good separate crystals of this felspar are sometimes obtained. In the same neighbourhood at Ornavasso is a quarry of fine white crystalline marble, little inferior to that of Carrara; from this came the stone used in building Milan cathedral. A very pretty mottled claret and buff marble is worked near Guilestre (Dauphiné), and good black marble in the Rhone valley near Aigle.

CHAPTER V.

FEW perils are more dreaded by the inhabitant of the Alps than those of the avalanches[1]. The summer traveller who only sees them in the far distance, plunging like a foaming cascade down some barren mountain-cliff, and listens for the distant roar which announces their fall as a pleasant interlude in his day's journey, has little idea of what that white streak of foam is composed, or how terrible is the danger when the snows lie deep on every mountain-side. For him, the falling mass only breaks the silence of the higher peaks, and its shattered fragments are strewed harmlessly over some glacier waste, or buried in some barren ravine; but there are times when it hurries down into the valleys, sweeping before it pine-tree and châlet, and burying often whole families in a snowy grave.

Avalanches may be divided into three classes; the first of which is the ice-avalanche, that most familiar to the tourist, caused in the following way. The glaciers in many parts of the Alps, especially those smaller glaciers which cling to the upper

---

[1] *Lawine*, German—*Laue* or *Lauine*, Swiss Patois—*Lahne*, Tyrol Patois—*Lavigna*, Romansch.

slopes of most of the higher mountains, frequently terminate abruptly on the brow of some tremendous precipice. Over this the icy mass, ever moving slowly downwards, is gradually protruded, till at last the heat of the sun and its own weight cause large fragments to break off; these, as they bound down the cliffs, are dashed into innumerable pieces, which leap from crag to crag high into the air; now the falling mass, like some swollen torrent, dashes with sullen roar through a gully; now emerging, crashes over a precipice, or spreads itself out like a fan, as it hisses down a snow slope. These avalanches, as I have already said, spend their force in the higher parts of the mountains, and are harmless, unless anyone is unfortunate enough to be crossing their track when a fall takes place.

Accidents of this kind, however, are very rare; for the danger can almost always be avoided, either by making a slight détour, or by taking care to pass before the sun has heated the air. Often and often as I have seen them fall, and have had to cross their paths, I have only once known a fragment to fall anywhere near me. At a distance they resemble a waterfall of the purest foam; if approached, they are found to be composed of fragments of ice of every size, from one or two cubic yards downwards. Of all that I have ever seen, the grandest were, one from the precipices of the Lyskamm above the Gorner glacier, and one down the flank of the Aiguille du Midi, which faces the Grands Mulets. On no place, however, are they more frequent than on that tremendous wall of precipices which rises on the other side of the Trümmletenthal, opposite to the Wengern Alp. Here daily, during the summer, groups of travellers gather on the greensward, to watch their fall from a distance of about a mile. With this distant view everyone was satisfied, till in 1862 Mr F. Galton discovered a way whereby the actual channel, down which the majority of these avalanches slide, could be approached in perfect safety. His description of the scene is so interesting, that I cannot resist making a short extract[1]. "I stood at one time so near to it, that, had I been equipped as a fisherman, I could have thrown a fly over the avalanche. I waited for the third and finest avalanche under one of the overhanging slabs of rock I have already mentioned; but though I had persuaded myself of the absolute safety of my position, I freely acknowledge that the advent of the avalanche alarmed me. It gave notice of its coming by a prodigious roar, and the appearance of an exceedingly menacing cloud of snow-dust, that was shot out far above my head. I knew not what was coming, and I ran away as fast as I could, till I was reassured that all was right by the appearance of the ice-cataract in its wonted channel; when I hurried back again to its side, to rejoice in the storm and uproar....The hurtling of the ice-balls in the depths of the ravine, and the crash of the huge hail-storm that issued at its foot, were almost frightful. The storm was remarkable for the irregularities of its outbursts. Frequently these were accompanied by vast gushes of water, due, I suppose, to some sub-glacial reservoir, whose foremost wall had toppled away and partly supplied the avalanche. Wind, in moderate blasts of cold air, accompanied each outburst. I was surprised there was not more of it, after the tales one is accustomed to hear about such things."

Occasionally, however, this phenomenon is produced on a larger scale, with fearful results. Instances have been known of a considerable portion of a glacier descending *en masse*, and dealing destruction in the valley below. Every traveller to Zermatt by the Visp Thal will remember the little village of Randa, which stands about 250 feet above the stream on a grassy slope at the feet of the Mischabel-hörner. On the other side rises a grand wall of ice-worn cliffs, forming a buttress of the Weisshorn, above which may be seen the steep and crevassed ice-fields of the Bies glacier. In 1636 a large part of

---

[1] *Alpine Journal*, Vol. I. p. 184.

this came thundering down into the valley, and almost wholly destroyed the village, killing thirty-six persons. Again, on the 27th of December, 1818, a mass of ice broke away from the glacier, and, falling into the valley below, produced the most disastrous effects. The following extract, translated and occasionally abridged from an official letter of M. Venetz to the Conseil d'Etat of the Canton[1], will give the best idea of the destruction caused by the blast, which was produced by the avalanche. "The village was not struck by the fall of the glacier, but the force of the wind was so intense that a mill-stone was carried a considerable distance up the mountain, together with large larches, torn up by their roots. Blocks of ice, 4 feet cube, were hurled half a league from the village up the slopes; the point of the steeple was carried away; houses were levelled with the ground; and the beams of which they had been built flung to a great distance in the forest. Eight goats, carried away together with their shed, were found a hundred yards from Randa; only one still lived ... 9 houses are wholly destroyed, 13 more or less damaged, besides outhouses of various kinds, 114 in all: those which are not destroyed are so injured as to be of no further use: no food is left for man or beast. Of 12 persons buried in the ruins, 10 have been taken out alive, one was dead, another cannot be found. The débris of ice, snow, and stone, forming a mass of 360,000,000 cubic feet, has covered all the cultivated land below the village for a space of about 2400 feet long and 1000 wide." He concludes by citing previous instances of a like disaster, and advising that the village should on that account be abandoned, a recommendation which does not seem to have found favour, since it has been rebuilt on the same site.

The other two kinds of avalanche, called respectively the dust and the ground-avalanche, are composed of snow. The dust-avalanche (*staub-lawine*) falls usually in the winter-time,

---

[1] *Conservateur Suisse*, No. XXXIX. p. 205 (Vol. X.).

when, after long-continued storms, the mountains are covered deep with freshly fallen snow. The ill-composed mass rests unstably upon the icy slopes, hangs in festoons and curtains over the peaks, and lies thick on the smooth banks of pasture-land, till a gust of wind or some other accident breaks the spell, and the whole slides down into the valley below. These falls are accompanied by fearful blasts of wind, which destroy houses and bridges as effectually as the explosion of a powder-magazine. According to Berlepsch, almost the whole of the village of Leukerbad was destroyed by one of these, on the 14th of January, 1719, and 55 of its inhabitants perished. In 1749 more than 100 persons were killed in the village of Ruäras (Grisons), which during the night was overwhelmed by an avalanche. So silently were some of the houses buried, that the inhabitants, on waking in the morning, could not conceive why the day did not dawn. It is said, too, that in the time of the Suabian war, A.D. 1498, one of these avalanches swept 400 soldiers over a cliff: strange to say, they all escaped without serious injury. The army of General Macdonald, in his celebrated passage of the Splügen in the month of December, 1800, suffered severely from avalanches of this kind. One cut completely through a troop of horse, while on its march from the village of Splügen to the top of the pass, and precipitated 30 dragoons into a gulf below the road, where they all perished. Again, some days afterwards, in the descent through the gorge of the Cardinel, the columns were repeatedly severed by avalanches, and more than 100 soldiers, with a number of horses and mules, were lost. It is said, that on one of these occasions the drummer of a regiment was among those carried away; who for some time was heard beating his drum in the gorge below, to summon his comrades to rescue him. Help, however, could not be given, the sounds became fainter and fainter, till at last the frost destroyed what the avalanche had spared.

The ground-avalanches (*grund-lawine*) differ considerably

from those last described; since they consist of dense and almost solid masses of snow, which for a considerable period has lain exposed to the elements. These avalanches as may be supposed, fall only in the spring, when the increasing warmth of the sun and the hot *föhn* cause large fields of snow to slip down the flanks of a mountain; just as it does off a house roof during a thaw in an English winter. Being much heavier than the dust avalanches, they are proportionately more destructive, and great pains have often to be taken to protect life and property in those places which by the configuration of the surrounding country are exposed to them. The forests, which clothe the lower slopes of the mountains, are kept sacred from the woodman's axe in order to check their fall, and not unfrequently massive triangular dykes are built on the hill-side behind the village, in order to stem the descending mass and cleave it asunder as a river is parted by the pier of a bridge. In some parts of Switzerland, for many years after the French war, the inhabitants suffered terribly from these avalanches; owing to the havoc which the invaders had made among the forests.

The roads are often blocked up and communication impeded by both these kinds of avalanches. Mr T. Kennedy[1], in his description of a winter visit to Zermatt, mentions one, over which he walked, that was 200 feet thick. In fact the remains of them may often be found at a comparatively low elevation till quite late in the summer. If indeed the season be an inclement one, or the place little exposed to the sun's rays, they will sometimes remain unmelted throughout the year. I recollect seeing the remains of an avalanche, between Bourg d'Oisans and Vénosc, during the month of August 1860, at a height of certainly not more than 3000 feet above the sea; and in July 1864 the torrent in the upper part of the Val Grisanche was completely bridged over by large masses of

---

[1] *Alpine Journal*, Vol. I. p. 77.

old snow. The stained and dirty surface of these relics renders them anything but picturesque additions to the landscape. The summer traveller of course is never in danger of the ground-avalanche, but those who climb the higher peaks are sometimes, especially after recent snowstorms, exposed to considerable risk from the other. For instance, the most direct route (called the 'Ancien Passage') from Chamouni to the summit of Mont Blanc is often rendered very dangerous by these avalanches. In 1820 a large party, consisting of 3 travellers and several guides, was swept away by one, was carried down a distance of 1200 feet, and three of the guides were entombed under a mass of snow in a deep crevasse. In 1863 some remains of them were found at the surface of the Glacier des Boissons, after having descended over a distance of not less than $5\frac{1}{2}$ miles. Soon after that accident a more circuitous, but perfectly safe route to the summit was discovered, and the 'Ancien Passage' was practically abandoned, being only used now and then by experienced travellers in very fine weather. Greater familiarity with the Alps and the lapse of time seemed to have partly effaced the remembrance of its dangers; and the calamity of October 13, 1866, was the consequence, when Captain Arkwright and three guides perished. It is impossible to stigmatize severely enough the conduct of the guides on this occasion. They must have been aware, if they knew anything of their business, that to attempt the Ancien Passage in the month of October, after an unusually wet summer, was little short of madness; and it was their duty, however much their employer might have wished it, positively to refuse to conduct him by that route. They would have risked little or nothing by this resistance, for all experienced mountaineers would have praised instead of blaming them[1].

---

[1] Three years before one of my friends was ascending Mont Blanc, and was strongly urged to go by the 'ancien passage' by one of his guides, who said he would "warrant it safe." Another, however, strongly opposed him, and the

In the summer of 1865 a porter was killed by an avalanche, and the rest of the party had a narrow escape, on the higher slopes of Monte Rosa. The sad accident on the Col du Géant may be considered as partly due to a slip of the snow. There three guides were conducting the same number of weary travellers down the steep ridge, or buttress, which leads from the summit of the pass towards Courmayeur. Usually this part of the journey is all rock-climbing of a very simple and easy kind, but on this occasion, owing to the inclement season (August, 1860), a quantity of snow still remained, forming at one place, a steeply inclined slope of considerable length, which terminated in a rocky descent, abrupt though not absolutely precipitous. The guides, according to their own account, wishing to save the travellers as much fatigue as possible, deserted the rocky arête for the smooth snow slope; the party were tied together, but the first and last guide held the rope in their hands instead of having it fastened round their waists. Very soon one of the travellers slipt upon the snow and overthrew the others; their fall started a small avalanche, and they all slid down together with it. The first and last guide, being hampered by the rope which they held, were unable to arrest the fall of the party, as, if both hands had been free, they in all probability could have easily done, and at last were obliged to let it go, in order to save their own lives. The three travellers, and Victor Tairraz, the guide who was attached to them, were dashed down the steep rocks at the bottom of the slope and were all killed. Of course usually an accident of this kind would in this place be quite impossible. Commonly the ascent or descent of the south side of the pass is only a scramble along the edge of a buttress of bare rock, which from a distance looks rather formidably steep, but in

more prudent course was adopted. They had not gone very far when they saw the 'ancien passage' so completely swept by an avalanche that escape would have been impossible.

reality can be traversed by any lady who is a tolerable walker. When however I crossed the pass, in July 1864, I was able to understand how the accident had occurred; for there was then an unusual amount of snow; and though, by keeping to the arête and occasionally proceeding with a little caution, there was not the slightest danger, it was obvious that the slope below was sufficiently steep to render a slip perilous to fatigued or inexperienced travellers. In the same way, in 1864 Dr Tyndall with two friends, and Jenni (the well-known Pontresina guide) and another, had a narrow escape in descending the Piz Mortaratsch, one of the peaks of the Bernina group. One of them, by slipping, set in motion some snow that was lying on an ice slope, and the whole party slid away with it. After descending for more than 1000 feet they fortunately came to rest within a short distance of some fearful precipices, a happy result in great measure due to the skill and strength of Jenni. Dr Tyndall has given an interesting description of the accident in a letter which he addressed to the *Times* newspaper[1]. In 1867 I descended by the same slope, at a time when the snow was not in a good condition. It is exceedingly steep, looking from below almost impracticable; and though the greater part of it is so perfectly safe, that we simply sat one behind another on the snow and slid down several hundred feet as a living sledge, the upper portion, where one crosses from the foot of the actual peak to the top of this 'slide,' requires great caution. On this the slope itself is very steep, and is broken here and there by a projecting crag; below are ice cliffs or crevasses; and, to make matters worse, there are some overhanging séracs above, which evidently sweep it occasionally from top to bottom. We crossed this part, fortunately not more than one or two hundred yards wide, very carefully; each step being cut through the loose upper coating of snow into the hard ice below, and every precaution taken to avoid

[1] Reprinted, *Alpine Journal*, Vol. I. p. 437.

the slightest slip. The detached fragments started small avalanches, which flowed down the slope and spread themselves like waterfalls over the rocks, with a stealthy serpent-like hiss that was peculiarly unpleasant to the nerves. A very melancholy accident also took place, Feb. 28, 1864, on the Haut-de-Cry, in which a Russian gentleman and J. J. Bennen, one of the best Swiss guides, lost their lives. The following account is abridged from a description written by Mr Gossett[1], one of the survivors:—The Haut-de-Cry is a mountain rising to a height of 9698 feet on the west side of the Lizerne, a torrent which enters the Rhone valley near to Sion. The travellers started from this town, ascended the valley, and, after working their way through a pine forest, in which they were much impeded by deep soft snow, gained a châlet at the height of about 7000 feet above the sea. The next three hours only took them up another 1000 feet; for the snow beyond the pine wood, though frozen at the top, was not generally strong enough to bear their weight. After ascending the N.E. arête of the mountain for a while, they determined to cross over to the eastern one. In order to gain this, they had to mount a steep snow-field about 800 feet high; it was a sort of *couloir* on a large scale, about 150 feet broad at the top and 400 or 500 at the bottom. When they were nearly on the other side of this the snow gave way under them, and Bennen expressed his apprehension of an avalanche, but was overruled by the local guides. They accordingly advanced a few steps further, when the snow-field suddenly split across, about 14 or 15 feet above them, with a deep cutting sound. "An awful silence ensued; it lasted but a few seconds, and then it was broken by Bennen's voice, *Wir sind Alle verloren*[2].... They were his last words,...the ground on which we stood began to move slowly, and I felt the utter uselessness of an

---

[1] *Alpine Journal*, Vol. I. p. 288.
[2] "We are all lost."

alpenstock. I soon sank up to my shoulders, and began descending backwards. With a good deal of trouble I succeeded in turning round." Mr Gossett goes on to say that he was then overwhelmed by the snow and was on the point of being suffocated, when he was providentially thrown up again to the surface. He now saw the avalanche before him as he descended; the head alone was preceded by a thick cloud of snow dust, the rest of the avalanche was clear. All around him he heard the horrid hissing of the snow, and far before the thundering of the foremost part of the avalanche. To prevent himself sinking again, he made use of his arms, as though he were swimming: soon after this he saw the snow in front of him come gradually to rest, and heard a sound similar to the creaking noise produced by a heavy cart passing over frozen snow in winter. The pressure of the snow behind, before it came to rest, nearly crushed him: he was again covered up, but fortunately he had previously thrown up his hands in order to protect his head. The avalanche froze as soon as it ceased to move, and he was almost stifled; but at length with much difficulty he succeeded in clearing away enough snow to allow him to breathe, and then one of the guides, who had escaped from being buried, came to his assistance. Two of the other guides were also able to disengage themselves easily, and after some time they set Mr Gossett free; but the snow had to be cut away with the axe down to his feet before he could be taken out. They then partly uncovered the body of his Russian friend, but he was quite dead. Bennen also was buried so deep that help could not be given, for by this time their feet were all severely frost-bitten. The freezing of an avalanche, as soon as it stops, is caused by the pressure of the hinder part, which is still in motion, upon that which has been brought to rest. Of course this greatly increases the danger, because the person overwhelmed may be suffocated before help can reach him.

M. Joanne, in the Introduction to his valuable *Itinéraire de la Suisse* (p. lxxviii), gives a list of twelve of the most destructive avalanches that have fallen in Switzerland, from which I select a few, in addition to one or two already noticed, to shew how terrible a scourge the Lawine can be in many villages which to the summer traveller often seem so calm and peaceful, —fit sites for an ideal arcadia of pastoral life.

In the year 1500 a caravan of 600 persons were swept away in crossing the Great St Bernard. In 1624, 300 were buried under an avalanche which fell from Monte Cassedra (Ticino). On the 18th February, 1720, one at Obergestelen (in the Rhone valley, about two leagues from the foot of that glacier) destroyed 120 cottages, 400 head of cattle, and 88 persons. The corpses were collected and buried in a large pit in the village cemetery, on the wall of which was engraved the following brief but pathetic inscription, "O God, what sorrow! eighty-eight in a single grave!" (*Gott, welche trauer! acht und achtzig in einem grab!*)[1]. About the same time 40 persons perished at Brieg, lower down the valley, and 23 on the Great St Bernard. The neighbourhood of Obergestelen was again ravaged in 1827, during the night of January, 16-17, when 46 houses in the villages of Selkingen and Biel were destroyed, with 51 of their inhabitants.

There are many strange stories of the instinctive prescience which animals have shewn when danger from this source is impending. Dogs and horses are said to be especially sensitive; Berlepsch tells a story of a pack-horse on the Scaletta pass, which, though at ordinary times most tractable, became restive when an avalanche was likely to fall. This made him very valuable to his owners, who in bad weather relied almost entirely upon his instinct. One day, however, he was conveying some travellers in a sledge over the pass, and when near the summit suddenly stopped. They foolishly insisted on proceed-

---

[1] *Conservateur Suisse*, XLVI. p. 478 (Vol. XII.).

ing; the horse after resisting for a time started off at full speed, as if to try and escape the danger; but the effort was vain; in a few seconds the avalanche descended and buried all beneath it.

Among other places, the Grimsel Hospice (now an inn) is often endangered by avalanches. This building stands at the bottom of a steep caldron of rock, down the sides of which they often rush with terrific force. The wall chiefly exposed to them is immensely thick, and the windows are protected by strong iron bars. Yet in 1858 I saw one of these which two years before had been bent by an avalanche, which had burst in the shutters and filled the room with snow. At the same time I heard the following strange story, which was said to have happened some thirty years before. The servant who remained there during the winter was in one of the rooms on a stormy evening, when he thought he heard a voice calling him, in another part of the building. Believing that his ears must have deceived him, he at first did not obey the summons; still, being rather startled, he continued listening attentively. Presently the cry was repeated, and he at once, though very much alarmed,—for he knew that he was alone in the house, and that no traveller would be out at such a season,—went in the direction of the sound. Directly after, an immense avalanche descended upon the house, crushing in the roof of the room in which he had been sitting and filling it with snow and débris.

It is a popular notion, that the slightest cause, such as the sound of the voice, the crack of a whip, or the report of a gun, is often sufficient to set the balanced masses of snow in motion and create an avalanche. Accordingly, we often read in the earlier accounts of mountain ascents, how in certain places the guides solemnly enforced silence on the party. No doubt, when great masses of snow are collected on the mountain crests or on steep slopes, the poise is so nice that a very slight cause may destroy equilibrium; it is perhaps hardly too much to say that, early in the year, places might be found where a snowball could originate an avalanche. This however is not the case in summer, at any rate in weather fit for mountain ascents; and the caution was only one act of the solemn farce which used to be played by the Chamouni guides during an ascent of Mont Blanc, with a view of overawing the victimised traveller, and of maintaining a tariff which,—now happily in a great measure a thing of the past,—was one of the most impudent codes of swindling and extortion ever framed. The following amusing extract from an account written by Mr Leslie Stephen of the ascent to a dangerous pass in the Bernese Alps, between the Eiger and the Mönch, shews the opinion of one of the most skilful Oberland guides on this point. The party, led by three guides, two of whom were from Chamouni, the other from Grindelwald, was threading some dangerous séracs in the upper part of the glacier, when, as Mr Stephen says, "the Chamouni guides warned us not to speak, for fear of bringing some of the nicely-poised ice masses down on our heads. On my translating this well-meant piece of advice to Lauener (the Oberland guide), he immediately selected the most dangerous looking pinnacle in sight, and mounting to the top of it sent forth a series of screams, loud enough, I should have thought, to bring down the top of the Mönch—they failed, however, to dislodge any séracs[1]."

A yet more awful calamity than the avalanche sometimes, though happily not often, befalls the dwellers in the Alps; this is the fall of huge masses of earth and stone. Not a breeze sweeps over the crags of the 'everlasting hills' but it brushes away the dust which has crumbled on their surface; scarce a drop of rain trickles down them, but it bears to a lower level some flake of mica or grain of sand; and in addition to this there are very few, down which stones, singly or in volleys, do not come thundering at intervals all day long, if not by night as well. Some mountains, however, spread ruin abroad on a much

---

[1] *Peaks, Passes, and Glaciers.* Second Series, Vol. II. p. 18.

vaster scale, when thousands of tons of rock and soil come crashing down at once, sweeping away and overwhelming everything in their course. Among the most noted of these bergfalls or éboulements, as they are called, are those from the Diablerets and the Rossberg. The former mountain is one of the westernmost of the Oberland chain. It is a long flattish ridge, garnished with several small peaks, which overhang very steep walls of rock on either side. These are built up with a kind of masonry of beds of limestone and shale, dipping roughly southwards, that is, towards the head of a small valley which runs up from the Rhone and terminates at the foot of one of these precipitous walls. Hence it is evident that if anything weakens one of these shale beds,—the mortar, so to say, which binds the courses of stone together,—there is always danger of a landslip.

This has actually taken place on two occasions. The first of these happened in the afternoon of September 25th, 1714. For two whole days previously loud groanings had been heard to issue from the mountain, as though some imprisoned spirit were struggling to release himself, like Typhoeus from under Etna; then a vast fragment of the upper part of the mountain broke suddenly away and thundered down the precipices into the valley beneath. In a few minutes 55 châlets, with 16 men and many head of cattle, were buried for ever under the ruins. One remarkable escape has indeed been recorded, perhaps the most marvellous ever known. A solitary herdsman from the village of Avent occupied one of the châlets which were buried under the fallen mass. Not a trace of it remained; his friends in the valley below returned from their unsuccessful search, and mourned him as dead. He was, however, still among the living; a huge rock had fallen in such a manner as to protect the roof of his châlet, which, as is often the case, rested against a cliff. Above this stones and earth had accumulated, and the man was buried alive. Death would have soon released him from his imprisonment, had not a little rill of water forced its way through the débris and trickled into the châlet. Supported by this and by his store of cheese, he lived three months, labouring all the while incessantly to escape. Shortly before Christmas he succeeded, after almost incredible toil, in once more looking on the light of day, which his dazzled eyes, so long accustomed to the murky darkness below, for awhile could scarcely support. He hastened down to his home in Avent, and knocked at his own door; pale and haggard, he scarcely seemed a being of this world. His relations would not believe that one so long lost could yet be alive, and the door was shut in his face. He turned to a friend's house; no better welcome awaited him; terror seized upon the village; the priest was summoned to exorcise the supposed demon; and it was not till he came that the unfortunate man could persuade them that he was no spectre, but flesh and blood.

A second fall took place in 1749, before which the subterranean groans were again heard; but this time the herdsmen took the alarm and fled at once with their cattle. Five Bernese, however, who were at work in a saw-mill down the valley, at a distance of six miles from the mountain, paid no attention to the warnings. The éboulement took place, and they and their mill were buried beneath the ruins. On this occasion forty châlets were destroyed, more than a square league of forest or pasture land was covered with ruins, the waters of the river were dammed up and formed the lonely tarns now called the Lakes of Derborence.

The valley is still one of the wildest scenes of desolation that can be imagined: for two hours one walks along a path winding in and out among the enormous masses of stone of every shape and size with which the bed of the valley is completely filled. The savageness of the lower part is now indeed somewhat softened by the firs and Alpine shrubs which have found root among the débris, but at the upper end the scene of ruin still remains in all its dreariness, while the steep cliffs and stone-strewn slopes of the Diablerets, which rise full in front during the whole walk, seem to shew that another catastrophe is by no means impossible. One feels a certain sense of relief in passing beyond the range of these terrible engines of destruction.

The second mountain, the Rossberg, of equally evil reputation, and perhaps more celebrity, rises near the lake of Zug. Its upper part consists of sloping strata of *Nagelfluh*[1], underlaid by beds of clay. This rock, though very hard, splits rather easily under the influence of the weather, so that in rainy seasons the water penetrates readily through it to the clay below. This then, becoming soft, gives way under the weight of the rock above, and a landslip is caused. The worst of these happened on the 27th of September, 1806, and the following account of it is condensed from a description published by Dr Zay, of Arth, a neighbouring village. The summer had been a very wet one, and on the first and second of September the rain fell incessantly. New cracks appeared on the flank of the Rossberg, from which deep groaning sounds were heard to issue; stones started from the earth, and rocks rolled down the slopes. At two o'clock in the afternoon a large rock fell down into the valley and raised a cloud of black dust. At the base of the mountain the ground seemed pressed down violently from above, and sticks thrust into it moved of themselves. Soon a large chasm was seen to open out on the side of the Rossberg; the streams ceased to flow, and the birds flew away terrified: then, about five o'clock, the surface of the mountain glided down into the valley, slowly enough, however, to allow some persons to save themselves by flight. The part which fell was about three miles long, 350 yards wide, and 33 thick. In

---

[1] Nailrock: it is a kind of pudding-stone or solidified gravel, the pebbles in which are so firmly cemented together that they are often split through more easily than torn from their beds.

five minutes one of the most fertile valleys in Switzerland was changed into a stony desert: three whole villages and part of a fourth, six churches, 120 houses, 200 stables or châlets, 225 head of cattle (many of those out at pasture had saved themselves by a timely flight), and 111 arpents of land[1], were buried under the ruins of the Rossberg. Among the dead, 484 in number, were seven visitors, who were members of some of the noblest families in Bern. A party of eleven were on their way from Arth to Goldau, one of the villages destroyed; these seven were a little in advance, and were just entering the village; the others, who were about a furlong behind, attracted by something strange in the appearance of the Rossberg, halted, and took out their telescopes to see what was the matter. Suddenly a volley of stones hurtled over their heads, a cloud of dust filled the valley, and a fearful crash was heard. They fled for their lives. When tranquillity was somewhat restored, they returned to seek their friends; but they and Goldau were buried beneath a hundred feet of débris. Of that village, nothing but the church-bell was ever found.

From this calamity too were some remarkable escapes: one woman, with her child in her arms, ran out of her cottage just in time to see it swept away into the valley below; a child, the sole survivor of a family, was found sleeping on a mattress upon the top of a mass of mud and stones; while another child and a servant girl were dug out from under the ruins with comparatively slight injuries, after being buried for fourteen hours.

In the seventh volume of the *Conservateur Suisse* (p. 184) a list is given of fifteen of the most disastrous éboulements that have occurred in Switzerland, among which are the three just mentioned. The earliest recorded happened in 563, and is thus described by a contemporary, Marius, Bishop of Lausanne, from whose chronicle the following account is translated. "In the

---

[1] An arpent is 40,000 square feet (French).

consulate of Basil...the great mountain of Tauretunum, in the territory of the Valais, fell so suddenly that it covered a castle in its neighbourhood, and some villages, with their inhabitants; it so agitated the lake for 60 miles in length and 20 in breadth, that it overflowed both its banks; it destroyed very ancient villages, with men and cattle; it entombed several holy places, with the religious belonging to them. It swept away with fury the Bridge of Geneva, the mills and the men; and, flowing into the city of Geneva, caused the loss of several lives."

Perhaps the most fatal to human life of all these catastrophes was that which overwhelmed Pleurs. This was a town near Chiavenna, which enjoyed great prosperity, being a convenient depôt for German and Italian merchandise. The inhabitants therefore were rich and luxurious; the situation of the town was smiling and beautiful; still, above the vines and forests that clothed the surrounding hills, rose the drear and furrowed head of the Monte Conto. Its ill-omened scars, and the warnings of some peasants who fed their flocks on it, appear to have been alike forgotten, and the inhabitants to have lived, till August 30, 1618, without a thought of danger. Then, after several days of heavy rain, a fragment of the Conto suddenly fell upon the neighbouring village of Schillano, and buried beneath it 78 houses with their inmates. Terrified at this awful catastrophe, the people of Pleurs crowded to the principal church at the hour of vespers; but, while they were at prayers, the greater part of the mountain "gave way, with a crash that shook all the country round, sweeping along forests, rocks, and fields, and buried the whole town for ever under the ruins." Scarcely any escaped alive; in all, about 1500 persons perished. Five churches (including those belonging to convents), two hospitals, and five bridges, with many handsome houses, were buried under a mass of débris some hundred feet deep. The course of the river Maira was obstructed, and the inhabitants lower down the valley, fearing a flood, escaped to the mountains. Most fortunately the river speedily forced its way through the barrier, so this further disaster was avoided. Many attempts were made to excavate in the ruins; first, in the hope of saving any who might be buried alive; then, of recovering some portion of the valuables which the town had contained; but all in vain. A few mangled corpses, and a church-bell, were all that could be reached[1].

It must not, however, be supposed that Switzerland is peculiarly exposed to calamities of this kind; few of the Alpine districts are without their tale of sorrow. Several éboulements are recorded to have happened in Dauphiné; one of which will be described presently. The crystalline districts, however, are less liable than those where shales or conglomerates abound. One of the most fearful scenes of ruin that I have ever seen is on the Ampezzo road, in the Italian Tyrol. Just on the east of this rises Monte Antelao, a fine pyramidal peak of grey rock and shale, capped with slopes of snow and ice. From one of its buttresses an enormous mass fell in 1814, overwhelming two or three villages and their inhabitants. Several square miles of country, covered with broken rocks and white dusty rubbish, which is only just beginning here and there to nourish a scanty verdure, shew the extent of the devastation. One very remarkable escape was related to me. Two persons, a father and his little son, were walking towards one of the villages that were overwhelmed, when they were startled by a loud crash, and by several stones whizzing past them. Close at hand a mass of rock rose by the road-side, and they instinctively rushed under its shelter. The next moment the fields and houses in front disappeared under a black cloud of dust, and the road on either side was covered with fragments of stone. The younger of the two was alive in 1866, and told this story to my companion, as he drove him past the spot.

The thriving little town of Cortina, in the same neighbour-

[1] *Conservateur Suisse*, I. 181; VII. 200.

hood, has not always been free from anxiety of this kind. The cliffs of an outlier of the Sorapisse, a grand mountain S. E. of the town, consist of dolomitic limestone resting on shale, and consequently often fall. These cliffs, indeed, are too far away to be likely to do any damage of themselves, but their débris has choked up the mouth of a slight hollow just at their feet, and converted it into a tarn. After some very heavy rain in 1842, this became unusually full, and the dam began to yield. As the quantity of water was happily not great enough to cause a flood, it converted the soil and débris into a stream of mud, which advanced at a much more gradual rate. As the evening approached, it came near Cortina, following the course of a torrent which descends through the pastures just on the south of the town. So far all was well; but the danger was that it might overflow the low banks of this ravine, and spreading itself out over the sloping pastures, roll down upon the town; when, in all probability, most of the houses would have been seriously injured, if not swept away. It was an awful night; the churches had been stripped of their furniture, the houses were deserted, the people, carrying away what could be removed, had most of them taken refuge in the neighbouring villages; the rest were praying, or watching the advance of the stream of mud and rolling boulders. It rose higher and higher in the ravine, which, just outside the town, was spanned by a handsome stone bridge. It reached the crown of the arch; this stemmed the current for a moment; then yielded, as if blown up by gunpowder, and disappeared. The stream rose up to the brink of the ravine, but fortunately did not overflow its banks; and so the commune escaped with the loss of their bridge, and a good many acres of valuable land, which were utterly ruined. It appeared to me that, though the danger may recur at any time after an unusually wet season, a few 'navigators' might, in a week or two, cut a trench that would drain the tarn, and make Cortina as safe as Venice. These mud-avalanches, though less dangerous to life, on account of their slower motion, are quite as destructive to property; and many hundreds of acres of arable and pasture land, besides houses and châlets have been utterly destroyed by them. The scene of one of these is well known to all who have travelled along the Rhone Valley, above the Lake of Geneva, for both the rail and the carriage roads cut through its remains. It was caused by a large mass of rock and shale which fell from the Dent du Midi, sweeping along with it a quantity of snow, ice, and moraine, and was converted by the swollen mountain torrents into a slimy mud, which descended to the Rhone just like a stream of lava.

The floods which, as we have seen, are sometimes caused by these berg-falls, are often even more widely destructive. One of the most fatal, to which I have already alluded, happened in the valley of the Romanche. Some 30 miles above Grenoble the mountains around this river, owing to the influx of the Vénéon and the Olle within a short distance of each other, retire so as to form a sort of amphitheatre around a rich alluvial plain. They, however, soon close in again upon the narrow defile of the Combe de Gavet, the northern portal to which is a mountain called the Voudène. A landslip from this in the twelfth century dammed up the narrow gorge and converted the plain into a lake, in some places 30 feet deep. This remained for many years, till, on the night of September 14, 1219, the dam suddenly burst, and the accumulated waters rushed down the valley sweeping everything before them. Many villages were destroyed with their inhabitants; and at Grenoble itself numbers were carried off by the flood. A similar lake was formed in 1512 in the Val de Blegno, which was 12,000 paces round, and so deep that only the tops of the church steeples stood above the water. This lasted for two years, and then burst, spreading ruin over the whole valley between it and the Lago Maggiore, and bringing death to more than 600 persons.

The inundation in the valley of the Dranse in 1818 is also well known. This, however, was not caused by a berg-fall, but by the advance of the glacier of Gétroz, which dammed up the river and formed a lake about 10,000 feet long, 400 wide, and 200 deep; containing, it was estimated, about 800,000,000 cubic feet of water. It was well known what the result of this would be, for in 1595 a similar barrier had been formed, which had at last given way and devastated the valley for miles below. The only chance therefore was to 'tap' the lake, desperate as the remedy might seem. This was done under the superintendence of M. Venetz, an eminent Swiss engineer. A brave band of labourers, working day and night, cut a tunnel 600 feet long through the glacier, which was completed just as the waters of the lake reached the level of its opening. The current quickly deepened and enlarged this, and between the 13th and 16th of June, about two-fifths of the water was drawn off. The cutting, however, thus formed, so much weakened the barrier, that on the latter day, at half-past four in the afternoon, it suddenly gave way and the remaining contents of the lake swept down the valley. In two hours the flood reached Martigny, and poured into the Rhone; by which it rushed down to the Lake of Geneva, reaching this at eleven; thus passing over about 18 leagues in six-and-a-half hours. It is said to have issued from the defile of Lourtier (a few miles below the glacier), like a moving wall or mound, a hundred yards high, the head of the column of water being entirely masked by the confused mass of mud, stones, beams, and trunks of trees which it swept along, and overhung by a dense cloud of dust[1]. The people in the valley had been warned of their danger, nevertheless 50 lives were lost. Besides this, 500 houses and cottages, with several bridges, were destroyed; and a great quantity of land rendered useless, at any rate for many years.

The violent storms which break upon the mountain districts

[1] *Conservateur Suisse*, No. xxxvii. (Vol. ix.) p. 865.

often cause floods, which, though less disastrous than these, would, if they occurred in England, be as noted as the bursting of the Holmfirth reservoir. Hardly a year passes without considerable damage being done; bridges are swept away, roads are buried under torrents of mud, and fields overwhelmed with débris. I well remember the storm of August, 1860, which among other mischief, seriously damaged the magnificent Splügen road. I was then at Zermatt, where it began with a thunder-storm and rained for about thirty-six hours; after which, as may be supposed, the torrents were swollen far beyond their usual size. Lower down in the valleys much harm was done, but there one bridge only was swept away. It was, however, an awful sight to see the Visp roaring under one of the bridges that remained, and to hear the groans and heavy thuds of the boulders that were being hurried on and dashed against one another by the torrent. The traces of this storm were visible when I crossed the Splügen the following year; and I had a few weeks before seen broken bridges and large tracts of stone-strewn land in the valley of the Romanche, which marked the course taken by a flood in 1856.

A letter, written by an eye-witness, relates how the pleasant town of Vevay[1] on the Lake of Geneva was once inundated. The torrent, which here descends from the mountains and passes through the town, overflowed its bank, rising in some streets to a height of nine feet, filling many houses and cellars with mud, and drowning several persons. Locarno, in the Canton Ticino, appears, on the 2nd September, 1556, to have been the scene of a yet more destructive storm and flood. The day began by several shocks of an earthquake, followed, about five o'clock, by a terrific gale from the south. Part of the old castle was blown down; the doors of St Victor's church were burst open by a blast while the priest was at the altar, and everything within

---

[1] On July 5, 1726. *Conservateur Suisse*, No. XXXVI. (Vol. IX.) p. 214.

was overturned. Towards midday thick clouds covered the sky, so that it was almost as dark as night; then came a violent thunder-storm, followed by torrents of rain, which lasted from two to six o'clock in the evening. Every rivulet was changed into a torrent; the stream which flowed through the town was so choked by uprooted trees and rocks, that its waters poured over their banks and inundated the streets, almost burying them under mud and gravel. Many lives were lost, and an immense quantity of property destroyed. In fact this calamity, following immediately upon the expulsion of some 300 of its inhabitants, who had adopted the Reformed faith, dealt a blow to the prosperity of Locarno from which it has never recovered; and it now numbers less than a third of the inhabitants that it did in the 14th century[1].

As may have been observed from the above notices, earthquakes are not very uncommon in the Alps, and are sometimes productive of considerable damage. In the year 1356 the town of Bâle was almost overthrown by one, and some 300 persons perished in its ruins. The last shock of any importance was in 1856. It was especially severe in the Visp-thal. At Visp an eye-witness[2] describes the Hotel du Soleil as "shaken from top to bottom, every wall split, mortar and stones brought tumbling to the floors...the two churches suffered grievously; the whole interior of the roof of one had fallen, crushing everything in its way; railings, seats, organ-loft, and altar-steps, all had been destroyed and the main walls cracked from top to bottom"...At St Nicholas also, about 12 miles up the valley, the houses were much injured and the church-tower so seriously shaken that it had to be rebuilt. A smart, but harmless, shock was felt at Zermatt; and what is more curious, the little village of Stalden, about half-way between the two places injured, escaped almost without damage.

[1] *Conservateur Suisse*, No. XLVI. (Vol. XII.) p. 431.
[2] Hinchliff, *Summer Months among the Alps*, p. 84.

One of the greatest dangers which the traveller has to dread on the Alpine passes, during unsettled weather late in the year, is the *Tourmente*. This is a sudden storm of snow, accompanied by violent gusts of wind, which fill the air with drifted flakes; so that, becoming bewildered, he loses his way, and at last sinks down benumbed with cold and dies. There is hardly a frequented pass which has not witnessed more than one death from this cause. In 1830 two Englishmen perished on the Col du Bon-Homme in one of these storms. Exhausted with fatigue and overcome with cold, they sank down by the wayside; and their guides, after having in vain endeavoured to urge them on, were compelled to leave them to their fate and press forward to save their own lives.

I had once a slight experience of a tourmente, and am not anxious to repeat the trial. It was on the well-known path which leads from the Grimsel Hospice to Obergestelen in the Rhone valley. One cold and rainy evening in the month of August 1858 I arrived, with a friend, at the former place, where we slept. On looking out next morning we found to our surprise that the ground was covered several inches deep with snow. Being however anxious to proceed on our journey and not supposing there would be any particular difficulty in crossing so comparatively low a pass, we shouldered our knapsacks and started directly after breakfast. On reaching the top of the rocky wall above the Grimsel Hospice, where the paths to the Rhone glacier and to Obergestelen divide, we at once saw that there was harder work before us than we had anticipated. All traces of the track were obliterated, a thick mist concealed everything beyond the distance of a few yards, and a cold wind swept in violent gusts over the plateau, driving the snow before it. Two or three fir trunks, forming a rude bridge across a stream, served to start us in the right direction; and a little while after we came in sight of an upright pole. This shewed us that for some distance at any rate the road was marked, and so we pushed on from pole to pole; for we could rarely see further than from the one to the other. Occasionally one was missing, and then we had to wait for a lull in the storm in order to catch sight of the one beyond it.

All this time the weather was getting worse and worse, the wind blew furiously, cold as ice, and raised such clouds of drifted snow and sharp frozen sleet that it was often impossible to see more than twenty or thirty feet ahead. Our hair was covered with this frosty dust, it even hung on our eyelashes; and had we been inclined to laugh, our appearance must have been sufficiently droll. The drifts too became deeper and deeper every step; we often plunged in above the middle in trying to cross them, and were obliged to make circuits to avoid those which we could not venture to pass. At last, thinking matters were looking serious, I suggested to my companion that perhaps we had better return. His reply was not encouraging, "I do not think we should ever get back, for it would be impossible to face this wind." Accordingly we pushed forward as before, halting now and then to raise a pole which had fallen, in case we were after all forced to attempt a return, and once or twice to drink a mouthful of brandy from our flasks. At last after descending a little we suddenly came to the end of the poles. This was by no means pleasant, for there was not a trace of the road; nothing but rock and drifted snow, with the mist as thick and the tempest as violent as ever. Return being now out of the question, we pushed on, always taking care to work downwards as much as possible, in order to avoid entangling ourselves in the hollows so frequent in the upper parts of mountains, and determining, in case there seemed no hope of finding a path, to follow the first running water which we could find. This would of course have been, in this place, the simplest way of getting out of our difficulties; but we did not know what was below us, and in an unknown country there is always a risk that taking a stream for a guide may bring you to a precipice, down which you can only go as it does; a mode of descent which, though speedy, would be the reverse of satisfactory, since the atoms of the human body do not reunite so readily as the drops of water. We therefore kept on following the line which seemed the most probable one for the path to take; driving our poles into the snow to sound for it, occasionally scraping the drift away if we fancied we saw any traces, and searching with special care along the edges of streams. At last we hit upon it and followed it for some distance, when it suddenly disappeared; the cold however was now less intense, the wind less violent, and the snow not so deep; so after some little difficulty we again found the path, and pressed rapidly on. At length a tree appeared through the mist, and a few minutes after this welcome sight we got clear of the snow and reached the verge of the pine-woods, through which we hurried in a drizzling rain till we reached the bottom of the valley at Obergestelen: thus terminating an adventure which might very easily have produced serious consequences. We afterwards learnt that another party, which later in the day had attempted to cross with a guide, was driven back, and all the guests at the Grimsel were weather-bound for the day; the guides pronouncing the pass to be impracticable. This account of what happened in summer on a pass hardly more than 7000 feet above the sea, may serve to give some idea of the danger of a tourmente later in the year, and at a higher elevation.

The wind often blows with great force on the tops of the highest mountains even in the finest weather: in fact, the north wind, generally the mountaineer's best friend, is sometimes in this respect his enemy. Not unfrequently an expedition has had to be abandoned when success was all but attained, because the gale rendered the passage of some exposed slope or ridge too dangerous, or because the intense cold produced frostbites. In the summer of 1864 I was buffeted by one of these gales in the Corridor[1] of Mont Blanc. The cold was something horrible; the wind seemed to blow **not round but** through me, freezing my very marrow, and **making my** teeth chatter like castanets; and if I stopped for a moment I shook **as if in an ague fit.** It whisked up the small spiculæ **of frozen** snow and dashed **them** against my face with such violence that it was hardly possible to look to windward. Thin sheets of ice as large **as** my hand, were whirled along the surface of the glacier like paper. During the whole ascent we were in the shade, **but** at the head of the Corridor the sun's rays were shining **with** full force upon the snow. Therefore I kept consoling myself with the hope that when once we arrived **there the cold would** be much less intense; but to **my astonishment when I** stepped out of the shade into the **sun I was not** conscious of any difference. A short time **afterwards one of** our party became exhausted and **was** frostbitten; whereupon by our guide's advice we abandoned the expedition and returned as fast as possible to a more genial climate. On several other occasions the cold has been so great that I have only been able to stay a few minutes on the exposed side of a lofty **peak**; once too I was caught by a gale in descending the narrow **ridge** along which is the way to **the** highest **peak of Monte Rosa.** This is not exactly a pleasant **place for an adventure of this** kind; for it is in many places only a few inches wide, with the slope on one side very steep, and on the other almost a precipice. We advanced as fast as we could during the lulls; then, when a blast came, anyone who was luckily near a projecting rock made a dash for it and sheltered **under its** lea; and the others either dropped on one knee or on all fours and anchored themselves as firmly as possible with their alpenstocks. When these gales are raging the drifted snow is blown far to leeward

---

[1] A sort of wide gully **or glen** on the north side leading up to the watershed between France and Italy, **at the foot** of the Calotte or actual peak of Mont Blanc. It is about 14,000 feet above **the sea.**

of the peaks in long streamers like delicate cirrus clouds; and on such occasions the mountain is said by the guides *fumer sa pipe* (to smoke his pipe); this Mont Blanc was doing to some purpose the day that we were upon him.

Not the least curious part of these gales is the way in which they are often confined to the crests of the mountains. A raging north-wind may be seen whisking the snow off the peaks while there is comparative calm on the slopes a few hundred feet lower down. On the occasion mentioned above there was but an occasional breath on the Grand Plateau of Mont Blanc while the storm was raging about 1000 feet above. Its violence apparently did not depend upon the absolute height of the mountain; for it seemed equally furious upon the upper part of all the peaks in that neighbourhood. Some of my friends at the same time were attempting the ascent of an Aiguille a few miles off, which was about 13,000 feet high; and they told me that the storm burst upon them also with comparative suddenness when about 2000 feet below the summit. They too were compelled to turn back when only a few hundred feet from their goal. In the same way the clouds in the upper regions of the sky may be seen scudding along impelled by a brisk gale, while lower down they are resting quietly among the peaks. Not unfrequently the configuration of the country affects the direction of the storms and causes them to break with peculiar fury upon certain spots. Such is the case with many of the squalls so dangerous on the lakes, which come rushing down the valleys from the mountains and burst suddenly on the waters. The form of a valley of course often modifies the direction of a wind, and causes it to apparently blow from a quarter quite different from its true course; and even on the calmest and hottest days a cool current of air may always be found rushing along above any large glacier stream.

A few words may also be said here on some of the prevailing Alpine winds. The chief of these is the Föhn, the best known and most efficacious of all the winds. It is a hot blast from the south, as some think from the African deserts. On its approach the air becomes close and stifling; the sky, at first of unusual clearness, gradually thickens to a muddy and murky hue: animals, both wild and domestic, become restless and disquieted by the unnatural dryness of the hot blast which now comes sweeping over the hills. It is said that in some villages all the fires are extinguished when this wind begins to blow, for fear lest some chance spark should fall on the dry wooden roofs and set the whole place in a blaze. The precaution is not a needless one; for the town of Glarus has been more than once greatly injured by fire during one of these storms. On the last occasion, May 10th, 1861, almost the whole town was consumed. Still, dangerous as the Föhn sometimes is, it is a welcome visitant in spring; for under its warm touch the winter snows melt away as if by magic. Tschudi says that in the valley of Grindelwald this wind causes a snow-bed two feet thick to disappear in about a couple of hours, and that it produces a greater effect in 24 hours than the sun does in 15 days. Indeed there is a Swiss proverb which rather profanely says, "If the Föhn does not blow, the golden sun and the good God can do nothing with the snow." The south wind, however, is never welcome to the mountaineer in summer time: for the vapours which it bears with it from the Italian plains are condensed by the snows of the Alps and stream down in torrents of rain. Tschudi also mentions a singular phenomenon partly due to the Föhn; which, during the early part of the year, often prevails for a considerable time at and above a height of some 6000 feet, while the air below is either calm or gently moved by the north wind; hence the snow is melted off the upper parts of the forests and the higher pastures, while it lies thick on all the lower slopes and on the bed of the valley. There is also a wind of a very opposite character called the Bise; this is a cutting blast from the north-east, which is held in much the same estimation by the Swiss as an east wind is by us.

A thunder-storm is always a grand spectacle, but nowhere is it so magnificent as among the mountains, where also it is much more frequent than on the plains. It cannot be better described than in Byron's well-known lines :

> "Far along,
> From peak to peak, the rattling crags among,
> Leaps the live thunder! not from one lone cloud,
> But every mountain now hath found a tongue,
> And Jura answers, through her misty shroud,
> Back to the joyous Alps, who call to her aloud![1]"

Often, during a summer which I spent at Lausanne, used I to admire the truth of the description of which these are the opening lines; for almost all the storms that approached the lake, either took their stand in the valley of the Rhone or settled down upon the long ridges of the Jura. Less awful than these, though more beautiful, were the distant storms which we used to see raging in the direction of Mont Blanc, while the lake itself was calm and the sky immediately above it almost unclouded. One in particular, I remember, the most beautiful that I have ever seen. The night was still and dark; a storm was evidently gathering, and so we waited watching for it to break. Suddenly a flash or rather sheet of unutterable brilliancy lit up the sky, and the whole chain of the Savoy Alps on the opposite shore rose clear before us; while a ghostly pale blue light glimmered over the surface of the lake and played upon the vine-clad slopes that stretched down from our terrace to the water side. Again and again the magic sheen returned, revealing for a moment this vision of beauty, and then letting the pall of night close over it again. Brilliant as was the lightning, the storm was so distant that only the faint rumble of the thunder could be heard.

---

[1] *Childe Harold*, c. III. 92.

No words, however, can adequately express the awful grandeur of these tempests when they burst among the mountains. I have often been out in them, in fact, far more frequently than was pleasant, but perhaps the grandest of all was one that welcomed me for the first time to Chamouni. As we entered the valley and caught sight of the white pinnacles of the glacier des Bossons, a dark cloud came rolling up rapidly from the west. Beneath it, just where two tall peaks towered up, the sky glowed like a sheet of red-hot copper, and a lurid mist spread over the neighbouring hills, wrapping them, as it seemed, in a robe of flame. Onward rolled the cloud; the lightning began to play; down the valley rushed a squall of wind driving the dust high in air before it and followed by a torrent of rain. Flash succeeded flash almost incessantly; now darting from cloud to cloud; now dividing itself into a number of separate streaks of fire and dancing all over the sky; now streaming down upon the crags, and at times even leaping up from some lofty peak into the air. The colours were often most beautiful, and bright beyond description.

It has happened sometimes that travellers have been actually enveloped by the thunder-cloud, and placed in situations of no little peril. One thus describes his sensations[1]: "A loud peal of thunder was heard, and shortly after I observed that a strange singing sound like that of a kettle was issuing from my alpenstock. We halted, and finding that all the axes and stocks emitted the same sound, stuck them into the snow. The guide from the hotel now pulled off his cap, shouting that his head burned, and his hair was seen to have a similar appearance to that which it would have presented had he been on an insulated stool under a powerful electrical machine. We all of us experienced the sensation of pricking and burning in some part of the body, more especially in the head and face, my hair also

[1] Mr Watson in *Alpine Journal*, Vol. I. page 143. See also Forbes, *Travels in the Alps*, p. 323.

standing on end in an uncomfortable but very amusing manner. The snow gave out a hissing sound, as though a heavy shower of hail were falling; the veil on the wide-awake of one of the party stood upright in the air; and on waving our hands, the singing sound issued loudly from the fingers. Whenever a peal of thunder was heard the phenomenon ceased, to be resumed before its echoes had died away. At these times we felt shocks, more or less violent, in those portions of the body which were most affected. By one of these shocks my right arm was paralyzed so completely that I could neither use nor raise it for several minutes, nor indeed until it had been severely rubbed, and I suffered much pain in it at the shoulder-joint for some hours."

The colours of the snow and sky in the higher Alps have already been incidentally noticed, but it may be well to add a few words on what is one of the traveller's greatest delights. The appreciation of pure colour no doubt varies greatly in different persons, but it is certainly quickened and rendered more delicate by observant travel in the Alps, for in no other parts of Europe are the hues more varied, more changeful, or more brilliant. I believe also that there is no faculty which is better worth cultivation, or which is more conducive to a pure and healthful state of mind; and yet thousands are from mere negligence practically almost colour-blind, and miss the rich visions of glory, which are so often before their eyes. To live among mountains and beautiful scenery cannot be the lot of all, but the sky is ever above us, and almost daily glows in the east before the rising sun, and flushes in the west with its departing rays. To return, however, to the Alps. The snow when seen from near is of course a dazzling white, so bright as to scorch the skin and inflame the eyes of those who walk over it without due protection. The cause of this is that the tiny facets of the ice crystals scatter around the beams of light which fall upon them; and thus not only is the traveller exposed to the direct rays of the sun, but thousands of little mirrors, as though guided by mischievous schoolboys, dart their reflected flashes upon him. A brief experience also shews him, that a foggy clouded day is comparatively little protection. Even though he has never once so much as seen the sun,—a pale globe through a dark mist,—his face will burn and his eyes smart that night unless he has taken all the usual precautions; for strange as it may seem, a very large portion of the light, which reaches us, does not come directly from the sun, but is reflected to us by the vapours of the atmosphere. An increase of vapour, that is, an increase in the reflecting power of the atmosphere, may therefore in some respects compensate for the loss which it produces by the obstruction of the direct sun-rays; and so the light reflected from the snow and made by its crystal mirrors to converge on any one spot on a cloudy day may not be so very much less than on a clear one. Principal Forbes[1] mentions some very interesting experiments which tend to establish this fact, and to shew that the burnt faces from which we Alpine travellers suffer, are not so much due to the greater nearness of the sun or to the thinner veil of atmosphere, affording less protection from its heat, as to the mirrors of the snow crystals, which collect the light usually absorbed by the soil or herbage and throw it back upon us.

In the chinks and holes of the snow, as we have already said, in speaking of the glaciers, the light appears a delicate blue, often with a slight tinge of green; its intensity depending upon the purity of the snow. The ice crystals deprive the light which passes through them of its red rays, and so change it to blue or bluish-green. Water in a pure state, whether liquid or crystallized, has an affinity for these red rays of the spectrum, and absorbs them during their passage; hence the depths of the lake of Geneva and of the glacier crevasses appear equally blue, and the predominance of a green tint appears to depend

[1] *Travels in the Alps*, p. 416.

mainly upon the greater or less amount of fine detritus in the one case and of minute air-bubbles in the other. At times the effect of the transmitted light in deep, fresh snow is almost magical; it is thus admirably described by Dr Tyndall[1]: "This morning as I ascended Monte Rosa, I often examined the holes made in the snow by our batons, but the light which issued from them was scarcely perceptibly blue. Now, however, a deep layer of fresh snow overspread the mountain, and the effect was magnificent. Along the kamm (the last ridge) I was continually surprised and delighted by the blue gleams which issued from the broken or perforated stratum of new snow; each hole made by the staff was filled with a light as pure, and nearly as deep as that of the unclouded firmament. When we reached the bottom of the kamm, Lauener came to the front and tramped before me. As his feet rose out of the snow and shook the latter off in fragments, sudden and wonderful gleams of blue light flashed from them." On this occasion, he adds, the sky was clouded and the air misty. The same flashes of blue light may be seen in the waters of a clear lake, when they are dashed up by the paddles of a steamer. The reason why the blue light was only conspicuous among the fresh snow is doubtless that the consolidated old snow not only deprived the light of its red rays, but absolutely forbade it to pass. According to the well-known law in optics, light can only emerge from a denser to a thinner medium, by striking the surface of the former in certain particular directions. Hence, in a tightly packed mass of snow prisms, the greater part of each pencil of rays fails during some part of its journey to fulfil these conditions, and is sent to wander hopelessly and perish by dashing itself against the walls of its icy prison. The feathery fresh snow and the transparent ice, wherein all these prisms are welded together, are alike more easily traversed; hence the greater beauty of their recesses.

[1] *Glaciers of the Alps*, p. 132.

A singular phosphorescence is also occasionally visible on the snow-fields during the night. Mr Tuckett[1], who observed it during an ascent of the Aletsch-horn, describes it as a "soft lambent glow" over all the snow-fields round, "something like that produced by the flame of naphtha;" besides this, at every step, he goes on to say, "an illuminated circle or nimbus about two inches in breadth surrounded our feet, and we seemed to be ploughing our way through fields of light and raising clods of it, if I may be allowed the expression, in our progress." Another observer, Mr Holland[2], speaks of the snowy particles falling from their shoes in a "little luminous shower. Except that the sparks were of a pale phosphorescent yellow colour, the effect was much the same as that of the sparks seen at night when a horse strikes his shoe against a stone." On the latter occasion neither moon nor stars were visible.

Red snow, so often mentioned in accounts of Arctic voyages, is not very uncommon in the Alps. My first acquaintance with it was on a snow-field near the Viso; and so far as I know it is rather more frequently found here, and in the neighbouring district of Dauphiné, than in any other Alpine region. There was a reddish-brown tinge upon the snow, which at first I took for dust blown from some rocks which were at no great distance; but when we walked over it, our foot-marks were distinctly of a dull crimson-red colour, as if we had first stepped upon some wet gravel—such as is common in the red sandstone districts of our midland counties. On taking up a little of this staining matter, I at once saw that it was not dust from any rock, and a closer examination shewed its real character. Under the microscope it appears as a minute crimson boss, something like a full-blown rose. Its true nature has been much disputed; originally it was supposed to belong to the vegetable world, and classed among the lowest botanical orders, under the name of

---

[1] *Peaks, Passes, and Glaciers.* Second Series. Vol. II. p. 52.
[2] *Alpine Journal*, Vol. I. p. 143.

protococcus nivalis. Recent researches have, however, established the fact that under this title several kinds have been confounded, most of which are infusoria of the genus *discercea*, having a silicious carapace and two trumpet-shaped appendages, which form their organs of motion. Some state that the colouring matter is developed on the pollen grains of the *Pinus pumilio*, which serve as a nidus[1]. If this be the case, it is not confined to the pollen of this species, for I have seen red snow most abundant in districts where this shrub is wholly wanting. A yellowish dust, which may also be observed upon the snow, appears to be entirely inorganic.

In the far distance the snow assumes a delicate primrose hue or pale cream colour. The same change of tint may often be noticed on massy cumulus clouds, and it is due, I suppose, to the invisible vapours with which the atmosphere is always more or less charged. The blue also of the sky varies considerably in intensity, and becomes deeper as we ascend higher. Occasionally, though only in the clearest weather, it appears a dark gentian blue, reminding us of Shelley's description:

> The sun's unclouded orb
> Rolled through the black concave.

It was thus, the first time that I ascended Monte Rosa. The day was perfectly clear, except for the sea of mist that as usual lay far below us shrouding the plains of Italy; and the colour of the vaulted firmament above, as we stood on the peak, was as deep as, though far more brilliant than, the richest hues of the bell-gentian[2]. The blackness noticed above, as well as this increase in the depth of the blue in the sky, are due doubtless to the thinner shell of atmosphere, capable of reflecting and dis-

---

[1] *Alpine Journal*, Vol. I. p. 152.

[2] *Gentiana acaulis*—the only one often grown in English gardens, and a very common flower in the higher Alpine regions.

persing light, which interposes between the observer and the vast dark space of unilluminated ether. On the southern slopes of the Alps the blues of the sky are generally very different from those on the northern; owing, I am inclined to think, to the greater quantity of vapour which is in solution in the air. Though not less beautiful, indeed by many they are preferred to the colder northern tints, they are not quite so deep in tone, are softer, sunnier, and yet—if one may be allowed the expression—more solid, resembling the turquoise rather than the sapphire. From the same cause probably proceed the exquisite blue tints of the distant landscape, which are always one of the greatest charms of the Italian valleys. The neighbouring Ligurian and Adriatic seas, and the marshy plains of the Po, must often reek under the summer sun like steaming caldrons, and fill the air with suspended vapour, which is only rendered visible when it drifts against the Alpine snows. Hence doubtless come those baffling sheets of mist just mentioned, which, lying at a height of about eight or nine thousand feet, almost invariably cut off all view of the Italian lowlands from the summits of the Pennine Alps; though they are often, I believe, so thin as to form a diaphanous canopy, which against the bright sky is almost invisible to those beneath.

But it is at the hours of sunrise and sunset that the sky and Alps assume their greatest glory and are wrapped in royal robes of crimson and gold, their Father's 'coat of many colours.' The hues on these two occasions are very different, but of course the distinction consists in minute graduations of tone which it is almost impossible to describe. As a broad division it may be enough to say that in the sunrise the tints generally incline rather to gold or orange, in the sunset to crimson or violet-pink. Travellers should never omit to see some sunrises as well as sunsets. The fact alone that the horizontal light falls upon the mountains from the east instead of the west, makes a marvellous difference in their appearance; and beautiful as it may be to watch the rosy flush lingering on the peaks, it is yet more delightful to see the golden gleam striking upon their summits, and kindling a hundred altar fires to the approaching day. Besides this the mind, perhaps half-unconsciously, rejoices in the triumph of light over darkness, and sighs in sympathy when night, the emblem of death, again prevails in the alternate round. So, Alpine traveller, 'shake off dull sloth, and early rise,' and in fine weather your heart must be cold indeed if, when the sun glances upon the mountains rising above the silent valleys or a level sea of clouds, it does not 'pay its morning sacrifice.'

Usually one is too much occupied in drinking in the beauties of the scene and in watching the changeful glories of the sky and mountain to think of noting down, watch in hand, each variation of tint; the delight is so intense that one abandons oneself to simple enjoyment and silent adoration. A very careful description, however, of a sunset on the Lake of Geneva, has been drawn up by M. Necker[1], and though it is rather long, I am tempted to translate it, if only to shew some of my readers how full of beauty are those sunset scenes, at which perhaps they scarce cast a glance.

"'The sun, from the instant of the contact of its lower edge with the ridge of the Jura, to that of the total disappearance of its upper, takes at Geneva (as a mean) 3 minutes to set, the greatest time being $3^m. 30''$, the least 3^m.

"As soon as it has disappeared, the eastern sky, if clear, continues to gleam with a brilliant white light, or is only slightly tinged with a yellowish hue. If there are any scattered clouds, their edges, which are still illuminated, assume a vivid golden-yellow, or orange, or red hue. But the sky itself in the intervals between them does not as yet share in these brilliant colours; and remains white, without undergoing any noticeable change, save a diminution in the intensity of its illumination,

[1] *Annales de Chimie et de Physique* (Feb. and March, 1839).

until all the phenomena which take place in the eastern quarter of the horizon have completely ceased.

"Let us now turn our eyes towards the east; the plain is in shadow, and the mountains, brilliantly illuminated, are conspicuous for the intensity, and as painters term it, the warmth of their tints. It is, in fact, the contrast between the lights and shades which gives this intensity and effect to the colouring, and it is the tinge of red or orange in it which produces this warmth. This tint is especially conspicuous upon the limestone rocks (yellowish-white) of the nearer mountains, and above all upon the eternal snows of the central chain of Mont Blanc. On the intervening chain the sombre hue of the woods, meadows, and rocks, and the greater thickness of the interposing stratum of air, give to this tint a purpler hue.

"However, the shadow steals rapidly up the nearer chains of the Salèves and Voirons, and simultaneously, the effect and warmth of the tints, as well as the illumination, fade away on those parts which it has occupied. A sombre shade, uniform and dull, replaces them; and it is by this rapid change from one condition to another so different, that one can estimate with certainty for each place the exact moment when its illumination ceases[1].

"In from 9 to 12 minutes, the shadow has passed over the first ramps of the Salève; and in 17 minutes, it reaches at the same time both the Piton, which is its culminating point, about 2,999 feet above the plain, and the summit of the Voirons, which is 3,281 feet, and is about 3½ leagues further to the east than the Piton. In 20 minutes it has reached the summits of the Môle and of the Brezon, distant nearly 5 leagues, and about 6,014 feet in absolute height. One minute later it has crept up to the ridges of the Vergis, which—more than

---

[1] On more distant mountains the change is not always so rapid. I have sometimes observed a sensible diminution in the brightness of the light, as though there were a zone of penumbra. T. G. B.

8,314 feet in elevation and 7½ leagues distant—are conspicuous by the brilliant hues, reflected from their limestone rocks.

"This progressive extension of the region of shadow, as well as the monotony and obscurity which accompany it, and the continual diminution of the parts still illuminated, are accompanied by a circumstance which was observable, though less distinctly, on the nearer mountains; namely an apparent increase in the brightness, intensity, and colour of the parts still illuminated, produced by contrast with the cold, sombre, dull, uniform bluish-grey tint of those which are so no longer. Then the snows of the distant illuminated mountains, are tinged with a bright orange-yellow, and their rocks with a ruddier orange. When the first chains of the Alps, those which do not rise into the regions of eternal snow, are wholly in the shade, the rocks and especially the snows of the central chain assume a tint which constantly becomes redder and more intense. On the snows it is first a bright orange, then a ruddy glow. On the rocks the tint is similar, but is a little mixed with grey. Bathed as they all are, snow and rocks, in the same orange-red light, their contrast is not too harsh, too striking; but their various hues harmonize together in the most pleasing manner. The part of the sky against which these mountains stand out, which rises to a height of three to four degrees above the horizon, already assumes a slightly red hue which now continues constantly increasing in intensity and ruddiness.

"By about 23 or 24 minutes after sunset, the shadow has reached the lowest snow-peak of the central chain, the snow dome of the Buet, which is elevated about 10,089 feet above the sea, and distant 12½ leagues from Geneva. Three minutes later, or 27 minutes after sunset, it reaches the summit of the Aiguille Verte, 13,389 feet in absolute height. It is then that Mont Blanc, which remains alone illuminated now that the whole surface of the land lies in deep shadow, seems to glow with the most intense orange-red light, and under certain circumstances, with a fiery red, like a glowing coal. One would hardly think it a thing of this world. One minute later, the Dôme du Goûter (a part of it) is in the shadow; and at last the sun, about 29 minutes after it has set upon the plain, disappears from the summit of Mont Blanc, which is 15,784 feet above the sea and 15 leagues distant from us.

"From the instant that the shadow steals over the snowy summits, beginning with the Buet, a striking change takes place in the appearance of each of them, just as it is obscured. These colours, so warm and bright, this so harmonious effect of illumination and colour, which confounds the snows and the rocks in the same glowing hue, of which they do but seem different shades, all vanish and are replaced by an appearance, which may be termed truly corpse-like; since nothing can more resemble the contrast between life and death on the face of man than this change from the light of day to the shadow of night on these high snowy mountains. The snows have become a wan and livid white, the ridges and peaks of rock which furrow or pierce them are in harsh contrast with the white drapery of their snows. Every effect is at an end, all relief has disappeared; there is no more contrast of light and shade, no more rounded contours; the mountain is flattened, and like a vertical wall. The general tone of the colour is now become as cold and as dull as it before was warm and brilliant.

"It is this sudden transition, this startling metamorphosis, which has now for a long time rendered the sunset on the immense snowy mass of Mont Blanc, a spectacle so interesting; and that not only to strangers, but also to those of the country; who, though born at the foot of this mountain, and long accustomed to the sight, do not for all that cease to admire it. But a third condition of light succeeds, which still further adds to the interest of this spectacle.

"The part of the sky near these mountains, against which

they are projected, which we have already observed to wear a ruddy tint, has been assuming, since the peaks became dull and overshadowed, a constantly increasing brilliancy and ruddier colour. If we continue to observe it attentively, we shall see that one or two minutes after the light has disappeared from the summit of Mont Blanc, there appears, in the lower part of this red sky, a horizontal band, dark and blue; which is at first very narrow, but which rapidly increases in height, and seems, as it were, to drive in front of it the red vapours which it supplants. This band is the shadow which falls upon the higher regions of the atmosphere of countries at a distance behind Mont Blanc. These regions of the air, though elevated, appear nearer to the horizon because they are at a greater distance from us; these were at first reflecting for us the red colour. When the shadow reaches them, they become obscured, and only appear as a sombre horizontal band of the ordinary blue colour of the sky near the horizon[1]. Regions, equally elevated but nearer to us, have as it were inherited the red colour which the former were lately reflecting. Thus the light, or the red vapour, has appeared to mount up and rise above the horizon. But soon the horizontal dark band, or the shadow, has also reached these last; this band has also gained in height, and the red vapours are still more elevated.

"When the horizontal blue band has reached an elevation, the angular magnitude of which I cannot exactly determine; but when it has risen considerably above the summit of Mont Blanc, or, when it has advanced on an average during five minutes, reckoned from the obscuration of that summit, or $33\frac{1}{2}$ minutes from the sunset for the plain, then we see Mont Blanc and the other snowy summits again tinted, again recovering a

---

[1] It would perhaps be more correct to say that, being now in the shadow of the earth, they are deprived of all direct and of very much reflected light, their tint is therefore deeper than the ordinary blue of the sky, when the atmosphere is illuminated, and may be seen to deepen into the dark violet hue of night, as the reflected light diminishes. T. G. B

kind of life. The mountain again appears in relief, of a warmer tone,—a yellow, more or less inclining to orange,—though far more feeble than it was before sunset. Again we see the contrasts between the rocks and snows disappear; the former assume a warmer and yellower hue, and are again in harmony with the snow. Little by little the same effect is produced upon the nearer mountains, in proportion as the zone of red vapours rises; and with the latter rises also, increasing in size, the horizontal dark band on which it reposes. Then, in the mountains fringing the Alps,—the Môle, the Voirons, &c., only the woods and meadows still retain the cold grey or bluish tint, which previously had spread over everything except the snow; and up to nightfall all the mountains resume and retain the same proportions of colour, of tints of light and shade, the same general effect that they had before their discoloration and obscurement.

"The red vapours steadily continue to rise eastward till about 42 minutes after the sun has set on the plain. Then, under ordinary circumstances, they wholly disappear in that region of the sky; the dark band, or the shadow, occupying at that time all the eastern region up to the zenith. The ordinary evening phenomena are at an end for that part of the sky, and are commencing for the western half."

The after-glow, described above by M. Necker, is no doubt caused by the reflexion of the red rays from the surfaces of sheets of vapour in the neighbourhood and to the west of the zenith. Although these may often be so fine and transparent as to be invisible to the eye, they are quite capable of reflecting light. Were it not indeed for the watery veil which envelopes our world, we should be ever alternating between insupportable glare or thick darkness. This statement may be illustrated by a simple experiment. Go into a room by night, take a piece of magnesium wire, place it in a dark lantern, or a closed box, with an aperture in one side only, and light it. One part of the room is brilliantly illuminated, the rest is impenetrably dark. The light is not brighter than the sun at noon-day, and yet the shadows thrown by it are far blacker. The reason is that the layer of air between the flame and the illuminated objects in the room is not thick enough to disperse the light over the whole room;—therefore when we want a general and well-diffused light, we place over the gas-jet or the flame of the lamp a globe of ground glass, which performs for the room the function of the atmosphere for the earth, moderating the intensity of the direct light, and scattering it over every corner and in every direction from the facets of the tiny prisms by which its surface is roughened. Thus each wave of light that rolls through space from the sun is broken on the oolitic shell of atmosphere that envelopes our globe, so that, while the main tide still sweeps on and floods each encountering surface, tiny ripples eddy in every recess and soften the darkness of every shadow. If it encounter any denser layer in the vaporous mass, part of the stream is at once turned aside, and illuminates some object, which it could not otherwise have reached. While the sun is setting, the temperature of the air above us is falling; therefore its suspended vapours are condensing, and so reflecting surfaces are being formed. Every one must have noticed how commonly filmy clouds make their appearance just after sunset; and careful watching of the sky will shew that, even on the finest and clearest days, it becomes perceptibly more misty as the sun sinks below the horizon; as though the vault above us, beginning from its eastern verge, were changed from transparent glass into translucent porcelain.

It may therefore readily be inferred that some of the grandest effects of colour are seen in stormy weather, when rolling clouds form vaporous screens, on parts of which the illuminations are displayed, while others lie in deep shadow, which is no longer grey, as in the noontide hours, but a purple, the tone of which depends upon the hue of the contrasted light. The more orange that is, the more blue the shadow will appear; so that while the glowing light changes in tone from yellow to red, the shadow is modulated in responsive harmony. I recollect that, during a glorious sunset which I watched from the Grands Mulets, when the first zone of colour came creeping up to us over the basin of the Glacier des Bossons, and flooding its pure snows with a delicate yellowish-orange light, every shadow upon them became an exquisite blue, the exact complement of the illuminated surfaces. Indeed, the same effect, though not so perfectly, may often be seen on a fine winter afternoon in England when the sun is approaching the horizon, and the ground is covered with snow[1].

Not the least interesting peculiarity of an Alpine sunset is the frequency with which its most beautiful effects are revealed quite unexpectedly. Often at the close of a rainy afternoon, the clouds, just before the sun goes down, break, roll up, sometimes disperse, as if by magic, in the glory of those crimson rays that come darting upon them, and piercing every rift. Many a time have I watched the vapours around a mountain-peak curling lightly upwards and melting away into the sky, till at last the unclouded summit glowed with flushes of orange or rose, ere it grew pale and dead in its shroud of fresh-fallen snow.

---

[1] Dr Tyndall records, *Glaciers of the Alps*, p. 37, an instance where, the red glow being very marked, the shadows on the snow were green, and I have myself seen an approach to the same colour.

CHAPTER VI.

THOUGH some of the larger wild quadrupeds have disappeared from the Alps during the period of history, and others are rapidly being exterminated by the assaults of the hunter and the advance of cultivation, yet several still linger among them which can no longer be found in the neighbouring more level parts of Europe. Chief among these in size is the Brown Bear (*Ursus Arctos*), which is still occasionally found in the Alps. It is, however, exceedingly rare, except in the Grisons and in the districts of Tyrol and Italy bordering on that Canton, where it is still a terror to the shepherd. Some also believe that it even lingers among certain rocky fastnesses in the Jura. According to Tschudi, Bruin's head-quarters lie in the triangle of mountains between the Inn valley and the upper part of the Etschthal, and especially in the forests which clothe the sides of the Ofenthal. He says that when he visited this district in September 1853, he came upon their traces almost every day, and a week never passed without his seeing one or more in some lonely glen. The mountains here are densely covered with the creeping pine (*P. pumilio*), whose snaky branches form a barrier to the hunter or the shepherd almost as impassable as an Indian jungle.

There is, properly, only one species of bear in the Alps; but according to Tschudi the hunters commonly speak of three —the great black, the great grey, and the small brown. The second is, of course, merely an accidental variety of the first, but between that and the third the distinction appears to be more strongly marked, though not sufficient to constitute a distinct species. They assert that the black bear is not only considerably larger than the brown, but is also different in its habits. It is less ferocious, and prefers a vegetable diet, feeding on herbs, corn, and vegetables, with the roots and branches of trees. Instinct, standing in the place of science, points out the fattening properties of saccharine substances, and makes the bear a gluttonous plunderer of the beehives; and as a corrective to over-much sugar it harries ants' nests, formic acid being, one may suppose, the ursine vinegar. It delights in strawberries and all kinds of fruits, to obtain which it often makes long nocturnal expeditions, plundering the orchards, and at times even descending to the vineyards of the Valtelline, from which, however, it always retreats before dawn. Unless irritated or ravenous with hunger, it does not attack either cattle or man. The brown bear, however, is a much more dreaded foe, prowling by night about the sheepfolds, lying in ambush and rushing upon the flocks, and causing them in fright to fall down the precipices. Favoured by mist or brushwood, it springs upon a stray cow from behind, clinging to its victim's head and tearing at the neck, till the animal falls from loss of blood. Its attacks are usually made by stealth; if the herd perceive their enemy, they surround him, bellowing and making hostile demonstrations; upon which he in general retires. Horses are rarely molested, since they shew their heels to the aggressor in more senses than one. Goats, when they scent their foe by night, leap bleating on the châlet-roofs and arouse the shepherds; so that when Bruin rears himself against the wall, to snuffle at the door or window, he not unfrequently receives a bullet from within by way of a welcome. So long as bears existed in the neighbourhood of Chamouni they were in the winter time frequently shot in this manner. When a track in the snow shewed who had been prowling round a châlet during the night, the hunter fastened a piece of raw meat to the outer wall, and ensconced himself within in a convenient watching place. The bear came, reared himself up to snatch the prey, and at the same moment received a rifle-ball, that generally put an end to his thieving. Sometimes, however, the chase takes place by day; and as the bear is by no means easily disabled, the hunter occasionally gets the worst of it, and there are many stories on record of fierce wrestles for life between man and beast. I will quote one as a sample of many. It happened among the mountains on the north side of the Rhine valley, near Dissentis, in the year 1838. One evening a hunter named Riedi, after tracking a bear for a whole day, arrived at the edge of a precipitous wall of rocks. Here the trail disappeared, but the lair of the beast was evidently in the gorge below; probably, as he conjectured, behind a projecting crag at no great distance, which was approached by a narrow path. Not caring to risk a duel *à l'outrance* with an ambushed enemy, in a situation whence flight was impossible, the hunter tried to entice him forth by yelling and other offensive demonstrations. Bruin, however, was not thus to be moved; so at length Riedi cautiously descended the narrow ledge leading to the supposed lurking-place, and arrived at the mouth of a cave in the shade of the crags. Advancing cautiously towards this, he saw two eyes glittering in the darkness, and an enormous paw projecting from the hole, so close to him that he could have touched it with his hand. He raised his gun and pulled the trigger; it missed fire; but the eyes neither moved nor twinkled. Again he pulled; again it missed; yet still the eyes continued to glare at him. The third time the gun exploded, and an awful howl echoed through the gorge. The hunter retreated as fast as possible, expecting every instant to feel the claws of the beast tearing him down. He, however, regained the open ground unmolested, and reloaded his gun. The howling had now ceased, so he stole cautiously back to the den. All was dark; he listened; only a rasping noise, as of claws scratching the rock, broke the silence; but thinking discretion the better part of valour he again retreated in haste and returned home. Next morning Riedi retraced his steps with three companions; and two of them, feeling persuaded from what had happened that the wound was mortal, foolishly went unarmed. The other, by name Biscuolm, tying a handkerchief over the lock of his gun and slinging it behind him, climbed down the trunk of a fir-tree which grew close to the mouth of the cavern. Scarcely had he reached the ground, when with two bounds a huge bear sprang out, seized him in its paws, and threw him to the ground. Shouting for his companions, he wrestled with the beast, and at last by a tremendous effort thrust it off, leaped up, and unslung his gun. Before, however, he could free the lock, the bear again charged, so he thrust the butt end into its open mouth. At the same moment Riedi arrived on the ground, and discharged his piece into its side. The bear loosed his hold and retreated a few paces, to make a rush at this new assailant, but the diversion gave Biscuolm time to fire, and his ball was fatal. On examining the body, they found that Riedi's first shot had fractured the jaw, a result which probably saved Biscuolm's life; he had also had an almost miraculous escape from falling over the precipice together with his assailant, when they were rolling on the ledge in their wrestle.

The bear passes the winter in a torpid state, rarely quitting its den, and eating little or nothing; further north, indeed, the animal appears to abstain wholly from food for four or five months, and the stomach becomes blocked with a substance called *tappen*, chiefly consisting of the pinnules of fir. Its den is carefully prepared for winter quarters with moss, leaves, pine branches, &c., so that the cold may not disturb its repose. Bears appear to hybernate separately, and in January the female brings forth her young. The cubs, from one to four in number, are at first blind. They do not issue forth till the spring has set well in, and remain with the mother up to the following winter. It is said that the male does not diminish much in weight during his long fast; and even the female, after nourishing her young for two months or so, is very little out of condition when she quits her den. If, however, the 'tappen' is cast too soon, the animal rapidly becomes thin: the usual weight is from five to six hundred pounds. The bear is far more active than its unwieldy shape seems to promise, climbing well, digging quickly with its long claws, and running faster than most men.

Concerning their sleep there is a certain 'pleasant vulgar tale,' according to Gesner[1], which appears to have originated in Switzerland. "There was a certain cowherd in the mountains of Helvetia, which, coming down hill with a great caldron on his back, he saw a bear eating of a root which he had pulled up with his feet; the cowherd stood still till the bear was gone, and afterward came to the place where the beast had eaten the same, and finding more of the same root, did likewise eat it; he had no sooner tasted thereof, but he had such a desire to sleep that he could not contain himself, but he must needs lie down in the way, and there fell asleep, having covered his head with the caldron to keep himself from the vehemency of the cold, and there slept all the winter time without harm, and never rose again till the spring time."

A bear is the coat of arms of Canton Berne, and the chief city might be denominated (literally, of course, not figuratively) a bear-garden. Two giant bears guard the western gate, a

---

[1] *History of Fourfooted Beasts and Serpents collected from the Works of C. Gesner*, by E. Topsel, p. 30 (London, 1658).

pigmy troop marches in procession round a throned figure in front of the clock tower, at the stroke of noon; Bruin also presides over the corn-hall, sits above the fountains armed cap-à-pie, looks on approvingly at the ogre swallowing children[1], stands by the side of Duke Berthold, watches at the feet of Von Erlach, and, finally, is maintained *in propriâ personâ* in a convenient den close to the bridge over the Aar, where he forms, if we may be allowed the expression, one of the principal lions of Berne; being a legatee of property to the amount of nearly thirty pounds per annum, and protected by laws, which forbid the populace to offer anything to their favourite except bread and fruit, lest his health should suffer. Wooden bears look at you from every toy-shop window: bears smoking, bears carousing, bears carrying burdens, keeping a school and inculcating bearish morality, nay even, forgive the bad pun, licking an unbearable cub into shape, in a way that shews the schoolmaster to be at home in his profession. In a word, the motto of the good old city seems to be 'Bear and For-bear.'

The wolf (*Canis lupus*) is rapidly becoming rare in Switzerland, though it still lingers in several lonely parts of the Pennine and Oberland chain, and is most common in the districts about the Engadine and in the Jura. It also is, or was very lately, found in the French Alps, and is not rare in parts of the Tyrol. In summer it roams in the loneliest solitudes among the mountains, skulking among the forests and rocks, and it is only in the winter time, when hard pressed by hunger, that it approaches the haunts of man. Then it wanders far in search of prey, and descends in bands even into the lowlands of Switzerland or to the verge of the Italian plains. It is said to be by no means particular in its food—foxes, hares, rats, mice, birds,

---

[1] The Kindlifresser-Brunnen; a noted statue crowning a fountain, which represents an ogre swallowing a child, while several others are stuffed into his pockets ready to be devoured in their turn. Below is a troop of armed bears. The two next mentioned statues are near the cathedral.

lizards, frogs, and toads; all is fish that comes to the net; the larger cattle and man are only attacked when it is desperate with hunger or banded with several others. Sheep and goats are at once a favourite and an easy prey; and the track of a wolf in the snow puts a whole village in a ferment. A hunt is at once organized, a chief chosen, men armed with firearms are posted in convenient spots, and the rest of the *chasseurs* beat the woods. At Vallorbes, in the Jura, there is a wolf-club, with an elaborate code of laws, of which no one can become a member until he has taken part in three successful hunts. Tschudi states that the death of the wolf is proclaimed by a flourish of six trumpets, and celebrated by a feast at the inn, whereat, among other 'high jinks,' all convicted of disobedience to the captain during the chase are put in straw fetters and condemned to drink nothing but water.

The same author tells a story of a Grison in the Val Misocco, who, one winter day, after a warm altercation with his wife, walked into the snow to cool himself. A few yards from his house a famished and ferocious wolf sprang upon him. This Grison Samson apparently considered a wild beast a much easier creature to manage than a woman, and saluted his new assailant with a blow of the fist, which killed it at once; then, taking the carcase by the tail, he opened the door, and flung it at his wife's feet. We are not told how this gentle hint or delicate compliment was received.

The young are brought forth in April, under ground, generally in the enlarged burrow of a fox or badger; they are blind for some days, are covered with soft woolly fur of a ruddy colour, and lie at the further end of the den packed together as closely as possible. To give the wolf his due, he is an affectionate parent, by no means of a Saturnine temperament; and the sire and dam alternate, like Darby and Joan on the weather indicators, one going abroad to forage while the other stays at home to guard the nurslings; a necessary precaution, since their relations are apt to prove 'a little more than kin and less than kind,' and terminate a morning call upon the interesting 'little strangers,' not with the orthodox cake and caudle, but by eating up the babies.

The fox (*C. vulpes*) is very common in many parts of the Alps, though like his English relation, he is not often seen by chance travellers. There is only one species, though the hunters speak of two varieties; one, haunting the forests and lower valleys; the other keeping always on the higher parts of the mountains, ranging over the stony wastes above the upper pastures, and only descending into the cultivated regions when driven down by heavy falls of snow in the early part of the year. The fox is, like the wolf, monogamous; the young, from five to nine in number, are born in the spring, generally early in May, and at first are blind. The burrow, their birthplace, is inhabited during the whole year, and it is said that Master Reynard quite holds to the truth of the proverb that 'fools build houses for wise men to live in,' and often contrives to take possession of a badger's hole, serving a writ of ejection upon the owner by various cunning devices. As Tschudi quaintly observes, "he has far too much imagination and poetic sentiment to like so monotonous and laborious an occupation as burrowing." The cubs, when a few weeks old, accompany their dam outside, and at first feed upon small birds, lizards, frogs, and worms, which are caught for them by her; but when they are about three months old they begin to forage for themselves, and during the autumn quit the domestic earth. The first winter is spent *en garçon*, and they pair in the spring. The mountain fox eats whatever he can catch,—reptiles and birds, hedgehogs, marmots, hares, kids and lambs, and even snaps up such unconsidered trifles as beetles, flies, and bees. Sometimes, though very rarely, he contrives to surprise a young chamois; generally these animals are too cunning and fleet for him. The bodies of sheep or goats that have died on the mountains, or been killed by falls from the rocks, are a rich feast; sometimes, too, the corpse of some unhappy person who has perished in an avalanche becomes his prey; and it is said that the wounded of his own species are torn in pieces and devoured. Tschudi tells a story of a peasant in Appenzell who used to amuse himself in the winter by placing a bait in a wooden box, and fastening it against a rock so that only a morsel could be torn away at a time. The hungry foxes came by night, sometimes eight or ten together, and held a sort of witch sabbath round it, leaping up like mad creatures, seizing the wood in their teeth, trying to tear it away or pull the box down, and practising every art to get at the flesh within. Frequently he shot some of them, and, though this made the survivors more cautious for a while, they still returned. If the shot was not fatal, the wounded fox was at once followed by the others, who rushed in a body upon it and tore it to pieces.

The fox of the valleys lives more luxuriously than his mountain brother. He devours game and plunders the hen-roosts, as in England, upsets the hives for their honey, and is a terrible robber of orchards. As were his forbears in Judea in the days of the Wise King, and in Sicily in the time of Theocritus, so is he a great pest among the vineyards, and from the mode of training the vines is not often in danger of finding the grapes sour. When rendered bold by hunger in winter time, he skulks near the hen-coops, and as soon as the fowls are let out, pounces upon a straggler and makes off with it at full speed. He is caught by the hunters in traps; but it is diamond cut diamond, and no little skill is needed in deceiving a 'vieux Reynard.' Sometimes he is hunted by dogs, and when he takes to earth is worried out again by terriers. Of course, as the object is to kill the beast, guns and weapons of all kinds are used, as in Scotland; and an Alpine foxhunt must closely resemble the scene so vividly described by Sir Walter Scott in *Guy Mannering*.

The lynx (*Felis lynx*) is still occasionally found in the Alps; but the only place where it is anything but very rare is in the mountain district about the upper part of the Inn. Next to this appear to be the less frequented valleys of the Pennine Alps, to the south of the Rhone, between Martigny and Visp. It is fortunate for the shepherds that they are not common, since the ravages committed by them on the flocks are very serious. One lynx, which was killed in Canton Schwytz during the early part of 1843, had destroyed, during the few weeks previously, 40 goats and sheep; and, some thirty years earlier, three or four of these animals are recorded to have killed not less than 160 of the same during a single summer. In winter it will even burrow under the châlet walls to get at its prey. Besides these, it devours almost all kinds of birds and smaller animals, being by no means particular. It rarely hunts, but prefers to lie in ambush and spring on its victim as it passes; seizing it by the neck, and killing it almost instantaneously by biting through the spine or carotid artery. It generally passes the day couched upon the branch of a tree; apparently half asleep, but wakeful enough if any prey approaches. It shuns the face of man, only fighting when wounded: then the strength of its claws and jaws makes it a formidable opponent. A dog has no chance with it; if, however, the hunter comes suddenly upon a lynx, it does not endeavour to escape, but remains stretched on its bough staring at him until he fires. It is said that if he have not his gun at hand, it is enough to hang some parts of his dress on a stick, and the animal will continue to stare at the 'mawkin' until he returns. The young, two or three in number, are born about April, in some secret crevice in the rock or in the deserted burrow of a fox or badger. They are blind at first. The full-grown animal is about $3\frac{1}{2}$ feet long, and weighs about 50 pounds. The flesh is eaten in the Grisons, and is said to be good.

The wild cat (*F. catus*) still lingers in the most unfrequented parts of Switzerland, being commonest in the Alps of Glarus and the forests of Canton Bâle. Its flesh is sometimes eaten; the fur is valuable, and used as a protection by persons with rheumatic affections. The colour is ruddy, or yellowish grey, with an irregular black band down the back, from which rib-like streaks branch off along the flanks; the tail is ringed and tipped with black; and there is a pale spot under the throat. It passes the day stretched out upon a branch, ready to pounce on whatever prey may come within reach of its spring. It can beat a dog in a fair fight, but does not attack men unless provoked. When wounded it flies at the hunter's face; spitting, scratching, and biting, until it is killed; and the wounds from its claws, like those from the domestic cat's, are often difficult to heal.

The badger (*Meles taxus*) is far from uncommon in the Alps, but from its nocturnal habits is rarely seen. It ranges from the border of the cultivated land to a height of several thousand feet above the sea; being found at a greater elevation in the Eastern Alps than in any other district. Its burrow is carefully excavated in slopes with a southern aspect, is provided with from four to eight outlets, and is lined with soft moss and dead leaves. The long curved claws and strong muscles of the fore feet enable the badger to work at a great rate; it loosens the earth with its sharp muzzle, scrapes it away with the fore-paws, and flings it still further back with the hind. The young are born in January, are from three to five in number, and are blind for some days; the female occupies a separate burrow. During the day the badger coils itself up at the end, and only comes forth occasionally to bask in the sun. The skin is valuable for its tenacity; the flesh, after being steeped in running water, is good, resembling pork in flavour: it is in the best condition towards the end of autumn. The fat is used as an ointment for sprains; from 5 to 10 pounds are taken from a single animal. The badger feeds on roots, vegetables, acorns, nuts, and fruits of various kinds. It is a sad robber of vineyards, biting off the branches to obtain the clusters which are out of reach. The maize-fields also suffer greatly from its depredations. Towards the end of autumn it collects together a quantity of moss at the end of its burrow, and passes a considerable part of the winter in sleep. Owing to its nocturnal habits it is not often shot. The hunter's only chance being to watch its hole in the evening or early morning. It is also very cunning in avoiding traps, so that it is generally either dug out, drawn by dogs, or pulled out by a pole with nippers or a hook at the end. In Canton Glarus, according to Tschudi, they adopt a very barbarous method of capturing it. "The hunters introduce into the burrow a long pole, having at the end a kind of double corkscrew; this is twisted round and round till the unfortunate beast is transfixed, when it is drawn like a cork from a bottle and killed by a rap on the muzzle." The same author says, "Of all its enemies the badger hates the fox most cordially, since the cunning rascal often disturbs its repose by depositing stinking ordure in the mouth of its den. The badger carries to excess its love of cleanliness, and even prefers to desert a warm and comfortable dwelling to having its nose offended by the arts of this infamous master Reynard. So it comes growling out of its burrow and sets to work to dig another—meanwhile the fox and its family take up their quarters in the old one, while it is still warm."

Of the less ferocious quadrupeds the otter (*Lutra vulgaris*) is common along the borders of the rivers and lakes; the beech marten (*Mustela foina*) and pine marten (*M. martes*)—supposing them to be distinct species, a very doubtful matter—are not uncommon in the forests; while the polecat (*M. putorius*), the weasel (*M. vulgaris*), and the stoat (*M. erminea*) are often more abundant than is agreeable to the keepers of poultry. The last turns white in the winter, as it often does in the mountain districts of Great Britain. The squirrel (*Sciurus europæus*) is common enough in the forests, and I have often watched them leaping from branch to branch. They vary greatly in colour; some being a very dark brown approaching black upon the back. Of 'rats and mice, and such small deer,' there is no lack.

Whether the beaver (*Castor fiber*) also still lingers by some lonely stream in the Alps, I am unable to say positively. It is mentioned in a list of Swiss mammals, published in 1817[1], as found, though rarely, in the most lonely spots on the banks of the Sill, Reuss, Aar, and Sarine, the lakes of Brienz and of the Klonthal, and the streams of Mont Pilatus. It also used to frequent the Rhone, and I have seen specimens of it from that river in the Museum at Grenoble, but I much doubt whether it can now be found in any Alpine district.

The rabbit (*Lepus cuniculus*) is far from common in the Alps. Not so the hare, of which there are two species—the brown hare (*L. timidus*), which appears to be seldom found beyond a line of from four to five thousand feet above the sea (I have seen it near Bormio at about the former elevation); and the blue or variable hare (*L. variabilis*), which I have met with in various districts up to a height of about nine thousand feet; an instance indeed is recorded of its having been observed on the Wetterhorn, in the Bernese Oberland, at a height of eleven thousand feet. In summer its fur is of a dull bluish-grey, and it frequents the stony and desolate tracts bordering on the snow regions; in winter it becomes perfectly white, and is forced to descend into the forests, whence, however, it retreats as soon as possible.

The marmot (*Arctomys marmota*), called *marmotte* by the French, *marmotta* by the Savoyards, *murmelthier* by the Germans, and *montanetta* by the Romansch, is common in all the higher Alpine districts. Often, when the traveller is breasting some slope of coarse turf far above the highest châlets, or crossing the stone-strewn floor of a lonely glen, he is startled by a

---

[1] *Conservateur Suisse*, Vol. VIII. p. 271.

long shrill whistle which breaks the silence of the mountain solitudes, and is unpleasantly suggestive of a bandit's signal. This, however, is nothing more than a sentinel marmot warning its companions that an intruder is approaching. The cry is perhaps repeated twice or thrice, and then a quick eye may detect the little creatures loping off towards their burrows, but it is no easy matter to distinguish them from the grey rocks, among which they are making their way. Occasionally, however, I have approached them unperceived and been able to watch them for a few minutes; but they soon scent danger, utter the signal, and disappear. They generally take up their position on some flat piece of rock, exposed to the sun, where they bask and play, scratching and combing themselves, now and then sitting up on their sterns with their fore-paws hanging down in a very droll kangaroo-like fashion. The fur is a yellowish or brownish grey, with black on the head and face, and a little white on the muzzle; the tail is short, bushy, and tipped with black. The fat is believed to have medicinal virtues, and the flesh is not at all bad eating; in taste it is not unlike rabbit. Marmots are caught in traps, and sometimes hunted down by trained dogs; more frequently, however, they are shot; but the watchfulness and caution of the little animal make it no easy matter for the hunter to get within range. The best plan generally is to lie concealed behind a stone to leeward, at a convenient distance from the mouth of a burrow, and wait for the occupant's coming out.

Usually the marmot does not inhabit the same hole all the year round. The summer burrow is excavated somewhere in the zone of rough pasture, which intervenes between the snows and the upper limit of the tree region. The entrance, according to Ladoucette[1], always looks to the south or the east; it is sometimes, like a rabbit-hole, in the face of a slope, but more frequently under some fallen block, which at once affords con-

---

[1] *Les Hautes Alpes*, p. 413.

cealment and protection. So far, in fact, as my experience goes, the marmots always prefer the most stone-strewn ground for their haunts. Towards the end of autumn they descend to the pastures which the herdsmen have just abandoned, and there excavate their winter dwellings. These are much larger than their summer burrows. The entrance gallery is from ten to twenty-five feet long, but only just large enough to let the owners pass, and leads up to an oven-shaped chamber, which is from three to six feet in diameter, and is well lined with dry leaves and hay, which have been collected before the snows begin to fall; the contents being often a heavy load for a man. The burrows are generally, like those of rabbits, provided with a bolt-hole.

About the middle of October, when the cold weather sets in, the marmots retreat into winter quarters; not as in summer going in pairs, but in companies of ten or twelve, and sometimes fifteen in number. The passage is plugged, a few feet from the entrance, with a mass of earth, stones, and hay; and the marmots rolling themselves up in balls, nose on tail, snuggle together, and go to sleep for six months or more. During this long period of torpor the vital functions are almost suspended; digestion ceases, the stomach being absolutely empty; the blood becomes thin and diminishes in quantity; the action of the heart and lungs slow. It respires, it has been calculated, about as many times during its six months' slumber as it does in two days when awake; and consumes in the former case only 1·82 times as much oxygen as it does in the latter. The temperature also of the body is of course, during this period, greatly lowered, not being higher than about 49° (Fahrenheit). In fact, its life seems then in many respects to approximate to that of a cold-blooded animal, especially in what may be called its tenacity; for it has been observed that, in the case of an animal killed when dormant, the head did not become perfectly motionless for half an hour, and the heart continued to beat for three hours after death. The hunters do not let them alone, even while they are hybernating, but sometimes succeed in digging down to their cave and extracting the sleepers,—generally more than seven in number. So sound is their repose that, according to De Saussure, they may often be taken out, placed in the game-bag, and carried home without being roused. They wake up again about April, not so much the worse for this long fast as might be expected; and the young, three or four in number, are born in June. Being not difficult to tame, they sometimes make their appearance in London streets with a poor Savoyard lad as keeper; and are also one of the numerous devices for getting pence from the traveller and training up children in the way they should not go—that of covert mendicancy—which has found so much favour at Chamouni and in the Oberland.

The chamois (*Capella rupicapra*), the gems of the German districts and *camoscio* of the Italian, seems to be the animal which, beyond all others, is identified with the High Alps. In the wood-carvers' shops, chamois, great and small, singly and in groups, are perched on every shelf; finding favour in the eyes of visitors, even beyond the bears, and almost to the exclusion of every other animal. Who ever forgets the time when he first, perhaps after many disappointments, caught a glimpse of a chamois; and however commonly he may afterwards come across them, 'where I saw those chamois' will be generally found to be in his mouth as a mark to identify some stage in an excursion. The chase appears to exercise a fascination over its votaries that no hardship or danger can overcome, and even the most phlegmatic of Teutonic guides become excited when once the word *gems* is pronounced.

This animal, the sole modern representative of the antelope family in Western Europe, is found in almost every part of the Alps, as well as in the Pyrenees, Carpathians, and Caucasus. Owing, however, to the persecution which it has undergone of late years, it is now much rarer in the Alps than it used to be, and has almost disappeared from some of the more frequented districts. Even in the days of De Saussure, chamois were becoming scarce in the neighbourhood of Chamouni, and now they are probably quite extinct. In such unfrequented dis-

(Fig. 9.) Chamois.

tricts as Dauphiné, the Tarentaise, and the Graians, and in parts of the Swiss, Tyrolese, and Bavarian Alps, they are still far from uncommon; and the traveller who deserts the beaten tracks will not unfrequently fall in with them. Sometimes they are seen singly; generally, however, three or four are together. The largest number that I ever observed at once was seventeen: these were in a secluded amphitheatre of rock and snow in the heart of the Dauphiné Alps, into which probably no traveller had ever before penetrated; and I saw a herd of fifteen on the slopes high above the east side of the Val Roseg in 1867.

The chamois stands at the shoulder about two feet from the ground. The hind legs are longer than the fore, rendering its gait awkward on level ground, and not very clever on a steep descent, but exactly fitting it for mountain climbing. The muscles, especially of the former, are exceedingly powerful, enabling it to check itself almost instantaneously when at full speed, and to spring with extraordinary agility. The hoof cloven, long and pointed, with sharp edges, is not well adapted for traversing the ice; the chamois therefore, if possible, always avoids the glaciers, and is obviously often ill at ease on them. On the snow, provided this be tolerably hard, it spreads its cleft hoof as wide as possible, and so gets on better, but it is only thoroughly at home on the rocks. It is very shy of venturing on the upper part of a glacier, having a great fear of the concealed crevasses; and the track which it leaves on the snow in these places often shews, by its windings and abrupt turnings, that the animal has found it no easy matter to escape from among so many hidden pitfalls. Travellers not unfrequently find this a useful clue to indicate the safest way of threading the maze. So I found it once in Dauphiné when ascending to a pass called the Col de Sais. We had taken a guide from La Bérarde, and the man, as is common in those parts, was almost useless; and when we came to some masked crevasses in the upper part of the glacier, declined to proceed further. We determined not to go back without an attempt; and espying from a distance the track of a chamois in the most broken part, made for it, and by following this, reached the smooth snow-fields above the icefall without much difficulty.

Its agility is something extraordinary; it can spring across chasms six or seven yards wide, and "with a sudden bound leap up against the face of a perpendicular rock, and merely touching it with its hoofs, rebound again in an opposite direction to some higher crag, and thus escape from a spot where, without wings, egress seemed impossible. When reaching upwards on its hind legs, the fore hoofs resting on some higher spot, it is able to stretch to a considerable distance, and with a quick spring will bring up its hind quarters to a level with the rest of the body, and with all four hoofs close together, stand poised on a point of rock not broader than your hand[1]." Mr Cowell[2] mentions an instance where a mortally wounded buck in four bounds cleared a space of more than forty yards. The gambols of a herd of chamois are most diverting; they leap up, springing like skipjacks from their long hind legs, run round and round, up and down, and even sideways, with great nimbleness, reminding one with their tricks and 'buck-jumps' not a little of the antics of a party of lambs. If disturbed, they gaze fixedly towards the spot whence the noise comes, till they have discovered what is wrong; then, unless danger is imminent, with a shrill Phew! move up leisurely towards their rocky fastnesses, halting now and then to look back, and again uttering the cry as they renew their march.

A full-grown chamois, in good condition, weighs about sixty pounds. Mr Bonar mentions instances where they have reached from seventy to more than eighty pounds; these are generally old bucks. The hair is thick, and changes colour with the season, being a red yellowish brown in summer, and almost black in winter. That about the nose, forehead, lower jaw, under the belly, inside the legs, and overhanging the hoofs, is of a yellowish brown, and does not alter; and the dark stripe, partly enclosing each eye and reaching from it to the adjacent corner of the mouth, is permanent. The outer hairs are rather coarse; on brushing them back, the thin wool below is seen to incline to a mouse-grey tint; and those along the ridge of the spine are in winter longer than the rest, and tipped with white;

---

[1] Bonar, *Chamois Hunting in Bavaria*, p. 97; a fascinating work, written by a thorough lover of nature and Alpine beauty.

[2] *Vacation Tourists*, 1860. p. 260.

from these is made the *gems bart*,—a tuft of hair, which forms a favourite ornament in the hat of a Tyrolean peasant.

The horns, which are pot-hook shaped, rise from the head above and between the eyes to a height which rarely exceeds seven inches; an average pair will be barely six inches high, and about eight and a half in length, measured along the outer curve. Their section at the base is very nearly circular, the curve being sometimes slightly flattened at the sides. This flattening becomes much more marked towards the upper part of the horn, but is again diminished in the immediate neighbourhood of the point, which is sharp and polished. The horn is plainly marked by transverse horizontal rings of growth for about the lower half, and is finely striated longitudinally to within an inch or two of the tip, both rings and striæ being gradually obliterated as they go upwards. When the kid is about three months old the horns make their appearance, and at first are not nearly so hook-shaped as they afterwards become; a pair in my possession, about three inches long, are very nearly semicrescent, and in general form resemble a miniature cow-horn. Mr Bonar[1] thus describes those of the fullgrown animal. "They do not stand up perpendicularly, but slant forwards at a right angle with the forehead; their points, which are very sharp, being bent back and downwards. This feature is not peculiar to the buck alone; there is, however, considerable difference between the horns of the male and female, which often assists the sportsman in distinguishing the two. The horns of the male chamois are thicker and altogether stronger-looking than those of the female; and, instead of diverging from each other in so straight a line as hers generally do, their outline describes a slight curve as they rise upwards and apart from each other. But a still more striking characteristic of the buck is, that the points of his horns are bent much more inwards than those of the doe; hers form a semi-

[1] *Chamois Hunting in Bavaria*, p. 89.

circular curvature towards the back, while his, turning over abruptly, form rather a hook."

The chamois feed on various mountain herbs, and on the buds and sprouts of the rhododendron and latschen (*Pinus pumilio*). During the night they couch among the broken rocks high upon the mountains, descending at day-break to pasture, and retreating, as the heat increases, towards their fastnesses. They are very fond of salt, and greedily lick any saline efflorescence from the rocks. In the winter season they are forced down to the higher forests, where they pick up a scanty subsistence from moss, dead leaves, and the fibrous lichen, which hangs in long yellowish-grey tufts from the firs, and bears the name of 'chamois-beard.' While browsing on this, they sometimes get their horns hooked on a bough, and so, being unable to disentangle themselves, perish with hunger. I have indeed heard of an instance of the dead body of a chamois being found suspended by the horns from a projecting ledge of rock, with its feet just touching the ground, which apparently had perished in the same way. I have also been told, on the authority of a chasseur in the Val d' Aoste, that sometimes, when they have retreated during a snow-storm under a fir-tree for shelter or for food, the branches, bending down under the weight of snow, enclose them on all sides; and being imprisoned in this snowy wigwam, they are starved to death, instinct not teaching them how to escape. When spring returns, their bodies are found, sometimes three or four together, at the foot of the tree. Owing probably to the resin contained in so much of their food, and its fibrous character, a hard, dark-coloured ball, from the size of a walnut to that of an egg, of a bitter taste, but pleasant odour, is often found in their stomachs. This is called Bezoar, and it was anciently supposed to cure all evils, and be a protection even against musket-shots. A sceptical age has, I fear, expelled it from the pharmacopœia.

The senses of hearing, smell, and sight are exceedingly acute, so that the hunter must exercise all his craft to approach the chamois. The general plan is to stalk them, by making a circuit out of sight, and creeping within shot up the wind, under cover either of rocks or of brushwood. Now and then, however, they may be taken off their guard. One day I was with a friend and two guides at the top of a pass called the Col de Cristillan, which crosses, at the height of about 9700 feet, a lonely range on the right side of the valley of the Ubaye. As a rather keen wind was blowing from the north, we sat down to rest and dine, just under the cover of a few projecting rocks which were close to the narrow opening forming the pass. We had risen up to continue our journey, and were still standing a few feet below the ridge, when I heard a clatter over the loose stones on the other side, and, turning round, saw a chamois leap up into the gap. For a moment it stood staring at us, apparently horror-stricken at finding itself face to face with its most dreaded foes; then, with a series of desperate bounds, leapt away down the rocks to the left, while our guides yelled and hurled stones after it. Generally, however, the chamois-hunter must endure hardship and fatigue, risk his life by scrambling up crumbling cliffs and along dangerous ledges of rock, happy if, after a day or two's labour, and perhaps a night spent in the open air, he return home with a chamois slung on his back. Often, when, after long watching and much toil, he is almost within range, the wary animal takes the alarm before he can fire, and retreats to rocky fastnesses where pursuit is hopeless. Pages might be filled with the hair-breadth escapes and fearful accidents which have befallen hunters. This following story, though it has been often told before, will perhaps serve better than any others as an example. Two chasseurs of the Sernfthal, Manuel Walcher and Rudolf Bläsi, were one day out hunting, when they perceived a chamois at some distance from them. In order to prevent its escaping, they determined to separate, and approach it from opposite directions. Bläsi, in the excitement of the chase, leapt across a chasm on to a narrow ledge on the face of a cliff; once there, he found that it was impossible to proceed further, and to his horror discovered that, as the side on which he stood was lower than the other, and the footing not good, it was impossible to spring back again. He was in a trap, and, to make matters worse, the ledge was so narrow that he could neither sit nor lie; therefore he was obliged to stand against the cliff, leaning on his rifle, and shouting for help, with the yawning gulf below, into which, when once his strength failed, he must inevitably fall. Tears, prayers, cries, seemed all in vain; slowly the sun crept towards the horizon, but no help came; evening darkened into night; a storm drifted up, and broke upon the mountains, increasing the horror of his fearsome vigil; but at last the dawn brightened in the east. Then the sun rose, and hope revived; his companion would surely come in search of him; but still the hours wore on; he grew sick and faint from hunger and fatigue; his head began to swim; and in a few minutes all would have been over; when a shout from above recalled him to life, and he saw Manuel looking down upon him. A rope was soon lowered to Bläsi, who with trembling hands secured the noose about his body, and was hauled up to a place of safety. He was sound in limb, but the horror of that one night had done the work of years, and blanched his hair.

Though horns, flesh, and skin are all worth money, yet it is rare that a chamois-hunter finds his occupation profitable. Tschudi, indeed, tells of one instance where a considerable sum was amassed by the produce of the chase. This was by a noted hunter, named David Zwicky, of Mollis near Glarus, who was said to have scraped together by the sale of this and various other game, combined with strict economy, a sum of £560, besides other property; having received from his father a patrimony of only £12. He, however, was said to have killed in his lifetime more than 1300 chamois and an immense quantity of marmots, hares, grouse, partridges, and other game; and so perfectly did he know the haunts of the first animal, and so skilful was he in his craft, that it was a rare thing for him to miss securing his prey when once he had started in pursuit. At last one Saturday evening, when he was seventy-five years old, he failed to return home as usual. Fearing something was amiss, his friends searched for him, but in vain: for nine months nothing more was heard or seen of him; then one day a skeleton was found in a lonely part of the mountains, which was recognised as his by the gun, watch, and fragments of clothes that lay around it. No bones were broken, but one foot was tied up in a handkerchief, and the corpse was resting on one arm as if asleep. Probably he had been lamed by a sprain or a severe bruise, and, becoming exhausted, had sat down where he was found and died from cold or hunger. Numbers of other hunters have been killed, but all seem to be animated with the spirit of the young peasant of Sixt, who said to De Saussure[1], "My grandfather met his death while out on the hunt, my father did the same, and I am so persuaded that I too shall die in this pursuit, that I call this bag which you see, Sir, and which I carry with me on the hunt, my winding-sheet; because I am sure that I shall never have any other; and yet if you were to offer to make my fortune on condition that I would abandon chamois-hunting, I would not accept your proposal." Two years after, says De Saussure, his presentiments were fulfilled, and he was found dead at the foot of a precipice.

In many cases the dangers of the chase are greatly increased by the feuds between the hunters of neighbouring cantons or states. Formerly, a trespasser was often shot without the slightest compunction by the native hunters, and so might think himself very lucky if he escaped with the loss of his rifle and being beaten within an inch of his life; nor did it go much better

---

[1] *Voyages dans les Alpes*, § 736.

with the rightful owners, if the intruders were the stronger party or caught them unawares. De Saussure, in the passage to which I have just referred, tells a story which he heard from a chasseur of Sixt, who had been the chief actor in it. This man was following up a chamois, which he had already wounded mortally, when two intruders from the Valais also saw it and gave it the *coup de grace*. Still, according to all the laws of the chase, it belonged to the Savoyard, who came up just at the moment, took it on his shoulders, and walked away. The others, owing to the nature of the ground, could not come straight towards him; they however shouted to him to put it down, and sent a ball whistling about his ears by way of enforcing their orders. Without heeding this, he was pressing on; when another ball whizzed close by him; whereupon as he could not get on quickly, owing to the roughness of the ground, and had no ammunition left with which to fight for his prize, he thought it wiser to obey their orders. Vowing vengeance, he went away to a hiding-place, whence he could watch their movements; feeling sure that the day was too far advanced for his spoilers to return to their own country. Things fell out as he expected; and he marked them down in a deserted châlet on the upper pastures; then he went in all haste home, two leagues away, got powder and ball, loaded his double-barrelled gun, and cautiously stole up to the châlet. Peering through the chinks in its timber walls, he soon saw his enemies seated by the fire; inserted the muzzle of his gun in such a way that he could fire right and left; aimed at one, and was on the point of pulling the trigger, when it suddenly occurred to him that these men, not having confessed since they had fired at him, would die in mortal sin and therefore be lost eternally. On consideration, this appeared to be a punishment so out of proportion to the offence, that he abandoned his project; and entering abruptly into the châlet told them of the danger which they had run. They, thanking him for their lives, owned that they had been in the wrong, and gave him half the chamois!

Even more deadly was the hatred between the keepers and the poachers in the Bavarian highlands. The former shot the latter with little compunction, whenever they could not easily take them prisoners; and if, as was often the case, the intruders were from the Tyrol, they were treated with no more ceremony than a vulture. Nor were the latter slow to retaliate when they got a chance. Several instances of this have a place among the Alpine scenes in the well-known novel 'Quits;' and Mr Bonar's book contains still more. I shall venture to make an extract from the latter as a sample[1]: the incident happened near Braunenburg, a village just within the Bavarian frontier.

"One of the keepers, while out on the mountain, saw three Tyrolese cross the Inn. He at once suspected what was their intention, and instantly set off for a pass among the rocks, where, if he was right in his conjecture, he knew they would surely come. For an hour or more he waited, without hearing or seeing anything of them. At length however he espied the poachers advancing up the mountain, and, keeping close to avoid being seen, let them approach. The place where he stood was a narrow path, with rocks rising on one side and on the other a precipice. When the men were at a short distance from him, he stood forth and called to them to lay down their rifles. As they did not obey, he shouted that, cowards as they were, he would lay down his, and challenged them, if they dared, to do the same and come all three of them armed only with their poles. They did so, and the three advanced upon him. Calm and collected, he watched his opportunity, and, as they approached, thrust his iron-shod pole two inches deep into the breast of the foremost man, and sent him toppling down into the abyss. The others, terror-stricken, sprang back to seize their

---

[1] *Chamois Hunting in Bavaria*, p. 419.

rifles, but the keeper was too quick for them; he had already grasped his own, and levelling it threatened to send a bullet through the first who should dare to raise his weapon. There was nothing left them now but to retreat; and as they did so the keeper fired at one, sending a charge of coarse shot into his back and wounding him badly."

The bouquetin or steinbock (*Capra ibex*) was once abundant in the greater part of the Alps, but is, I believe, now restricted to the Graian chain in the neighbourhood of the Grivola and Grand Paradis, where they are most strictly preserved by the king of Italy. They disappeared from the Tyrol about a century ago; in Switzerland, the last in Canton Glarus was shot in 1550; they were becoming rare in the Engadine and neighbouring districts in 1612, when it was forbidden to hunt them under a penalty of fifty crowns; one was shot on the St Gothard in the middle of the last century; and they lingered still longer in the Pennine chain. De Saussure observes that in his time they had ceased to be found near Chamouni; but Mr Hinchliff says that one was shot on the south side of the Grandes Jorasses in 1856[1]. The Dent des Bouquetins, between the heads of the Val Pelline and the Val d' Annivièrs, takes its name from them, and Tschudi states[2] that a few years since they were met with in the neighbourhood of Monte Rosa. This, however, Mr King[3], who devotes several interesting pages to their history, denies. In the district already named they are not very rare. I have never, although I have been several times among their haunts, had the luck to see more than the track of a bouquetin, but some of my friends have been more fortunate, and two among them have even found their skeletons. The laws concerning them are very strict. It is even forbidden to possess any part of them; and twenty-four pounds fine and nine years at the

---

[1] *Summer months among the Alps*, p. 207.
[2] *Les Alpes*, p. 645.
[3] *Italian Valleys of the Alps*, p. 338.

galleys is the penalty for killing one. Mr King, however, managed to purchase a pair of horns, but he had some trouble and several amusing adventures in smuggling them out of the country. The horns of a full-grown buck are at least two feet long, and curve very gracefully backwards as they rise from the head, spreading slightly outwards. Along the flattened front of each horn is a row of knobs or horizontal ridges, culminating on the well-defined line between it and the inner side; these are the rings of annual growth. Mr King states that on his pair, which are two feet long, there are eight of these marks; on a smaller pair now before me, which are fifteen inches long, there are six; these I purchased at Aosta three or four years ago. The horns of the female are much smaller in proportion, less curved, and less prominently ringed than those of the male; those of a specimen belonging to Mr King, whereon are fourteen rings, are only seven inches long.

(Fig. 10.) Bouquetin.

Of course a weight like this on the head requires a corresponding frame to carry it; and the bouquetin is consequently far more muscular than the chamois. Its whole build is remarkably strong, giving it a sturdy self-reliant look, differing greatly from the slender and rather fragile appearance of the chamois: still it is not less, perhaps is even more, agile than that animal; for a young one has been known to take a standing leap as high as a man's head; and its sureness of foot is equally surprising. The bouquetins are, however, calmer and less restless in their habits than the chamois, and all who have come across them have noticed their stately and almost disdainful gait. Their time of feeding is also different; they descend towards the pastures in the evening, browse during the night, and retire very early in the morning to the higher peaks, where they pass the day among the rocks. They are generally found in small troops; but the bucks lead a solitary life during the early part of the year. They pair in January, at which time the males fight furiously; they will also couple with the common goat, and the hybrid offspring are fruitful. The kid is born in June, and may be tamed; it does not, however, seem to be healthy in captivity, and is liable to diseases of the feet and nostrils. A closely allied species, *C. pyrenaica*, exists on the Pyrenees, differing slightly in the form of the horns, which is probably identical with the *C. hispanica* of the Sierra Nevada. Another species, *C. caucasia*, is found in the Caucasus, and a fourth, *C. bedens*, in Crete, in some of the islands of the Archipelago, and on Mount Olympus.

The bouquetin, like every other rare animal, has had a plentiful halo of legend thrown around him. The blood was supposed to be a medicine of marvellous virtue in cases of stone; the horns were imagined to act as buffers when the animal precipitated itself from a crag; an aged buck[1], when conscious of the approach of death, climbed to the summit of some lofty mountain, and there hooking itself on to a rock with one of its

---

[1] *History of Fourfooted Beasts and Serpents: collected from the works of C. Gesner* by E. Topsel, p. 349 (London, 1658).

horns, twirled round and round, like a dancing Dervish, until the tip was worn away, whereupon it expired. As a bathos of equal absurdity, and more unpardonable ignorance, take the following extract from an 'Own Correspondent's' letter in the *Times* of Aug. 16, 1861 (p. 8), describing the exploits of the present king of Italy when chasing the bouquetin. "The horn is wound, the hunt is up, and away he rides as fast as the nimblest mountain nag can carry him, and then takes to his legs, and the race is between him and the swiftest quadrupeds, over crags and along gullies common men shudder only to look at. He came back to Turin a few days ago in great glee, telling his friends he had given chase to a bouquetin for two whole days, had parted company with his aides-de-camp, his guides, his huntsman, every man in his suite; he had followed the coy mountain goat, he had pressed closer and closer, he had driven it higher and higher and higher up; he had knocked it up, blown all the wind out of its panting body, and had at last brought it back triumphant, the prize of that untamed strength which has no match in these regions." It is really delightful to find such a refreshing oasis of viridity in the dry desert of a sceptical age; the author of the above must have been a very prince among *gobemouches!*

The roe (*Capreolus capræa*), the fallow deer (*Dama vulgaris*), and the red deer (*Cervus elaphus*) have, it is said, quite disappeared from the French and Swiss Alps. All of them still occur in the Bavarian and Austrian highlands. They belong, however, rather to the sub-alpine region, being found among the forests which clothe the lower slopes, and do not often wander into the more rocky districts. The first, I believe, has rather the highest range. The wild boar (*Sus scrofa*), also, only now and then makes its appearance across the Rhine, although it is common in the sub-alpine forests further east; its habits, however, hardly qualify it for admission into the list of Alpine quadrupeds.

CHAPTER VII.

CHIEF among the birds of the Alps is the bearded vulture (*Gypaetus barbatus*), the lämmergeier of the Germans. Once common, it is now gradually disappearing before the hunter's bullets, and only here and there holds its own in some lonely mountain fastness. It does not seem to be confined to any particular district, but occurs occasionally in the wilder parts of the Alps. Although its neck is feathered, and it is said to prefer living prey to carrion, still in many important characteristics it is closely allied to the true vulture. The upper part of the body is a greyish-brown hue, the under white, tinged with reddish-brown. The neck is of a still lighter colour, the top of the head white, the beak and part round the eye black, and the tail feathers are an ashy-brown. From the lower mandible projects a bristly tuft, whence its specific name. The nest, built in some inaccessible ledge on a dizzy cliff, consists of a substratum of straw and fern, resting on sticks placed crosswise, on which is placed a kind of wreath of branches lined with moss and down[1]. It contains two or, at most, three orange-brown eggs, clouded with a darker brown tint.

It is but now and then that the traveller, by approaching it unperceived, obtains a near view of this monarch of the Alpine birds. Owing to the great size of its wings, which are sometimes as much as nine feet in span, it does not rise very readily, but when once off, its flight is very stately. Its voracity is only surpassed by its digestive powers, which are something extraordinary. According to Tschudi[2], the stomach of one lämmergeier was found to contain five fragments of a cow's ribs, two inches wide and from six to nine long, a mass of matted wool and hair, and the leg of a kid perfect from the knee downwards. Another had bolted a fox's rib fifteen inches long, as well as the brush, besides a number of bones and other indigestible parts of smaller animals. These were being eaten away, layer after layer, by the gastric juice, which was dissolving all the gelatinous parts and leaving behind only the brittle calcareous fabric. The bird's usual food consists of almost any of the smaller quadrupeds and birds. One clutch of those claws, and the victim is secured; one blow from that ponderous bill, and its skull is crushed; one gape of those hungry jaws, and it is swallowed whole. Lambs, kids, and young chamois meet with the same fate, or, if not devoured upon the spot, are carried off to its eyrie and there consumed. Sheep, goats, and full-grown chamois, are not generally attacked at once with beak and claws, but the bird, watching a favourable opportunity, dashes against them, and endeavours by the shock and the violent buffets dealt with its long wings to precipitate them down the cliffs. This done, it swoops down upon the mangled prey and tears it to pieces; then, when gorged, it floats lazily up to some inaccessible crag, and perches itself with an air of tranquil indifference, to wait till the gnawings of the gastric juice compel it to seek another meal. It is said to be some-

---

[1] Bree, *Birds of Europe*, Vol. I. p. 18.
[2] *Les Alpes*, p. 409.

times bold enough to attack a man, when it finds him asleep, or climbing in any dangerous place; but if the first swoop is unsuccessful it rarely repeats the attack.

Cases, however, have been recorded in which it has succeeded in carrying off young children. Tschudi[1] has collected several instances which he states are unquestionably true; the most remarkable of which happened in the Bernese Oberland. Two peasants, named Zurbuchen, were at work making hay upon the Alpine pastures, and had taken with them their daughter Anna, a child about three years old. They laid her on the turf near the hay châlet, where she quickly fell asleep; so the father, after covering her face with his broad brimmed hat, went on with his labour at some little distance. On returning with a load of hay he found that the child was gone; and it needed but a brief search to prove that she was nowhere in the neighbourhood. It happened just at this time that a peasant, of Unterseen, named Heinrich Michel, was walking along a rough path in a glen, at no great distance from the alp, when he was startled by the cry of a child. Advancing at once towards the place whence it came, he saw a lämmergeier rise from a neighbouring summit and hover for some time over a precipice. Thither he climbed in all haste and found the child Anna lying on the very brink. She was but little injured; some scratches on her hands and on the left arm, by which she had been seized, and the loss of her shoes and cap, being the only ill consequences of her flight of more than three-quarters of a mile through the air. She lived to a good old age, and was always called Geier-Anni (Vulture's Annie) in memory of her escape. The particulars of it are inscribed in the registers of the parish of Habkeren.

The golden eagle (*Aquila chrysaetus*) is also not very uncommon in most parts of the Alps, although the traveller cannot often obtain a near view of it. I have many times noticed it wheeling about in the air high over a valley, but have

---

[1] *Les Alpes*, p. 414.

only once been near enough to one to see it distinctly. Its food resembles that of the lämmergeier; and it is said to have a special liking for hares, which it chases and captures with great address. As in Great Britain, it is accused of having carried off children; but I am not aware that there is any case in which the crime is to be positively attributed to it; generally its larger brother, the lämmergeier, is reputed to be the robber.

The kite (*Milvus regalis*), with more than one species of buzzard and falcon, are occasionally seen. Several species of hawks also occur; the commonest of which is the kestrel (*Falco tinnunculus*). There are at least ten species of owls, among which is the magnificent eagle-owl (*Bubo maximus*), marked as found in Switzerland; but from their nocturnal habits they are rarely seen, and I do not think that they ascend very high. The Alpine birds of prey correspond very closely with the British.

The hoarse, bell-like croak of the raven (*Corvus corax*) is often heard in the lonelier glens, and the bird itself may be seen wheeling about the crags, or be disturbed from an unclean meal of dead lamb on the mountain side. It is not unfrequently tamed, and is an arrant thief, with an amount of shameless impudence that is very amusing. One day we were suffering from that most doleful of afflictions in mountain travel, a thoroughly wet day, in a not too comfortable auberge, at San Chiaffreddo, near the head of the Vallon di Po. Whatever may be said about the pleasures of a day of rest, I certainly prefer it to be a fine one; and always find that the combined effect of unexpected delay and uncomfortable quarters is to incapacitate one, in spite of the most virtuous resolutions, from devoting the whole day to writing journal and letters, finishing drawings, and other indoor work. Accordingly we, with two or three Piedmontese gentlemen from Turin in the same plight, were glad enough to amuse ourselves with the tame raven of the establishment, which soon fraternised with us, and ate *gressini*[1] from our hands. It greedily bolted bits of these two or three inches long, until its throat was full; then, when no more could be stowed away, it flew off to dispose of its load, returning after a short interval for a fresh supply. At last one of the Turinese presented his pocket-knife to the bird instead of the expected morsel. Very much to the disgust of the owner it made a sudden snap at it, twitched it out of his hand, and flew away, disappearing over the brow of a cliff just below the terrace on which we were standing. We followed, hoping to mark the thief down, but were too late. Before long it came flying back, and perched between us with its usual air of demure self-complacency; whereupon the owner of the knife, perhaps wishing to be even with it, held out a box of matches. Another snap and this too was gone. This time I managed to keep the rogue in view, but when I came up, the box was already torn open, the matches were scattered about, and master raven was biting off the heads one by one, and to all appearance swallowing the brimstone pills with an appetite. The cunning bird, however, had stowed the knife away in some hiding-place, which we failed to discover.

Two other members of the same family are not uncommon in the High Alps. These are the chough (*Pyrrhocorax graculus*), now becoming so rare in England, and the Alpine chough (*P. alpinus*). These birds may be seen flying about the higher peaks; and are only distinguished by the former having a red bill, the latter (a slightly smaller bird) a yellow; both have red legs. They ascend to great heights; I have seen a pair,—of which species I could not be sure, but I think the latter—at the top of the Piz Languard (10,715), and another pair flying about the Höchste Spitze of Monte Rosa, the highest bare

---

[1] A sort of bread or biscuit eaten commonly instead of bread in the Piedmontese valleys. It is made in long stems which look not unlike a bundle of unbaked 'churchwarden' pipes without the bowls. I wonder it has not been introduced into England, for it is far more wholesome than bread.

rock in the Alps. The jackdaw (*Corvus monedula*) is also common.

It is not my purpose to attempt a complete list of the Alpine birds, since in these limits it could be little more than a bare catalogue of names, uninteresting to most readers, and would include a great number of species which would never be seen by ordinary travellers. In fact, one is often struck by the comparatively small number of birds that, even in a long day's walk, are seen in the Alps. The most remarkable of these are the nutcracker (*Nucifraga caryocatactes*), which haunts the Alpine forests, feeding on the pine cones, especially those of the arolla (*P. cembra*), from the recesses of which his note 'crack,' and at certain seasons 'curr,' is constantly heard resounding. It is a shy bird, and difficult to approach, so that it is not easily examined. It is only of late years that the nidification of the nutcracker has been observed[1]. The reason of this is that the bird builds very early in the year (March), before the snow has melted off the ground in the pine forests; and during this time changes its habits, being very silent and stealthy in its movements instead of rather noisy. The jay's (*Garrulus glandarius*) harsh cry breaks now and then the stillness of the woods; the white-breasted swift (*Cypselus alpinus*) plys its untiring wing high in the air, and the dipper (*Cinclus albicollis*), yet more conspicuous, with throat and breast of white, sits perched on a boulder by the torrent, or darts arrow-like up the stream. The Alpine accentor (*A. alpinus*), its throat white, with crescent spots of black; the wheatear (*Sylvia œnanthe*), and the common and black redstart (*S. phœnicurus* and *S. tithys*), enliven the stony tracts above the Alpine pastures; the beautiful wall-creeper (*Tichodroma muraria*), with its ash-coloured back and breast, crimson and black wings, and black tail tipped with white, may be seen ranging to above 10,000 feet; the snow-finch

[1] See a paper by Professor Newton, *Proceedings of the Zoological Society*, 1867, pp. 162—4.

(*F. nivalis*), as its name implies, mounts to the borders of the snows, and is commonly mistaken by observers for the snow bunting (*Emberiza nivalis*), which there is no reason to believe inhabits the Alps; and by rare good fortune the beautiful rose-coloured pastor (*Pastor roseus*) may be noticed. I believe that I saw a specimen of the last on the precipices of the Grand Som, above the monastery of the Grande Chartreuse. The common starling (*Sturnus vulgaris*) is very much more frequent.

Of the game-birds, the capercailze (*Tetrao urogallus*), the black grouse (*T. tetrix*), and the hazel grouse or gelinotte (*T. bonasia*), are not uncommon in many of the forests which usually clothe the lower parts of the Alps, especially on the southern slopes; and ranging far above them is found the ptarmigan (*Lagopus vulgaris*), which, like the variable hare, haunts the waste stony tracts on the borders of perpetual snow. These birds seem to delight in the cold and solitude of the mountains, playing on the snow-beds, and feeding on the scanty vegetation which here and there takes root among the rocks. They are generally seen in flocks, varying in number up to about fifteen. They fly rather low and straight, with a whirring noise, more quickly than the black grouse, and they rise to the wing much less noisily. In the winter they turn white, with the exception of a patch about the eye and the outer tail feathers, which are black; and even in the summer, when the prevailing colour is a greyish-brown, a good deal of white remains.

The pheasant (*Phasianus colchicus*) is, I believe, not found in the Alps; the quail (*Perdix coturnix*), the grey partridge (*P. cinerea*), and the red-leg or French partridge (*P. rufa*), which are abundant in many parts of the lowlands, can hardly be said to be Alpine birds; although they may be sometimes found on the level plains which form the beds of valleys, surrounded by lofty mountains, along which many species of birds and animals penetrate into the Alpine region, without actually ascending the mountains themselves. There is, however, one species of partridge which may be called an Alpine bird; this is the Greek (*Perdix græca*) or bartavelle, which closely resembles the red-leg, but may be distinguished by its larger size, and the absence of the mottled plumage below the black mark on the neck. It is by many naturalists identified with the *P. chukar* of Asia, which ranges from Armenia to China; but of late some eminent authorities have considered them distinct[1]. If the former hypothesis be true, the range of *P. græca* is very extensive, for it is found in most of the mountain districts in the countries bordering on the Mediterranean, as far west as the Pyrenees. It runs quickly, and is flushed with difficulty; once risen, its flight is strong, but not prolonged. The flesh is said to be very good.

The various water-birds and gulls are by no means common in the High Alps, so far at least as my experience goes. To see them it is necessary to descend to the lowland country, where storks, herons, and many birds of these families are far from rare. It may be worth remarking that the course of the migratory birds over the Alps has given rise to considerable discussion; some asserting that they seek for the marked depressions in the mountain chains, crossing in fact like man by the easiest passes; others that they simply go over in the direct line of their course, without turning aside to seek for a gap in the intervening barrier. The subject can hardly yet be regarded as finally settled.

The lower orders of vertebrata do not call for many very special remarks. A great number of the mountain streams and tarns contain excellent trout; and most of the larger lakes are well stocked with fish; chief among these are the lotte (*Lota vulgaris*); the perch (*Perca fluviatilis*); the ambre of Auvergne (*Thymallus vexillifer*), which mounts up in some parts to a height

[1] H. B. Tristram, in *Ibis*, 1868, pp. 213, 214.

of more than 4000 feet above the sea; the pike (*Esox lucius*) which, according to Tschudi, is found at a height of about 3400 feet, and frequently weighs from 12 to 15 pounds; the salmon-trout (*Salmo trutta*), which lives as far up the mountains as the village of Splügen (4757 feet), where specimens have been captured weighing a dozen pounds; and the eel (*Anguilla latirostris*), of which I have seen a very fine example caught in the Lago d'Alleghe near Caprile (3000 ? feet). Some of the trout of the Swiss and Italian lakes attain to a very great size. In the former an excellent fish, called the fera (*Coregonus fera*), is not rare, and the Lombard lakes furnish the delicate little agone (*Cyprinus lariensis*). In the *Conservateur Suisse*, Vol. XII. p. 310, a list is given of the fishes of the lake of Geneva, twenty-one in number, and probably many of the others are equally well provided. Small perch are so common therein, that near Ouchy they may be taken in the following manner: a line having at the end an ordinary unbaited pike gorge-hook is lowered into the water, and jerked smartly up and down; the flash of the metal weight attracts the perch, so that they come swimming about it and are speared by the hook. In the paper mentioned above, a curious document is quoted, which fixes the value of several species of fish. From this it appears that in 1376 the price of trout was, during Lent, six deniers; from Easter to All Saints' day three deniers, and for the rest of the year five deniers; the prices of the perch during the same seasons being respectively four, two, and three deniers. The price of pike, fera, and other fishes is also contained in the tariff.

With a few exceptions, reptiles do not appear to be very common in the higher Alps. The common frog (*Rana temporaria*) is said to range up to an elevation of 10,000 feet. It literally swarms in some parts of the Rhone valley. One hot day I happened to be travelling alone to Zermatt, and set off to walk from Leuk to Visp, an expedition which I cannot recommend to any of my readers, unless they desire to be nearly suffocated with heat, choked with dust, and to risk a subsequent fever from the **miasma of the frequent** marshes. A strip of grass divides the **road** in **many places from a** stagnant ditch; and along this I walked, whenever it **was possible, in** order to cool my feet. Every step that I took flushed **the** frogs in twos **and** threes, like pheasants in a warm corner of a cover; up they got, little and big, baby squeakers and patriarchal croakers, taking a **hop** and a header into the stinking water. **Another** species (*R. alpina*), with a brown back and bright orange **belly,** frequents the mountain tarns. It is found abundantly **in the** Todtensee (7090 feet), on the Grimsel Pass, and in the Oberalpsee (6663 feet), and is said to be even more delicate in flavour than the next species. The green or edible frog (*R. esculenta*) is also not uncommon, at any rate in Switzerland; but I believe it does not range so high **as the last-named** species; while the beautiful little **tree frog** (*Hyla arborea*) **is** rarely seen beyond the lower slopes. **I have** found it **in** the bushes **on** the verge of the Lake of Geneva.

According to Tschudi **there** are three species of toads, besides the one common to England (*Bufo vulgaris*). Only the last-named, or a variety (which some have made a separate species under the name of *B. alpinus*), ascends to any great height: this has been found up to about 6000 feet.

A flat-headed slimy black lizard may sometimes **be seen** sluggishly crawling about, especially in **damp places on the** mountains, which is evidently very different **to** the newts and lizards familiar **to most English**. This is the salamander (*Salamandra*), first **cousin to** the peculiarly ugly creature from Japan, which was, if it is not **still, to be** seen in one of the reptile-cases in the Zoological Gardens (London). There appear to be two varieties in the Alps. **One** (*S. maculosa*) marked with orange spots on the flank and belly; **the** other (*S. atra*), which is all **black**; and the latter is said to **have** a much higher range than the former. I have seen it in most parts of the Alps; the highest station being near the little lakes forming the sources of the Po, about 7700 feet above the sea. These reptiles are very abundant near Cortina d' Ampezzo. On a damp evening I used to see dozens of them crawling about a low wall by the road-side just outside the town—into the crevices of which they scrambled, if disturbed, with a slow, wriggling, awkward gait. They were generally from four to six inches in length, but occasionally specimens may be found a couple of inches longer. Tschudi says that they are considered to be weather-indicators, and that when they are seen abroad in considerable numbers in the morning during dry weather, rain may be expected before sunset. In Dauphiné, where it is called *l'alabrène*, it is believed to be blind; in some parts of France it is also thought to be deaf, and called *le sourd;* the common people suppose it, most unjustly, to be very venomous. There are, according to Schinz[1], seven species of newts (*Triton*) in Switzerland, some of which range high.

Of the true lizards (*Lacertidæ*), Schinz mentions five species as belonging to Switzerland; one of which, *Lacerta pyrrhogastra*, ranges up to a height of at least 8000 feet. It is five or six inches long, with a brownish back, marked with black striæ and dots, and a bluish throat. In the male the belly is a greenish-blue, dotted with black, in the female it is a bright orange. *Lacerta muralis* is very common, though I believe it is not found at so great a height above the sea; and the beautiful green lizard, *Lacerta viridis*, which is often more than a foot long, occurs in some of the warmer regions. Some of these species have the power of throwing off their tails with the greatest ease, and afterwards reproducing the lost member. I have often seen them running about the walls with the stumps in various stages of growth. One day as I was walking in a lane, near Lausanne, by the side of a garden-wall, on which a number of little lizards, probably *L. muralis*, were disporting themselves, I caught hold of the tail of one, which the owner

---

[1] *Neue Denkschriften der Allg. Schweitz. Gesellsch.*, Vol. I. (1837).

had incautiously left sticking out of a crevice. I neither jerked nor pulled it hard, but to my surprise it was instantly cast off without apparently the slightest effort. It twisted violently to and fro, and after I had thrown it down, continued for some time wriggling in the dust. I have known an instance in which the muscles of the tail contracted on being pricked with a needle, at least six hours after it had been separated from the body.

The blind-worm (*Anguis fragilis*), so common on many of our English heaths, is not rare in the Alps. They are said to hybernate, twenty or more together, in subterranean burrows, the apertures of which are closed by moss and grass. There are also five species of snakes (*Coluber*), among which is our English ringed-snake (*C. natrix*, or *Natrix torquata*), and two of adders; the English species, *Pelias berus*, being one, and *P. redii*, the other. They are, however, as a rule not often seen; although the common adder is found up to a height of more than 7000 feet, and some of the snakes also appear to ascend to a considerable distance. I do not suppose that I have fallen in with a dozen of these animals in all my walks; and of these half have been lying dead by the road-side. Ladoucette[1] says that near Monêtier (Dauphiné) certain persons "summon the adders by means of a shrill whistle, and then seizing them in their gloved hands cast them into a bag to sell them to the apothecaries of Genoa and Turin." It is perhaps hardly necessary to state that the adders are the only venomous reptiles found in the Alps: all the rest, salamanders, newts, frogs, toads, lizards, and snakes are perfectly harmless, though they are often doomed to destruction on this charge by the ignorant peasants.

It is of course impossible in a work of this kind to attempt a detailed account of the invertebrata of the Alps, even if I possessed the requisite knowledge and had access to the needful materials. To give an idea of the magnitude of such a task

[1] *Les Hautes Alpes*, p. 417.

it may be enough to quote a statement from Tschudi to the effect that in the Canton of Glarus alone there had been described, in addition to 213 species of vertebrate animals, 5000 articulata, 50 worms, 100 molluscs, and 200 zoophytes. Of these articulata, 300 species belonged to the arachnidæ (spiders), and about 50 to the crustacea. There were 1500 coleoptera, 1000 diptera, 800 lepidoptera, and as many hymenoptera, 100 neuroptera, 100 porthoptera and 300 hemiptera.

Of the mollusca several species ascend to a considerable height—among which are *Vitrina diaphana* (7,500 feet), *Helix arbustorum alpicola* (7000 feet), and *Bulimus montanus*, about 6000 feet. The great edible snail (*H. pomatia*) is very abundant in the lower Alpine regions, and occurs up to at least 4000 feet. In Italy it is cooked, and is considered a dainty, of which however our countrymen seem generally rather shy.

The lepidoptera are very abundant, the number of species in Switzerland alone being at least double of that in England. Meyer-Dür[1] gives a list of 162, which includes almost all those found in Great Britain, and the excess is chiefly supplied by additional species, not by new genera. Many of those which are rare, or very local in England, are common among the Alps; and it is with no small delight that the entomologist sees insects on the wing in numbers, which at home are, and probably always would be, only known to him from cabinet specimens. The beautiful Swallow-tail (*Papilio machaon*) is common, but does not ascend very high; and still more restricted in its range is its more delicate brother (*P. podalirius*), whose claims to a place in our British fauna are by many naturalists somewhat peremptorily rejected. It is most abundant in the sunny valleys on the Italian slopes. The handsome Apollo (*Parnassius apollo*), with his downy plumage and lazy, yet regal flight, is common between 2500 feet and 5300 feet; and his smaller kinsman (*P. delius*) is said to range from 4000 feet to 7000 feet; indeed,

---

[1] *Neue Denkschriften der Allg. Schweiz. Gesellsch.* Vol. II. N. S. (1852).

I believe that I have seen it still higher. The difference in size is very marked, so that the species are easily distinguished. *Colias paleno*, or a closely allied species, abounds on the upper pastures up to above 7000 feet. It much resembles *C. hyale*, the Pale clouded-yellow, which is also found, but in much lower stations. *Pontia rapæ*, the Small-white, is found up to 7000 feet; the more delicate *Daplidice*, our rare Bath-white, does not go so high, but I have found it in the Visp-thal, at between three and four thousand feet. A species of Anthocaris (*A. Belia*) mounts up to 7000 feet, leaving our Orange-tip (*A. cardamines*) below. Some of the Coppers ascend to even the highest pastures, chief among them being *Lycæna chryseis*; and the Blues are also very common; of these *Polyommatus adonis* is said to reach 4000 feet, *P. corydon*, the Chalk-hill Blue, the same, and *P. acis*, now extinct in England, 3000 feet. I believe that I have seen the second of these at still higher stations. Another species closely resembling *P. alexis*, abounds in the upper pastures. It appears to like water, and I have often seen numbers of this and a species of Copper by some damp spot in the pathway, apparently so stupified, that they could hardly be induced to take wing; in fact, they seemed to be drunk. So far, however, as my observation goes, the butterflies in the Alps are much tamer than in England. I have often stood over them as they were feeding or fluttering from flower to flower, without their taking the slightest notice of me. Hence it is generally easy to examine them, without subjecting them to even a temporary captivity. Last summer a Bee-hawk moth (*Sesia fuciformis*) worked through a whole flower-bed in a garden near Innsbruck while I stood over it. The Painted Lady (*Cynthia cardui*) wanders up to nearly 9000 feet, and some of the *Vanessæ* range high. The beautiful *V. antiopa*, however, does not go above 2500 feet, at which height I have myself seen it. The Ringlets are very abundant, and of numerous species. The Scotch Argus (*Erebia blandina*) and the Small-ringlet (*E. cas-*

siope), being, with some allied species, not easy to distinguish without careful examination, very abundant on the mountains. The latter insect is said to range from 5600 feet to 8500 feet; sometimes indeed it descends lower; but I have never seen it in districts where the peaks do not rise above 5000 feet. The former species occupies similar but rather lower zones, and may consequently be found in districts where the above condition is not fulfilled. The Fritillaries are numerous; the larger species, as in England, fluttering over the brushwood. Common among them are the, to us rare, Queen of Spain (*Argynnis lathonia*), and the noted *Melitæa dia*, or Weaver's fritillary, the claims of which to English citizenship are more than disputed by many entomologists. They both have a very extensive range, and the latter is abundant in some parts of the Alps. Stragglers indeed often ascend far above the limits here mentioned. *E. blandina* and *E. cassiope*, as well as two *Fritillaries*, probably the last named, flew by me over the top of the Strahleck Pass (10,994 feet); and when I was on the top of the Grivola (13,028 feet) a Small-tortoiseshell (*V. urticæ*) and a blue-bottle fly were sporting merrily about crags, on which the sole signs of vegetation were a few lichen spots.

Of the Sphyngidæ, the Burnet-moths are exceedingly abundant, and ascend to the higher pastures, being found at a height of certainly not less than 6000 feet above the sea. Among them I have observed the Five and the Six-spot Burnets (*Anthrocera trifolii* and *A. filipendulæ*), and the more delicate *A. minos*, which in our own isles is chiefly confined to the west of Ireland. I have also noticed one of the Foresters (*Procris*). With the exception of the Humming-bird (*Macroglossa stellatarum*), which is exceedingly abundant in the lower and warmer parts of the Alps, I have not observed many of the Hawk-moths, and think they are generally confined to the vine regions, among which I have seen the Death's-head (*Acherontia atropos*) and the Oleander (*Chærocampa nerii*).

Once, however, I saw a good many caterpillars of *Deilephila euphorbiæ* on the ascent to the Great Scheidegg above Grindelwald; and found a fine specimen of *Sphinx convolvuli* dead on a snowfield at the head of the Val Pellice, near the Viso, at a height of about 9000 feet above the sea. As for the remaining lepidoptera, diurnal and nocturnal, I cannot attempt to describe them; and will therefore only mention one of the most striking, which ranges up to at least 4000 feet, namely, the beautiful Jersey tiger-moth (*Callimorpha hera*).

Beetles are of course abundant enough, but I dare not attempt to particularise; and so are grasshoppers of various kinds up to the higher pastures. Two species are very conspicuous: the great green grasshopper (*Acrida viridissima*), and a stouter and more portly species, which I have seen in the Italian Alps, over 4000 feet above the sea. The noise made by some of these insects is very great, being a shrill whirring whistle; and their habit of biting whatever they come across is often very destructive to ladies' dresses. I have seen the firefly at a height of 4544 feet, near Crissolo in the Val di Po; and the glow-worm is common in most of the Alpine valleys. In the lower parts of some of those on the Italian slopes the scorpion (*Scorpio europæus*) may occasionally be found. I saw one in 1861 at Baveno; it was sitting upon a bed in a room occupied by one of the ladies in our party; she at first mistook it for a specimen out of her herbarium, and took hold of it by the tail. Finding that it moved, she dropped it, fortunately before it had time to sting, and summoned me to look at her strange visitor. After a little management I slipped it into a a bottle of spirit, in which it is still preserved.

The ants make their mounds almost everywhere in the forests and on the meadows—those constructed by a large brown species (*Formica fusca*) being often five or six feet in diameter and two or three high—up to a height of some six thousand feet at the least.

F. rufa establishes its nest under stones. The solitary large *F. herculanea* is said to range above 8000 feet. Of spiders, *Opilio glacialis* has been found on the summit of Piz Linard (10,516 feet). The excellence of Alpine honey is proverbial, and bees thrive well up to about 4000 feet. Humble-bees, wasps, flies, and gnats are abundant; the last ranging very high. The common cray-fish (*Astacus fluviatilis*) is found in the streams up to at least 4000 feet. The brick-red mite (*Rhyncholophus nivalis*) is said to have been found at a height of 10,000 feet in the Grisons.

The ubiquitous flea must not be forgotten. This pest of the tired traveller haunts almost every châlet and far too many inns, and is even found, with an appetite whetted by frequent abstinence, in the hut on the Grands Mulets, 10,000 feet above the sea. One naturally asks Do they winter there? I am inclined to answer the question in the negative, and to suppose that a fresh supply is brought up annually in the skin knapsacks, not to say on the persons, of the porters. It happened that in the summer of 1864 I was one of the first party that spent a night there. The hard boards and stuffy air, combined with a knapsack pillow that seemed to be all edges and, lie as I would, to be bent on decapitating me, effectually banished sleep; but though, remembering the evil reputation of the place, I waited long in uneasy anticipation, not a flea came to the banquet; and I am sure that, had there been one in the hut, it would have found me out.

There is yet another little insect, which is able to support a still greater degree of cold, living in a temperature which can never rise much above the freezing-point. This is the glacier flea, which, though bearing some slight general resemblance to its agile namesake, is in reality no relation, and may be watched without fear of after consequences. The scientific name of this minute insect—not half the size of a common flea—is *Desoria glacialis*, but according to M. Nicolet, who has carefully examined them, there is more than one species[1]. This one, when magnified, appears as a long thin earwig-shaped creature, with two rather thick and short antennæ pointing forward and somewhat outwards from an oval head, in the upper part of which are two eyes. The first joint of the thorax bears a pair of short stout legs, and is so small, that they appear to start from between the head and the second joint of the thorax; this is shield-shaped, with the point upwards, and is about as large as the head. Another pair of legs is attached to it. The third plate is smaller than the last-named, and is oblong in form; it bears the third pair of legs. The abdomen appears to consist of four plates, from a knob at the end of the last of which spring two caudal appendages, like a pair of shears. These insects may be found in great numbers in the shallow pools of water which form under the isolated stones lying on the surface of glaciers; and one generally has not to turn over very many before coming upon a society, the members of which instantly begin to leap and kick about, and generally scurry together at the bottom of the pool, where they form an animated patch of wriggling black dots. De Saussure[2] was, I believe, the first to describe these little insects, which he referred to the genus *Podura*. I doubt, however, whether those which he observed belonged to the same species, seeing that he speaks of them as having long and curved antennæ, and describes them as running and leaping among the grains of snow. He found them on the summit of the Petit Mont Cervin, a minor peak of the Breithorn (Valais), at a height of 12,749 feet above the sea. Mr King[3] also observed them, together with some *aphides*, in the same neighbourhood, on the Col of the Théodule pass (10,899 feet), where they were on the snow and under the slaty schist.

---

[1] *Neue Denkschriften der Allg. Schweiz. Gesellsch.*, Vol. v. (1841).

[2] *Voyages*, § 2249.

[3] *Italian Valleys of the Alps*, p. 212.

CHAPTER VIII.

Our glance at the botany of the Alps must necessarily be even more brief than at the zoology. The subject may conveniently, though not scientifically, be treated under the five following heads:—(1) deciduous trees; (2) coniferous trees;—these two forming pretty nearly the leaf-wood and needle-wood of the Germans; (3) brushwood; (4) flowers; (5) ferns, mosses, and lichens. The statistics contained in this section are in great part taken from Tschudi, but I am able to confirm almost all of them from personal observation. It is of course only possible to speak in general terms when attempting to fix either the upper or lower limit of any plant, for so much depends upon local circumstances. The aspect of the site, its position with reference to prevailing winds, the nature of the soil, the height of the neighbouring mountains, and numbers of like causes may enable a particular plant to flourish at a level in one neighbourhood many hundred feet above what it can reach in another.

The majority of the deciduous trees can hardly be said to belong to the Alpine region, though of course they clothe

the lower slopes of the mountains; and in some cases penetrate deep into their recesses up the comparatively level beds of the larger valleys. Thus the vine flourishes freely in the Val d'Aoste between the great ice-capped walls of the Graian and Pennine Alps, and, to the north of the latter chain, clothes the lower slopes on either side of the Rhone valley, even penetrating the Visp-thal as far as Stalden (2,736 feet). In the neighbourhood of this village is probably its highest station in Switzerland. On the southern slopes of the Alps, and in the Italian Tyrol, it may rise a little above this level; but it can rarely be said to thrive above 2,500 feet, and in many places fails to reach it by several hundred feet.

The Spanish chestnut, in the same way, grows to nearly 3000 feet on the Italian slopes, under favourable circumstances; and the walnut occupies about the same zone, perhaps rising slightly above it. The apple and pear are confined to much the same limits; but the cherry, especially a small black variety, flourishes much higher. I have eaten it from trees in the village of Claux, in the Val Louise (Dauphiné), at a height of about 4000 feet. The oak is confined to much the same limits as the chestnut; the lime advances rather beyond it. There is a very fine old tree in the village of Macugnaga, in the Val Anzasca, at a height of 4369 feet. The maple cannot grow above 5000 feet, but the aspen advances some 200 feet above it as a tree, and even higher than this as a shrub; while the birch flourishes up to 6000 feet, and thrives as a shrub in some places almost up to the snow line.

The following interesting extract from Tschudi[1] gives the limits of several trees in different localities (the heights are in French feet; 1000 = 1066 English feet nearly: the temperatures are reduced to the Fahrenheit scale):

---

[1] *Les Alpes*, p. 43. Some interesting details about the age and history of several Swiss trees will be found in an article in the *Conservateur Suisse*, Vol. x. p. 333.

"The walnut rises in the northern part of the Swiss Alps to a mean level of 2500 feet, and a maximum of 2900 feet; the mean temperature being 45°; in the Central Alps, where the mean temperature is the same, it reaches 2700 feet, and as a maximum 3600 feet; lastly, in the Southern Alps (Mont Blanc and Monte Rosa), where the mean temperature is 44°, it rises to 3600 feet. The cherry-tree reaches a mean of 3500 feet in North Switzerland, though some isolated plants grow even at 4580 feet; in the Bernese Alps this limit mounts up to 3900 feet; in the Grisons it attains a maximum of 4500 feet; in the Valais of 4164 feet; in the Val de Saint Nicholas, the last cherry-trees occur above Herbrigen at 3963 feet. The beech grows in North Switzerland at a mean altitude of 4200 feet; the mean annual temperature being 39·4°, and in certain aspects it even rises up to 4800 feet. In the Bernese Alps the limit is from 3700 feet to 3900 feet; in Canton Tessin it is 4666 feet. In the Valais and the Grisons, where the soil is formed of crystalline schists, beeches are very rare; on Monte Rosa they reach 4500 feet."

Of the coniferous trees, we may place first the larch (*Abies larix*), which is also deciduous; it is very common in nearly every part of the Alps; large forests being almost wholly composed of it. It is particularly abundant in the Tarentaise and the Engadine; but in the former place has suffered much of late years from a kind of blight. In 1864 I saw hundreds of acres of forest, the trees of which were brown and apparently dying. It grows freely up to about 6000 feet, and in some localities, such as the Engadine, as far as 6700 feet. Speaking generally, the zone of larch forests extends from 4000 to 7000 feet. Like all the coniferous trees, it disappears rather suddenly at the upper limit, without any considerable fringe of stunted growth. The traveller not unfrequently falls in with magnificent specimens in the woods, giants rising to a height of from 100 to 120 feet above the ground, with a diameter, measured about a yard from the soil, of four or five feet.

THE SPRUCE FIR.

The common spruce (*Pinus abies*) is also abundant in the Alps; sometimes mingled, but more frequently alternating with the larch, which generally ranges a little above it. Perhaps is it nowhere more beautiful than in the limestone zone which extends along the northern face of the Alps from Savoy to the Tyrol, where the vast sweeps of purple forests, broken here and there with exquisitely green Alps, and surmounted by grand crags, offer some of the most beautiful combinations of wild and pastoral scenery that can be conceived.

Travellers not unfrequently complain that the pinewood scenery is monotonous, and perhaps on level ground the remark is just. I have, however, never yet found it so in the mountain districts; the exquisite curving outlines of the wooded slopes, the beauty of which is enhanced by the fact that no one of them is a continuous line, but is composed of an almost infinite number of slightly varying angles,—is the edge of a sylvan frill,—the delicate play of colour and tone produced by each one of the myriad leafy spires being partly in light and partly in strongly marked shadow, the change through almost every tint of dark green and purple as the sun passes across the sky from its rising to its setting, together with the indescribable harmony between the trees themselves and the surrounding scenery, have always seemed to me inexhaustible sources of pleasure. Let me quote the testimony of one, who has not only the power of appreciating mountain beauty, but also the far rarer gift of expressing his feelings in the most appropriate words[1]:

"Other trees show their trunks and twisting boughs: but the pine, growing in either luxuriant mass or in happy isolation, allows no branch to be seen. Summit behind summit rises in pyramidal ranges, or down to the very grass sweep the circlets of its boughs; so that there is nothing but green cone and green carpet. Nor is it only softer, but in one sense more cheerful

[1] Ruskin, *Modern Painters*, v. 84.

than other foliage; for it casts only a pyramidal shadow. Lowland forest arches overhead, and chequers the ground with darkness; but the pine, growing in scattered groups, leaves the glades between emerald-bright. Its gloom is all its own; narrowing into the sky, it lets the sunshine strike down to the dew. And if ever a superstitious feeling comes over me among the pine-glades, it is never tainted with the old German forest fear; but is only a more solemn tone of the fairy enchantment that haunts our English meadows."

In the Dolomite region of the Tyrol and in Carinthia the lateral branches of the pine are smaller and altogether scantier than in the more western examples. Each tree being thus rendered more 'spiky' in form, the distant woods in these districts have a markedly 'horrent' appearance, which certainly does not add to their beauty. Messrs Gilbert and Churchill[1] state that this mode of growth is produced by the practice of cropping the side branches to obtain winter fodder for the cattle,—a custom almost as prejudicial to a landscape as the English one of pollarding trees. I have, however, examined pines high up on the mountains, which were certainly much more slender in growth than those that I had been accustomed to see further west, on which I could not detect any traces of the axe, so that I do not feel persuaded that this explanation wholly accounts for the peculiarity. Occasionally also their branches droop, or as we often call it, 'weep'; and the effect of one or two of these weeping pines in a cluster of other trees is very picturesque. The branches bend round rather sharply a few inches from the bole, and slope down almost parallel with it, curving slightly upwards near the extremity. I passed through a wood of such trees on the eastern side of the Tre Croci pass (Val Auronzo), some of which were veritable giants; lower down they assumed their usual growth. I also noticed that the larches in this neighbourhood appeared to have their side branches comparatively small.

[1] *The Dolomite Mountains*, p. 28.

The silver fir or **weisstanne** (*P. picea*) is more sparingly distributed than the **last named**. It is common in the Jura, and in parts of the Engadine and **Southern Tyrol, but I** do not remember to have very **often noticed it in the Swiss or other** districts of the **Western** Alps. In general appearance it resembles the **spruce fir**, but the silvery tint of its bark and of the under side of its leaf renders it easy to be distinguished. In the **Jura** it reaches a height of 5000 feet on the Dôle, but in **the Engadine** it has rather a lower range. It has, however, been observed in the Pennine chain up to about 6200 feet.

Sporadic also in its distribution, **but occasionally very abundant**, is the Scotch **fir** (*P. silvestris*), **which grows up to** about 6000 feet. **It is rare in the** French, Piedmontese, and Swiss Alps, where **it seems to be generally** confined to the alluvial land. **It is, however, occasionally found in the mountains**, but does **not generally form extensive forests.** In the Southern Tyrol **it is more abundant, and extends to** a considerable height **above the sea, perhaps not less than** 5000 feet.

Last comes the arolla **or arve** (*P. cembra*), one of the most beautiful **of** all, with its **glossy** dark-green brushes and dense clustered foliage. Though **in** many districts very abundant, it is decidedly a local tree. Tschudi mentions, as among **the most** celebrated habitats, the Frela above Livino, the **north side** of the Munster Thal, **the** neighbourhood **of the Bernina, and** the Stelvio. I can answer for the **abundance of it in the last** two localities; **for it is one of the great charms of the mountains** about Pontresina **and Trafoi (on the eastern side** of the Stelvio pass), where **it grows as far up as** 8000 feet above the sea. I have also seen **it near Zermatt**, especially in the Zmutt-thal, in Dauphiné, on the **south side of the** Dent Parasseé in the Maurienne, about the Ampezzo **Pass, and** indeed generally throughout the Dolomite districts. Tschudi states that it occurs sparingly **in the** mountains about **the** west of the Diablerets, (where **I have also seen** it), in the Gentel-thal and Engstelenthal, near the Grimsel, and in two or three spots in the Central Oberland. A well-grown arolla is from 50 to 80 feet high; the circumference of the trunk a little above the ground being a dozen feet or so. The cone contains some 20 or 30 little nuts with a white kernel, which has a pleasant taste, resembling that of an almond, but slightly resinous. The wood is said to be very durable; in the Grodner-thal it is worked up into toys and ornaments.

Among the brushwood may be named a species of dwarf alder (*Alnus viridis*), which is exceedingly abundant, clothing the mountain sides up to a height of at least 6000 feet, and not restricted to any particular district. It has, indeed, been observed in the Pennine chain at about 7200 feet. A cotoneaster (*C. vulgaris*) may also be observed, especially on limestone. A kind of ash-tree also rises up to a limit of about 5000 feet; and, as has been already said, birch scrub is very abundant in some neighbourhoods up to a height exceeding both of these.

In the Engadine and Eastern Alps the dwarf-pine or mughus (*P. pumilio*), the *knie-holz* or *latschen* of the German, is exceedingly common. Its growth is peculiar; for a considerable distance it trails along the ground (down-hill if on a slope), then it rises in a bold sweeping curve, throwing out branches, which all point sharply upwards, till their extremities are nearly vertical. This part might at first sight be easily mistaken for a young arolla. The long snake-like trailing trunk, of a reddish-brown colour, does not throw off any important branches; it is frequently 10 or 15 feet long, and sometimes even attains to 30 feet; near the root it is often from 4 to 5 inches thick. The upper part forms a bushy shrub from 5 to 15 feet high. Thus the whole length of the stem may be as much as 45 feet; but I should say that from 20 to 30 might be taken as a fair average; hence a dwarf-pine scrub generally a little overtops a man's head. Its colour is dark green, and the cones, which are small (about 1½ inch long), are chiefly produced on the upper part of the tree. The peculiar habit of growth makes the descent through a forest of it a comparatively easy task; except that its smooth round stems are very slippery, and if trodden upon, are apt to prove excellent 'shoots' and bring the incautious walker into a sitting posture with remarkable celerity, producing sensations suggestive of early efforts on the ice; but to force one's way up through them is a most heartbreaking business. I shall not quickly forget the time when, in my innocence of its habits, I started for a quiet stroll, as I fancied, up a steep hillside covered with latschen. The bottle-brush tops proved to be a natural *chevaux-de-frise*, and after about an hour's scrambling, pushing, and hauling, varied with an occasional slip on a stem and consequent sprawl, I formed a very clear opinion that 'it was not worth going through so much to get so little,' and succumbed.

Common in almost every district of the Alps, so far as I remember, is the dwarf mountain juniper (*Juniperus nana*), which occurs sparingly in parts of our British highlands, and is a little brother of the well-known shrub, from the berries of which schiedam is made. It grows on stony tracts, twisting and interlacing its snaky branches among the boulders till it has almost covered them with a dense matted coat of scrubby brushwood, rising from one to two feet above the ground. Its favourite haunt is the zone of coarse pasture land, which succeeds to the region of forest and alp. Gnarled, stunted, prickly, its bleached boughs bent hither and thither, in hard and obstinate angles of growth, interrupted here and resumed there, its whole aspect bears witness to the struggle between the stubborn life within and the deathful cold without. It forces its way almost to the verge of the snows. I have seen it growing by the side of the Glacier Blanc in Dauphiné, more than 8000 feet above the sea. Hence it is regarded with a friendly eye by the mountaineer, whose bivouac fire often depends upon it alone for a supply of fuel; to him juniper on the Alps means a cheerful evening by the crackling blaze, a cup of hot wine at night and of warm soup in the morning, after some hours passed in comfortable slumber instead of in shivering wakefulness. Still we must own there is a drawback in it. Nature, in kindly constructing holes in the rocks as refuges for houseless vagabonds, has forgotten to provide chimneys; it is therefore needless to observe that the bedroom fire smokes; whose would not if you built up the flue, shut the window, and took the door off its hinges? Now the smoke of juniper is peculiarly pungent, and the effect of putting on more wood, especially if it be green, gives one some little idea of what Pelissier's Arab friends must have felt, when he let them taste the blessings of civilisation.

Another species of juniper (*J. sabina*) is more local in its growth, but still by no means rare. It is, I remember, abundant among other places, in the Val Savaranche (Graians), the Nicolai-thal and in part of the Valle di Livinallungo (on the eastern side above Caprile). I was the more struck with it in the last case, because I had not remarked it in the adjoining valley near Cortina; there the other species was not uncommon, but the scrub consisted mainly of latschen, which was here wanting and was replaced by the sabine. It appears to occupy a rather lower zone than its kinsman, and is a much richer and more graceful plant, covering the slopes with its long curving boughs; not hard and rough, as with purpose obstinate though often baffled, but lissom and undulating as though life went easily, with but difficulties to overcome enough to prevent it being monotonous. The leafage too is not bristly, coarse, grey, and dull in colour; but full, rich, and green, more like that of a procumbent cypress. The long tapering curves with which the branches end are especially beautiful, just such as the pencil of Turner never wearied in rendering.

Growing along with the sabine among the forests, and reaching far above it to almost the limit of the other juniper, come the dwarf rhododendrons, the roses of the Alps as they are often called—rather unfairly, **seeing there is a** true Alpine rose (*R. alpina*), far from rare, **with a flower about the** size of the ordinary English dog-rose, **and of** a deep crimson, surpassing in colour any that we can shew. These sturdy little **shrubs strike** their roots into the most sterile soil, among **the** boulders and crumbling splinters of fallen rock, and are to the Alps what the **heather is to** the hills of Britain. There are two species; one is *Rhododendron ferrugineum*, which is rarely seen **below 3000 feet, and may** be said to flourish from 4500 feet to 7500 feet. **This** is readily recognised by the rust-coloured under **side of its leaf;** which, combined with the darker hue of its flower, gives **it a** more sombre appearance than the other species; indeed a reddish-brown hue so much predominates in this rhododendron that, at a little distance, whole **patches of it in the** higher Alps might easily be supposed to **be withered.** The other species (*R. hirsutum*) descends a thousand feet **lower, and is chiefly** found in a zone between **3500 feet and** 6500 **feet,** rarely occurring above 7000 feet. Its leaves are covered with a multitude of fine hairs, whence its name; and its **flowers are of a more** delicate pink; so that on the whole it is the more beautiful shrub. It is much more abundant in the Tyrol than in Switzerland. I have **seldom seen it** grow more freely than on the Sponda-lunga slope, **on the** western side of the Stelvio road. Words are **inadequate** to describe the beauty of these rhododendron flowers when they **clothe whole acres of the mountain slopes with a robe of dappled** crimson, rivalling in hue the flush which **is kindled in the upper** sky by **the last rays of** the setting sun. It blossoms in the latter part of June and **in July.** August travellers can form but little idea of its richness. The red-berried *Hippophae rhamnoides* is a striking shrub in **many valleys,** growing on the stony plains overflowed at times by the mountain torrents; the 'screes' in Dauphiné up to about 4000 feet, **are** in many places almost **masked by the** sweet-scented tufts **of** lavender; and, in the Bernina, the mountain air is **perfumed** by the blossoms of

Daphne striata, which flourishes considerably above 7000 feet. Another species, *D. alpina*, is less conspicuous.

Nor must we forget the fruit-bearing shrubs, delights of the mountaineer. Who does not remember pleasant pasture among gardens of Alpine raspberries; daintier, though smaller, than those at home. These we find almost everywhere, up to a height of some 6000 feet. The finest plantation that I ever saw was on the southern side of the Giéta, a mountain that rises near to Sixt (Savoy). Wandering down one summer's afternoon from its summit towards the gloomy Lac de Gers, we found that the hill-side was literally clothed with raspberry plants,—a garden of fruits apparently never visited save by the birds and insects. We must not pass by its dwarf congener, the slender *Rubus saxatilis*, with its little red berries, called in the French-speaking district *griffes de chat* (cat's-claws), doubtless from their flavour. Acid though they be, they are pleasant to the thirsty wanderer; and to many are quite irresistible. Nor must the bilberry (*Vaccinium myrtillus*) be forgotten, which is abundant in many districts. How refreshing is its black, lip-defiling juice when the mouth is parched by toiling up a steep slope, and how often have its fruits proved apples of Atalanta to the youth whose motto ought to be 'Excelsior,' and seduced him—not to 'stay and rest his weary head upon maiden's breast,' but to sprawl among the pliant tufts and browse upon their purple berries. This friend or foe, as you like to take it, of the Alpine climber is very hardy, and ascends up to a height of more than 7000 feet. Strange to say, the peasants make very little use of its fruits, though they may often be gathered in gallons within a few minutes' walk of the upper villages. More sparingly distributed, but still common, is the little Alpine strawberry, which may be here mentioned for convenience, and in virtue of its being a member, though a lowly one, of the family of the rosaceæ; its fruit, however, cannot complain of neglect, for it is a great source of revenue to the village children, and so well are strawberries hunted, that it is no easy matter to find any in the neighbourhood of tourist-haunted spots. Like nearly all other fruit, it should be eaten from the plant to be tasted in perfection. After it has been gathered awhile, the slightly resinous aroma becomes a little too pronounced. Occasionally also one finds wild gooseberries, bearing a hairy yellow fruit, much smaller than that of the corresponding English garden plant, but of an excellent flavour. Among other localities for it may be mentioned the Val d'Anniviers and the Val Louise (in Dauphiné); in the latter place it grows some 4500 feet above the sea. Let me here say a word for the astringent sloe, which ranges rather higher, especially on the southern side of the Alps. The traveller, when any part of his walk lies through one of the hot Italian valleys, will do well not to despise this berry. If eaten, it will of course make his palate and teeth like a file; but if simply held in the mouth, it promotes saliva, as does a pebble, and at last by melting away almost imperceptibly, produces a slight acid taste which is very refreshing. Useful for the same purpose are the brilliant scarlet and orange clusters of the barberry, whose thorny shrubs are very abundant in the sub-alpine regions, and range in many places up to nearly 6000 feet.

To write of Alpine flowers, even of the commoner species, would be little more than to give a catalogue of names which would be dry enough to all but botanists. A few words, however, must be said about them, for it is impossible for any one to walk many hours in the higher Alps during the months of June and July without being struck with their extraordinary profusion, variety, and beauty. To see them at their best, it is necessary to leave England earlier than is possible to most travellers; still, even in the beginning of July, when the stream of outward-bound holiday-makers begins to flow from our shores, though the flowers are fast disappearing from the lower meadows, the Alpine pastures are decked with their tapestry of many colours. Who cannot recall many a happy hour spent in rambling from cluster to cluster on the side of some great alp; the scent of sweet herbage or of sweeter daphne perfuming the invigorating air; the melody of the cattle-bells borne up from some far off pasture; while the great blue vault of heaven above seems reflected in the gentian clusters at his feet. The love of flowers seems natural to almost every human being, however forlorn his life may have been, however far it may have missed its appointed mark. It may well be so; they at least are fresh and unstained from their Maker's hand; the cry of 'Nature red in tooth and claw' scarce breaks their calm repose; side by side they flourish without strife, none 'letteth or hindereth another'; yet so tender and delicate, doomed to fade all too soon, a touch of sadness is ever present to give a deeper pathos to our love.

Those then who in Britain feel each year a new delight when they see the great lent-lilies nodding heavy-headed above the springing grass, the cowslip's cluster and the ranunculus' cup, broidering the meadows as with beads of gold, the pale primrose stars and the wood-anemone snow-flakes spangling every glade, the bells of countless hyacinths purpling the woods, the corn-fields scarlet with the poppy flowers, and the moorlands blushing with ling or crimsoning with heather, will find still greater treasures awaiting them in the Alps. There the pale lilac crocus studs the meadows; the pink dianthus and the purple aster, orange-eyed, spangle the banks; the stone-crop of many kinds, yellow, white, and crimson, clings to the rocks, thriving where all other plants would wither. There are golden-ball flowers by the marshy spots; pink persicara in the fields; poppies, larkspur, and corncockle among the grain crops; blue chicory by the road-side, with harebells even richer in colour and more varied in species than in England. Nor must the gentians be forgotten. One, a great herb with flower of purple or of saffron, and huge leaves, from which the *Eau-de-gentian* is distilled;

another, dwarf-like, **with spike of lilac flowers; a third** with long trumpet bells of **richest blue, and** many other varieties, of which more anon. **Nor must we forget to look for the** martigan lily, or the pale yellow foxglove, **which replaces** our **sturdier friend, or,** if **we are** near the Eastern Alps, the matted tufts **of the** *Saponaria ocymoides*. Several of these have a considerable **vertical range, in** some districts **up to** full **6000 feet. You would,** I believe, gather **them all within a** short **walk of** Pontresina (5,915 feet).

One of the pleasantest regions for a botanizing **ramble in** the Alps lies at a height of between about **6000 and 8000 feet,** on the zone of pasture-land immediately above the forests. In that grow great anemones, white and sulphur-coloured; gentians of deepest blue; **campanulas, geums,** alpine soldanellas and forget-me-nots, asters, **ox-eyed daisies, pale pink** primulas, and purple heartsease, **which make the Alps like a** great flower garden. **Among the spots peculiarly noted for** their botanical treasures are the pastures of **Dauphiné** and the Viso, and the Val del **Fain** in the Engadine. **Beyond** this region the flowering plants begin to disappear **from the** coarse turf; but still two species at least of gentians (*G. verna* and *G. nivalis*) hold their own; the mossy saxifrage and androsace (*S. oppositifolia* and *A. pennina*) have their home; the turquoise **clusters of the** *Eritrichium nanum* **gem the rocks,** and **the beautiful** *Ranunculus glacialis* flourishes **in damp places. Besides these, we find the** yellow **poppy,** also the Alpine toad-flax (*Linaria alpina*), purple with **yellow eye; and, in the Eastern Alps,** the silver-leaved, pink-flowered *Potentilla nitida*, **and** *Thlaspi rotundifolium*, a favourite food of the chamois. **The** mountaineer, when about to dine, should not forget to look **for the** Alpine cress, *Passerage des Alpes*, or *Cresson* in patois (*Lepidium alpinum*), which grows up to at least 8000 feet **on** damp banks and moraines. **The** edelweiss (*Gnaphalium leontopodium*) must not be forgotten, a plant so often associated in poetry with the mountains. It may be found up to about 8000 feet; but is rather local. It is abundant in several parts of the Pennine Alps, especially near Zermatt: also in the Italian Tyrol, and in the mountains near the Bavarian frontier. The handsome monkshood (*Aconitum napellus*) is very common, and grows up to nearly the same height. I remember a particularly fine bed of it on the Gemmi Pass at about 7300 feet.

Many of these grow up to the level of the snow. As a rule, however, flowers become rare in any part of the Alps after a height of about 9000 feet, but still I have often gathered them on spots far above this; for example, I found two or three flowering plants, among which was *Pedicularis* (*verticillata?*, I have unfortunately mislaid the specimen), on the Col de Séa (10,154). Not far below the summit was *Eritrichium nanum*, which I have noticed in other places not much below 10,000 feet. We gathered *Saxifraga bryoides* and *Androsace glacialis* on Mont Emilius at about 11,670 feet, and on the Ruitor at 11,480 feet, and *Campanula cenisia* on the Grivola at about 12,000 feet, the highest locality in which I have seen a phanerogamous plant.

Among the above-named, few plants are more beautiful than the gentians, the two most conspicuous members of which family are *G. verna* and *G. acaulis*. The former is a star-shaped flower, about half an inch across, of the richest dark blue, on a stem from one to three inches long. So intense is its colour, and so profuse are its flowers, that I have seen a patch as large as a saucer, in which the green of the leaves could not be distinguished. The other is the common garden species in England; in the upper pastures of the Alps it is almost as abundant as are daisies in our meadows. This also is a very free flowerer; I have counted as many as twenty-seven bells on a single plant.

Turning now to the last division, the apparently flowerless or cryptogamic plants, I will venture on a few notes upon the ferns, which, as in all mountain districts, are abundant in the

Alps. The majority of them are identical with those of Great Britain, but the collector will find species growing in profusion here, which, at home, are either very rare or, at best, confined to one or two localities.

Of the polypodies, the beech-fern (*P. phegopteris*) and oak-fern (*P. dryopteris*) are generally common; and so is the limestone polypody (*P. calcareum*) in districts where that rock prevails. Another species, *P. alpestre*, which at first sight might easily be mistaken for the lady-fern, grows plentifully in many places. I have gathered it in profusion—generally at a height of from 5000 to 6000 feet, near the Col des Sept Laux in Dauphiné, in the tributary glens of the Val d'Orco (Graians), near the Col de la Croix (Val des Ormonds), and in several other places. *Allosorus crispus*, the parsley fern, is common, especially on the crystalline rocks, and ascends to above 7000 feet. *Polystichum lonchitis*, the holly fern, is perhaps above all others the one most characteristic of the higher Alps. It is abundant in almost every district from the Viso to the Tyrol, ranging from about 5000 to nearly 8000 feet; but, so far as my experience goes, is not found unless the general level of the surrounding peaks considerably surpasses 6000 feet. At about that elevation it seems to flourish in perfection. It thrives in both the crystalline and limestone districts; but on the whole the finest fronds are to be seen in the latter; especially in places where the rock, as is so often the case, weathers into channels, two or three feet deep, with parallel walls only a few inches apart. Nestling down in these, it shoots out great fronds, often more than eighteen inches in length, which are giants compared with the stunted specimens on the rock-work in our own gardens. Some of the finest that I have ever gathered, grew on the limestone plateaux between the Faulhorn and the Lake of Brienz. The various members of the families *Lastræa* and *Athyrium* do not as a rule ascend very high up the mountains.

Of the spleenworts, *Asplenium septentrionale* is exceedingly common in most of the crystalline districts, but I do not think it flourishes much on the limestones. I particularly remember that, in the Badia-thal (S. Tyrol), I did not see a plant of it during a walk of some hours over the dolomite limestone, but found it abundantly as soon as I came upon the mica slate. Its near relative, *A. alternifolium*, is much rarer; I have found it near the châlets of Ailefroide in the Val Louise (Dauphiné), near Salvent in the Val de Trient, near Chiavenna, and on the Col di Colma; rather plentifully in the last two localities. The wall-rue (*A. ruta-muraria*) is generally plentiful on buildings and rocks; and the common maiden-hair (*A. trichomanes*) is abundant, though it does not ascend high, being succeeded by the delicate *A. viride*, which ranges as far above the sea as the holly fern. *A. fontanum* is local; I have found it abundantly in the Combe de Malaval (Dauphiné), between St Laurent du Pont and the Grande Chartreuse, at Les Etroits du Ciel (above Moutiers in the Isère Valley), and near Sepey in the Val des Ormonds. *A. lanceolatum* is also local, and so is the black maiden-hair, *A. adiantum-nigrum*. The hart's-tongue (*Scolopendrium vulgare*) is hardly to be called a mountain fern, and the scaly *Grammitis ceterach* is not common except in the lower districts. *Blechum boreale* may be also found in places. The common brake (*Pteris aquilina*) is confined to the lower slopes, and so is the beautiful *Adiantum capillus-veneris*, which I have only seen in the Italian Alps; *Cistopteris fragilis* and *dentata* are common, and ascend well above 5000 feet, and the more delicate *C. alpina* is not very rare. I have gathered it above the Dauben See (on the Gemmi Pass) at about 7400 feet. *C. montana*, which may easily be mistaken for a variety of *P. calcareum*, is common in certain localities, as for example near Rosenlaui, about the Diablerets, and near Landro and Cortina. I have gathered it at a height of considerably above 5000 feet in the last two places. The woodsias are difficult to find, owing to their manner of growth. I have never seen the *Hymenophylla* in the Alps, and the kingly *Osmunda regalis* keeps to the warmer valleys. The moonwort (*Botrychium lunaria*) abounds in the upper pastures. I have seen them tawny with its fronds at about 6800 feet. The adder's tongue (*Ophioglossum vulgatum*) I have never found. Besides these there are several species which do not occur in Great Britain; such as *Struthiopteris germanica* in the lower valleys; *Polypodium rhæticum* and *Botrychium matricarioides* in the Rhætic Alps; *Woodsia glabella, Asplenium halleri*, and *A. scelosii* in the Eastern Alps.

The club mosses (*Lycopodium*) which are found in Great Britain are common in most parts of the Alps, especially the sturdy *L. selago*, which grows up almost to the verge of the snows. Lower down is the delicate *L. helveticum*, which creeps among the damp mosses under the shade of the forests. The long chamois-beard lichen, which drapes the aged firs with a vesture of pendulous threads, has already been noticed, and many of the smaller species stain with spots of crimson, orange, and purple, the rocks among the snow-fields and glaciers, and gem the summits of peaks more than 13,000 feet above the sea, reaching even to the highest rocks in the Alpine chain. Of their beauty and effect upon the scenery I feel sure that I cannot do better than again quote Mr. Ruskin's words[1].

"We have found beauty in the tree yielding fruit and in the herb yielding seed. How of the herb yielding no seed, the fruitless, flowerless lichen of the rock?

"Lichen, and mosses (though these last in their luxuriance are deep and rich as herbage, yet both for the most part humblest of the green things that live),—how of these? Meek creatures! the first mercy of the earth, veiling with hushed softness its dintless rocks; creatures full of pity, covering with strange and tender honour the scarred disgrace of ruin,—laying quiet finger on the trembling stones, to teach them rest. No

---

[1] *Modern Painters*, Part VI. Chap. X. (Vol. V. p. 102).

words, that I know of, will say what these mosses are. None are delicate enough, none perfect enough, none rich enough. How is one to tell of the rounded bosses of furred and beaming green,—the starred divisions of rubied bloom, fine-filmed, as if the Rock Spirits could spin porphyry as we do glass,—the traceries of intricate silver, and fringes of amber, lustrous, arborescent, burnished through every fibre into fitful brightness and glossy traverses of silken change, yet all subdued and pensive, and framed for simplest, sweetest offices of grace. They will not be gathered, like the flowers, for chaplet or love token; but of these the wild bird will make its nest, and the wearied child his pillow.

"And, as the earth's first mercy, so they are its last gift to us. When all other service is vain, from plant and tree, the soft mosses and grey lichen take up their watch by the head-stone. The woods, the blossoms, the gift-bearing grasses, have done their parts for a time, but these do service for ever. Trees for the builder's yard, flowers for the bride's chamber, corn for the granary, moss for the grave.

"Yet as in one sense the humblest, in another they are the most honoured of the earth-children. Unfading as motionless, the worm frets them not, and the autumn wastes not. Strong in lowliness, they neither blanch in heat nor pine in frost. To them, slow-fingered, constant-hearted, is entrusted the weaving of the dark, eternal tapestries of the hills; to them, slow-pencilled, iris-dyed, the tender framing of their endless imagery. Sharing the stillness of the unimpassioned rock, they share also its endurance; and while the winds of departing spring scatter the white hawthorn blossom like drifted snow, and summer dims on the parched meadow the drooping of its cowslip-gold,— far above, among the mountains, the silver lichen-spots rest, star-like, on the stone; and the gathering orange-stain upon the edge of yonder western peak reflects the sunsets of a thousand years."

CHAPTER IX.

THE following statistics taken from the work of MM. Legoyt and Vogt (*La Suisse*, 2me Partie), may be interesting, although they include of course more than the mountain district. To them I have added some particulars concerning the other parts of the Alps, derived from personal knowledge and from various sources. In Switzerland the surface is divided according to the following table:

	hectares.
Arable land	581,400
Meadow land	636,610
Vineyards	27,720
Forest	712,800
Pasture land	792,000
Waste land, water, roads, and ground built upon	1,240,230
	3,990,760

With regard to the crops raised upon the arable land; it is estimated that 39,501 hectares are devoted to wheat; 23,626 to barley; 106,205 to oats; 159,768 to rye; and 71,995 to potatoes.

The wheat grown is the horned variety; the limit up to which it may be cultivated with success varies from about 4,000 to 5,000 feet according to the districts. In Switzerland it rarely passes, and often falls below, the inferior number; but in many places towards the south and the east it rises above the superior. In Dauphiné it is chiefly cultivated on slopes with a southern aspect, which, owing to the burning heat of summer, are often too parched to be of any use as pasture land. Thus the effect looking down a valley which runs east and west is very remarkable; one side being all yellow, the other all green. The Tyrol is distinctly more of a corn-growing country than Switzerland; and it is not easy to imagine a richer scene than is presented towards the end of July, by the Pusterthal near Brunecken,—a wide undulating valley, with the green Alpine slopes and snow-streaked crags above keeping ward around this field of the cloth of gold. At Cortina d'Ampezzo considerable quantities of wheat are grown, at a height of at least 4800 feet. In Switzerland, if it could be got to grow at all at that level, it would be stunted and poverty-stricken. Oats and barley are both able to flourish at a higher level than wheat, and may be seen, though not very luxuriant, above 5,000 feet; and in a few places towards the Eastern Alps, up to 5,500 feet. Rye also grows up to about the same level, and the potato will ripen at about 5,000 feet. I have seen it growing a little above that altitude in Dauphiné. Cabbages, carrots, spinach, lettuces, and other garden vegetables, thrive pretty well in stations about the same height; and they are often cultivated with success in some spots a little above 6,000 feet. I remember seeing gardens in which were growing spinach, lettuces, &c., at Bonneval in the Arc valley, a village just on that line. At Pontresina in the Engadine, vegetables are plentiful, and Tschudi[1] states that in that district lettuces, celery, spinach, salsify, radishes, carrots, and flax, flourish in gardens between 5,300 and 5,600 feet, and

---

[1] *Les Alpes*, p. 324.

that lettuces and carrots mount up to nearly 7,000 feet. Hemp is also cultivated in considerable quantities, especially in the Italian valleys; it does not however flourish in stations above about 4,000 feet, though it may often be seen higher. The smell of the stagnant ponds, in which it is left to steep, is most offensive; and the traveller will do well not to linger near them. After being sufficiently soaked, it is hackled with a rude wooden instrument, something like a pair of nutcrackers. The women may be often seen employed with it as they walk. Flax is generally spun with the old-fashioned distaff and spindle; and the sound of the loom may not unfrequently be heard. In some of the Viso valleys, where the harvest is necessarily late, great racks are constructed on which the corn is hung out to dry; somewhat similar racks are used in the South Tyrol for harvesting beans, which are largely cultivated in that district. In the Tyrol also, sticks some four feet high, with two or three sets of cross pegs at right angles, are commonly stuck into the ground, on which corn, hay, and especially clover, are piled in a tall 'cock' to dry.

In the Alpine meadows, and indeed in the more level flats in the valleys, the hay harvest is not, as with us, almost wholly confined to the month of June, with a possible aftermath in the autumn; but the grass is mown whenever it is about four or five inches high, so that the haymaker is at work all the summer. The crop, when dried,—a process which does not take long,—is generally bundled up in a piece of sacking and carried on the head to a store châlet, whence it is sent down to the valley below on sledges. In many cases this is not done at once, but a load is fetched from time to time during the winter when required; the ease with which the *traîneau* descends the smooth slope compensating for the increased labour and danger of the ascent.

The mower's task is pleasant enough on the sweet alps, with the morning mists curling up from the valley below, the snowy peaks softly gleaming through the illuminated haze, and the rich scent rising from each swathe of his scythe; not so that of the wild-hay cutter. In the early morning he is off with his scythe or sickle to the mountains; passing by the pleasant swards he comes to the great cliffs, along whose ledges he creeps and clambers, by paths more fit for the chamois than for man, in order to gain the grassy cornices and shelving banks, which break here and there the face of the precipice. On these,—often steep slippery slopes, to which he can only cling by crampons,— grow mountain-grasses, full of Alpine flowers; these produce a hay, coarse enough in appearance, yet toothsome to the cattle, and best food of all for the milch cows, seeing that from it comes the richest butter. His task done, he gathers his store into a cloth and binds it firmly together. If the cliff below be sheer, bare, and not too high, he simply casts his bundle over its edge to await him below; if, however, projecting rocks or trees would arrest its fall, or, by tearing it open, scatter its contents to the winds, he poises it upon his head, and betakes himself to the yet more dangerous task of retracing his steps. If it was difficult before to pass along some narrow ledge, with a wall of rock rising up on the one hand and a dizzy depth below on the other, or to turn a projecting crag, clinging to some knob or crevice, and feeling with one foot for the unseen stepping-place, how much worse is it now with a heavy burden balanced upon the head; how sure must be the hand and foot, and how nice the poise, to escape the overbalancing which must inevitably lead to a fatal fall. Hence the occupation of the wild-hay cutter is one that, like the chamois hunter's, too often proves fatal. One day a stone yields, or a limb fails; a despairing cry and a heavy fall break the mountain silence; and something that was a man is lying upon the rocks a thousand feet below. In certain districts the mower's task is dangerous, even upon the larger alps; where the mountains are formed of huge terrace walls of rock separated by steep slopes of turf. These, in the heat of summer, become almost as slippery as ice, and the workman, neglecting to wear his crampons, or stepping incautiously across some steeper spot, loses his footing, and slides downwards, vainly clutching at the short dry herbage, till he reaches the verge of the cliff and takes the fatal plunge.

The vine, as may be supposed, is only cultivated with success on the lower slopes of the mountains; still, in a few places, it ascends the open valleys for a considerable distance into the heart of the Alps. On the northern side it is generally trained in the German manner, on a short pole; so that, colour excepted, a vineyard appears not unlike a garden full of raspberry plants. On the southern side a more picturesque plan prevails. Upright posts of wood, or, very commonly, of rough-hewn mica-slate, are fixed into the ground, placed in two rows, a dozen or fifteen feet apart, and upon them a rough framework of poles is arranged, forming a kind of skeleton roof over which the vines are trained. These pleached walks, cool and shady, with pendent clusters of purple grapes, often rising terrace above terrace up the slopes, are very picturesque, especially at vintage time; when the people turn out *en masse* to gather the fruit in deep baskets (*hottes*) carried upon the back. These, when full, are emptied into tubs, and the grapes are crushed with a kind of fork made by lopping near the stem the side branches of a stout bough or sapling. The juice is then collected in skins or barrels and taken down to the houses, where it is emptied into pans, and stirred every day, until fermentation takes place. Few of the wines are of any value; but a very fair red *vin ordinaire* is made in the neighbourhood of Montmélian in the Isère valley; and a rather pleasant and strong white wine, with a flavour of the muscat grape, is obtained from the vineyards at the entrance of the Vispthal. The *Vin du Glacier* of the Rhone valley, near Bex, is also good, and deserves notice because of the peculiar process in its manufacture from which its name is derived. "The casks of wine are taken up, before the winter, to safe hiding-places among the rocks in the neighbourhood of a glacier; here they are left till the following spring; and during the severe frosts all the inferior parts of the wine freeze to the sides of the casks, the purest parts remaining unfrozen in the middle. With the help of an axe the ice is broken, and the choicest wine obtained[1]." In this neighbourhood the grapes are crushed in presses, and the process has been described as follows[2]: "The wine-press is made entirely of wood, and consists of two strong upright posts, the one I saw being about twelve feet high and ten apart, fixed in the ground, supporting a cross beam with a screw in the middle. Between the posts is a square trough on four legs, and in this a perforated moveable frame, for the reception of the grapes, is placed, and then boards, whose dimensions allow of their being pressed into the frame, are piled on the fruit till nearly on a level with the screw, which is worked by two or more men, according to the pressure required. Each lot of grapes is stirred up and pressed three times; the juice, passing into the trough, runs thence through a hole into a large tub, which is again emptied into the barrels, where it is allowed to ferment for ten days or a fortnight before it is closed, and in six weeks they consider it fit to drink. The white grapes are pressed as they are brought from the vineyards, but the black, of which comparatively very few are grown in the Vaud, are allowed to lie and ferment for several days previous to the pressing, in order to improve the colour of the wine. From the residuum a common sort of brandy is distilled called *eau-de-vie-de-marc*, from the name given to the pressed grapes, and if kept some years,—a rare occurrence in this country as regards both wine and brandy,—it has the flavour of good cognac."

While on this subject one may mention that several kinds of liqueur are distilled from the mountain herbs; four

---

[1] *Peaks, Passes, and Glaciers*, 1st Series, p. 343.
[2] *Village Life in Switzerland*, p. 96.

being manufactured at the monastery of the Grande Chartreuse; two of these, the *liqueur verte* and the *liqueur jaune*, are very good; and a *petit verre* is an excellent restorative for the tired traveller. A very common spirit is that distilled from cherries, by crushing them when fresh, stones and all; it is called *kirchwasser*, but I cannot recommend it. The Swiss beer is not worth much, but in the Tyrol a light and pleasant kind may be often obtained. I have also occasionally been served with very fair cider, especially in Savoy.

The forests still form no inconsiderable portion of the wealth of the inhabitants of the Alps, although they have in some places been much diminished by over-cutting. This has especially happened in the neighbourhood of mines, and in consequence the people of the unfrequented communes have become so alive to this, that some jealousy is felt of strangers wandering about the mountains, lest they should discover metals and cause the destruction of the woods. Mr Wills relates[1] that this apprehension gave him some trouble when he was treating for the purchase of the site of his lovely Alpine home, the Eagle's Nest (near Sixt); and I remember in a remote Dauphiné village being straitly questioned by the *maire* as to whether my rambles had anything to do with mines. Their fears are not unreasonable, for the forests, besides producing some effect upon the rainfall, form natural defences against the rush of the spring avalanches; and it is recorded that after the war of 1799, in which many of those near the St Gothard pass were destroyed, the neighbouring villages suffered terribly from this scourge. Hence the laws do not allow of timber being cut in certain forests called *Bannwalde*, and in most places the right of felling trees is strictly regulated, and the woods are under the inspection of officials, communal or cantonal. In spots high upon the mountains, to which the only access is by difficult winding paths, the timber is at once converted into charcoal,

[1] *The Eagle's Nest*, Ch. ii.

which is then brought down in sacks by horses and mules. The men engaged in this occupation are a grimy rough-looking lot, but I never heard any harm of them. Besides this, however, a vast quantity of timber is felled for building and other working purposes; in 1853 Switzerland alone exported 659,220[1] metrical quintals; and the huge waggons loaded with planks or vast boles, fit for an argosy's mast, may be seen daily toiling over the Ampezzo Pass on their way to Venice and the north of Italy. The French Alps are on the whole not so well wooded as the districts further north.

Timber is generally conveyed down from the forests in one of two ways; either it is cut up into logs some five feet long, and thrown into a neighbouring torrent, which bears it down cliff and gorge to the valley below; or else trough-like slides are constructed along the mountain sides, down which the trunks themselves are launched. The passenger by the steamer on the Lake of Brienz may often notice a perfect shoal of logs floating on the water at the foot of the Giessbach falls; these have been sent down the cascade from the upper forests, and will presently be conveyed away in boats or rafts to the depôts at Interlachen or Thun.

The woodman's life also is not without its dangers. His work is generally begun in the winter; so there is always risk from the avalanche, as he wades through the snow, often waist deep, to 'blaze' the trees. These, when felled, must be conveyed to the border of a torrent, either by rolling them down the slopes or by the aid of a slide, called in the patois of the French-speaking districts a *rize*. This is a long channel constructed of pine-trunks, placed side by side and supported upon strong posts. Down this the logs thunder like arrows from a bow. Suppose them to have reached the brink of the torrent, the worst part of the work then begins. If its stream is not strong

---

[1] *La Suisse*, Legoyt et Vogt, p. 44.

enough to transport them, a dam is constructed somewhere above, and when this is suddenly opened, the rush of the accumulated waters sweeps all before it. But the greatest danger is when the torrent is full and strong. Here and there it rushes through deep narrow gorges, thundering among great masses of fallen rock; among these a trunk may easily become wedged, and the barrier once formed rapidly increases. Into these gorges the woodsman must descend, armed with his *grespil* (a long pole terminated by two iron spikes, one in the same line, the other at right angles to it); then, supported if possible by the cord by which he has been lowered, or if not, standing on some slippery rock above the roaring stream, he disengages the entangled trunks. Woe to him if his foot slip or he lose his balance, while making an incautious wrench! Once in the torrent his fate is almost sealed. The strongest swimmer could not breast that rush of water, and in a few minutes his body, battered and bruised, is flung among the logs below as lifeless as they.

The slides, mentioned above, are often very long, and evidence no small engineering skill. The most celebrated was that of Alpnach, by which timber was conveyed from Mont Pilatus to the Lake of Lucerne. It was constructed by M. Ruepp, and was nearly eight miles long, passing over some most difficult ground. A large tree would traverse its whole length in two-and-a-half minutes. Professor Playfair[1] thus describes its descent. "We stood close to the edge of the trough, not being more interested about anything than to experience the impression which the near view of so singular an object must make on a spectator. The noise, the rapidity of the motion, the magnitude of the moving body, and the force with which it seemed to shake the trough as it passed, were altogether very formidable, and conveyed an idea of danger much greater than the reality. Our guide refused to partake

---

[1] Quoted by Beattie; *Switzerland*, Vol. II. p. 119.

of our amusement; he retreated behind a tree at some distance, where he had the consolation to be assured by M. Ruepp that he was no safer than we were, as a tree, when it happened to bolt from the trough, would often cut the standing trees clean over. During the whole of the time the slide has existed, there have been three or four fatal accidents; and one instance was the consequence of excessive temerity." This slide was destroyed in 1819, and has not since been repaired. At the first convenient spot a saw-mill is erected, worked by a water-wheel, and all the trunks, which are not intended to be sold whole, are sawn up into planks or logs, and sent thence to the depôt in the village below.

(Fig. 11.) Châlet Village with the Sasso di Pelmo, from near Caprile.

The pasturages and cattle of the Alps can hardly be separated from the villages, and particularly from the châlet-life, so important a feature in the eyes of the mountain peasant. And here be it observed that an alp is not a lofty peak, as its

English use would seem to imply, but an upland pasture above the forests, one of those great banks of sward which extend for miles like a green riband between the party-coloured fringe of cliff and pine below and of crag and glacier above. In winter they lie buried deep in snow, and in early spring, down those long slopes where one was wont to bask dreamily in the summer sun, secure among the harebells and the daphne, the avalanche rushes thundering down, bearing destruction to all that may cross its path. A few weeks later, when,—though the snow yet lies deep among the peaks and even dapples here and there the upper pastures,—the lower slopes are green with growing grass and already beginning to shew the first blooms of spring flowers, it is time to be off to the alps. The weary winter is over, with its long dark nights; not indeed wholly cheerless around the fireside, while the pinewood crackled on the hearth, and outshone the dull light of the primitive oil-lamp; but still at times dreary, when the tempest whirled the snow-wreaths high above the eaves, and the roar of the avalanche woke many a remembrance of devastated fields and lost friends. It is a hard life in winter in a mountain village; every peasant, much as he may love his home, will tell you that; '*Un mauvais pays, un pays des montagnes*,' is the common complaint uttered sadly and apologetically, yet with a touch of affection in the tone, while your host places his scanty fare before you. And no wonder that it is hard: wages are low; the simplest luxuries dear, or unattainable, for they must be brought up miles of rough mule-paths. Rye ripens tolerably well when the summer is fine; wheat imperfectly; so the peasant's bread must be made of the former. Baking too is a serious business; and fuel, likely enough, is too dear to allow of the oven being often heated. Bread therefore is made only once or twice a year, *Toussaint* being a favourite season. It is baked in large cakes, half a yard or so in diameter, like gigantic buns, which are stored on shelves in an airy loft in the same way as cheeses. They are a dark brown colour, and they soon become dry, remaining perfectly sweet and wholesome for six or even twelve months. In fact, I believe that the former period is generally the shortest for which a batch is made; and I can see no reason why the bread should not remain good for years. It is very hard, as formidable to weak teeth as sea-biscuit, and to try to slice it with an ordinary knife is lost labour: a hatchet may be used with advantage, but the correct instrument is a sort of cutter, which terminates in a hook fitting into a ring on a piece of board, so as to give a leverage. An enterprising member of the Alpine Club thus records his experience of one of these loaves[1]. "Oyace yielded but one small rancid sausage, two bottles of wine, and a loaf of black bread. The last may be excluded from the list. We tried to chop it with an ice axe, and it hopped about the châlet like a marble: we boiled it for four long hours, while we glared greedily at the pot, and at the end a quarter of an inch of the outside was turned into gluey slime, and within it was as hard as ever. No fragment of that loaf was ever mastered by guides or travellers."

This bread then, or in the Italian Alps, polenta,—a sort of porridge made of maize meal,—with a little goat's milk or a scrap of cheese, is the staple of the Alpine peasant's food. Now and then it is varied by a slice of dry sausage or of raw bacon, or by a bit of smoked mutton, a perquisite from one of the flock that has been accidentally killed, or sometimes, if report say true, has died a natural death. Fresh meat he seldom tastes, except on some rare festival, such as a wedding, or a baptism, or the great day of Mi-Août[2]. Times are often hard enough to the English labourer, but I am inclined to think that an Alpine peasant is still more poorly fed and housed. I am,

---

[1] *Alpine Journal*, Vol. I. p. 222.

[2] August 15th, the Assumption of the Virgin Mary; a general holiday in Roman Catholic countries, and kept with double honour in the French Alps, since it is also the Emperor's *fête* day.

of course, now speaking of the higher villages, in those remote districts where travellers rarely come to spend money, and where shops are almost unknown. Near the great roads and favourite places of resort, life appears to go more easily; visitors and their wants furnish plenty of work for the steady and able-bodied men in summer, and a fair heap of francs may be laid up against the winter. But in such places as the lonely glens in the French and parts of the Italian Alps it is a different story. In these also fuel is often scarce, the soil and climate being unsuited for forests; so that in winter the people herd together with the cattle, occupying a room partly underground. This is the case to my knowledge in the upper valley of the Arc and in the mountain villages near the Val d'Aoste, and is probably a practice far from uncommon.

And then the cottage itself, built in many parts of the Alps of rough stones, stuck together with coarse mortar, sometimes not even plastered within; its fireplace without a grate, possibly without a chimney[1]. For furniture, one or two common tables, half a dozen chairs, or perhaps only a bench and a few stools, a shelf with some odds and ends of crockery; and a *crochet* fastened to the wall above the fire, to hold the *marmite* or big pot in which everything is cooked;—there is an Alpine home. What wonder then if the people are as afraid of fresh water as a dog with the hydrophobia, and walk about protected from the cold by a permanent coat of dirt? I really doubt whether many of the villagers take off their clothes from week's end to week's end; in the châlets they certainly do not. Slovenly fashions spread naturally, like all bad habits; thus I have been in cottages—owned by men of the yeoman class, who possessed several acres of corn land, a large number of cows, sheep and goats, with extensive rights in pasture and forest,—to which

---

[1] This latter is a common fashion in the Val Auronzo (Italian Tyrol), quite respectable houses being without this, as we should think, necessary accommodation.

that of an ordinary English farm labourer would be a palace. For instance, the house of the principal peasant in La Bérarde —a village some 5,700 feet above the sea in Dauphiné—is just such a place as I have described. It has only one room for living and sleeping, and in the wall is a kind of recess, fitted up with what look like closets with the doors off. These are the beds. The resemblance is increased by large drawers below, which I at first supposed were solely devoted to the fête-day raiment; a subsequent visit, however, disclosed their true use; for, happening to go in at daybreak, I found that the son and heir, a boy about eight years old, was asleep in one of them. Wishing to ascertain one or two toilet mysteries, I watched him dress (with the maternal aid). The process was simple; he put on his trousers, waistcoat, jacket, and shoes, all equally tattered and too large for him, clapped a scarecrow cap on his head, took his stick, and went off after his goats.

In many parts of Switzerland, especially in the Oberland, the smaller houses are built entirely of wood, with the exception of the chimney, and are much more picturesque than those in the French and Piedmontese Alps, where stone is more commonly employed. The latter is also much used in the Southern Tyrol, but there the larger dwellings have often wooden gables, so that the loft or garret is of this material; as are the barn and stalls, which are usually under the same roof, and form the rear half of the house. There also not unfrequently the inner walls are faced with planks instead of plaster; and where the folk are cleanly, as in good Frau Ortler's inn at Trafoi on the Stelvio, it has a very comfortable look; though sometimes one seems to be living in a big box, and has a vague notion that the proper way to get out is to lift up the lid. To see the cottages of the Alps in picturesque perfection we must go to the neighbourhood of the Bernese Oberland. There a wealthy peasant's house is quite a gem. The walls of the ground-floor are usually built of stone, plastered and whitewashed. In this are the kitchens and offices. Above this level all, with the exception of the chimneys, is of wood. On the first-floor are the parlours, the best bed-rooms, and often, towards the back, some chambers for grain and other stores. Besides the staircase from the entrance below, access is commonly obtained to the house by an external flight of steps which leads from the front to a railed gallery running all along the side, into which a door opens from the first floor. Very commonly there is a gallery of this kind on both sides of the house, each with its door; one giving more direct access to the living-rooms, the other to the store-chambers. The windows, glazed with small panes in wooden casements and provided with jalousied shutters, often painted green, are placed close together along the front of the house. The second floor is partially in the roof, which is low in pitch and is covered with wooden shingles,—the eaves projecting for at least four feet; and under their shelter another railed gallery runs along the front and sides of the house; on this stage also, the windows, as far as possible, are made to look front. Above this floor there are generally two or three garret-rooms in the apex of the roof, used for bed-rooms or for stores. In many houses the beams are richly carved, the walls panelled, and ornamented with sculptured or painted devices, the balustrades of the balconies carefully worked, and even the ends of the shingles on the roof are cut shield-shape. Owing to the force of the wind, it is often found necessary to secure these last by long beams or heavy stones arranged in rows and lashed firmly down. Often on the beams and panels the builders' names are inscribed, together with appropriate texts of scripture; such as, "Except the Lord build the house, their labour is but lost that build it;" or couplets like the following:

> In Gottes Hand stehet dieses Haus;
> Gluck komme herein und Ungluck heraus[1].

[1] Nearly this:
> This house in God's hand standeth stout;
> Bide weal within, and woe without!

The corner posts and brackets also which support the roof are frequently very richly carved, particularly in the Val des Ormonds. The stables, cart-house, barn, &c., are in a separate building, after a similar but plainer pattern; but in a poorer house all are under one roof; the horses, &c. being on the ground-floor, and the hay stored at the back. This arrangement is very common in every part of the Alps,—the ground-floor in the old-fashioned inns both in Dauphiné and in the Tyrol being generally devoted to the horses and carriages, and perhaps to the kitchen, and the living rooms above. In the Italian Tyrol I noticed that usually the rooms on each floor were arranged to open into a tolerably wide gallery, which ran from back to front of the house, with the staircase at one end and a glass door, opening into a little balcony overlooking the street, at the other. This gallery was used as a kind of house-place, a table being placed at the upper end, on which your meals were served.

Every district of course has its local peculiarities, but the domestic Alpine architecture may be epitomized with tolerable correctness as follows: In the French and Vaudois Alps, stone is used much more than wood, and the houses are mean and unpicturesque. In the Pennine chain both are employed, but the latter rather for small châlets, barns, and outbuildings. In the Oberland (using the term in a wide sense) wood is the favourite material, and nearly every cottage is a study of quaint picturesqueness. In the Grisons and the adjoining Tyrol the houses are usually large and plain, without beauty, but comfortable looking, built of stone, plastered and white-washed; wood being chiefly used for internal decorations. Further east, in the Tyrol, more use is made of the latter material, the houses being often about half and half; and in some of the larger villages or towns, such as Sterzing on the Brenner Pass, the numerous quaint oriels and bay-windows produce an excellent effect. Speaking generally, the use of wood denotes

German, and that of stone Italian, influence in the population. In the former case the larch, the red spruce, and in some districts the arolla are the usual materials; the last named assumes with age a peculiarly rich ruddy-brown hue.

(Fig. 12.) Swiss Châlet.

Such being the villages, let us return to the châlets, which form the summer quarters of a numerous class among the people. They are dotted about on the mountain pastures, sometimes singly, sometimes in little clusters; the number of course depending upon the extent of the surrounding pasturages. They may at once be divided into two classes; those whereat cows are kept, and those where they are not—a very important distinction, as is well known to all mountaineers. 'It is a cow-châlet,' is as significant an expression to them as 'he keeps his carriage' would be in England. It means that you can get a roof to shelter you, hay, or perhaps a bed—if you don't mind fleas—to sleep upon; perchance even white bread and ham, certainly cheese and plenty of milk, possibly even spoons to eat it with. In the sheep or goat châlet you may find nothing but black bread or polenta, it may be not even a roof over your head, but only a sort of kennel just large enough for one man, under the lee of a huge boulder. The men also at the cow-châlet, are generally much brighter and more intelligent than those at the others; not unfrequently their wives and children are with them *à la montagne*, and right healthy do the little ones look from the glorious mountain air, in spite of dirt and poor fare. The châlets, built of rude beams, or rough stones without mortar, are generally small and low, consisting often of only one room, lighted by a minute window, the glass of which is never cleaned. Hence perpetual twilight reigns within. In one corner is the fireplace, but the chimney is often omitted as a needless luxury; for there are so many chinks in the walls and roof that the smoke escapes readily enough. Here hangs the huge copper caldron in which the milk is boiled to make the cheese. In another corner is a low platform of boards, covered with hay and a dirty rug or two; this is the bed;—don't lie on it if you can find any dry hay. A bench, rough table, and stool, with a hanging shelf for the crockery, complete the furniture, and the chinks between the beams or stones in the wall form extemporary cupboards for spoons, knives, and oddments. The dairy is either an inner room or a separate châlet, which, if possible, is built against a rock for the sake of coolness. In other hovels near, the cows and goats are folded, and the hay is stored. Here some of the châlet folk often sleep; and the traveller will do well to decline if he can the use of the bed which his hosts, in kindly meant courtesy, too frequently insist upon vacating for him.

'Necessity makes strange bed-fellows' is a proverb often true in the Alps. One night our châlet was shared by a couple of our hostess' children, who slumbered peacefully on an adjoining heap of leaves, while I lay awake envying them and making ineffectual pounces in the dark at my agile tormentors; another time I woke up at daybreak early enough to see two bouncing lasses roll out of the hay at the other end of the room and perform their toilet for the day—it only consisted of a shake or two; another, we occupied one corner of a large loft, in a second of which slept our guides, in a third two shepherd lads, and in the fourth a big dog; another night was spent with an invalid goat, and yet another, with three remarkably healthy ones, each of which had a bell of a different note and kept it ringing during the best part of the night. Another evening, on arriving at a sheep châlet in Dauphiné, we found that our party, which was seven strong, in addition to the three shepherds already there, would more than fill it. We travellers, not being of the order pachydermata, accordingly determined to bivouac outside. My companions skilfully constructed a couch in a stack of brushwood, to which they kindly invited me; but as the sharp ends of the sticks appeared quite certain to wriggle upwards, so that one would probably dream all night of being tossed upon pikes, I gratefully declined, and spread my cape on the softest bit of ground that I could find. Covering myself with a plaid, a guide tucked me up by arranging a fringe of heavy stones near its edge, and I soon slept the sleep of the unfleabitten. This went on till past midnight, when plash came something cold on my nose, about the only feature exposed, and I woke up in a thunder-shower. Any thing, even a legion of fleas, is less formidable than sitting in wet clothes, so gathering up my traps I softly opened the châlet door, and saw that, though the sleepers lay on the floor like herrings in a barrel, there was just room for one more in the windiest place. Coming in after supper-time, my foes were less alert, and before long I was fast asleep.

One cannot, however, always reckon upon finding even this much accommodation at a *châlet des bergers*, as the following extract from my diary will shew. It relates the story of two nights and a day which we spent in a certain den on the upper pastures of the Pelvoux. The ascent of this mountain had never before been attempted by English travellers; and all that we could learn at the principal village below was, that we must sleep at a certain *Cabane des bergers de Provence* some two hours above the valley. Supposing from this name that we should have to pass the night in a hay châlet, we packed up a few necessaries in one knapsack and left the rest of our things in our landlord's charge—a great mistake as it afterwards proved; we also got as large a store of bread, meat, and wine, as we could, and a porter to carry it.

"A stiff climb now commenced up some very steep rocks, on which both skill and care were occasionally requisite; we however made rapid progress, till at the end of about an hour and a half we came to the end of the rocks and emerged upon a slope of turf, thickly spread with huge blocks, to one of the largest of which the guide pointed, saying '*Voila le cabane*.' I confess to having felt disgusted. I had not hoped for much, still I had expected a hut and a truss of hay for a bed. Nothing of the kind was here. Only a huge mass of rock, that in former times had fallen down from the cliffs above, and had rested so as to form a shelter under one of its sides. This had been still further enclosed with a rough wall of loose stones; and thus a sort of kennel was made, about nine or ten feet by five or six, and about four feet high at the entrance, whence it sloped gradually down to about two feet at the other end. Our thoughts turned regretfully to some extra wraps left down below, but there was no help for it, and 'what can't be cured, must be endured' is excellent philosophy for the Alps. Accordingly we put the best face on it, and set to work to make all comfortable for the night. Dead juniper boughs were collected for a fire, and the guides began to clean out the cave, which, being frequented by the sheep as well as by the shepherds, was in a sufficiently filthy condition. The first who entered quickly emerged again, holding at arm's length the mortal remains of a defunct mutton in a very lively condition, which he lost no time in sending over the precipice for the ravens **to sup on, if** they had any fancy for it. The floor was then swept and strewed with fern and dock leaves, and a fire lighted to sweeten the place. Evening drew on, **and one by one my** companions retired into the cave; but not fancying **the look of our** night quarters, I stopped outside as long as possible. **It was a strange** wild scene: overhead **hung the crags of the** Pelvoux, splintered in flame-like **points; and** from their base sloped down **vast banks of fallen blocks,** overgrown **with serpent-like branches of old junipers, and broken** here and there with slopes **of turf;** a few feet in front of me steep precipices, overhanging the **fatal 'Baume¹,'** led down into the valley below, beyond which **rose another mass of** rocks and pine-covered slopes, surmounted **with a ridge of** cliffs somewhat overtopping **us.** A fine pyramid of snow-streaked rock, from which a large glacier descended, closed the valley.

"Night however came on, the sky grew wild and stormy, and it became too cold to remain out longer; so, mustering up my resolution, I crawled into the cave, and almost instantly retreated much faster, more than half-choked. A fire is a very comfortable thing on a cold night, but has its drawbacks when the house is without a chimney, and **the smoke has to escape by the door.** If, in **addition to this,** the **house be about four feet** high, and **the fire of damp juniper wood, matters are still worse.** However, **human nature can adapt itself to a good deal, and so** by lying down, **and thus avoiding the** thickest **part** of the smoke, I contrived to endure **it after a time.** Supper over, we prepared for the night. My attire was simple, but certainly not ornamental: a travelling cap, with the flaps tied **over** my ears, **a huge** woollen 'comforter' about my neck, and a **spare** flannel **shirt over** my usual costume; **my** boots were **taken** off and **placed in a safe** corner, a second **pair of socks drawn on, and**

---

¹ See page 101.

my slippers worn during the night; then spreading my gaiters on the ground I lay down on them, having picked the softest stone that I could find for a pillow. My companions did the same; and despite the blasts of the storm, which howled round our cabane, we did not suffer from cold. It was a strange sight, when stiff and cramped by my hard bed, I woke from time to time during the night. The flame, flickering with the wind, lit up the faces of the sleepers and the rocky walls of the cavern with a weird unearthly light. Croz (our Chamouni guide) alone was generally on the alert, smoking his pipe and feeding the fire. Now and then he would step outside to examine the state of the night, and return with a hearty curse on the bad weather. So passed the night, wearily and drearily, to give birth to a drearier day. The dawn did but reveal thick banks of clouds and mist, above, below, around, pouring down a steady, hopeless rain. One by one we roused up with a true British growl at our ill-luck. Then we held a council of war; the expedition was for that day evidently impossible; what then was to be done; should we give it up altogether, or await better weather? Angry at a recent disappointment, we unanimously resolved that we should wait at least one day before retreating. This, however, would require a fresh stock of provisions. Accordingly, we sent the two local guides down to Ville de Val Louise to bring up what they could get, and composed ourselves to watch out the weary day. Sleep was tried again, but not much was done that way. Breakfast was spun out as far as possible, but that cannot be carried on long when the fare is bad. Happily I discovered that the lining of my coat had been much torn in climbing over the rocks, and that I had a needle and thread with me; so I spent an hour in tailoring. Presently the rain began to find its way through various cracks in the rock, and obliged us to set out the cups of our flasks to catch it.

"About mid-day snow fell at intervals, and the rain became less heavy. Our French friend, who had a liking for botany, sallied forth occasionally for a few minutes and returned with a handful of weeds (I cannot dignify them with the name of flowers). Then would commence a botanical argument between him and M. After diligently turning over two paper-covered volumes he would declare a plant to be so and so. This assertion was generally controverted by M., whereupon after the manner of opposing 'savants' they recklessly pelted one another with long names; till M., who was a good botanist, in most cases forced his antagonist to confess himself vanquished. These discussions helped to pass away the time till dinner. During the meal H. suddenly remembered that it was his birthday; we accordingly drank his health, and sincerely wished that he might never again spend so dull a day. Late in the afternoon it ceased raining, and we strolled about the broken rocks near our cave, hunting for plants and minerals, with very little success. However, we collected a good store of dead juniper boughs for fuel during the night, which I placed near the fire to dry, not caring to be choked with the smoke of wet wood. Soon after our return to the cave the guides came in with the provisions. Night at last brought the day to an end, and we prepared for bed. This time we had to vary our proceedings, for the earth was too wet to lie upon; we therefore placed smooth stones upon the floor and sat or reclined upon them. In consequence of this, we were more uncomfortable than on the previous night; we were crowded closer together; our legs, which all pointed to the fire, frequently getting into a hopeless tangle. I woke up once so stiffened with the pressure of my stony seat that for some time I could not identify my own legs. However all things come to an end, and so did this night; morning dawned again; not indeed exactly 'smiling morn,' but still giving us some hopes; so about four we bid adieu to the 'Hotel du Mont Pelvoux', which we agreed had but one recommendation, that of having no bill to pay when we left it." After all, the mists gathered again, and we did not reach the summit.

To return, however, to the general question of châlet-life, from which we have rambled in indulging these reminiscences. The first move in taking the cattle to the mountains from the byres in the village, where they have been stall-fed all through the winter, is generally made towards the end of May; and it becomes the occasion of a kind of fête. The *senner* (cowherds) are drest in their best clothes, with nosegays in their hats; the household goods, conspicuous among which is the great cheese-caldron, are heaped upon a mule or pack-horse; the cows are carefully groomed, all their coats are sleek and shining, large bells are suspended by embroidered collars round the necks of the three finest in the herd, and a procession is formed, the progress of which is thus spiritedly described by Berlepsch[1]:

"A concourse of people takes place in the villages through which the procession passes, for old and young wish to pass in review Korde-Urche-Bübli's (Conrad Ulrich's) or Franz-Anthony-Lismet-Seppeli's beautiful cows, and examine their shape and *g'schlachtheit* (breed) with the air of connoisseurs. The mountain-peasant has his cows' æsthetics, which distinguishes the finest shades of colour, position of feet and horns, and other peculiarities with close discrimination. Jumping and springing as if they knew that they were going up to the rich nourishing Alpine pastures, the whole herd of cows, goats, lambs, follow in long procession. Roaring and grumbling, in the midst goes the Sultan of the Seraglio, the '*Muni*,' to-day the scape-goat for universal amusement; for it has been the popular custom from of old to bind the milking-stool, adorned with flowers, between his horns. The '*gaumer*' or herd, and the *hand-bub* go with the procession in linen shirts and rough cloth hose, supporting the '*zusenn*' with cries and '*jodels*' (the peculiar mountain-shout). The pack-horse, with the cheese implements brings up the rear, with the possessor of the herd, unmistakably conscious of the triumph that is being celebrated."

[1] *The Alps*, p. 310 (Stephen's translation).

The following interesting extracts from the same book give an excellent account of the different duties of the herdsmen: "In all the moderate sized Alps of Switzerland there are generally three men and a boy; women look after them, as we have already said, only in the Eastern and Austrian Alps[1]; and in some valleys of the Valais. The *Senn* is major-domo, either as himself possessor of the herd, or as appointed by a society; he is commander of the regiment, takes care of the cheese and the magazine, and is at the same time book-keeper of the concern." (The herd is often composed of cows belonging to several owners, among whom the produce is divided at the end of the year in proportion to the number of their animals). "Memorandum-book, day-book, list of current prices, and ledger-books, generally are either united in a calendar of the quarter, interleaved with paper, and stuck behind a flat board nailed to the wall, or some kind of small pocket-book contains the hieroglyphics of the whole management of the business. His help and supporter is the 'Senn-bub, hand-bub, schorr-bub, junger,' or, in the Valais, the 'pató,' who, like the Senn, spends the greatest part of his time in the châlets; he has to clean the vessels (which, in contrast with the ordinary habits of the châlets, are kept perfectly clean, because the goodness of the cheeses, &c. depends upon it), and to help the Senn, but is not always a lad (bub) of fourteen or fifteen, but often a tough fellow of thirty or more. The mediator between valley and mountain, the cheese-mercury and telegraph to home, is the 'Zusenn,' who has to carry down all the productions of the alps, and to bring back wood and victuals. In the Valaisan patois he is generally called 'Lamiciy' (*l'ami*). Where things are well ordered, he has a pack-horse to help him. Finally, the proper herd is the 'Chüener, gaumer, Kühbub,' or 'Rinderer,' or in the

---

[1] I have also often seen women at châlets in the Savoy, Dauphiné, and Viso Alps. T. G. B.

Valais, 'Vigly' (*vigilantia?*). His exclusive duty is to drive out and look after the cows."

According to Tschudi[1] there are four kinds of cattle in the Swiss Alps: (1) The Simmen-thal breed, distinguished for their size and their excellence as milkers. The head is short and sturdy, the colour red or bright black, marked with white; these prevail in the western Oberland and north-west Switzerland. Professor Rutimeyer[2] remarks that this breed does not appear to be indigenous; for it is only found in one or two of the most recent Lake settlements; (2) the Grindelwald breed, varieties of which are met with in most parts of the Oberland and in the Valais; (3) the Entilbuch breed, large, colour usually brown, with a yellowish stripe down the back; (4) the Zug and Schwytz breed, also large and fattening well; (5) the brown cow, small, with short horns and legs, dispersed over most parts of Switzerland, not above named, and of the neighbouring Alps. This breed appears to have been established during a very long time in the country; for its remains have been found extensively in the Lake dwellings. According to Legoyt and Vogt[3], Switzerland possessed a few years ago 919,524 head of cattle; this being at the rate of 36·28 per hundred inhabitants.

The cattle, on arriving at the châlets, graze at will on the pastures: during the night they are generally housed in the neighbouring hovels; but occasionally they are only collected for milking in the evening, and remain out of doors. They are milked twice a day—at about ten in the morning and late in the afternoon. In many places the herdsmen use a droll, but convenient stool, consisting of a wooden circular seat, about eight inches in diameter, supported by a single leg. A broad leather strap is fastened on each side of the seat and then buckled round the milker's loins. Thus he has no need to pick

---

[1] *Les Alpes*, p. 666.
[2] Keller, *Lake Dwellings*, p. 358 (Lee's translation).
[3] *La Suisse*, p. 41.

up his stool. He sits down, and the peg, with his legs, form a tripod; he gets up and walks away, with the peg sticking out behind, and wagging to and fro, **exactly like** a stumpy tail, producing the most ludicrous effect. **Novices, however, when seated in** this way, find overmuch laughter **dangerous, for a momentary loss** of balance is sure to be followed **by a roll on the dirty floor.**

Cheese is made always once and sometimes twice a day. The milk is warmed in the great caldron before the rennet is put in, and then stirred for half-an-hour. The curds, after draining a little, are at once put under the press. The cheeses are turned daily, and salt **is said** to be **rubbed into them with a stiff brush.** There are generally three qualities, the rich (*gras*), the *demi-gras*, and the *maigre*. The first is made of new milk, or new milk with **cream added**; the second of equal parts of new and skim milk; and **the third** with skim milk alone. When the curds have been removed (which **is done by the hands** or by a strainer) **some more** rennet is added to the whey, and from the curds thus obtained a kind of cheese is made, called ***serret*** or *sérac*, which in taste resembles the poorest English cream-cheeses. This **forms** one of the herdsmen's perquisites; it is **sometimes** eaten fresh, sometimes salted for keeping; **the latter being to my taste the more palatable.** The milk, when first cracked, is called *niedl*, *brousse* or *fleurette*, **and is a noted mountain luxury.** It is well however not to yield too freely to its seductions, as it is apt to **cause remorse on the morrow.**

The **most** celebrated cheeses are the **Gruyère, made in** Canton Fribourg, and the Schabzieger **of Canton** Glarus, which is coloured greenish-blue with melilote flowers. **There** are also several other varieties **of local fame. I particularly** remember one, in taste rather **resembling Stilton, which was served to us at Chateau Queyras, in Dauphiné; but the common cheese is poor, like an inferior Gruyère, with a slightly sour taste.**

Due subordination is maintained among **the herds by the**

chief bell-cow, who always heads the string on going to or returning from pasture. Should another attempt to take precedence of her, a battle-royal would begin at once; and when a new cow is introduced to the herd she has to fight for a place among the others, just like a boy at school. If the leader were deprived of her usual bell, she would pine and become ill; this bell, however, is not the one carried on the fête days; for these are too heavy for general wear, and are therefore reserved for such occasions. As much as a hundred or a hundred and fifty francs is sometimes given for the set of three.

One must not forget the *Ranz des vaches* or *Kuhreihen* (cow rows), pastoral tunes, at the sound of which the cows fall into their ranks or rows after the bell-cows to return from the pasture. There are many forms of these airs, according to the different localities; but the general title is associated with Switzerland as much as "God save the Queen" is with England. They are most in use in the northern part of the country which skirts the Oberland, and are properly played upon the long Alpine horn. The general characteristic of these airs is 'a great simplicity, accompanied by a slow and melancholy measure¹'; their effect in producing home-sickness, as it is well known, was so great on the Swiss soldiers formerly in the French service, that it was forbidden to play them. There is an interesting account of these tunes in the *Conservateur Suisse*, with a specimen of one and its accompanying song, in an almost unintelligible patois. It consists of a number of couplets, followed by a chorus, which relate how the cattle bound for the mountains come to a dangerous part of the path; whereupon one of the herdsmen is at once sent back to beg the priest's prayers, which are promised after a little rather comic bargaining. This done, the cattle proceed on their way, and, on arriving at the châlet, yield an abundant supply of milk.

¹ *Conservateur Suisse*, Vol. I. p. 425.

Here is the first couplet and the chorus, as a sample of the patois:

(*Couplet*) Lé zarmailli dei Colombetté
Dé bon matin sé san léha.
(*Chorus*) Ha ah! ha ah!
Liauba! Liauba! por aria!
Vinidé toté,
Bllantz' et nairé,
Rodz' et motailé,
Dzjouven' et otro,
Dézo **on tschâuo**
Io vo z'ario,
Dézo on treinbllo
Io ie treintzo.
Liauba! liauba! **por aria!** (bis)[1].

Above the richer pasturages **devoted to** the cows lie those frequented by the sheep and goats. These can find abundant food among the coarse herbage which **extends up** to the limits of the snow, and springs up here and there over many an acre thickly strewn with fallen rocks; they too can reach ledges and banks unapproachable by larger cattle. There is hardly any spot so lonely but that in summer you will find a few sheep or goats in **possession of it.** If the surrounding precipices prevent them **from straying,** they are often left entirely to themselves for **two or three months;** but usually some unfortunate **lad is condemned to a sort of solitary confinement** with **them;** a hole under a

---

[1] Translation

The herdsmen of Colombettes
At early morn have **risen.**
Ha ah! Ha ah!
Cows! Cows! to milking!
Come ye all,
White and black,
Red and mottled,
Young and others,
Beneath an oak
Where I milk **you,**
Beneath an aspen
Where I drain it, &c.

stone, such as that on the Pelvoux, which I have described, being his sole shelter from the storm, and a shout from some distant hunter or shepherd his only intercourse for days together with his fellow-men. A little dry cheese and drier bread (or polenta) is his food, his clothes hardly hang together, and a few francs at the end of the year are his wages. The flock which he guards is often a joint-stock affair belonging to several villagers not so very much richer than himself. Sometimes the access to one of these Alpine oases is so difficult that the animals have all to be carried singly over a glacier upon men's backs, or be hauled by a rope up a cliff. There is such a place above the western side of the Mer de Glace (Chamouni). Hither when the snows have melted some thirty sheep are carried, and left to spend the summer. When their owners return for them, though two or three are generally missing, having fallen down the rocks, the rest are so fat that the loss is more than compensated. Were it not for their stupidity and pig-headedness, which often prevents them from finding their way back, when they have wandered too far, they could take pretty good care of themselves. The agility of a goat is proverbial, but that of a mountain sheep is scarcely inferior. I remember that one day as we were descending from the Grandes Rousses (Dauphiné), we met a flock on a narrow track along the face of a cliff, which fell down some forty feet or more. It was not absolutely a precipice, but a very steep slope of gneiss rock, which had apparently been smoothed at some former time by glacial action, and it now seemed impossible that either they or we could maintain a footing on it for a moment. The path too was only a few inches wide, so it was distinctly a case of "suppose you come, we go." We advanced, and they for a moment stood still; then, scorning to turn tail, broke and 'skedaddled' down the rock at a run, as easily as if it had been a gentle slope of turf; stopping themselves once or twice by some almost imperceptible crack or knob, and turning round to watch us. Both sheep and goats on the mountains seem to be almost without fear of man, and come running up to the stranger to see what he has got for them. The shepherds, when they visit them, generally bring some salt; thus the sheep run up to all comers, snuffing about them in hopes of getting a pinch of their favourite dainty, and will often follow one for a long way. This amiable tendency is sometimes rather a nuisance; for they have a habit of keeping along a slope, parallel to, and a few yards above the path, and thus not unfrequently detach stones which are apt to be dangerous.

Besides the small native sheep, which are not unlike our Welsh breed, there are also some of the Suabian, Flemish, and Merino breeds, the latter being rare. The most interesting in many respects, and the finest looking, are the Bergamesque sheep, which are annually driven up from the lower valleys and plains of Lombardy to summer in the Engadine. The wool of this breed is soft, abundant, and white; a kind of fringe extends from the chin to the breast; the nose is blunt, the ears droop, and the head is carried high; they are much larger and less lively in their movements than are the common sheep, and utter a deeper sounding bleat. When the snow melts, these sheep come streaming up the various Alpine highways in immense flocks. Their shepherds, men chiefly from the neighbourhood of Brescia, form quite a separate class; generally tall, well-made, and swarthy, often very handsome; they are rather silent and reserved in manners, but have a kind of native dignity that becomes them well. They wear a rough suit of dark woollen stuff, short breeches, hats with high pointed crowns and broad brims, carry a large mantle or sheepskin for a wrapper, and generally shew just one bit of bright colour about their necks. At the head of each company is a chief called the *pastore*, who goes in advance to engage the sheep-walks, keeps the accounts (the flocks, it must be remembered, belong to several owners), and arranges all the business. When a flock is on the march, one shepherd leads it; the others, helped by their large dogs, and accompanied by some stout donkeys, bearing their chattels, bring up the rear. On arriving at the mountains, the flock is separated into four divisions, to each of which is assigned a separate district; these are, the ewes with lambs, the rams and young ewes, the milch ewes and wethers, and the sheep for the slaughter. The mutton of the Bergamesque is inferior in flavour to that of the native sheep; but the wool is valuable, and there are two shearings annually. The milk—though very small in quantity, a ewe, according to Tschudi[1], only yielding five or six table-spoonfuls a day, and troublesome to obtain, since the beast will not stand to be milked, but must be held a prisoner—is esteemed; for, when mixed with three times the quantity of goats' or cows' milk, it makes a cheese, the flavour of which is much admired. Although this breed is most abundant in, it is not confined to, the district above named; but may be seen in many of the valleys which descend towards the north of Italy. The Cottian Alps are supplied largely with sheep from the plains of Piedmont, and great numbers also visit the Dauphiné mountains from Provence; large flocks annually deserting the hot, stony, mirage-covered plains of the Crau, near Arles, for the cool, rich Alpine pastures. They are conducted by their shepherds in much the same way as the Bergamesque sheep; and here too the keeper of the flock walks in front after the Eastern fashion.

Goats, of course, are to be found almost everywhere in the Alps; in Switzerland alone there were, a few years ago, not less than 368,000. They make themselves as much at home as pigs in an Irish cabin, and pervade every place. Far more intelligent, lively, and sociable than the sheep, they would be general favourites with travellers, were it not for their disagreeable odour. The natives, however, do not seem to mind it; and certainly after a time it does become less offensive. The goats

[1] *Les Alpes*, p. 704.

may be separated into three classes: those which are kept up in the villages; those which are daily driven to the mountains; and those which pass the whole summer at the châlets. The last are smaller, but much more lissome and active than the stay-at-homes; their colour is generally ruddy-grey or brownish-black, pure white or black are rare. The horns are often very fine. Tschudi[1] mentions a pair which measured $2\frac{1}{2}$ feet along the curve. I have certainly seen them not less than two feet, the finest examples being in a flock at the head of the Guil valley, near the Viso. Occasionally the goat is four-horned, one pair growing in the usual way, the other more like those of a sheep. Very early in the morning the goatherd, generally a ragged lad, about ten or twelve years old, drives his charges to the mountains, returning at night-fall to the village; and a pretty sight it is to see them trotting along the narrow paths in single file, their bells tinkling pleasantly, and gathering around their stable for milking: snuffing and poking their noses into every corner in their usual restless, inquisitive manner. Many are fed on the rough ground just outside the villages, browsing on the coarse grass, wild flowers, and brushwood which clothe the space between the meadows and the alps. These, in order to prevent their straying into the crops, are either tethered, or more frequently tended by an old man or woman, or by one or two little children, who are not yet strong enough to be employed as regular goat-boys. The she-goat yields a good pint or so of milk in the evening; if drunk while still warm it is nearly free from the musky taste which renders it so unpleasant to many; its medicinal properties are well known, but where there is no demand on it for this purpose it is chiefly used for cheeses, in which the flavour is unmistakable. The flesh is frequently eaten, but, apart from the inevitable smack, is in every way inferior to mutton; it however figures to the profit of the innkeeper on the table

[1] *Les Alpes*, p. 684.

of the 'regular tourist' hotels, under the name of chamois; and therefore finds a pretty ready sale.

The only other domestic animal that calls for any remark is the St Bernard dog. These magnificent animals, as large as a full-sized mastiff, are generally classed along with the spaniels, but the origin of the breed is uncertain. Some think them sprung from a cross between a Spanish pointer and an English mastiff; others from one between a Danish dog and a Bergamesque sheep-dog. As the name implies, they are especially connected with the celebrated monastery in the Pennine Alps, but they may also be seen at some of the other hospices on the summits of the Alpine passes: in these however the breed generally has not been kept quite pure. About a dozen years ago there was great danger that the pure blood would be altogether lost, owing to a murrain which reduced the stock to a single pair. I believe, however, that they have since considerably multiplied. In stormy winter weather these dogs accompany the servants of the company—called Marroniers—and one or more of the monks along the road leading from the last châlets to the convent. The dogs, guided by their scent, track with wonderful skill the unfortunate travellers who have wandered from the way, and have even been known to discover them when overwhelmed in the snow-drifts. This done, their barking soon draws the men to the spot, whose timely aid often recalls the benumbed sleeper to life. One of the most famous of these dogs, called Barry, whose skin is now in the museum at Berne, is said to have once discovered a child asleep in the cold, to have succeeded in waking him, and at last induced him to mount upon its neck, whereupon it bore him off in triumph to the convent. Be this anecdote true or not, there is no doubt that the sagacity and courage of these noble animals have from time to time saved many lives.

CHAPTER X.

In the first chapter the main Alpine ranges were spoken of as constituting a number of closely connected groups rather than a single chain. In fact, nature, by way of facilitating communication, has breached in several places the great fortress-wall with which she has girdled Italy. These gaps are commonly about 6000 feet above the sea; the lowest of all, which lead out of the basin of the Po, being the Col des Echelles de Planpinet (5873 feet). This pass indeed is lower than any other over the main chains, except the Reschen-scheideck and the Brenner, which unite the basin of the Adige with that of the Inn. A carriage-road has not as yet been carried over it; perhaps because a small portion of the descent on the Italian side is rather precipitous and the route is a little less direct than that by the Mont Genèvre. This last is the southernmost carriage-road leading over the Alps from Italy to France, unless we include the Col di Tenda. It was in use in the Roman times, and is said to have been crossed by Julius Cæsar; but the present carriage-road was only commenced in 1802, and was completed in 1807. From one side of the tolerably level plain forming the summit (6102 feet) the Dora Riparia starts in its course towards the Adriatic; from the other the Durance to the Mediterranean. The approach from Piedmont, and the descent towards the fortresses of Briançon, by which France protects herself from Italy, are picturesque, but on the whole the Mont Genèvre is not a very interesting pass. On arriving in the valley of the Durance the traveller, bound for Central France, finds the *massif* of the Dauphiné Alps interposed between him and his destination. Fortunately this barrier can be readily crossed at the narrow and comparatively low isthmus which unites it to the main Alpine chain. Accordingly a carriage-road starts from Briançon, and before long commences the ascent to the Col du Lautaret (6740 feet); whence it descends through the magnificent glacier scenery of La Grave and the grand gorges of the Combe de Malaval and the Combe de Gavet to the fortresses of Grenoble. This road was commenced by the first Napoleon; but was not quite completed till 1861. Its importance to France is obvious; for in case of war with Italy it would greatly facilitate the concentration of troops from both the central and southern provinces at the foot of the Genèvre.

The next pass, going northward, is the Mont Cenis (about 6772 feet), which, starting like the Genèvre from Susa, leads into the valley of the Arc, a tributary of the Isère. The carriage-road was constructed by orders of Napoleon I. in 1803-10; and during the year 1867 rails were laid down upon a part of the road-way, so that it is now crossed by trains, the locomotives being constructed after a pattern invented by Mr Fell. As regards scenery, it is one of the least interesting among the Alpine passes.

In connexion with this pass may be noticed the 'tunnel under the Mont Cenis,' as it is popularly, but incorrectly named. In reality, its northern opening is fifteen miles below the spot where the zigzags begin, by which the slopes of the Mont Cenis Pass are scaled; and its southern opening is in a valley, which does not join the one followed by the carriage-road till it reaches the town of Susa. Of course the usual mode of excavating at several points along the line of work by a series of vertical shafts was, in this case, absolutely impossible; and the galleries have to be driven straight on from each end till they meet in the heart of the mountain. The northern opening is near Modane, at the height of 3904 feet above the sea level; the southern near Bardonnèche[1], at 4344 feet. Between these points the tunnel rises from the former end by a gradient of 2 in 91, to a height of 4377 feet above the sea, whence it descends again by gradient of 1 in 2000; its total length being 13,031 yards, nearly $7\frac{1}{2}$ miles. The main purpose of this peculiar form is to facilitate drainage and ventilation. The tunnel, which is lined throughout with masonry, is in section very nearly a semicircle; the greatest width, a short distance from the ground, being nearly $26\frac{1}{4}$ feet, and the height about 25 feet. Beneath the roadway an arched culvert is constructed for drainage; and the upper part of the curve will be cut off with a brattice, to form a ventilating shaft.

Had the mines for blasting the rock been made by hand in the usual way, the tunnel would have taken at least thirty-six years; but some very ingenious machines have been constructed, by which the work is performed much more quickly. The principle of these is simple, though the apparatus could not be explained without elaborate drawings. Immense condensing engines outside the tunnel, worked by water-power (of which there is of course no lack), drive compressed air into a long tube, which is connected with the drills placed against the rock at the end of the excavation; these are worked—just as by steam —by the elastic force of the confined air, which, when liberated, ventilates the tunnel, and by creating a draught removes the powder-smoke. The drills are fitted with a number of 'jumpers' or chisels, which revolve as they strike; and these, by

---

[1] The design is due to the late M. Medail, a native of this place.

means of adjustments, can be applied to any place on the face of the rock. When I visited the works in 1863, they had advanced 1244 yards from the northern and 1640 yards from the southern entrance. The following extract[1] describes the condition of the works at that time.

"We come to the end of the vaulting, and before long find the water nearly ankle deep in every part; we make our way as best we can, now clinging to the rocky side of the tunnel, as we step from knob to knob; now balancing ourselves on a rail, or climbing over an empty train of ballast-waggons,—long low cradles, like magnified horse-troughs,—gathering dirt plentifully on hands and clothes; and now and then slipping with a splash into the muddy pools. The excavation contracts, the air becomes closer and ladened with the fumes of gunpowder, lights gleam fitfully ahead through the fog, and a hissing and a tapping are more and more distinctly heard. Soon we pass a strong door, the shield to protect the workmen and the machine from the explosion of the mines; figures are seen moving through the smoke, the rocky roof of the vault seems almost to touch our heads, and we reach the drill, a long carriage all wheels and bars; with the attendant sprites crouched beside and below, more like dusky gnomes than human beings. Crawling cautiously by the side, we peer forward and catch a sight of the chisels pertinaciously stabbing the hard, black slate, streaked here and there with white veins of quartz. The heat and noise do not tempt us to prolong our stay, and we are not sorry to struggle back to a purer atmosphere." At that time the daily advance was about a yard at each end; since then further improvements have been made in the machinery, and it is hoped that the tunnel will be ready for use in 1871.

The carriage-road leading from the Val d'Aoste over the Little St Bernard (7123 feet) into the Isère valley is still not quite finished, Italy apparently being in no hurry to complete

[1] From a paper by the Author in *Once a Week*, Oct. 1, 1864.

her part of the work, now that her good friend and ally is on the other side of the crest. **Many think that** this was the scene of Hannibal's celebrated **passage, but the** topographical difficulties cannot in my opinion be reconciled with Polybius' **account; and** the Little Mont Cenis, a pass corresponding in part with **the one just** mentioned, appears to have much stronger claims. **The scenery of** the Little St Bernard is pleasing, **and on the whole rather** superior to the Mont Cenis.

Further to the north, the **Pennine Alps oppose a barrier** which has not as **yet** been surmounted by **a carriage-road**; and it is not until we come to their eastern **extremity that** a convenient depression is found. **Over this,** 6628 feet above the sea,—a pass frequented from very early times,—the great highway of the Simplon **was planned by Napoleon I.** who, after his troublesome **passage of the Great St** Bernard, and narrow escape **from** being wholly foiled **by the** resistance at Fort Bard in the gorge of the Val d'Aoste, **had no** wish to run so great a risk a second time. The works were commenced in 1802, **and** completed in about **five years.** The engineering difficulties on both sides were considerable: there are 613 bridges between Sesto Calende, at the south end of the Lago Maggiore, and Brieg, where the bed of the Rhone valley **is reached**; but although the torrents and avalanche paths **on the northern slopes have necessitated** some very long détours and more **than one extensive gallery, the greatest difficulties were** found in the narrow **gorge through** which **the road ascends from** the Val d'Ossola. Here **a mountain** torrent rushes between vast walls of compact gneiss, seamed with waterfalls, which leap from the towering peaks above. Sometimes the slope of the rock is sufficiently gentle to allow the road to run for a while along **a kind of excavated terrace**; then some projecting crag interposes, **descending sheer for hundreds of** feet, through which a **gallery has had to be driven.** The grandeur of this gorge, the **views** of the glaciers of the Fletschhorn, the wonderful contrast of these with the smiling slopes of the Val d'Ossola, within so short a distance, and the fine prospect of the Bernese mountains from the Swiss side, make this pass deservedly celebrated.

The next in order, proceeding eastward, over the main chain is the St Gothard. This pass appears to have been known from very early times, but the carriage-road over it was not completed till 1832. It is the most direct communication between the lakes of Lucerne and Maggiore, and consequently between many parts of Central Europe and Milan. The gorge of the Reuss, in which is the well-known Devil's Bridge, on the Swiss side, and the Val Leventina on the Italian, offer some fine scenery, but the actual passage of the mountains is rather dull and dreary. This remark indeed applies to nearly all the Alpine highways; because their upper part generally lies over an upland plateau surrounded by higher mountains, so as to form a kind of trough or channel, the sides of which exclude all view of the grander peaks and glaciers, while its elevation above the sea, generally from 6000 to 7000,—at once too high for the pine woods and too low for perpetual snow,—brings us to the region of coarse grass and stunted scrub. No doubt among these there are often many beautiful flowering plants; but the passing traveller who cannot search for them, finds this part of the Alps, unless it wear its winter dress of snow, the least pleasing of his whole journey.

The parallel passes of the Bernardino (6769 feet) and Splügen (6945 feet) lead from Italy into the valley of the Rhine, a little above Coire; the one from the head of the Lago Maggiore by the Val Misocco, the other from the Lago di Como by the Val di S. Giacomo. The grand feature of these two roads is the wonderful gorge of the Via Mala, which is on the part common to both, below the village of Splügen. Here the torrent of the Hinter-Rhein forces its way through a narrow and deep gorge, high up on the sides of which the road is carried along the face of awful precipices, passing through several tunnels, and crossing and recrossing by lofty bridges, from three to four hundred feet above the water. At one of these, called the Verlornes-loch, the gorge is so narrow that the torrent beneath is almost hidden. On the whole I think this, though several run it hard, the grandest ravine in the Alps. The Bernardino was known to the Romans, who avoided by a circuitous route most of the Via Mala; and the present carriage-road was commenced by the Swiss in 1819 to facilitate commerce with Piedmont. The Austrians, fearing that it would interfere with the advantages which they derived from the much frequented path over the Splügen, endeavoured by threats and bribery to prevent its being carried out. They prevailed with the authorities of Canton Tessin, but were deservedly snubbed by those of the Grisons, and at last were obliged to make the whole of the Splügen route at their own expense. The difficulties on the southern side of this, especially in the avalanche-swept gorge of the Cardinel, were very great.

Besides the Splügen, two other great roads, the Maloya and the Stelvio, take their departure from near the head of the Lago di Como; the former, one of the easiest and most ancient in the Alps, branches off from the Splügen route at Chiavenna, and after crossing the watershed between the Mera and the Inn, at a height of about 5942 feet, descends very gradually into the latter valley. The most remarkable feature on it is the long trough, leading by a very gradual and slight descent from the summit of the pass to St Moritz, in which are situated the lakes of Sils and Silvaplana. The former of these, some three miles long by one wide, is the largest in the Alps which lies so high (5887 feet) above the sea. They obviously once formed a sheet of water more than nine miles long. The Stelvio ascends the valley of the Adda, the principal affluent of the Lago di Como; as, however, it descends into a valley, the waters of which also flow to the Adriatic, I pass it by for the present.

The Inn it will be remembered drains into the Danube;

hence in this part of the Alps is the junction-point of three great watersheds, those separating the affluents of the Adriatic, the North, and the Black Sea[1]. The passes over two of these, between the first and second and the first and third, have already been described: it remains to mention those between the second and third. These are two in number, the Julier and the Albula, both starting from Coire in the Rhein-thal, and descending into different parts of the Inn valley. Owing to the somewhat confused arrangement of the valleys in this district, it has been found most convenient to strike the upper part of one of the affluents of the Rhine, by crossing a low range immediately to the south of Coire. The level of this stream, the Oberhalbstein-Rhein, is reached at Tiefenkasten, where the roads divide; the Julier following a direction a little east of south, while the Albula turns off much more towards the east. Opinions differ as to the relative merits of the two passes, but though leading through a good deal of interesting scenery, they are both inferior in beauty and grandeur to several of those which have been already mentioned. The Julier, though 7503 feet above the sea, is an unusually easy and safe pass at all seasons, being very free from avalanches, and the snow melting early. On this account it has been used from very ancient times. The Romans carried a military road from Chiavenna to Coire over the Maloya and Julier in preference to the more direct route by the Septimer; and on the summit of the latter are two rough-hewn stone columns, to which some assign a Roman, others a Celtic origin. The present carriage-road was

[1] The Julier, Maloya, and Septimer Passes (the last a very ancient horse-track well known to the Romans) form a triangle uniting the heads of the valleys draining into the North Sea, Black Sea, and Adriatic. The little mountain mass therein included is therefore a knot-point in the water system of Europe. One of its peaks, the Pizzo Lunghino (9121 feet) supplies water to three seas. Only one other mountain in the Alps does the same; this is the Pizzo Pesciora, south of the Upper Rhone Valley, which gives birth to streams running respectively to the North Sea, Mediterranean, and Adriatic.

constructed in 1823; that over the Albula pass was only completed about two years ago.

The Bernina Pass (7658 feet), one of the highest and also one of the most beautiful among the Alpine roads, leads from the head of the Inn valley to that of the Adda. The former stream is left at Samaden, and the road ascends gently up a lateral glen to Pontresina, whence is a fine view of the glaciers at the head of the Val Roseg. About three miles beyond, it zigzags up a steep slope commanding magnificent views of the Piz Bernina, the culminating point of the chain, and its attendant peaks, from which the Mortaratsch glacier descends to within three or four hundred yards of the road. Beyond this is the usual rather barren upland scenery until the bleak tarns near the summit of the pass are reached, when the Cambrena and Palü glaciers come well into view. The descent is at first rapid; before long, signs of a more genial climate appear; and the road passes through scenery at once rich and grand till the Val Telline is reached at Tirano on the Stelvio route.

Three more passes remain, connecting great water systems; these are the Reschen-scheideck, the Toblach-plateau, and the Brenner. The first and second of these lead over comparatively level plateaux, destitute of the ordinary features of a mountain pass; the one from the valley of the Inn to the Vintschgau, the other from the head of the Puster-thal to that of the Drave. They are in fact little more than interruptions in the bed of a trough, owing their origin to some cause quite independent of those which have produced the general configuration of the district. The third pass, the Brenner, crosses at the lowest point of a deep and strongly-marked depression in the Noric chain, its summit being only 4700 feet above the sea. In scenery it is the least interesting among the Alpine roads; from where it quits the Puster-thal to where it gains sight of the broad meadows by the Inn, there is only one striking view, that of the Stubayer Ferner, from near Sterzing. The rest of the road, though it would be considered fine in Wales or Cumberland, is surpassed by almost every other part of the main Alpine chains. Still, the causes which have made it poor in scenery have made it rich in historical associations. The lowest depression in the whole Alpine girdle of Italy, it has been from the most remote antiquity the great highway of nations, the natural portal between the north and the south. Through it the Roman legions marched to plant their eagles in Germany. Through it, when the days of retribution came, the barbarian hordes poured down upon the Italian plains: in quick succession swept on Allemanni and Goths, Attila with his Huns, Odoacer with his Heruli, Theodoric with his Ostrogoths. Following them, army after army, too many to enumerate, passed and repassed in the varying contests of the Middle Ages. It became again memorable in the desperate struggles of the war of Independence, when the Tyrolese peasantry, undisciplined but undaunted and unerring marksmen, made Sterzing, Mittewald, and Mount Isel, ill-omened names to the armies of France and Bavaria.

This pass is also remarkable as being the first over which a distinct railway has been carried. On the 15th August, 1867, the line from Innsbruck to Botzen was formally opened: the last link of the iron chain which unites the peninsulas of Jutland and Italy. Though the engineering difficulties have of course been very considerable, there has been no *tour de force* necessary, like that of the so-called Cenis tunnel, so that it is needless to give a detailed description of the works.

Among the high-roads over the lateral ranges there are, besides the Col du Lautaret already mentioned, the Furka and the Oberalp Joch. The former of these runs close to the magnificent glacier of the Rhone, and after crossing a ridge (7992 feet above the sea), commanding a splendid view of the Finster Aarhorn and some of the neighbouring snowy peaks of the Oberland, descends into the head of the Reuss valley at the foot of the ascent to the St Gothard Pass. The latter, the

Oberalp Joch (6732 feet), **mounts from this point of junction**, and after crossing a rather **dreary Alpine** plateau, descends into the head of the Vorder-Rhein-thal. Well-known bridle-paths for centuries, they have **only** been converted **into** carriage-roads during the last few years; and **if ever a war** should again arise in Europe, resembling the great contest at the end of last century, they may be found to possess considerable military value; since they connect by roads, passable by artillery, the valleys **of** the Upper Rhine and Rhone, **and** link each of these, **through** the glen **of** the Reuss, with the Lake of Lucerne **and Northern Switzerland**. Armies **can** now march, parallel **to the main chain**, through the whole mountain barrier between **Austria** and France.

We come next **to the Stelvio, the most wonderful among the** Alpine highways, and **the most** elevated carriage-road in Europe. Essentially a military road, it was constructed by the Austrian government to establish a direct communication between Milan, the capital of their (former) Lombard possessions, and the heart of the empire. On first entering the mountains, it is carried along the eastern margin of the Lake of Como, whose precipitous shores were often the cause of great trouble and expense; then up the broad and malarious Val Telline to Tirano, where now it is joined by **the** Bernina route **already described.** Hence **the Stelvio road continues to mount the valley of the** Adda, through **scenery which rapidly becomes wilder, until it** reaches Bormio, where **the great ascent may be said to commence**. A little above this place, near the well-known hot springs, the Adda, formed by the confluence of two torrents, rushes forth from a deep ravine, the precipices of which seem to forbid all access to the mountain solitudes beyond. High on the left **bank of this, and** up the easternmost of these torrents, **runs the road, burrowing here and** there through projecting **crags. Presently the valley opens** out a little, but **the cliffs** still rise, high, **brown, and bare on either hand,** varied here and there with dreary slopes of débris. Long galleries protect the road from the rush of avalanches or swollen torrents. A rocky wall, down which the main torrent leaps from step to step, now breaks the level of the valley. Up this, called the Spondalunga, the road climbs painfully by long zigzags till it gains an upland grassy basin surrounded by stony slopes. Here is a pause in the toilsome ascent, and an almost level reach leads to a large mass of buildings,—inn, custom-house, and barrack, standing on a hummocky plateau, which is surrounded by low rocky ridges, capped in many places with glittering sheets of snow. Being 8153 feet above the sea, it is the highest permanently inhabited house in Europe. Walk a few hundred yards to the north, and you look down upon the green slopes of the Munster-thal, which stretches away from beneath your feet towards the uppermost parts of the Vintschgau. This opening is the Wormserjoch, once a route of considerable commercial importance, and the course which Austria naturally would have preferred for her road. Unfortunately for her, a small portion of the upper Munster-thal belongs to the Grisons; and the sturdy Swiss absolutely refused either to sell this corner of their territory or to concede a right of way over it, so that their imperial neighbour, after vain negotiations, was forced to turn aside towards the less promising gap which leads into the Trafoi-thal.

Towards this the road slowly ascends, over an undulating plateau, a barren tract of scattered stones and patches of snow, with smooth slopes of imperfectly formed glacier on the right, and a rocky ridge on the left. Before long the road, which has for a while been hugging the latter, bears rapidly round it to the left, and a mass of snowy peaks rises suddenly in front. A few hasty steps, and you stand, by the opening of an avalanche gallery, above a slope falling almost precipitously down to a deep glen, across which—some four miles away—rises the Orteler-Spitze, a mighty roof of snow and ice, curving up to a glittering point full twelve hundred yards above you, and crowning a craggy wall of dark limestone-rock. **Deep** buried in the gorge beneath this wall are seen the upper slopes of a glacier, round the head of which a peaked ice-covered ridge circles round till it slopes down to your very feet. No Alpine road, perhaps **no track of** equal elevation, commands a view at once so startling and so magnificent, the effect of which is vastly enhanced **by** approaching it as **above described.** Then comes **the most** astounding part of the road itself. One steep unbroken stony slope forms the northern side of the glen which descends from the summit of the pass towards the pine-woods of Trafoi, already visible far below; down this, in zigzag after zigzag, the road descends; protected in many places by galleries from the avalanches, which must at certain seasons sweep the slope from top to bottom. **Two** thousand feet lower down is **a small alp,** occupied by the ruined post station **of** Franzenhöhe, which causes a short break in the almost incessant zigzags; **but these** soon recommence, and lead down through scrub and pine-wood, till the bed of the valley is approached; when a more gradual descent through a forest of magnificent pines brings us to the green meadows around the village of Trafoi.

Between this and the summit, a distance of about 4100 feet in vertical height, there are no less than forty-eight **zigzags.** Still, startling as the descent appears to **the traveller, as he** winds down these, **or hurries from angle to angle down the** slope itself, I think **the audacity of the undertaking can only** be fully appreciated by gaining some point high up on the opposite side of the valley, and by a single glance comprehending every twist **of the** road from Trafoi to the Col. As I stood one evening at **the** door of a châlet **on the** sides of the Orteler, and saw the pass with its avalanche-gallery standing **out above** that enormous slope, **cold and grey in** the fading light, I marvelled **more** than ever **at the** daring genius which had projected and executed the design of making that deso-

18

late and apparently almost inaccessible gap a highway for carriages[1].

One road only remains which can fairly be reckoned among the Alpine Passes; that which, turning off from the plateau in the Puster-thal near the watershed between the Adige and the Danube, ascends gently through the magnificent limestone scenery of the Hollenstein-thal; and then, after crossing a scarcely marked col, surrounded on all sides by great precipices, descends by two or three zigzags into the trough of the Ampezzo valley, and follows the stream of the Piave to the Venetian plains. The pass, considering the general height of the surrounding mountains, is a low one (about 5064 feet), and the construction of the road does not appear to have presented many of the usual difficulties; but it is remarkable as leading through the very heart of the Dolomite district. Generally the line of a carriage-road is about the worst that can be chosen by anyone wishing to gain a good idea of the physical features of a mountain region; here, on the contrary, almost all the grandest and most characteristic peaks rise on either side of the road and are well seen from it.

There are several other roads in the sub-alpine regions, which pass through very beautiful scenery; but those above described are all that have as yet been constructed in the strictly mountain districts. Others will no doubt from time to time be completed; some have already been a good while contemplated; among which are a carriage-road to connect the valley of the Rhone and the Val d'Aoste by the Col de Menouve, and a railway over the Luckmanier Pass to link the Rhine region to Northern Italy.

[1] Now that Austria has lost her Lombard dominions, the Stelvio has ceased to be of value to her, and to repay the great cost of keeping it up. She therefore takes no pains to repair the road on the eastern side of the pass, and several parts of it are already much injured; in fact when I crossed it in 1867, one or two places looked rather unsafe for carriages. It is to be hoped that she will not suffer this great triumph of engineering skill to fall wholly into ruins.

Perhaps here may best be mentioned the hospices or religious houses which have been established, many of them from very early times, near the summit of frequented passes, for the succour of travellers belated or overtaken by storms. The most celebrated of these is that on the Great St Bernard, a pass which has formed the highroad between Western Switzerland and North Italy from the most remote antiquity; for we know that the Celtic Veragri worshipped their mountain god Pen at a spot near its summit, where afterwards was erected the shrine of Jupiter Penninus. A hospice appears to have been built near this at a very early period, but the present foundation dates from the year A.D. 962, when it was established by the pious care of Bernard de Menthon, Archdeacon of Aosta, the Apostle of the Alps. The convent is a huge quadrangular building of rough stone, without any architectural features, with a smaller and more irregular appendage on the opposite side of the road. To the north rises the snowy ridge of the Vélan; a few yards from the convent on the south is a half-frozen tarn; around are bleak, bare, snow-streaked rocks. When the mists are driving over these, and the dark water, troubled by the wind, laps against the boulders, it is indeed a dreary scene. On the hill-side behind the convent is a small cell, wherein are placed, exposed to the air, the bodies of those who have sunk down to die upon the road and have never been claimed by their friends. The keen wind dries them up, and the flesh, shrivelled and withered like shrunken leather, is a more ghastly spectacle than any skeleton.

The convent is mainly supported by voluntary contributions; and the brethren who inhabit it are of the Augustinian order. Although the opening of other passes has somewhat diverted the stream of travellers that once flowed across this one, there is still work for them and their trusty dogs, and nearly twenty thousand persons annually come to the convent; many of whom would perish in stormy weather were it not for its shelter and relief. Whatever opinions we may hold upon the merits of convents in general, and I for one am no friend to them, we must all agree in reverencing the self-denial and Christian charity of these men; for the severity of the climate and the other necessary privations of the life are such, that every one who becomes an inmate of the St Bernard Hospice knows that he is dooming himself to a premature death or a crippled and painful old age.

Besides the roads constructed for carriages and generally traversed by regular services of lumbering diligences[1], a sort of amalgamation of coach, omnibus and waggon, there are hundreds, perhaps thousands of by-ways, some of which are just passable by rough country carts, others only bridle-paths.

(Fig. 13.) Swiss Carts, &c.

These traverse the Alps in every direction, except where snow-fields and glaciers interpose, or the rocks are unusually precipitous. Their altitude of course varies considerably, but as a rule the crest of a great chain—one in which the peaks rise much over eight thousand feet above the sea—rarely sinks below six thousand feet; and very few horse-paths

---

[1] In the winter months sledges are used upon the upper parts of most of those that remain open.

will be found to surpass nine thousand. Foot-tracks, which do not involve the passage of large snow-fields or glaciers, or anything that may be called scrambling, will be found in many places up to a thousand feet higher; but beyond this the mountain chains can rarely be crossed by the ordinary pedestrian. Hence in many cases the only direct communication between places, but a few miles apart on the map, is over trackless glaciers and rocky ridges. Not many years since, these barriers were supposed to be generally impassable; now there are comparatively few notches remaining in them which have not been crossed. Some of these expeditions involve little more than several hours of rather laborious walking. Of such a kind is the Col de St Théodule in the Pennine Alps (10,899 feet), which, though the track lies for two or three hours over a vast snow-field, is sometimes crossed by cattle; others are exceedingly difficult, and can only be undertaken by practised mountaineers with skilled guides. In order to give some idea of the general character of these, I will extract from my note-book an account of a two-days' journey in the Pennine Alps, over passes which, without being particularly dangerous, presented most of the usual difficulties.

"A glance at a good map of Switzerland will shew that the Rhone valley and the highest part of the Pennine chain from the St Bernard to the Matterhorn are almost parallel, and that several valleys run from the former nearly at right angles to it, becoming shorter as they approach the east. Around the granitic mass that has upheaved Monte Rosa, the mountains extend in different directions, thrusting forward three large chains towards the Rhone valley, between which the two branches of the Visp-thal are squeezed. Zermatt is in the western of these, and consequently the heads of some of the smaller valleys mentioned above can be reached from it. The nearest is called the Val d'Anniviers, and this we determined to visit. Just beyond Zermatt, the valley, on arriving at the foot of the Matterhorn, breaks into two ravines running right and left; in the former is the Zmutt glacier, in the latter the Gorner[1]. Therefore the chain of mountains on the right-hand side of the valley turns abruptly round, and runs (towards the Dent Blanche) at right angles to its former course; enclosed within the angle thus formed is the Glacier de Zinal and the head of the Val d'Anniviers. There are then two routes from Zermatt to Zinal, one on either side of the Gabelhorn, a mountain forming the apex of the angle; we determined to go by one and return next day by the other. Enough for topography—now for our journey. We had with us our trusty attendant, Michel Croz, of Chamouni, and had engaged a local guide, Johann Kronig, and we determined to start as soon after four as possible. Good intentions, however, in the matter of early rising are sometimes hard to carry into effect; especially when you have been up between two and three the previous morning; so from one cause or another we did not get off till 5·30 A.M. The sun had long lit up the obelisk of the Matterhorn and had even begun to creep down by the dark crags of the Hörnli into the valley before we started; so when once off we lost no time, and hastening through the meadows, fresh with dew and gay with the lilac flowers of the autumn crocus, crossed the torrent and entered the pine-forest on the left side of the Zmutt valley.

"Let no visitor to Zermatt forget this walk. Here he may saunter along at his ease, shaded by the dark arollas, and peer over now and then into the ravine at his feet, glancing down the crags half-hid with feathery ferns and rhododendron bushes, red with flowers, till he sees the torrent tumbling among the green blocks of serpentine two hundred feet below. Or, if he like it better, he can lie on the mossy turf, and watch the nutcrackers at work on the pine-cones, or admire the peak of the Matterhorn towering above him, and the glaciers and pinnacles around the Dent Blanche. We, however, have no time for this

---

[1] Described in Chapter III.

now, '*vorwärts*' is the word, and Kronig's caution of '*langsam, langsam,*' as he perspires after us is little heeded. We emerge from the wood, and are in the pastures just above the Zmutt glacier. Our work is before us; just across the valley, from a point of the range between the Dent Blanche and the Gabelhorn, comes a steep crevassed glacier, called the Höchwang, above which lies our pass.

"We run down to the Zmutt glacier, and are soon upon the extremity of the great ice-stream. Fancy a river a mile or so wide, frozen hard, ploughed up here and there with crevasses, and then covered with stones of every size from a cricket-ball to a cottage. Macadamisation on a small scale is all very well on a road, but I disapprove of it when carried to an excess on a glacier. You go slowly,—it becomes intolerably tedious, and the opposite bank will not get any nearer,—you try to go faster by jumping from stone to stone; you leap on one, it slips; on another, it totters; on a third, it rolls over; you twist your feet and ankles; till at last you lose your footing and your temper together, and come down ignominiously on all fours, 'barking' your shins in the process.

"However, we get across in about half-an-hour, and toil up the steep bank on the other side. A long pull now begins up turf slopes varied by patches of rock; uncommonly hot work, but we comfort ourselves with the thought that we are rapidly rising in the world. In about three-quarters-of-an-hour we begin to be conscious that we breakfasted more than four hours since; so we sit down and make what would be a *déjeûner à la fourchette*, if only we had any forks. We lose no time about this, but press on; now the lower part of the Höchwang glacier is well beneath us, but it is too much crevassed to tempt us on it. We climb rocks steeper than before, or scramble clattering up banks of loose stones, till we reach a few patches of snow, and see that we are above the ice-fall and just under the edge of the snow-field which feeds it. Here we rest a few minutes and feast our eyes on the glorious view before us ;—far below us lies the Zmutt glacier, the dazzling whiteness of its upper fields in strong contrast with the foulness of its lower end, a sad parable of many a life. To the extreme right are the Col d'Hérens, the Tête Blanche, and the Col de la Valpelline. Opposite, across the Zmutt-glacier, rises the tremendous tower of the Matterhorn, a steep white slope of snow leading from the right-hand side to a small glacier, that girdles the mountain with an outwork of icy crags, from which now and then an avalanche is fired like a warning gun. The Matterhorn from this point of view loses its spire-like shape, and appears as a corner-tower, terminating a long line of ruined wall. Beyond this is the wide field of glacier stretching to the Théodule pass, above which rises the head of the Petit Cervin and the snow-cap of the Breithorn; next are the Twins, vested in robes of purest snow; beyond, the ridge of the Lyskamm; then the broken masses of the Lys glacier, among which we had been wandering the day before[1]; and rising above it, the rock-tipped petals of Monte Rosa. This is the place for seeing the Queen of the Alps in her true beauty; the subordinate ridges of the Gorner and Höchthaligrat are reduced to their proper position as mere buttresses of the chain, and her coronet of peaks is better seen from here than from the usual points of view. Next comes the hump of the Cima di Jazi, the cone of the Strahlhorn, the jagged wedge of the Rympfischhorn, the little peak of the Allaleinhorn, and then the flat top of the Alphubel closes the view on the extreme left.

"We stand for some time unable to tear ourselves away from the scene, tracing out the paths of many pleasant excursions and planning new expeditions. Time, however, is passing, so we turn to the snow; a few minutes' scrambling and we look on a wide basin of névé. The Dent Blanche rears its unpromising triangular head to the left and the cliffs of the Gabelhorn are on the right; in the ridge connecting them are two distinct

[1] See Chapter III.

depressions, apparently a few hundred yards apart. We desire to try the one to the left, being evidently the lower; Kronig asserts that the one to the right is that usually passed, so we follow him. We plunge through the soft snow, toil up the slopes, and at 11.50 are on the Col Durand (11,398 feet). Here we rest on a little patch of rock (chloritic slate), which protrudes through the snow, and luxuriate for a while.

"The view behind us is much less extensive than it was from below, but we look down now on to the basin of the Zinal glacier and along the Val d'Anniviers, till in the purple distance our view is closed by a snow mountain on the other side of the Rhone valley. Rested, we commence our descent,—at first we run merrily down a snow slope, this however gets rapidly steeper, and we go more cautiously; suddenly there is a cry of 'halt,' and we find it a case of 'no road this way.' A few steps below us the slope terminates abruptly, and a cliff of ice, at least sixty feet high, cuts us off from the glacier below. We glance to the right, the precipice rises higher there, so we turn to the left; we walk cautiously for a hundred yards or so along the edge, looking out for a means of escape; and at last discover a promising spot, where the cliff is not quite vertical, and a steep bank of snow, like a buttress, joins it to the glacier below. Croz sets to work and hews steps out of the ice; we follow. The position is unpleasant, for the cliff is so nearly vertical that we grasp at its icy wall with our hands, in order to secure our footing; the snow slope beneath looks steep and hard, and below it a lot of crevasses grin open-mouthed at us. Step by step we advance very cautiously, and now only about half-a-dozen notches remain to be cut, when 'crack, whirr,' and off flies the head of Croz's ice-axe, and scuds down the snow slope towards the crevasses. We all look rather blank as he holds up the broken handle, but fortunately are not defenceless. We are both armed with good stout alpenstocks, not the flimsy things that the unwary tourist is deluded into buying at the

Rigi or Chamouni, but stout poles, of English ash, with a four-inch spike of tempered steel at the end, the heaviest of which is handed to our guide,—he pecks out a few steps, yet more diminutive than before, and after a minute or two we are safe on the glacier. Fortunately the broken head of the ice-axe has escaped the crevasses, and is soon recovered.

"We hasten on, making for a snow-capped patch of rock in the middle of the glacier, sinking deep in the soft snow, and sometimes grumbling at it more than a little, for floundering above the knees in loose snow under a hot sun does try the temper. In course of time, however, it becomes thinner, and the hard ice appears; we hurry down the glacier, get on to the pastures, and after an hour's walk reach Zinal about 5 P.M. While coming down the glacier we saw that we should have descended more easily had we taken the lower gap."

We had expected to find only a châlet at Zinal, but were ushered into a newly-built little inn with two rooms. Everything was scrupulously clean, and an excellent dinner was served up to us, with capital muscat wine from near Stalden in the Visp-thal.

We started at 3.45 A.M. next morning, and, after retracing our steps till we got some distance on the glacier, turned sharp to the left, and took to that bank to avoid an ice-fall; we then struck across the tributary glacier that descends from between the Rothhorn and Gabelhorn. "Before us is a steep jagged wall of rocks, perhaps a thousand feet high, in which is a deep cleft, looking as if some Paladin of old had hewn it out with two blows of a magic axe. This is the Trift-Joch.

"The sky was lowering, so we press on quickly, and before long reach the steep snow slopes that form the glaçis of the wall; up these we go as fast as we can. '*Il faut dépêcher,*' says Croz, and there is no need to impress the warning on us, for the slopes and the glacier below are spotted with stones of every size. We are within range of the cliffs of the Rothhorn, and if it fires a volley while we are on the slope, skill and courage may avail but little. We reach the foot of the wall, and as we grasp the rough crags breathe more freely, for we are out of range now. The next hour-and-a-half is spent in contemplating the boots of the man in front, and trying into how many contortions it is possible to twist the human frame. Here we make spread-eagles of ourselves; there we wriggle up a chimney; here crawl under a projecting ledge; there climb on all fours up a smooth sloping bit of rock; now we require a friendly shove in the rear; now a haul from an alpenstock in front. At last we come to the top of a steep couloir of snow, terminating in free space two or three hundred feet below, which has to be crossed; this however causes no difficulty, as some thoughtful guide has fastened a chain to the rocks on each side, and so saved his successors from the trouble of using a rope. A few more scrambling steps upwards, we turn a corner, and look down towards Zermatt.

"The view is not so extensive as from our pass of yesterday, but is very fine, and includes the Mischabel range. The clouds, however, are gathering; and though the most difficult part of our work is done, we see that we must not waste time if we wish to return unwetted to Zermatt. The Col (11,614 feet) is a mere notch in the rocks, you can almost sit across it; and the cliffs by which we have ascended from the Zinal glacier look awfully steep from where we stand. The rock is a very pretty green-grey gneiss with pale pink lumps of felspar.

"A steep slope of snow connects us with the Trift glacier; down this we descend cautiously for a time, till at last we see that we may venture on a *glissade*. Some rocks jutting out of the snow threaten to break the continuity of our slide, so we make a flank movement to get beyond them; the snow is hard, and I expect every moment to commence my voyage 'promiscuously.' I object strongly to this; sliding along, sprawling on the back or face, is, to say the least, undignified, and may be detrimental; so I place my feet together, put the rudder on hard with my alpenstock against the snow, and sweep round the corner in first-rate style. This done we unite our forces again, and trudge over the glacier, till we come to a very large crevasse with one side rather higher than the other. Croz jumps at it, forgetful of the old proverb 'Look before you leap;' he alights upon the snow, which breaks under him, and he is engulfed up to his middle. In an instant he throws himself forwards, and supports himself on the edge of the crevasse; in another moment he springs up again and is in safety. It was a narrow escape; had he jumped a few inches shorter and gone down, we could not have helped him, for he was carrying the rope. He knocks the treacherous snow away with his pole to shew where the ice is strong, and a good spring puts us by his side. Some more tramping through the snow, succeeded by another *glissade* or two, lands us on the lower part of the glacier; a short walk over it brings us to a place where we quit it for the pastures, and after racing down these we arrive at Zermatt just in time to escape a tremendous thunder-storm."

CHAPTER XI.

THE Alpine regions, like most other mountainous countries, have their fair share of legends. The wild huntsman's yell is still heard in many places by the shuddering peasant as his phantom-train sweeps by the châlet. There is also the wild goatherd, a wicked lad who crucified an old he-goat and drove his flock to worship it: lightning consumed him, and now he wanders for ever over the Alps, miserably wailing. When the glacier of Gétroz burst, the arch-fiend himself was seen swimming down the Rhone, with a drawn sword in one hand and a golden ball in the other; when opposite to Martigny he halted, and at his bidding the waters rose and swept away part of the town[1]. A vast multitude of imps was seen about the same time on a mountain in the Val de Bagnes by two mendicant friars from Sion, who hearing of this unlawful assembly, had gone out as detectives to learn what mischief was hatching. Many places also have their spectral animals; the Valais, according to Tschudi, being the head-quarters of these legends. There are also pygmies to be seen in the lonely mountains like the

[1] *Quarterly Review*, Vol. XXII. p. 362.

Norwegian Trolls; and Brownies who make or mar in the house, according as the goodwife is neat or a slattern. Of the Stierenbach (on the Surenen Pass) a wonderful story is told by Scheuchzer[1], setting forth how an impious shepherd baptized one of his sheep, whereupon it was changed into a horrible spectre which proceeded to devastate all the neighbouring pastures. The unhappy owner sought counsel of a wise man, who told them to feed a calf for nine years on milk; during the first year from one cow; during the next from two, and so on. This done, the animal was to be led to the haunted alp by a virgin, and there left. This being duly effected, a terrible battle ensued, in which the spectre was vanquished; but the victor died from quenching its thirst too freely in the waters of the Stierenbach.

Nor among the traditional marvels of the Alps must dragons be forgotten. In former days the dark woods and pathless gorges of Switzerland, at least, appear to have been favourite haunts of these monsters; and happily the old Zurich Doctor of Medicine, John James Scheuchzer, to whom we have already referred, has preserved ample records of them in his four quarto tomes, which were published at Leyden, under the patronage of our Royal Society, in the year 1723. More than this the effigies of several of these monsters are done after the life; wherein we see one dragon, serpent-like, with a head half human, half feline, contemplative and sardonic in aspect; another, four-footed, bearing, except for a nodding crest, a considerable likeness to the restorations of the iguanodon; a third, with feeble rudimentary legs, ill able to support its long snake-like body; a fourth, footless, but winged and fire-breathing, (this, I am able to state, on the authority of a fresco upon a church at Surava (Grisons), is the species slain by St George); a fifth, a yet more grisly monster, with a sketchy head and a number of rudimentary suckers in the place of its right fore-leg; a sixth, two-legged, with forked tongue, confronting a terrified peasant, and

[1] *Itinera Alpina.* Vol. I. p. 13.

standing up on his coiled tail in an attitude that 'means wenom,' as unmistakably as a rattle-snake, when it makes itself like 'a corkscrew with the handle off a sittin' on its bottom ring.'

Besides these are three or four portraits of other dragons, each with their specific characteristics; and last and best of all is a quadrupedal dragon, with cocked-up tail and arched neck, supporting a catlike head, which is advancing on its hind legs, smiling pleasantly, to salute a terror-stricken traveller. In several pages, interspersed with quotations from classic and other authors, Scheuchzer tells us how one John Tinner, armed with a sling and aided by his brother Thomas, did slay on the Frumsenberg the first-named monster; and how the fourth dragon was seen in the year 1649 to fly by night from Mount Pilatus across the clear sky. Lucerne, Berne, and Glarus also contribute their tales of wonder; and from the Grisons comes a story authenticated by the Reverend Petrus de Juvaltis, pastor of Stul, near Bergün, in a letter written Oct. 29, 1702, telling how one Bartholomeo Allegro of Ponte, near Plurs, did by the aid of sling and stone slay a certain hairy, four-clawed, and fork-tailed dragon, about two ells long, which he discovered at the bottom of a pit, near the summit of a high hill, being brought to bay and rendered courageous through desperation, after having vainly endeavoured to escape from the monster by running away. On returning to the spot three days after, he found the carcase already putrid and black with flies. More marvellous than all perhaps is the story connected with dragon number five; which tells how a certain Vietor, a cooper of Lucerne, while out woodcutting in a forest, lost his way; and being benighted, fell into a deep pit; the bottom of which was fortunately covered with soft mud, so that though sorely frighted and much besmirched, he sustained no present damage from the tumble. Still he was in an evil plight, for the walls of his prison were too steep to be scaled. Upon examining them he discovered sundry fissures in the rock, into which entering in search of shelter, he found himself to his horror face to face with a pair of dragons. In answer to his earnest prayers to heaven, these grisly beasts were not suffered to hurt him, but in this fearful companionship he passed six whole months, from Nov. 6th to April 10th, nourished only by a certain brackish liquid which exuded from the rocks, to which, following the example of the dragons, he applied his tongue. On the last-named day the dragons issued forth from the cave, and one of them flew up to the world above to seek a more generous diet; before the other could follow it Vietor grasped its tail, and was thus borne up from the pit and landed on the ground above. Thence he contrived to find his way home, and in order to record his escape had the portraits of the dragons and of himself embroidered on a chasuble, which he presented to the church of St Leodegarius, in Lucerne. Two months afterwards he died from the effects of his prison diet, the subterranean 'skilly' having ruined his digestive organs. Scheuchzer says, with a touch of the critical spirit, which now and then crops up drolly, while he is discussing the truth of these stories, "I have seen the two dragons, but not Vietor himself, and have made a drawing of one of them. But, if I may be allowed to express an opinion, the chasuble or planeta, at Lucerne, appears to be Chinese embroidery, and the figure of the dragon, that which is on the flags of that nation, especially those belonging to the Emperor." The date of this remarkable captivity, he goes on to say, has unfortunately been lost; but it is supposed to have happened in the year 1420[1].

But there is yet, according to Scheuchzer, a further confutation for the sceptical: the Museum of Lucerne possesses among

---

[1] *It. Alp.* III. p. 387. The story of a dragon, killed about A.D. 1250 by a certain Struth von Winkelried, may be found in the *Conservateur Suisse*, Vol. VI. p. 440, and there is another story bearing upon the same subject in Vol. IV. p. 414. A monument in Klagenfurt (Carinthia) records the death of a dragon which in the middle ages infested that neighbourhood. *Dolomite Mountains*, p. 337.

its treasures a genuine **dragon-stone**. This marvel is divided into three zones of **colour, the** two outside being brownish-black, like clotted blood, **the inner one** yellowish-white, with 'wonderful spots.' It can heal the **plague, if applied to the** boil, as well as diarrhœa, dysentery, **and other** malignant defluxions; and a long list of attested cures is given, shewing **that its discoverer must have** been no less a benefactor to **his species** than Dr Morrison or Professor **Holloway.** The history **too of** its invention is recorded; *videlicet*, the affidavit of **an honest** fellow, one Rodolph Stempflin, who, on the Monday after **St** Martin's Day, 1509, did depose that he had heard **from his** parents, how his grandfather, **when** a mowing in **a certain** meadow, beheld **a** dragon wing **its way past** him from **Mont** Pilatus, at which awful **sight** he fell terror-stricken upon his face. Reviving after **a while,** he beheld near him **a** clot of excreted blood, in the **midst of which lay the aforesaid stone**[1]!

Many Alpine stories have reference **to the sudden** destruction of pastures **by** the fall **of** rocks **or ice.** Hear, for example, the legend of the Clariden Alps. Once **upon a** time these were fertile pastures, on which dwelt a 'senn.' **He** grew rich, so that none could match him in wealth; but at the same time **he grew proud** and haughty, and spurned both the laws of nature **and** the commandments of God. He was so foolishly **fond of his** mistress, **that he paved the path from the** chalet **to the byre with** cheeses, **lest she should soil her feet;** and **cared so little** for **his mother that, when she lay at his door** fainting **with** hunger, he offered **her** only milk to drink **in** which he had thrown the foulest refuse. Righteously indignant, she turned away, calling upon heaven to punish such **an insult. Before** she reached her home, the rocks **and ice had** descended, **crushing beneath** them her **wicked son, his mistress, and** possessions. A very similar legend is told of the Blumlis Alp, where the proud **'senn'** built himself a staircase of cheeses, **and** insulted

---

[1] See also *Conservateur Suisse*, Vol. XIII. p. 290.

the parents of a damsel whom he had wronged. A fearful storm arose during the night, and in the morning the glaciers had overwhelmed the whole alp.

In the neighbourhood of Monte Rosa there is a tradition that a valley exists in the heart of that mountain, the entrance to which has been sealed up by impassable glaciers, though the floor of the 'cirque' within is still a rich pasturage. I heard of it in the Val Macugnaga, where they point out a spring, which bursts from the ground, as the outlet of the torrent by which it is watered. Once, said they, a *chasseur* found the bed of this stream dry, and creeping up its subterranean channel, arrived on the floor of the valley. It was a huntsman's paradise; chamois were there in plenty, bears also, and even bouquetins wandering over the richest pastures. He retraced his steps to announce the good news; but when he returned again, the waters had resumed their course, and the place has ever since remained inaccessible. De Saussure[1] mentions the existence of the same tradition at Gressoney in the Val de Lys, where the valley is said to have belonged to Canton Valais, and goes by the name of the Hohenlaub. Six years before his visit, that is in 1783, seven youths from Gressoney, after a toilsome journey, had gained on the second day a ridge from which they looked down on a fertile but deserted valley, surrounded by steep precipices, which they at once assumed to be the long-sought spot. On a second occasion they endeavoured to descend into it, but without success. De Saussure examined into the story, and found that there was reason to doubt their assertion that the valley was uninhabited. He conjectures that they may have seen some part of the Val Anzasca; Mr King[2] thinks that it was probably the head of the Visp-thal, a situation which agrees better with the description.

Of what may be called the historical legends, there is that of Mont Pilatus, near the summit of which is a tarn, in whose

---

[1] *Voyages*, § 2156. [2] *Italian Valleys of the Alps*, p. 437.

waters Pontius Pilate is said to have committed suicide. His unquiet spirit continues to haunt its shores, and is supposed to be infuriated by any intrusion upon their solitudes, manifesting his wrath by storms. So firmly was this believed in the fourteenth century, that severe penalties were inflicted on any one who set foot on the mountain, and the neighbouring herdsmen were bound by an oath not to guide any stranger thither. Even in the sixteenth century permission had to be obtained from the head of the police of Lucerne, before any one could undertake the expedition. The celebrated stone, which had such power over the heart of Charlemagne, and ultimately led to the foundation of Aix-la-Chapelle, was given to him at Zurich by a serpent, as a thank-offering for his destroying a huge toad that had robbed its nest. At St Maurice the soldiers of the Theban legion are said to have been martyred by the Emperor Maximinian. The giant St Martin, as has been already mentioned, is the hero of various legends, which commemorate his prowess and his conflicts with the Evil One; and the pretty story of Heiligenblut in Carinthia must not be forgotten. Thus it runs: a Dane, named Briccius, had so won the favour of the Emperor Leo at Constantinople, that on his returning home to preach Christianity to his own people, he bore away as a parting present a few drops from the store of the Holy Blood preserved in the church of Sta Sophia. On his way towards the Noric Alps, he was overtaken near Heiligenblut by a *tourmente,* and perished. Before long three ears of corn were seen growing out of the snow, on the spot where his body was concealed. This led to its discovery; the villagers placed it in a cart drawn by oxen; these, on reaching the spot where the church now stands, suddenly refused to go further; so the grave was dug there. In a little while the foot of the corpse was seen projecting from the earth; and on being examined, a small bottle containing a little dark fluid was found concealed in a bandage. This was taken away, and when enquiries were made, the value of the treasure was known, and the sanctity of the spot established. The reader must form his own opinion as to the genuineness of the relic, but the main outlines of the story of Briccius may be true.

A belief in witchcraft probably still lingers in many parts of the Alps. Ladoucette, in his history of the Hautes Alps, gives several instances of it. Among others, he says that the exhalations visible during the summer nights in the cemeteries of Puy St Pierre and Briançon are taken for vampires or ghosts, and the dancing lights, which we call jack-o'lanterns, are supposed to be magicians on their way to a 'sabbath.' One of the strangest outbursts of superstition or epidemic insanity, which has been known in modern times, took place some ten years ago at Morzine, a little village among the Savoy Alps. It lies, a few hours' walk south of the Lake of Geneva, up the valley of the Dranse, about 3000 feet above the sea, in a pastoral district, among bold scenery well worth a visit. This region was in former days the head-quarters of sorcerers, but for a century and a half things had gone smoothly. However, in the spring of 1857 a girl, previously known for her unusual intelligence and religious earnestness, was seized with a kind of cataleptic fit. The attacks recurred, and presently a young companion began to suffer in the same way. The symptoms then altered, and the children appeared to hold communion with invisible beings; after this they became convulsed, screamed, blasphemed, and predicted events, which in due course came to pass. Other children then became possessed, and in eight months' time twenty-eight persons, some of them adults, were under the influence of this strange epidemic. Many persons also, who were not attacked to so great an extent, appear to have suffered from hallucinations and unusual mental excitement, so manifestly exaggerated are many of the stories which describe the actions of those affected. Pilgrimages and exorcisms were tried with small avail, and the Sardinian government was at this time too busy with its own concerns to look after the matter. The country then passed into the hands of France; and when, in April, 1861, Dr Coustans, inspector-general of lunatics, visited Morzine, he found a hundred and twenty cases of persons possessed; their insensibility to pain and apparent invulnerability, as recorded by him, are something marvellous; and, though various means were tried, his success in mitigating the violence of the symptoms was only temporary. In 1864 the disease broke out more terribly than ever, and the scene in church at a confirmation held by the Bishop of Annecy is described as follows by an eye-witness: "The church became a perfect hell. Nothing was heard but cries, blows, oaths, and blasphemies...the victims of the disease, about a hundred in number, seemed to fall into simultaneous convulsions without any previous warning... the greater number were young girls and women from fifteen to thirty years old." The government now determined to try stronger measures. A troop of sixty soldiers was sent there; all the sick were removed, and distributed among distant hospitals; and thus the disease appears to have been successfully 'stamped out'[1].

A few of the peculiar local customs may be cited as examples of many; whether they all still exist, I am unable to say, but the authors in which they are mentioned are all of the present century. In Dauphiné, if a maiden wishes to signify to a swain that his visits are welcome, she sprinkles his soup thick with rasped cheese; if the contrary, she slips a handful of oats into his pocket. Should he still persevere, she turns the dead ends

---

[1] These details are taken from an interesting article in the *Cornhill Magazine*, Vol. XI. p. 468. The French government appears to have rather hushed up the matter. When I passed through Morzine in 1864, I was quite unaware of the existence of the malady, and supposed that the soldiers were there looking after some frontier questions. The disease was probably one of the varied forms of hysteria; and I well remember, many years ago, seeing a very similar case in England. The patient then was a youth of about 17, and several of the symptoms exactly resembled those of the Morzine 'demoniacs.'

of the firebrands towards him. In many parts of Switzerland and the Tyrol, courtship is carried on at night (*kiltgang*); the maiden receiving her lover in her chamber, into which he makes his way by the window; often sitting there till the small hours. If he be a stranger, the lads of the village often resist his attempts; sometimes they endeavour to carry off the bride and demand a ransom for her, so that not unfrequently sharp faction-fights break out. The wedding is generally a day of high festival; each place has its local usages, but shouting, feasting, and firing guns and pistols are pretty universal characteristics.

There are also some curious customs belonging to funerals. At La Grave (Dauphiné) the ground is too hard frozen in winter to allow of a grave being dug; so the corpse is slung up in the barn till the spring returns. In other places the funeral ends with a revel; and at Argentière (in the same province) tables were set in the cemetery; that at which the priest and relatives were seated being placed above the grave. After dinner the next of kin proposed the toast *à la santé du pauvre mort* (the health of the poor departed). The churchyards of Canton Zug are noted for the gilt and ornamented crosses erected instead of head-stones; and in several Cantons the practice prevails of exhuming the skeletons after a certain number of years, and placing them in an ossuary; the skulls being ranged apart on shelves, and ticketed with the names of their former owners. In Roman Catholic districts road-side crosses and crucifixes are of course frequent; but the general fashion of these varies considerably. In Piedmont the cross is generally without the figure, though it bears the various instruments of the Passion. In the Vintschgau the figure is commonly life-size and painted in colours; the wounds, streaming with blood, being depicted with an attention to detail that is simply disgusting; often also the knees, in order to enhance the effect, are represented as raw and bleeding. Sometimes the effigies of the Virgin Mother and the Beloved Disciple are placed on either side. In the Puster-thal the figures are much smaller; and by the side of the Ampezzo road they are not more than about a quarter life-size. A sort of roof resting on the head and arms of the cross protects the Christ from the weather.

The favourite amusements, especially in Switzerland and the Tyrol, are shooting and wrestling matches. The former are the great attractions on sundays and fête days, scarce a village of any size being without its rifle-ground: the practice is generally good, but the ranges are, as a rule, much shorter than those in England. The latter amusements, called *schwing-feste*, though less frequent, are very popular; those of the Hasli-thal are especially noted. Skittles and bowls, any part of the street, however rough, serving for the alley or green, are among the commonest diversions; and in the Italian Tyrol, *pallone*,—a game played with a leathern ball about the size of an English foot-ball, struck with the hand instead of the foot. Drunkenness is comparatively rare (Canton Vaud has the worst reputation for this evil), and an Alpine *fête* is in many ways a pleasanter sight to witness than an English fair. I am never so much ashamed of my own country as when I contrast these two scenes. Whence it comes, it is hard to say; but there is very commonly something of the gentleman about the mountaineer. He may be ignorant—though he can generally read and write a little,—he may be rather sharp at a bargain, he may be grossly superstitious and piggishly dirty, but for all that you find yourself instinctively treating him as if he were your equal. A genuine 'senn' has something of the sheikh about him. I have often had of the herdsman's best—not much it is true, but still his best, and found that payment had to be almost forced upon him, nay sometimes was absolutely refused. The traveller who goes prepared to be pleased and expecting to be treated with kindness, will rarely be disappointed; that is in the unfrequented districts; where many tourists come, especially English or American, the people are spoiled, and then the proverb, 'Worst is a spoilt best,' certainly holds. Nothing can be more disgusting than the systematized mendicity and chicanery of Chamouni and the Oberland. I am glad to see that in several parts of Switzerland the people are becoming fully sensible of what is already a national disgrace.

To return, however; the great vintage festival of Vevay, called the Abbaye des Vignerons, should not be unmentioned. It is held once in four years; the principal feature being a masked procession in which are represented the various personages, mythical and historical, connected with agriculture and the cultivation of the vine. Bacchus and Silenus, with Fauns, Satyrs, and Bacchantes; Vulcan and his Cyclops, Ceres, Noah and his children, the spies with the cluster of Eshcol, and the like. Nor must one forget the celebrated Mystery Play performed once in ten years at Ammergau in the Bavarian Highlands, whereat all the scenes of the Passion are acted;—almost the only relic of a practice once common in Christendom, though the memory of it still lingers amongst us, in Punch's puppets, and the Morris Dancers. There existed a few years ago, in a remote corner of the French Alps, a custom which went back even to pagan times. The village of Anderieux (in Val Godemar) is so enclosed by steep mountains that for one hundred days in the year the sun cannot shine there. On the 12th February, the day of its return, the head of each family prepares an omelette, which, at ten in the morning, he takes to the village 'place.' When they are assembled, a deputation summons the oldest man, entitled the 'venerable', to direct the fête, and on his arrival all dance round him omelette in hand. This done, headed by him and accompanied by rustic music, they go in procession to the village-bridge, on the parapet of which the omelettes are placed. A dance in a neighbouring meadow occupies them till the hour when the sun's rays begin to glitter above the mountain crest. The 'venerable,' bareheaded, then elevates each omelette towards the light, and when the whole orb is visible, the procession is formed again; and all return to their homes to pass the rest of the day in feasting, the omelette being one of the dishes.

Our sketch would be incomplete without a few brief notes on the antiquities of the Alps. The testimony of etymology, archæology, and history informs us that at a very early period they were inhabited by tribes of Celtic origin. I am not indeed aware that traces of this people have been observed among the mountain districts so frequently as in many parts of our own hill countries; perhaps in those days they found room enough in the fertile sub-alpine regions, and but rarely sought the fastnesses near to the cold wastes of snow and ice; though on the borders of the former, as Professor Keller has told me, earthworks are found resembling those common in Britain—obviously cities of refuge against marauding bands. There is, however, on the summit of the Little St Bernard Pass, a circle (about twenty yards in diameter) of unhewn stones some four feet long by two wide, and near it a rude column which also is generally supposed to be earlier than the Roman epoch. There are, besides, two columns on the Julier Pass, and one or two megaliths in other parts of Switzerland. But the most remarkable discoveries concerning the Pre-Roman, and indeed Pre-Historic, population of the Alps have been made in some of the Lakes, which, although occurring almost entirely in localities distinctly beyond the mountain region, as in Neuchâtel and Bienne, Zurich and Constance, the western extremity of Geneva, and the southern parts of the Italian Lakes, must not be wholly passed over without mention. In the shallows of these, and in certain other sheets of water (some of which are now morasses), remains have been discovered during the last fourteen years[1] which shew that the former inhabitants of their shores dwelt in villages, the log-huts of which were built on platforms of beams, which

---

[1] The first discovery—at any rate the first that was really used—was at Ober Meilen on the Lake of Zurich in the winter of 1854.

were raised above the water and supported by posts driven into the muddy bed of the lake. The immense number of remains which have been dredged up from beneath the water and dug up in peat moors enables us to form a tolerably clear idea of the habits of this bygone race. Its earliest members were ignorant of the use of metal; their weapons, tools, and ornaments, were all of stone, wood, horn, or bone. These, however, were often finished with much skill, the stone axes being carefully smoothed or polished. After which they were fitted into sockets of horn, and inserted into a wooden club; as is still the fashion with many savage nations. The not unfrequent use of flint and perhaps of nephrite, and the occurrence of amber and coral, shew a certain amount of commerce with other countries. They made cordage for nets, and wove tissues for covering; their pottery, of a very coarse paste, was rude in form, and ornamented only with a few knobs or hatched lines. After a while—how long we cannot say—bronze became known; some have thought it was introduced by an invading race, but the idea does not meet with general favour. Spear-heads, knives, daggers, swords, hair-pins, armlets, and many other bronze articles, useful and ornamental, often very skilfully wrought, became common, the pottery finer and more highly-finished; the settlements too were larger and built further from the shore; in a word, with the knowledge of metallurgy civilisation evidently increased. For some reason, which we cannot discover, the use of metal does not appear to have obtained so extensively in the pile-buildings of Eastern Switzerland as in those of Western. Most of the settlements appear to have been abandoned before the use of iron became general; still there is reason to think that some were inhabited up to and perhaps after the Roman invasion[1]. It is interesting to observe that during the 'stone

[1] There is no reason to suppose that the inhabitants of the pile-buildings were a different race to those who occupied the mainland and the hill forts, or that the two modes of life did not go on simultaneously.

period' the urus, bison, *bos longifrons*, elk, and bouquetin still inhabited Switzerland; and that the pile-folk possessed flocks and herds, the remains of sheep and goats, of three breeds of oxen and two of pigs, having been discovered. They also cultivated wheat, rye, and flax, living not only by hunting and fishing, but also by the produce of their fields and cattle. The remains of wild animals used as food preponderate in the earlier settlements of the stone age over those of the domestic animals, but the proportions undergo a change in the bronze age; during which the two great wild oxen disappear, and the domestic races come upon the scene[1]. Researches into the archæology of Switzerland are being carried on with great activity, and the next few years will probably largely increase our knowledge of the races who appear to have occupied so large a part of Europe in the ages when Troy was still standing, and Rome had not begun to struggle into existence as a petty Italian state.

In mountain countries, where the roads are bad and money is scarce, many examples of elaborate architecture cannot be expected; still here and there, in some remote village, one comes upon a fine old church or ruined castle; and more than one town, situated in the large valleys which extend into the heart of the Alpine chain, is rich in remains both Roman and mediæval. Dauphiné has not preserved many relics of the former epoch, the only one of any importance that I have seen being an arch by an ancient road high up on the pastures of Mont de Lans, above the ravine of the Combe de Malaval; but many of its village churches are of considerable interest. These generally follow one rather peculiar type, and may, I think, be referred to about the latter half of the twelfth century. The

---

[1] Keller, *Lake Dwellings*, p. 346 (Lee's Translation). The subject has also been treated by Troyon, *Habitations Lacustres*; Desor, *Les Palafittes du Lac de Neuchâtel*; Lubbock, *Prehistoric Times*, and several others. Collections may be seen at Zurich, Lausanne, Bâle, Neuchâtel, &c.

body of the church, with a square east-end, has often been much modernised; but the steeple is usually in its original state. The tower, rather high and slender, is divided into several stories, each lighted with round-headed windows, and resembles generally those so common in Lombardy: from it rises a rather short octagonal spire, occasionally crocketed, perhaps too, in some cases of later date, with dwarf pinnacles at the corners. These are peculiar: they may be defined as triangular pyramids, three of the sides of which are right-angled triangles (nearly isosceles), placed so that an edge is in the same line with one of the edges of the tower. In eastern Dauphiné an Italian influence is sometimes distinctly visible in the heavy porches supported by slender columns; as for example at Guilestre and Ville de Val Louise.

The great fortresses which defend the Alpine Passes in this country also claim a passing notice, as being more picturesque than is usual with buildings adapted to modern warfare; such are Chateau Queyras, Mont Dauphin, and Briançon. There is not much good ecclesiastical work of a later date than early in the thirteenth century; indeed this remark, so far as my experience goes, applies not only to Dauphiné, but also to the whole of the Alps, the best churches being Romanesque or at latest Transition. All the fine 'Pointed' churches that I remember to have seen are in the sub-alpine districts. In most of the larger mountain valleys, in all parts, ruined castles are tolerably abundant. I was especially struck with the number of them in the Tyrol, particularly in the Vintschgau; few, however, of them are extensive, or can be called more than picturesque. Roman remains are not numerous in the Swiss Alps; but two towers[1] and some fragments at Coire are of this age. The cathedral of this town, which stands within the Roman *castrum*, is most interesting. The crypt, and four figures stand-

---

[1] Still called Marsoël and Spinoël, said to be from 'Mars in oculis' and 'spina in oculis' respectively, names signifying their effect upon the natives.

ing on griffins, now placed at the western gate, are very early, probably about the ninth century, when the first cathedral was built. The greater part of the present building is Romanesque, rich but rather stiff, perhaps early twelfth century; but a strong classic influence is perceptible in it, some of the ornamentation being almost pure Roman, and one or two bits even reminding me of Byzantine work. Within are some fragments of stone, carved with the interlacing knotwork so common on British crosses; these have here unusual interest, when we remember that the cathedral is dedicated to Lucius, a British saint. It is quite a museum of shrines, monstrances, and other ornaments. The modern ecclesiastical architecture in the Swiss Alps is generally very poor, the churches being mostly ugly copies of the worst Italian Renaissance. The towers are often crowned with a bulbous cupola, which is frequently, especially in the western and central districts, covered with polished tin plates. In the Tyrol the tower commonly terminates in four gables, whence rises an attenuated wooden octagonal spire, usually painted dull red. With the exception perhaps of Sion, whose castle-crowned hills are more picturesque at a distance than from near, and St Maurice, where there is a fine abbey church, Coire is almost the only town in the Swiss Alps of architectural interest. Lovers of this study must confine themselves to the sub-alpine region, to Lausanne, Lucerne, Berne, and Zurich; and to those delightfully quaint old towns which lie on or near the Rhine from Bâle to Constance.

South of the Alps traces of the Roman domination become more frequent. The Val d'Aoste is unusually rich in remains of this people. There is a fragment of an aqueduct in the Val Tournanche, a bridge in the Val de Cogne, and in the principal town, Aosta, which in its plan and name still preserves a record of its origin (Augusta prætoria), there is a gateway and a triumphal arch, a bridge, portions of a theatre (?)

and an amphitheatre, a considerable part of the city walls, and several minor relics, which entitle it to rank very high among the Roman provincial towns. The church of St Ours, built, in great part with Roman materials, in the twelfth century, is also well worth a visit, the steeple and cloister being particularly fine. Some of the village churches in the hill-country about the Italian lakes are said to be interesting, as incorporating pagan or very early Christian buildings, but I have not seen any of them. The campaniles, however, in the Lombard and adjoining Piedmontese Alps, cannot fail to attract the notice of every traveller. In many districts nearly every village has its grey old tower, which adds much to the picturesqueness of the view, although the rudeness of the architectural details perhaps a little disappoints on a closer examination. The custom of supporting the street front of the houses on an arched portico through which the footway is carried, of constructing loggias or corridors on each floor with open arches, like a cloister, the general use of whitewash and colour, and of red pantiles for roofing, make the little mountain towns on this side of the Alps far more pleasing to the artist than those on the northern slopes. Some of the streets also in the Central Tyrol towns are rendered very picturesque by the frequent use of small bay-windows extending up the whole house front.

The fondness for colour which is characteristic of South European races, shews itself on the Italian slopes, sometimes offensively in imitated architectural ornament or statuary on blank walls, sometimes pleasingly in the greater delicacy and beauty of the frescoes so common on every church and wayside shrine. In several places, especially in the neighbourhood of the Val Sesia, these exhibit considerable artistic power. This region indeed has been the seat of a small school of painters, chief of whom is the celebrated Gaudenzio Ferrari[1], whose name

---

[1] Born at Valduggia in the Lower Val Sesia, A.D. 1484. A good account of him and his works will be found in King's *Italian Valleys of the Alps*, Ch. xx.

reminds us of the Monte Sacro at Varallo, in the adornment of which he aided considerably. This singular place is situated on a conical hill some 300 **feet above the town, and** is supposed to **represent Jerusalem and the various events of the** Saviour's **Passion.** These are portrayed by groups of terra-cotta figures about life size, clothed and coloured, which are arranged **in** small chapels **open** on one side to the air, the walls **being** adorned **with frescoes.** This singular conception is **due to** Bernardino Caimo, a Milanese, who visited Palestine to **obtain** drawings of the Holy Places; it was commenced A.D. **1491, and** the various chapels and their contents were constructed **during** the following century. The resemblance of this New Jerusalem to the Old is at best very superficial; **and in spite** of the occasional excellence of both the frescoes and the statues, the place has rather a **peep-show aspect; but** the quaintness of the design and the beautiful views over **the valley make it** well worth a visit. **There are two or three other Holy** Mountains among the lower slopes of the Italian **Alps;** the most important being the Monte Sacro at Orta, **where scenes** from the life of S. Francesco d'Assisi are depicted; and in all the Roman Catholic **districts it** is very common to see a convent church on the summit **of a** hill with a *via sacra* leading up to it, along which **are** little **'station'** chapels or shrines, each with its commemorative picture.

It would **be of course impossible in a work of this size to** attempt anything **like a detailed account of the nations inhabiting the various districts of the Alps, or** of the historical events of which they have been the scene. Still the following brief notes may be of some use **and** interest, as recalling **a few of the** more important **of these events, and** giving in a connected **form those which have already been** glanced at in the preceding pages.

Most **interesting, among those connected with the French** and Italian **Alps, are the struggles of the Vaudois or Waldenses** for liberty of conscience. The tributary valleys of the Upper Durance, especially the Val Freissinières, the Val Louise, and the glens of the Guil appear to have been the head quarters of these sufferers on the western side of the Alps. The earliest persecution of them on record is between 1238 and 1243, after which date there are frequent entries on the roll of martyrs. On the 22nd May, 1393, two hundred and thirty victims are said to have been burnt alive at Embrun[1]; the brutal outrage in the Val Louise has already been described[2]. In the latter part of the sixteenth century the Waldenses, under the guidance of Lesdiguières, took up arms in their own defence, captured Embrun, Guilestre, and Chateau Queyras; and after some hard fighting, in which, exasperated at previous cruelties, they were unfortunately guilty of taking severe vengeance on their enemies, they succeeded in establishing themselves in comparative peace. This lasted until the revocation of the edict of Nantes, when many of them were obliged to take refuge in Piedmont, and those that remained gathered themselves in secret places among the mountains for the worship of God. Descendants of these sufferers, whose piety, courage, and adventures remind us much of the better sort of English Puritans and Scotch Covenanters, still are to be found in parts of the above valleys, and the name of the saintly Felix Neff, of Dormillouse, a dreary hamlet in the Val Freissinières, will not soon be forgotten.

The Vaudois of Piedmont chiefly inhabited the valleys which are drained by the Pellice and its affluents; the settlements in the upper part of the Val di Po being unable to resist the attacks of their enemies. The persecutions first recorded took place early in the fourteenth century, when the Vaudois in the Val Angrogna appear to have successfully resisted by force of arms the encroachments of their enemies. Conflicts again took place in the same valley and in the Val di Pragelas

---

[1] *The Israel of the Alps*, p. 15.
[2] Page 101.

in the year 1487, under Alberto Cataneo, whose troops were defeated with great loss; one of their leaders being shot down on the heights of San Giovanni in a manner that reminds us of the death of Lord Brooke during the siege of Lichfield. The Vaudois, when the attacking party advanced, raised a cry to Heaven for help. "The enemy, who from a distance beheld their suppliant attitude, sent forth a contemptuous shout of laughter, and hastened their march. 'You shall be saved with a vengeance,' cried one of their chiefs, named from his black complexion, *Il Nero de Mondovi*, and as he spoke he raised his visor in scorn of the poor folk, whom he thought he could insult with impunity; but at the very instant an arrow, shot by a young man of Angrogna, called Peter Revelli, pierced the forehead of this modern Goliath between the eyes, and laid him dead on the spot[1]." After this the Vaudois appear for a while to have enjoyed comparative rest, although we read of isolated acts of cruelty, which are enough to make the blood run cold; but about the year 1556, another general persecution was commenced. The Vaudois as before took up arms, and after a valiant and protracted resistance, the most desperate struggles taking place at the ravine of Pra-del-Tor in the Val Angrogna, they succeeded in obtaining comparatively favourable terms of peace from the Duke of Savoy, though of course their best lands had been devastated, their property and cattle pillaged, many of their people slain or maimed, and the rest almost ruined. The next outbreak of the spirit of persecution was in 1655, when the atrocities perpetrated—if the descriptions be true—are so horrible that the tortures of North American savages would be tender mercies compared with the doings of those who called themselves the soldiers of Christ. It was in consequence of these cruelties that Cromwell intervened; and his letters, as well as the speech of Sir S. Morland, his ambassador, and the noble ode of Milton, his secretary, are

---

[1] *The Israel of the Alps*, p. 11.

protests of which England may well be proud. The Vaudois performed prodigies of valour, and repeatedly defeated their adversaries with great slaughter—the heights of Roccamanante and La Vacchera being the scenes of the fiercest struggles, and the defiles of the Val Angrogna proving more than once another, but more prosperous, Thermopylæ. The varying successes, the protracted negociations with foreign states, and the abominable duplicity of the persecutors, may be read at length in the histories of the Vaudois, but would be too long to relate here; suffice it to say that at last, when the greater part of the inhabitants of the valleys had been killed, hanged, or massacred, often after the most horrible tortures and outrages, the miserable remnant obtained from Victor Amadeus of Savoy permission to emigrate from their native land to any country which they might select, to receive back those who were imprisoned, and to be maintained to the frontier at the charge of the state. The population of the Vaudois valleys, no long time before, was reckoned at about 15,000; of these 2656 reached Geneva early in the year 1687, where they were most hospitably entertained, and near to which place the majority remained; though some were distributed among the other protestant states of Switzerland, and others were conveyed to Brandenburg, Wurtemburg, Holland, and even America.

And now I must briefly chronicle one of the most remarkable Alpine journeys ever made. The exiles, finding themselves ill-received in some of the above-named countries, and in consequence becoming a heavy burden upon their brethren in Switzerland, determined to attempt to reestablish themselves in their native valleys. Their leader was one Henri Arnaud, who was animated with much of the spirit of a Hebrew leader, and, in his own words, had girt on 'the sword of the Lord and of Gideon.' The enterprise had to be organized with the greatest secrecy, it being discouraged by the Swiss authorities, who naturally feared giving offence to their more powerful neighbours. At last a band of eight hundred exiles, after meeting at a secret rendezvous in the woods of Nyon, succeeded in crossing the Lake of Geneva and landing near Ivoire, on the opposite shore, during the night of Friday, August 16, 1689.

The following day they advanced southward through Savoy, with but little resistance, as far as St Jeoire, a town on one of the present roads from Geneva to Sixt, a short distance beyond which they rested for the night. The next morning (Sunday), they advanced into the valley of the Arve. The inhabitants of Cluses, who at first threatened resistance, were overawed, and were compelled to sell them food and furnish hostages. Thus the narrow defile beyond was traversed in safety; and the town of Sallenche, after much negociation and several attempts at treachery, was also frightened into letting them pass unmolested. The night was spent at a small village called Cablau. The next day was occupied in crossing an unfrequented pass, called the Portetta[1], the difficulties of which were increased by bad weather and treacherous guides, so that eventually they had to halt for the night in some miserable châlets. On the next day (Tuesday) they crossed into the valley of the Isère by the Col du Bon-Homme, and slept at Scez. Next morning they continued their march upwards along this picturesque valley: meeting, as on the day before, with occasional difficulty from the hostility of the people, but without finding it necessary to fight; and before evening reached Laval. The next day they climbed the long dull ascent which leads to the Mont Iséran Pass[2] (9175 feet). Descending thence into the valley of the Arc, after a little trouble at Bessans, they passed the night in

[1] The contemporary narrative calls this the Col de la Haute Luce, which according to Brockedon is a misnomer.

[2] Since celebrated for the neighbouring mountain, supposed to be 13271 feet high and streaming with glaciers, a creation of the Piedmontese surveyors. This impostor was effaced from the map by some members of the English Alpine Club, who after in vain trying to obtain a view of it, went to the place to look, and found that the highest point near did not exceed 11322 feet; this is moreover an unusually insignificant looking mountain.

one of the villages, and next day ascended the Mont Cenis. On the pass they captured, as a measure of precaution, the horses at the post station, and seized the baggage of Cardinal Angelo Ranuzzi, which, as it happened, was being carried over. This they afterwards restored, though some of his private papers were lost in the confusion. They descended from the Cenis plateau by the Col de Clairée, and were benighted on their way down. The next morning they met with their first serious opposition, and after losing several men in a skirmish in the ravine of the Jaillon, were obliged to retreat. Still undaunted, they pushed over the Col de Touille towards Salabertrand, where an unsuccessful attempt was made to draw them into a trap, on the failure of which a fight took place at nightfall with some 2500 French troops at the bridge over the Dora, in the narrowest part of a defile. The Waldenses, finding themselves between two fires, made a desperate charge, and utterly routed the enemy. After about two hours the ground was covered with their slaughtered foes, and the rest, with their wounded commander, were flying headlong over the Genèvre. The Waldenses, who had only lost about twenty-eight killed and wounded, obtained a quantity of plunder and military stores, and then pushed on towards a pass leading into the valley of Pragelas. Fatigue obliged them to halt before reaching the top, but the next morning (Sunday) they beheld once more their native mountains, and offered up their heartfelt thanks to God.

The succeeding days were spent in harassing expeditions and skirmishes in different parts of the valleys of Pragelas, St Martin, and Angrogna; but it would take too long to describe them in detail. Truth compels me to add that they were frequently stained by the slaughter of prisoners, a measure which, however it may be excused by policy or provocation, cannot be defended. The winter was passed in frequent skirmishes, and among the severest privations, but the spring brought them unexpected repose, Victor Amadeus and Louis XIV. having quarrelled; and so each prince sought to win over the Vaudois to his side by shewing them kindness.

The Swiss Alps can hardly be separated from the story of Tell, the Brutus of Helvetia, who, as is often the case, is a more popular hero than the three real founders of Swiss liberty—Werner Stauffacher of Schwytz, Walter Faust of Uri, and Arnold von Melchthal of Unterwalden. The Emperor Albert of Austria, hoping apparently to obtain an excuse for depriving the inhabitants of the Forest Cantons of their liberty by goading them to insurrection, or to compel them to barter it for present relief, had set over them as bailiffs two men of tyrannical character, Hermann Gessler of Brunnecken and Beringar of Landenberg. The former established himself at Altdorf, and the latter at Sarnen; who both, together with their creatures, grievously oppressed the people. The story of how Gessler, as a last insult, set up his cap on a pole in the market-place of Altdorf and bade the people doff their hats to it, how Tell the archer refused, and was condemned to shoot an arrow off his son's head as the price of pardon, how he hid a second arrow, and on its discovery avowed what its butt would have been, is too well-known to require recounting. Nor need I do more than mention the storm which arose in the Bay of Uri as Gessler was hurrying Tell to the castle of Küssnacht, and released him from his chains to take the helm of the boat; or the address with which he guided it to the narrow shelf on the Axenberg, and then sprang on shore and escaped; or the moment of vengeance, when in the hollow roadway near Küssnacht an arrow from his unerring hand went straight to Gessler's heart[1].

---

[1] The story of Tell has been questioned in modern times owing to a close correspondence with a Danish legend of the tenth century. Although some of its details may possibly be mythical, the evidence for its truth seems too strong to be resisted; and the similarity of the story is after all not a very weighty argu-

This assassination—justifiable, if ever one was—which took place towards the end of 1307, seriously embarrassed the three confederates, Stauffacher, Furst, and Melchthal, who in their midnight meetings on the little alp of Rütli had for some time past been planning a general rising; for their preparations were not yet completed, and they disapproved of bloodshed, save in self-defence. However in November they met again at the usual place; and then, raising their hands towards heaven, in the attitude which every Swiss village painter has helped to immortalise, they swore "to live and die for the rights of their oppressed countrymen; no longer to suffer injustice, and on their part to commit none; to respect the rights of the house of Hapsburg, and, without offering violence to the imperial governors, to put an end to the arbitrary acts of their tyranny." The rising was fixed for the first of January, 1308; on that day the castle of Sarnen was seized by stratagem, and in a very short time the oppressors were turned out of the country without bloodshed.

Albert of Austria now made preparations for invading the Forest Cantons, but while on his way, and separated from his suite, at Königsfelden, a ferry over the Reuss, he was murdered by some conspirators, the leader of whom was his own nephew, John of Suabia, whose inheritance he had refused to restore; and thus he received the 'reward of injustice.' It will be remembered how his amiable wife, after 'bathing in the dews of May' by slaughtering about a thousand persons, apparently with very similar motives to those of King Herod—on the chance that some might be guilty—founded a convent at the scene of her husband's murder, and died there in the odour of sanctity.

The Swiss made good use of the breathing time thus given, and when at last they were attacked they defended themselves successfully. Beneath the heights of Morgarten, by the shore of the Egeri See, they scattered the troops of Leopold. After

ment. History has a way of repeating itself, and *similia similibus curantur* is true in more senses than the medical one.

which they defeated their foes several times, not the least important being at Laupen near Berne and at Näfels in the Linththal. Other cantons joined the original three, till in 1352 the confederacy consisted of eight, distinguished long afterwards as the 'Old Cantons,'—Schwytz, Uri, Unterwalden, Lucerne, Zurich, Glarus, Zug, and Berne. The struggle was concluded by a battle on the sloping shores of the Lake of Sempach, where 6400 well equipped Austrian troops met 1300 badly armed burgers. These at first made little impression on the serried ranks of the enemy, till Arnold von Winkelried, clasping in his arms as many spears as he could embrace, pressed to his heart the harvest of death, and 'opened a way for the confederates.' The ranks once broken, the long swords and heavy halberts of the Swiss did their work, and Duke Leopold, with nearly a third of his army, including 676 members of the first families of Germany and Aargau, remained upon the field. After this the land had rest.

Appenzell obtained its liberty from the bishop of St Gall, after a struggle terminated by the battle of Am-Stoss, where Rudolph of Austria, his champion, was defeated with great slaughter; the women of Appenzell contributing to the rout by appearing in force on a hill which commanded the enemies' retreat. The Valais revolted from the Duke of Savoy and the Bishop of Sion about the same time; and a few years later the Grisons (Graubunden, or Grey league, so called from the dress of the inhabitants), shook off the yoke of the petty tyrants who lived in the castles of the Rhein-thals; and about the same time the Engadine obtained its freedom. The three leagues—that of the Caddea (Casa dei), formed in 1396 under Hartmann, Bishop of Coire, and including nearly all the district drained by the Hinter-Rhein, together with the Engadine, that of the Graubunden, or Vorder-Rhein country, and the League of the Ten Jurisdictions, consisting of places to the east and north-east of Coire, on the borders of the Tyrol—formed a solemn alliance in

1471, but did not join the Swiss confederation till 26 years later.

Perhaps however the most remarkable military exploits of which the Alps have been the scene occurred in the end of last century, when the armies of France, Austria, and Russia counter-marched and fought among passes trodden before only by the hunter and the shepherd.

The French Republicans had in the year 1798 admirably enacted the fable of the wolf and the lamb; and had afforded to the world the edifying spectacle, which they have repeated in the present century, of the friends of liberty doing their best to extinguish it in another nation. The Forest Cantons had resisted bravely, and Morgarten and Näfels had revived their ancient glories; but the power of France was irresistible, and she did her best to secure peace by making the country a desert. The Grisons however, relying on the aid of Austria, still refused to join the new 'Helvetic Republic'; and when war broke out in March 1799, between the Emperor and the Directory, the French troops invaded that district, and at first succeeded in driving out the Austrian force which had wintered there. Then the battles of Stockach and Feldkirch obliged them to retreat. After nearly three months' desperate fighting, in which the Forest Cantons did all that was in their power, the Austrians, headed by Archduke Charles, forced their way to Zurich, captured it, drove the French headlong down the St Gothard Pass, and occupied the heads of the valleys of the Reuss and Rhone. Having thus gained a decided advantage, they waited for the coming of the Russians, under Korsakoff, who was advancing from the east, and under Suwarroff, who was marching towards the St Gothard, intending to make a combined attack on the French army in September; this plan however was thwarted by the vigour of Massena, who took the initiative, and by the meddling of the Austrian Council, who in spite of the most earnest remonstrances of Archduke Charles, weakened his right by ordering a large number of his troops to the Middle Rhine. Massena on the 14th August drove the Austrians back on Zurich; Lecourbe, aided by a corps descending from the Surenen Pass, established himself at Altdorf; Loison crossed the Susten Pass and seized Wasen, thus dividing the troops that occupied the Reuss valley, and forcing those who had defended Altdorf to retreat by the Maderanerthal and Kreuzli Pass into the head of the Vorder-Rhein-thal; Thurreau attacked Prince Rohan, who was stationed at Brieg in the Valais, and drove him over the Simplon Pass; and this disaster having obliged Strauch, who was guarding the passes of the Grimsel and Furka, to weaken his forces by going to the aid of the Imperialists in the Upper Valais, General Gudin pushed up the Haslithal, and, availing himself of the guidance of a peasant of Guttanen, descended by a difficult route upon the summit of the Grimsel[1]. The Austrians were engaged against the rest of Gudin's troops, who had diverted their attention by an attack up the Haslithal, and so, being completely taken by surprise, retreated as fast as possible into the Valais. Strauch, being thus menaced on both flanks, was obliged to retire on to the south side of the Alps by the Nufenen Pass: Lecourbe then pushed on up the St Gothard to the Devil's Bridge, this the Austrians broke by blowing up one of the side arches, and made a desperate stand. The French, however, threw planks during the night over the chasm, and the Austrians, being now menaced by Gudin who was descending from the Furka into the basin of Hospenthal, retreated towards the Oberalp Pass. Here they made another stand, but the next day were driven by the combined forces of Lecourbe and Gudin some way down the Vorder-Rhein-thal. To effect this brilliant success Massena had been obliged to

---

[1] Wandering one evening up the line of this route we picked up two bullets on a grassy shelf beneath a rock: they were very slightly flattened, and were thus not improbably part of a volley fired at the Austrians, when they first made their appearance among the broken ground high above the pass.

weaken his left, and the Archduke Charles, now reinforced by Korsakoff, attempted to cross the Reuss and crush it. This attempt, admirably planned, failed through the neglect of the engineers, who had not taken proper precautions to bridge that river, and thus, as Alison observes[1], "the want of a few grappling irons defeated a project on which perhaps the fate of the world depended." Shortly after this, the Archduke was obliged to march for the Middle Rhine, and Massena advancing again drove back the Austrians to a defensive line, extending from the Lake of Zurich along by the Wallenstadt valley to Sargans in the Rhein-thal.

More defeats followed, during the month of September, in a series of battles near the Lake of Zurich, when the French, headed by Massena and Soult, and aided by the conceit of Korsakoff, captured that town, severed the combined Russian and Austrian armies, driving the former back to Schaffhausen and the latter over the Rhine, with immense loss in men, artillery and stores.

A few days before, on the twenty-first of the month, Suwarroff had arrived at the foot of the St Gothard, with twelve thousand veterans, having detached six thousand under Rosenberg to force their way into the Vorder-Rhein-thal, by the Val Blegno and Luckmanier Pass, and sent his artillery and baggage to the Grisons, by the Lake of Como and Chiavenna. The old marshal, after desperate fighting, succeeded in driving the French under Gudin over the St Gothard, into the Urseren-thal[2]. Rosenberg was equally successful, and on arriving in the head of the Rhein-thal, divided his forces, beating back the French troops from the summit of the Oberalp Pass into the Urseren-thal with one detachment, and sending another over

---

[1] *History of Europe*, ch. xxxviii. § 37.

[2] The words 'Suwarroff Victor' carved upon a granite rock near the top of a pass still commemorate this exploit. At one time the resistance of the French was so obstinate that the attack seemed likely to fail, and the marshal ordered a grave to be dug, vowing that he would be buried where 'his children' had been repulsed.

the Kreuzli Pass to Amsteg to cut off their retreat. These successes obliged Lecourbe to evacuate the upper part of the Reuss valley. After throwing his artillery into the river, he retreated, filling up the Urner loch with rocks[1], and breaking down the roadway at the Devil's Bridge; while Gudin, crossing the Furka by moonlight, again posted himself on the Grimsel plateau. The next day the Russian troops arrived on the bridge, where a yawning gulf arrested their advance; a desperate struggle took place here in the narrow defile, numbers of the Russians fell into the torrent wounded by the enemies' shots, or even thrust down by the pressure of their friends behind, who were hastening to the attack. At last Suwarroff succeeded in turning the post, by despatching some troops above the wall of rock which forms the left bank of the torrent, and a hastily constructed bridge having been thrown across the chasm, he forced the French back, effected a junction at Amsteg with the remaining detachment of his army, and then drove the enemy beyond Altdorf.

Unfortunately this brilliant success was a few days too late; and the old lion found that his valour had but brought him into the toils. One division indeed of the Austrian army attempted to effect a junction with him by advancing along the Lake of Wallenstadt, and another, crossing from the Vorder-Rhein-thal into the Sernf-thal descended towards Glarus; but both were compelled to retreat, and Suwarroff, unable to obtain boats to navigate the Lake of Lucerne, formed the desperate resolution of crossing the steep ridge of the Kinzig Kulm (6791 feet) into the upper part of the Muotta-thal. Thence he fought his way over the Pragel Pass and established himself in the Linth-thal. From this, after vainly endeavouring to drive the French, who had entrenched themselves at Näfels, out of the lower part of that valley, he retreated by the Sernf-thal over the Panixer Pass

---

[1] A tunnel through which the road passes a short distance above the Devil's Bridge.

(7967 feet); and after great difficulty and suffering, increased by a recent heavy fall of snow, succeeded in gaining the Rhine valley at Ilanz, on the tenth of October. One third of his army is said to have perished during the five days occupied in this exploit.

Two other passages of the Alps, which occurred about the same time, must not be passed over in silence; that of the Great St Bernard by Napoleon I., and of the Splügen by Macdonald. In the spring of 1800, the Austrians, under Melas, had succeeded after hard fighting in driving one body of the French troops under Suchet across the Var, and in blockading the other under Massena in Genoa, which eventually was compelled by famine to surrender. Napoleon, in the hope of raising the siege of this place, and of recovering Piedmont and Lombardy, determined to make a descent upon the Imperialists from the north. Concealing his plans with great success, he sent the left wing of his army, 16,000 strong, over the St Gothard, the right wing of 4000 over the Cenis, and determined to lead the centre down the Val d'Aoste. Of this, he conducted the main body, 40,000 in number, towards the Great St Bernard, and ordered the rest, a force of 5,000, to cross the Little St Bernard, and join him in the valley. Thus, as a glance at the map will shew, 65,000 men would converge on Turin; threatening the flank and rear of the Imperialists, severing them from their base of operations, and compelling them to fight in a position where defeat was hopeless ruin.

Large supplies of provisions were prepared; the cannon were dismounted and placed on sledges, extemporised from the trunks of firs; their carriages were taken in pieces and placed on the backs of mules, and on May 16th the army began the ascent. The passage, though of course difficult, was made without any serious loss, the most troublesome part being, as usual, the commencement of the descent; where much of the winter snow still lay unmelted. Each regiment occupied three days in the passage; the first night being spent at St Pierre, the second at St Remy or Etroubles, and the third bringing them to Aosta. Napoleon crossed on the 20th[1]. Fort Bard, a castle on a projecting pyramidal rock, that almost closes the Val d'Aoste, offered an unexpected resistance; and, had he not succeeded in passing it by stratagem, would have compelled him to retrace his steps. The victory of Marengo, on June 14th, was the reward of this difficult enterprise.

By this victory the Austrian forces were driven out of Piedmont and compelled to take up a defensive position within the Lombard frontier, resting in the rear upon the famous quadrilateral. On the cessation of the armistice of Alessandria, Napoleon determined to strike home at Austria, by marching from north-eastern Italy to Vienna, and dealing a death-blow at her heart, with the combined armies of himself and Moreau, who had already advanced through Bavaria to the Austrian frontier. The intense loyalty of the Tyrol and the strength of its defences made the task of forcing a way through it difficult and dangerous. Napoleon therefore determined to compel the Austrian troops by flank manœuvres and threatening the line of their retreat to evacuate 'without a combat the immense fortress of the Tyrol.' Macdonald, who was in command of the army in the Grisons, was accordingly ordered, though it was the depth of winter, to cross the Splügen and to proceed by way of the Lago d'Iseo, to threaten Trent and form the left wing of the army of Italy. The general concentrated his forces at Thusis, dismounted his artillery and placed it on sledges drawn by oxen, packed his ammunition on the backs of mules, and commenced the ascent. The leading companies arrived at the village of Splügen, where the road quits the Hinter-Rhein, on November

---

[1] He rode upon a steady mule, not, as a well-known picture ludicrously represents, on a prancing charger. Had he attempted anything of that kind, the battle of Marengo would probably not have been fought. The little inn at St Pierre still bears the sign *Au déjeuner de Napoléon.*

26th. Thence they mounted with immense difficulty, a company of pioneers, followed by a troop of dragoons, going in front to form a track through the deep snow. For a while they advanced without accident; then a *tourmente*[1] arose, and an avalanche fell, severing the column and sweeping thirty of the dragoons into a gulf, where they perished. Those behind were terror-stricken, and returned to Splügen. The *tourmente* raged for three days, blocking up the road; but when it subsided Macdonald, undaunted, recommenced the ascent; and after immense labour more than half the army, favoured by fine weather, succeeded in crossing on the first three days of December. The remainder, about 7000 in number, led by Macdonald himself, commenced ascending from Splügen on the 5th. Fresh snow had, however, fallen during the previous night; the track was effaced and had to be made anew; and worse than all the *tourmente* again rose. Two days the passage lasted, the wind often blowing a hurricane, and the frequent avalanches sweeping all before them. The descent through the gorge of the Cardinel was even more fatal than the ascent, and altogether about a hundred men perished. His efforts a few days later, to force a way by the Monte Tonale (6483 feet) to the Etschthal above Trent, was unsuccessful; owing to the vigorous resistance of the Austrian force which had occupied that important passage.

The western parts of the Tyrol, and the highlands of Saltzburg and Carinthia, had more than once been the theatre of battle during the operations above described; but the different character of the country made the warfare less exclusively Alpine. So, too, in the celebrated Tyrolese rising, the Brenner Pass was almost the only one where scenes resembling the Swiss mountain struggles were enacted. The desperate valour of these contests by untrained peasants, rendered all the more

---

[1] See ch. v. p. 138.

remarkable from the very fact that several of them were not waged among the mountain defiles, but in broad and open valleys like that of the Inn, and their ultimate failure, owing to the inability of Austria to cope with the combined forces of France and Bavaria, with Switzerland no longer neutral ground, and the quadrilateral gone, are too well known to need a detailed description. Of the three gallant leaders of the insurrection, Hofer, after being in vain solicited to take refuge in Austria, sheltered himself in a châlet on the upper portions of the Passeyerthal, alone among the winter's snow, till a friend betrayed him, sixteen hundred soldiers succeeded in arresting him, and Napoleon the Great had him shot at Mantua. Spechbacher, after lying hid through the winter in a cavern on the Eisgletscher, without daring to light a fire lest the smoke should discover him, had the ill-fortune to be swept down by an avalanche in the spring and dislocate his thigh. Compelled then to drag himself to a village, he gained, after marvellous escapes from being taken, the Austrian frontier, and reached Vienna; whither the remaining hero, Haspinger the Capuchin friar, had already arrived by a circuitous route through Switzerland.

CHAPTER XII.

THE first questions to be asked, before starting on an Alpine excursion, supposing a reasonable allowance of time and money, are when and whither to go. The season for pedestrian travel begins with June and ends with September. In the early part of the former month, there may be at times difficulty or even danger on the higher passes from the remains of the winter snows; at the end of the latter from the shortness of the days and the coldness of the nights. August is, from motives of convenience, the month usually chosen; but it is open to objections, one of which is the long spell of bad weather so frequent about the middle of it. In considering the second question, the Alps may not inconveniently be divided into districts, one or more of which may be chosen according to time, funds, and inclination.

These are, beginning on the south-west, the Viso district, in which are included the Vaudois valleys, and those of the Guil and the Ubaye, together with the northern part of the Maritime Alps; the Alps of Dauphiné, meaning more especially the *massif* between the Romanche and the Durance; the Tarentaise and Maurienne, that is, the region drained by the Arc and the

Isère; the Graians; the Pennine Chain, which may be subdivided into the Chamouni and Zermatt districts; the Oberland, with the Alps of Uri and Glarus; the Grisons and the Engadine; the West Tyrol Alps; the Dolomites, centering on the Marmolata; and the East Tyrol and Carinthian Alps, the most important peak of which is the **Gross Glockner**.

(Fig. 14.) View in the Graians. The Grivola from the Col de Chéeruit.

We come now to the best mode of making a tour. Imprimis, get a companion; and more than that, a friend. Many an excursion has had almost all its pleasure marred by an unsuitable companion, so, if you are wise, do not commit yourself to one whom you do not thoroughly know. To be alone for days with a morose man, to rough it with a constant grumbler, or to be among the beauties of nature with one who, though he considers it 'the thing' to 'do the Alps,' has no more appreciation of them than a gorilla, is a sore trial to temper and spirits. Solitude is better than such companionship; but solitude, especially

21

in unfrequented districts, has obvious inconveniences and occasional dangers; therefore get a trusty friend to go with you. Parties of three or four have advantages in tours through regions where travellers are few; but as in these the supply of accommodation is generally proportionate to the ordinary demand, they have often to undergo considerable inconveniences.

Having settled whither to go, look carefully to your kit. This should consist of a small portmanteau, to be forwarded from town to town, and a water-proof knapsack. The portmanteau is by many deemed an unnecessary luxury; it certainly is a slight additional expense, say of from sixpence to a shilling a day, but it is well worth this. It is not pleasant to be stinted in linen or clothing, to be unable to carry back occasional souvenirs of the places visited, to hurry post-haste through towns, or else to walk through churches, picture-galleries, and boulevards in tattered, weather-stained garments and hob-nailed boots; which latter are positively dangerous on the slippery floors and staircases of foreign hotels. Also carefully consider what will be wanted. Here is my idea of a pedestrian's necessary outfit. Two flannel-shirts, two pairs of woollen socks, one pair of cotton socks, a few pocket handkerchiefs and collars, a suit of tweed or of flannel (the coat having plenty of pockets), one pair of thin trowsers, for a change when wet through, a pair of walking boots, a pair of slippers, a mackintosh coat or cape, a flask, a leather cup, a compass, writing materials and note-books according to requirements, with a few simple medicines (these should never be forgotten), are about enough for the pedestrian, and will not make the knapsack too heavy. The woollen socks should be very thick and soft; the boots, of strong leather, with tips, should be made with low heels and double soles, both of which should project all round well beyond the upper leather. This is a very important point, because the foot is thus protected from being bruised on projecting rocks, and all unequal wearing down and twisting is prevented. They should be well garnished with hob-nails. If you purpose to ascend high mountains or sleep much in châlets and caves, a warm woollen comforter, night-cap, and gloves, are necessary. A semicircular mackintosh cape is then better than a coat, because when spread on the ground it ensures a dry bed; a small Scotch plaid is also a great comfort. For the alpenstock, take a strong ash-pole about five feet long, tipped with a ferule-shaped point of tempered steel; but if you intend to wander much on the glaciers without guides, or to undertake very difficult excursions, a *piolet*[1] is preferable.

We have next to consider what is to be avoided. First and foremost, over-fatigue. Alpine walking, like all other exercises which call for considerable exertion, requires some preparation and training. The pleasure of a whole excursion may be marred through too long a walk on the first day, either by blisters and abrasions of the skin, or by illness, the result of over-exertion. My own custom is to approach the region of the high peaks by some by-way, and to take two or three days' quiet walking in the charming sub-Alpine, or rather mid-Alpine districts, where, among summits ranging from six to eight thousand feet in height, there are exquisite combinations of cliff, pasture, and pine wood, with occasional glimpses of the distant snows, forming pictures of unsurpassed beauty. Let me venture to add a few hints, the result of experience; which, though obvious enough, are too often forgotten. After a day of severe exertion, take an easy day. An average of seven or eight hours per diem, for the six days of the week, is as much as is good for most men. Do not walk too fast, especially up hill, '*Plus doucement on monte, plus vite on arrive au sommet*' is a

---

[1] A sort of stout walking-stick tomahawk. N.B. Beginners cannot be too earnestly warned against rambling much on glaciers; but a little experience with good guides will teach them where they may go and where they may not. As a rule, however, it is always better to have a companion on a glacier.

very good proverb. Do not eat much meat or drink much wine after a day of severe exertion, especially on the snow. Very weak tea lukewarm assuages thirst better than anything else, being a slight febrifuge and sudorific. Do not drink much water while on the march; it is far better to wash the lips and mouth often, than to swallow. Red wine and water, or very weak brandy-and-water, are the best beverages; beer, with most men, only aggravates thirst. Do not smoke when walking up hill. Look well after the commissariat, you can't have a good fire without good coals. Avoid sleeping in châlets as much as you can; there, as a rule, the fleas and yourself are equally wakeful. Some of these may seem small matters; but the effects of over-exertion or of insufficient or improper food are often very bad; for they result either in fever at the time or in obstinate neuralgia or derangement of the digestion afterwards, and, it may even be, in serious injury to some of the vital organs.

The dangers incurred during excursions in the High Alps, which have been so painfully forced upon our notice during the last few years, have now to be considered. The most prominent of them may be thus classified: (1) from falling stones, ice, or snow, (2) from an insecure footing. There has not been, to my knowledge, any accident of late years from either falling stones or ice, though narrow escapes have not been unfrequent; the former is always possible in the vicinity of a precipice, but some mountains are more than others addicted to the bad habit of pelting visitors. When glaciers terminate above steep rocks, large masses frequently break off and tumble down in huge cascades of icy fragments. Such are the well-known avalanches of the Jungfrau, already described, and indeed most of those witnessed by the tourist; very grand spectacles when he is out of the line of fire, far worse than a discharge of grape when he is in it; they are most to be feared during the hot period of the day, but in many cases they can be entirely avoided by caution and previous study of the mountain. Snow avalanches, as I have said, are rare, but they are occasionally to be dreaded early in the season or after long-continued bad weather. Some of the accidents caused by them have been mentioned in a former chapter[1].

The dangers from an insecure footing are chiefly confined to the region of snow and ice, though sometimes the foot or the hand fails in its hold on rocks, especially in descending. On ice, if the steps are carefully hewn, and the traveller advance cautiously, the risk of slipping is very small. An ice-slope is often a great difficulty, but rarely a danger; except when it is covered with snow, of which more hereafter. When, however, the face of a sloping crag is glazed over with a thin layer of ice, which is not deep enough to allow of good steps being hewn, and the rocky projections are not sufficient to give sure hold to hand or foot, there is the utmost peril. It was a combination of this kind which caused the fearful accident on the Matterhorn on the 14th of July, 1865. The travellers had accomplished the ascent from the spot where they had passed the night (at a height of 11,000 feet), after about eight hours' actual walking. They had first mounted by the north side of the eastern face overhanging the Furgen glacier; they had then climbed, for some distance, along the *arête* which descends towards the Hörnli—this was to scale the wall of the house-like summit; and had accomplished the last part of the ascent by the shelving roof which terminates above the fearful precipices overhanging the Matterhorn glacier. On descending the steepest part of this slope, which was, as may often be seen from below, thinly covered with ice and snow, one of the party slipped and knocked over the leading guide; the jerk of the rope successively overthrew the next two, but the last three, Mr Whymper and the two Zermatt guides, stood firm in their steps. The rope snapped under the strain, and the result is too well known.

[1] Chapter v.

But more lives have been lost by treacherous snow than by any other means. The upper fields of the glacier look smooth and inviting. Surely, thinks the inexperienced traveller, no harm can lurk under those gently undulating plains of spotless purity! he treads heedlessly; suddenly he staggers and is gone; a crash of falling icicles followed by a dull thud comes up through the round hole that now marks the level surface, and very often help cannot be given till it is too late.

This danger, however, can always be obviated by tying the party together with a strong rope as soon as the snows are reached. An accident is then, I believe, impossible; and the travellers, whatever the guides may say, should always insist on this precaution; for, owing to their very skill, the best guides are often more inclined to neglect it than those that are inferior. I have seen three or four narrow escapes from the results of this carelessness.

Worst of all is fresh snow when it overlies inclines of ice. After continued fine weather the surface of the snow slopes, through melting by day and freezing by night, becomes ice, and the new deposit does not readily bind with the old. Hence the travellers' weight may be enough to disturb the nicely poised mass, the snow slips from their tread, and they slide down, riding, as it were, on a small avalanche. Accidents from this cause have already been noticed[1]. This is undoubtedly the greatest danger in Alpine climbing; no experience can entirely avoid it, and no skill avert it.

Such are the main sources of peril in Alpine travel; it remains to say one word on the use of the rope, a question which has been much mooted since the Matterhorn accident. On glaciers, especially on the upper snow-fields, it is always an advantage: on rocks, it is sometimes rather an impediment, but unquestionably a security. In a word, its great value is that it prevents serious consequences resulting from a slight

[1] Chapter v. pp. 120, 121.

slip. On steep snow slopes, if the steps are well hewn, it has the same advantage; but it should always be kept as nearly taut as possible. There are, however, occasionally places where a slip on the part of one endangers the whole party; in that case every man should go singly; or better still, the expedition should be abandoned. If life is to be deliberately exposed to considerable risk, there are many nobler causes in which it may be hazarded. I think that not more than four men should be fastened together; three ought to be able to hold up one, and if they could not, the momentum acquired by so many falling bodies would, in most cases, pull down the others. If some must perish, better few than many. Lastly, never undertake a difficult excursion with untried companions.

These precautions taken, I maintain that there is no more danger in Alpine climbing than in most other manly exercises. The mischief is that difficult excursions are often undertaken without proper preparation. The perils of crags and glaciers were formerly exaggerated; they are now perhaps underrated. There is an art in Alpine climbing, just as in all other exercises, which can only be learnt by practice; and the neophant must be content to serve an apprenticeship. But it may be asked, Granting the risk is small, what is the good of it? I reply that it is an exercise wholesome alike for mind and body. The little hardships inseparable from it—simple fare, hard beds, endurance of cold and heat, in a word, 'roughing it'—are no bad discipline for those who live in an over-luxurious age: while the nature of the work calls into play coolness and self-command in danger, prompt decision in action, perseverance under difficulties, and many other valuable qualities. The same steadiness of nerve which enables a man to glance calmly down a steep ice-slope, or to cling to the projections of a precipitous arête, accustoms him to distinguish between real and apparent dangers in the affairs of life, and trains him to estimate at their true value the 'bugbears' which will from time to time beset him in his daily walk. Anyone, who, like myself, has lived much among men of studious and retired habits, knows from experience how close the connexion is between some kinds of physical and moral courage, and how often the want of the former impedes the usefulness of such men, and even tempts them to pass by without protest, or acquiesce in, conduct of which their consciences secretly disapprove. But, besides this, the undulating wastes of lifeless snow, the frozen cataracts of the glaciers, the dark crags and splintered pinnacles of the higher mountains, speak to the soul in a language ill understood by those who view them afar off from the luxurious valley. They give rest to the fevered brain, peace to the weary heart, and life to the languid frame; but better still than this, few, I think, can return from wandering among their solitudes without a deeper sense of the infinite wisdom and lovingkindness of our Almighty Creator.

APPENDIX.

CHAPTER I.

IN the text of this work I have preferred to use general rather than special scientific terms; therefore the following notes, founded principally upon an article by M. Desor, in the Introduction to the *Alpine Guide*, may be of use to the geologist.

The metamorphic rocks in the Alps consist of gneiss, various kinds of mica, chlorite, talc, and hornblende slates, quartzite, crystalline limestones, serpentine, and grey and black slates, often with considerable quartz veins. These, as stated in the text, form the backbone of almost every important chain, and compose the highest peaks. In very many cases it has not yet been found possible to determine with certainty their geological epoch; in others they have been referred either to the carboniferous, triassic, or jurassic, age. Deposits older than the first of these have not yet been identified in any of the higher Alpine regions.

Carboniferous Formation.

The mountain limestone has only been identified in some parts of the Eastern Alps. The coal measures are largely represented—though generally so metamorphosed as not to be easily recognised—in the Central and Western Alps. They occur in Switzerland, Savoy, the Graians, Tarentaise, and Dauphiné; but are perhaps more extensively developed in the Maurienne, about the valley of the Arc, than in any other district. Though beds of anthracite occur occasionally, they are not nearly so productive as the English coal measures. Fossils are found in places. One of the richest localities for fossil plants is in the valley of the Dioza, near the châlets of Moëd, described by Mr Wills. (*The Eagle's Nest*, Ch. VII.)

Permian Formation.

Not yet identified with certainty. Possibly occurring in the Rhætian Alps.

Trias Formation.

Largely developed in the whole Alpine chain. To this age most of the vast masses of dolomite, the marls, and the sandstones, so abundant in the Eastern Alps, are referred, with the beds of stratified volcanic ash about the Fassa-thal. Some of these are rich in fossils, one of the most noted localities being St Cassian in the Gader-thal. This formation also occupies a large portion of the chain north of the Inn, composing the highlands of Tyrol and Bavaria. There is another great mass of it in the Lombard Alps between the Lago di Garda and the Lago di Como. It is also developed extensively in the Rhætian Alps, is wanting in the Oberland and Swiss Pennines, but reappears in the neighbourhood of Mont Blanc, and has recently been identified over a considerable portion of the Savoy Alps and in some places in Dauphiné.

Lias Formation.

The vast beds of pale fawn-coloured dolomite, named after the Dachstein, and so largely developed in the neighbourhood of the Ampezzo Pass, are by some referred to the lowest part of this formation, by others grouped with the Permian. Beds which have been identified with the lias also occur in other parts of the Eastern Alps, and occasionally in the Lombard Alps, the Oberland, the neighbourhood of Mont Blanc, and in parts of Savoy and Dauphiné.

Jurassic Formation

Occurs occasionally in the southern district of the Eastern Alps; more abundantly in the northern, especially in the Bavarian and Tyrol highlands mentioned above. There are patches of it in the upper part of the Inn valley and the Rhætian Alps. It fringes the

Lombard Alps as far as the eastern shore of the Lago Maggiore, skirts the south side of the Upper Rhone, and is largely developed along the northern face of the Oberland. Here it rises to above 12,000 feet in the outer peak of the Wetterhorn and the Blumlis Alp; the deposits composing these mountains, as well as the Titlis, Altels, and Wildstrubel, being referred to an epoch contemporaneous with our Middle Oolite. In Savoy it occupies a large part of the district between the Rhone and Arve, and fringes on each side the curving chain of crystalline *massifs* which extends from Mont Blanc to the Pelvoux group. South of this it occupies a considerable portion of the mountain country west of the watershed of the Maritime Alps, down to the sea at Nice and Monaco.

Cretaceous Formation

Is not much developed in the Eastern or the major part of the Central Alps, but in the latter there is one considerable zone, which, commencing near Immenstadt in Bavaria, extends to the Rhine, and crossing it runs to the Rhone between Martigny and the Lake of Geneva. On the south of this sheet of water it occurs less frequently, but is found at intervals in Savoy, being most extensively developed on the right bank of the Isère, about the lakes of Annecy and Bourget. The majority of the rocks are referred to the Neocomian age, supposed to be contemporaneous with the Lower Greensand of England. It is perhaps needless to add that the traveller must not expect to find much similarity in appearance between the deposits here and their English equivalents.

Eocene Formation.

Rare in the higher Eastern Alps; in fact, generally found in conjunction with the formation just described. A mass of it commences just north of the Arc, widens out between that river and the Romanche, rising to a height of nearly 11,500 feet in the summit of the Aiguilles d'Arve, which then, after fringing the eastern side of the Pelvoux group, occupies a large portion of the mountain district to the south-east of it. To this age belong the remarkable grey shales called *Flysch*, largely developed along the northern face of the Oberland; a bed in which, near Glarus, is celebrated for its fossil fish. The above-named deposit of Dauphiné, as well as that which forms the inner zone in the Oberland, and rises occasionally to a height of over 10,000 feet, forming the summits of the Dent du Midi, Dent de Morcles, Grand Moeveran, Diablerets, &c. belong chiefly to the lower part of the Eocene, or Nummulitic series, which was formerly referred by some to the preceding group.

Miocene Formation.

Found only in the Sub-alpine districts; forming the lowlands of Venetia, West Bavaria, Switzerland, and Savoy, consisting chiefly of beds of conglomerate (*nagelflue*) and grey sandstones (*molasse*); partly of marine, partly of freshwater origin. Between this and the preceding formation a long interval must have intervened, during which the first great rising of the Alps took place.

After this epoch the Alps appear to have remained continuously above the sea, but vast masses of drift have accumulated in their valleys, which have in places been again cut through by streams. These may be seen to great advantage in the mouth of the Kander-thal and in parts of the Puster-thal. I have already stated my opinion in the text that much of this drift must have been deposited under water. In some cases it may have been done just before the sea retired; in others the lakes may have been much more numerous and extensive than they now are; local alterations of level, and the sawing through of barriers by existing streams, would account for their present diminished area. Geologists distinguish these deposits into at least two groups, the *Ancient Alluvium* and the *Terrain glaciaire*. Some consider that the Alps were formerly much loftier than they now are; I confess I do not think the arguments in favour of this theory very strong, since I believe that very much of the work of denudation was performed as they were rising from the sea.

One other peculiarity in the Alps deserves notice; this is the fan-structure. In approaching many of the principal chains the usual geological order of the strata appears to be reversed; and the more recent and unaltered beds appear to be overlaid by the more ancient and metamorphic rocks. On crossing the chain the same structure is found repeated; so that a section through it would exhibit the beds arranged like an open fan, all dipping inwards; the oldest and most highly-inclined occupying the centre of the mass. A

APPENDIX.

glance at the following section[1] from the Brévent to the Mont Chétif, across the chain of Mont Blanc, will explain this better than any amount of description.

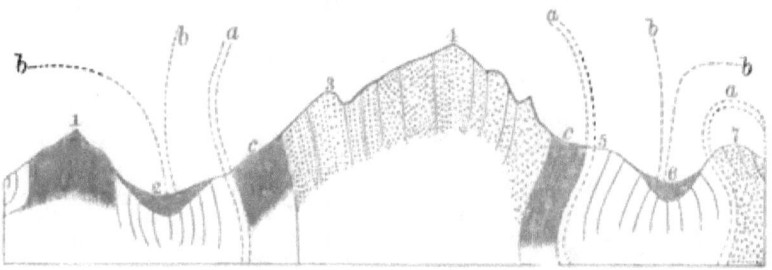

(Fig. 15.) Section through the range of Mont Blanc.

Explanation. 1, Brévent; 2, Valley of Arve; 3, Aiguille du Midi; 4, Mont Blanc; 5, Mont Fréty; 6, Val Veni; 7, Mont Chétif. The dotted parts are crystalline rock, shewing in Mont Blanc stratification and fan structure; dark shading, nearly vertical, crystalline schists (perhaps of triassic and carboniferous age); dark shading, horizontal, débris and alluvium. The wide lines represent folded beds of jurassic age; the dotted curved lines b, b, denoting the upper face of the top bed, and being supposed to have once formed a continuous horizontal line. The stratum a is a bed of carneguile on the north side, believed to be identical with a bed of dolomite on the south side, of Mont Blanc. The dotted lines denote the parts of the fold removed by denudation. The dark schists c, c represent identical beds; and probably correspond, though differing somewhat in mineral character, with the Brévent schists[1]. The beds of the Mont Chétif (7) are intermediate in character between these and the protogine of Mont Blanc, and probably contain representatives of both.

The same section will also give the explanation of this apparent anomaly, by shewing that it is really produced by the strata being rolled up in a series of folds, after which the exposure of underlying beds by fracture of the upper, and the removal of large portions of the surface by denudation, have obliterated the original structure. It will also be observed that the cause of upheaval appears to have been lateral rather than vertical pressure—a squeezing out rather than a forcing up;—and such has no doubt often been the case; some would consider this the principal agent in the elevation of mountain-chains, and attribute it to causes not immediately connected with the melting of subjacent beds; it must not, however, be forgotten that upheaval in one part would often produce lateral thrusts in others; and the question must be regarded as still *sub judice.*

---

[1] Reduced from a plate in M. Favre's work, *Recherches Géologiques dans les parties de la Savoie du Piémont et de la Suisse voisines du Mont Blanc*, one of the most valuable contributions to Alpine Geology that has as yet appeared.

CHAPTER II.

Strictly speaking, many valleys, such as those shewn in the woodcut above, are in a certain sense valleys of depression; but I speak in the text only of those which, even though considerably modified by denudation, at once strike the eye as owing their origin to this cause. It is only by careful examination that the origin of the valleys on each side of Mont Blanc can be detected.

CHAPTER III.

I have omitted to mention one phenomenon not unfrequently observed in glaciers, namely what are called the 'hyperbolic dirtbands'; because I do not remember to have noticed them on the Gorner glacier. These are successive 'wrinkles' on the glacier, which are rendered visible from a distance by the dust accumulating on them. Dr Tyndall considers them to mark the site of fractures, made when the glacier passes over a place which breaks it up into a 'cascade.' The 'hyperbolic' form is due to the swifter motion of the centre of the glacier, which gradually changes the straight transverse furrow into a curve with its vertex pointing downwards. They are particularly conspicuous on that portion of the Mer de Glace (Chamouni) which descends from the ice-fall of the Géant Glacier. Dr Tyndall also calls attention, *Glaciers of the Alps* (p. 413), to certain large seams of white ice, which are often conspicuous in a glacier. These he considers to be formed by the filling up of the channels of glacier streams by winter-snow, and the subsequent conversion of this into ice by pressure, due to the motion of the glacier.

The reader will find the various phenomena of glacier motion fully discussed in the above-named work of Dr Tyndall, and in Principal Forbes' *Travels in the Alps of Savoy*, and *Occasional Papers on the Theory of Glaciers*.

CHAPTER IV. p. 94.

I have once seen this prismatic structure in England, on the ice of a pond in the Fellows' Garden, Christ's College, Cambridge, Jan. 26, 1867. The following is an extract from a Note read before the Cambridge Philosophical Society: "A fragment from near the edge was about $\frac{1}{4}$ inch thick, and was a mass of prisms with their axes perpendicular to the surface. The ends of these in one part were very irregular polygons; and the lines joining opposite angles, speaking roughly, were on an average about one inch in length; but in another part the forms appeared rather more regular—hexagons being common—the diameters of which were about ½ inch. Another fragment was then obtained rather further from the edge; this was a little more than one inch thick, and consisted of prisms whose ends were about the same size as those just described. Though the number of sides in their polygonal ends was not constant, six was certainly a common number, and this appeared to be rarely exceeded; the angular points of the polygons were a little blunted, so that the sides were slightly curved. The angles were thus difficult to estimate, and I had no instrument, but I do not think that they were constant. The ice broke very easily along the sides of these prisms, and never through or athwart one of them. The ice contained a few air-bubbles and a chance bit of weed or bark here and there, but was in no other way remarkable. We carried a large piece of this last described to my rooms; and after hastily improvising a freezing bath of snow and salt, subjected some fragments of it to a temperature of about $-5°$ Cent. (for a short time the thermometer sank $3°$ or $4°$ lower, but this was the general temperature). After leaving it here for some time we examined it carefully; the prismatic structure was entirely obliterated, the only traces of it being the slight surface depressions here and there which marked the edges of the prisms, and certain vertical chains of small air-bubbles which had formed in the interstices at their angles. The ice was very hard, and, when broken, exhibited the usual conchoidal fracture. I was anxious to see whether the prismatic structure would return as the ice thawed again, but unfortunately the fragment laid aside for this purpose got in contact with some of the melted salt and snow of the bath, and was dissolved too rapidly."

The following table shews the temperature in the neighbourhood during the days of thaw preceding Jan. 26.

	Jan. 22.	Jan. 23.	Jan. 24.	Jan. 25.	Jan. 26.
At 9 A.M.	28·2	44·5	15·5	46	40
During past 24 h.					
maximum	30	44	53	55	50
minimum	26	22	43·5	42	34

CHAPTER V. p. 157.

Perhaps I should here have added something about the effects of the rarefaction of the air—but after some consideration I omitted it from the text. The reason is that I am inclined to consider these effects generally due far more to fatigue than to any change in the air. It is true I have never been on the summit of Mont Blanc, which appears to be most favourable to these symptoms—difficulty in breathing, excessive exhaustion, bleeding at the nose, vomiting, &c.—for I was driven back from the Mur de la Côte by a gale, but I have twice reached the summit of Monte Rosa, and been many times on other high peaks and passes, without being conscious of any inconvenience on them. I could eat, drink, walk, talk, smoke, and even sleep, as comfortably as down below. I have only twice felt the symptoms usually assigned to 'rarefaction of the air;' each time at an elevation of from eight to nine thousand feet. On one of these I had been living on insufficient food for nine days before, and for five of the nights had lain on hay or on the ground—so that I was suffering from a disordered liver and diarrhœa. On the other I was walking on a warm close morning, just after breakfast, up the slopes above the Riffel Hotel, and entered a cloud. The immediate effect was to make me gasp for breath, as usually described, and my two companions were affected in the same way. At the same time I have occasionally seen persons singularly affected on high mountains, and as the barometer stands at about 16 inches on Mont Blanc and 30 at the sea level, one would expect this great difference to be felt. Still I do not think it very easy to separate the inconveniences due to atmosphere from those caused by unwonted fatigue, and am inclined to attribute most of them to the latter. Inexperienced travellers often do not consider that it is a severe labour to lift the weight of their bodies through seven or eight thousand feet vertical—and walk too fast at first; or eat and drink too much—and so get easily 'blown.'

One kind of mountain sickness is peculiar and common; though I have rarely seen it noticed; but this always attacks people going down a mountain. The symptoms are, severe headache and sense of tension in the forehead, followed by pain in the stomach, and concluded by violent sickness. It generally comes on after a rapid descent from a high peak to the upper part of a glacier on a hot afternoon, and I think is chiefly due to the sudden change of temperature, and the glare of the sun reflected from the snow-fields. When once the sufferer has reached the more shady parts, the attack passes away, leaving no more ill effects than a short fit of sea-sickness; and after an hour or two's walk in the cool of the evening, he arrives at his journey's end as well as ever.

CHAPTERS VI. AND VII.

In Mr Morell's *Scientific Guide to Switzerland*, the number of the mammals of that country is given at 56, including domestic animals. The birds at 311. Many of these, however, belong to the lowlands, or only occur very rarely. The reptiles are given at 34: among which is included the curious *Proteus anguinus*, found in the limestone caverns of the Eastern Alps at Adelsberg, &c. The fishes at 42. To these also the same remark applies.

CHAPTER VIII.

The divisions which I have adopted, have caused me to mention some coniferous trees (as the *P. pumilio*), under the head of brushwood, instead of in their proper place.

It is difficult to find a complete work on the Alpine flora. The chief authority for the Swiss and the Eastern Alps is Koch's *Synopsis Floræ Germaniæ et Helvetiæ*. There is also for the Italian Alps, Bertoloni's *Flora Italica*. I do not know any special book on the French Alps. Wood's *Tourist's Flora*, is too concise to be of use to any but skilled botanists. A very pretty, and useful book to the non-scientific tourist—I do not feel qualified to say more—is Weber's *Die Alpen Pflanzen Deutschlands und der Schweiz*. 3 vols. (Munich).

One interesting point connected with the distribution of plants in the Alps may be noticed, namely, the occurrence, in exceptionally warm localities on the northern side of the Alps, of plants which are usually found at a much lower level, and that on the southern side. This is especially the case on the hot slopes of the Rhone valley, and again in the neighbourhood of Zermatt. These isolated colonies remind us of the occurrence of tropical and semi-tropical birds and plants in the Jordan valley and the basin of the Dead Sea, as well as of the boreal forms clustering around the summits of Hermon and Lebanon. Tristram, *The Land of Israel*. Ch. xxv. I believe that the more the Alps are studied, the more they will be found to shew that continuity of change, not catastrophe, has been the law which has governed the earth.

CHAPTER IX.

(P. 239). I might have added that the scarcity of fuel in some parts of the Alps compels the peasants to use dried cow-dung for fuel. It is done especially in the villages on the treeless slopes above La Grave (Dauphiné). The Bedawin use dry camels' dung for the same purpose.

CHAPTER X.

Brockedon's work, *Illustrations of the Passes of the Alps*, contains much information about the Alpine Passes; but the numerous engravings are far from satisfactory.

(P. 265). The latest works on the subject are :—For the Little St Bernard, *The Alps of Hannibal*, by W. J. Law; for the Little Mont Cenis, *A Treatise on Hannibal's Passage of the Alps*, by R. Ellis, and *On the Ancient Routes between Italy and Gaul*, by the same author.

In the *Alpine Guide*, Western Alps, § 7, Route C, will be found a summary (drawn up by myself) of Mr Ellis's arguments in favour of the latter pass. No doubt there are some difficulties in his theory, but none of them, I think, are insuperable; whereas, if we put any confidence in the topographical knowledge of Polybius,—and both disputants appear to agree in appealing to him,—there are two difficulties in the Little St Bernard theory which seem to me, after examining the ground, fatal to it. These are: the absence of a place from which Hannibal could point out any view, which would encourage his faltering soldiers. From the upper part of the Little St Bernard you see in front the crags and glaciers of the Mont Blanc range, apparently blocking the way; and behind, the comparatively smiling Isère valley. Everything suggests the idea of 'back' instead of 'forward.' The other difficulty is that of finding the locality of the dangerous slope described by Polybius. The gorge of La Thuile, where Mr Law places it, is not only rather too far down, but there also, unless we suppose the climate much altered, snow could not have remained a whole summer high up on the steep sides. The arguments

APPENDIX.

advanced only prove that it might have lain at the *bottom* of the gorge; where it would have helped Hannibal instead of hindering him. I uphold the Little Mont Cenis theory, not because I think it unquestionable, but because it seems much less open to objection than any other. The conclusion, which I came to after examining the Little St Bernard very carefully, was, that by whatever pass Hannibal might have gone, he could not have crossed this one; if at least any faith is to be put in Polybius.

CHAPTER XI.

(P. 303). The authorities which I have followed are:—*The Israel of the Alps*, translated from the French of Dr Alexis Muston. *Narrative of an Excursion to the Mountains of Piedmont*, by Dr W. S. Gilly. *The Waldenses*, by Dr Beattie.

It may be interesting to mention that the five volumes from the collection of Waldensian MSS., presented by Sir S. Morland to the University of Cambridge, which were for a long time missing, and were supposed to have been stolen from the Library shelves, were found in 1862 by H. Bradshaw, Esq. M.A.,—at the present time Librarian—during a minute investigation of the manuscripts belonging to the University. The books had been misplaced, and then wrongly described in a catalogue, made at a time when their value was not appreciated. One of the most interesting results of this discovery is that the date of the *Nobla Leyçon* is not, as it has been generally represented, the eleventh century, but the fifteenth (probably the early part); copyists not having observed an erased figure 4 in the text. See a paper by Mr Bradshaw in the *Report of the Cambridge Antiquarian Society*, Vol. II. p. 203.

(P. 309). The account of the struggle with Austria is founded on *The History of Switzerland*, by A. Vieusseux (Library of Useful Knowledge).

(P. 312). The remainder of the Chapter is mainly on the authority of *The History of Europe*, by Sir A. Alison. I have, however, endeavoured to correct his topography where it is vague: the reader of his work must also commonly substitute the words 'frozen snow' or 'ice' for 'glacier,' since he uses this term very loosely.

APPENDIX.

The following Table of the Altitudes of the Passes, mentioned in the text as crossed by the contending forces, may be interesting:—

Surenen	7578 feet.
Susten	7440 ,,
Kreuzli	7710 ,,
Simplon	6628 ,,
Grimsel	7108 ,,
Furka	7992 ,,
Nufenen	8009 ,,
Luckmanier	6289 ,,
St Gothard	6936 ,,
Oberalp	6732 ,,
Kinzig Kulm	6791 ,,
Pragel	5203 ,,
Panixer	7967 ,,

INDEX.

A.

AAR, R., effects of, on Lake Brienz, 46; geological features of the Valley of, 30; the fall of, 54

Abbaye des Vignerons, the vintage festival of, 296

Acronius Lacus, v. Constance, Lake of

Adamello, the, position of, 33

Aigle, marble quarry near, 112

Aiguille Verte, height and position of, 25

Ailefroide, the, shape of the peak of, 19

Air, rarefaction of, effects of, 336

Aix-les-Bains, the tepid springs at, 107

Albula pass, 268

Alder, the dwarf, 214

Allevard, the mineral springs of, 106

Alp, an, meaning of, 236

Alpenstock, the best kind of, 323

Alpine Regions, the: their physical and geographical importance, 2; general configuration of, 3; signs of upheaval in, 4; effects of denudation in, 6; action of glaciers upon, 7; sketch of the scenery in the principal districts of, 21; the waterfalls in, 53; the glacières or ice-caves, 85; caverns, 100; subterranean and salt springs, 104; mines, 111; quarries, 112; avalanches, 113; berg-falls or éboulements, 126; floods, 134; storms, 135; earthquakes, 137; the tourmente, 138; the winds Föhn and Bise, 142; colours of the snow, 146, and sky, 150; the quadrupeds remaining in, 160; birds, 190; fish, 197; reptiles, 198; numbers of the vertebrate and invertebrate animals, 201; the mollusca, 202; lepidoptera, ib.; sphyngidæ, 204; the insects, 205; botany of, 208; the trees, 209; brushwood, 214; flowers, 219; cryptogamia, 222; cereals and vegetables, 228; the harvest, 229; cultivation of the vine, 231; manufacture of wines, ib.; the forests, 233; the bread, 237; cottages, houses, and domestic architecture, 239—242; cattle and cowherds, 250; cheese-making, 253; pastoral songs, 254; sheep and shepherds, 255; goats, 258; the various passes, 261; by-ways and bridle-paths, 277; numerous legends of, 285; historical legends, 288; belief in witchcraft in, 292; peculiar local customs of, 293; favourite amusements, 295; pre-historic antiquities and lake settlements, 297; Roman and mediæval architecture, 299; the principal historical events of, 303; hints to tourists in, 320; the chief dangers of travelling in, 324; precautions to be taken, 326; good derived from Alpine climbing, 327; notes on the geology of, 329; works on the flora of, 337

Alps, the, vague notions regarding, 3; the three divisions of, *ib.*; scenery of the various ranges of, 21; convenient divisions of, for tourists, 320

Altdorf, the scene of the story of Tell, 309

Ammergau, the mystery play at, 296

Amusements, favourite, in the Alpine regions, 295

Anderieux, ancient custom at, 296

Ankogel, the, position and height of, 34

Annecy, lake of, 41

Antelao, Monte, landslip from, 132

Antiquities of the Alps, 297

Aosta, Roman remains at, 301

Appenzell, caverns at, 101

Architecture, domestic, of the Alpine regions, 242; Roman and Mediæval, 299—302

Argentière, curious funeral custom at, 294

Arlenbach and Aar, the, fall of, 54

Arnaud, Henri, leader of the Vaudois, 306

Arolla, or Arve fir, 213

Arve, R., earthy matter in, 8; its effect on the Lake of Geneva, 41

Atter See, the, 49

Auf der Platte, granitic rocks of, 12; situation of, 67

Auronzo, silver mine at, 111

Avalanche, the three classes of, 113; causes of, and accidents from, ice avalanches, 114; dust avalanches, 116; ground avalanches, 117; records of those most destructive, 124; farce of their being caused by talking, &c., 125

B.

Bad Gastein, baths of, 111

Badger, the, 170

Bâle, earthquake at, 137

Bear, the, of the Alps, rarity of, 160; its habits, 161; fierce encounter with, 162; its torpidity in winter, 163; numerous representations of, in Berne, 164

Beaume des Vaudois, the, 101

Beaver, the, rarity of, in the Alpine regions, 172

Bell-cow, the, use of, 253

Benacus Lacus, *v.* Gardo

Berg-falls, accounts of, 126; examples of, 127

Bernardino Caimo, originator of the Monte Sacro, 303

Bernardino Pass, 266

Berne, curious representations of the bear in, 164

Bernina, the, position and highest summit of, 32; the pass of 269

Bex, the salt mines and springs of, 105

Bezoar found in the Chamois, 180

Bienne or Biel, Lake of, 44

Birds of prey, Alpine, 190; various others, 195; game-birds, 196; water-birds and gulls, 197

Bise, the, an Alpine wind, 142

Blow-holes, *v.* Windlochs

Blumlis Alp, the, legend of, 299

Boar, the wild, 189

Bodamicus Lacus, *v.* Constance

Boden See, *v.* Constance

Bormio, baths of, 111

Botany of the Alps, 208; best regions for studying it, 221

Botzen, porphyry bed in the neighbourhood of, 13, 32

Bouquetin, the, strict preservation of, 186; its appearance and habits, 187; legendary ideas of, 189

Bourget, Lake of, 41

Brags, baths of, 111

Bread in the mountain-villages, 237

Brenner Pass, the, 269; struggle of the Tyrolese at, 318

Brenta Alta, the, 33

Brides-les-Bains, tepid springs at, 107

Brienz, lake of, 46
Brigantinus lacus, v. Constance
Brushwood of the Alps, 214, 337
Buet, the, position of, 29
Buzzard, the, 193

C.

Cabane des Bergers, **two nights and day in a**, 246
Campaign, the, of 1799, in Switzerland, 312—316
Campaniles, the, of Lombardy, 302
Carè Alto, the, 33
Carnic Alps, the, 35
Carts of Switzerland, 276
Cat, the wild, 169
Cattle, procession of, to **the mountains**, 250; **various kinds of, in the Alps**, 252; **management of, at the châlets**, *ib.*; use of the bell-cow, 254
Caverns in the Alpine regions, 100
Celtic Antiquities of **the** Alps, 297
Cereals, Alpine, 228
Ceresole, mineral springs of, 107
Châlet, the, two kinds of, 243; interior of, described, 244; strange bedfellows **met with at**, 245; cowherds' **life at**, 250; management of cows at, **252**; **to be avoided by the tourist**, 324
Chamois, the, the animal most identified with the Alps, 175; its gradual disappearance, 176; appearance and habits of, 177; the horns, 179; food, 180; difficulty of approaching it, 181; dangers and toils of the hunters of, 181
Chamouni, storm in the Valley of, 145
Chappet-sur-Villaz, glacière de, description of, 97
Charcoal, manufacture of, 233
Charlemagne, the serpent stone given him at Zurich, 291
Charpentier's theory of glacier motion, 74
Chaudière d'Enfer, the, 100

Cheese, process of making, and various kinds of, 253
Children, instances of their being carried off by vultures, 192
Chough, the, two varieties of, 194
Cirques, the, in Alpine valleys, **39**
Clariden Alps, the, legend of, **289**
Cogne, iron mines at, 112
Coire, the cathedral of, 300
Col des Echelles de Planpinet, 261
Col de St Théodule, 277
Col du Géant, the accident on, 120
Combe de Gavet, the, disastrous flood in, 134
Como, lake of, 49, 51
Companion, choice of a, **for an Alpine tour**, 321
Coniferous trees, 210, 337
Constance, lake of, **45**
Cortina, landslip at, 133
Cotoneaster, the, 214
Cottages of the Alps, 239; **their picturesqueness in the Oberland**, 240
Cottian Alps, the, **scenery of**, 21; **the** waterfalls of, 54
Courmayeur, mineral springs at, 107
Courtship, curious customs of, 293
Cowherds, **their life and duties at the** châlets, 250
Creux de Champs, the cirque of, an example of a limestone precipice, 20
Crevasses, the formation of, 58; difference of, in the upper part of a glacier, 72
Croda Malcora, the, limestone precipice of, 20
Crosses and crucifixes, road-side, in Roman Catholic districts, 294
Cryptogamic plants, Alpine, 222
Customs, local, of the Alpine regions, 293

D.

Dangers of Alpine travelling, 324; precautions against, 326

Danube, the, fed from the Alps, 2
Dauphiné, singular forms of the gneiss rocks of, 18; scenery of the high Alps of, 22; description of the valleys of, 37; the waterfalls, 54; mineral springs in, 106; curious customs in, 293, 294; Roman and mediæval architecture in, 299
Deer, red and fallow, 189
Dent Blanche, the, 27
Dent d'Hérens, the, 27
Dent du Midi, the, 29; berg-fall from, 134
Denudation, effects of, 6; its action in the Alpine valleys, 37
Derborence, lakes of, their origin from a berg-fall, 128
Diablerets, the, 29; destruction caused by berg-falls from, 127
Diet, for the tourist, 324
Dilatation theory of glacier motion, 74
Dogs, sensitive of an impending avalanche, 124; the breed of St Bernard, 260
Dolomite, effects of weather on, 18; grandeur of scenery caused by deposits of, 34
Dom, the, height and position of, 28
Dragons in the Alps, legends of, 286
Dragon-stone, the, at Lucerne, 289
Dranse Valley, the, inundation of, 134
Drunkenness, rarity of, in the Alps, 295
Dust avalanches, accounts of, 116

E.

Eagle, the Golden, 192
Earthquakes in the Alpine regions, 137
Eboulement, v. Berg-fall
Eburodunensis lacus, v. Neuchâtel
Ecclesiastical architecture in Dauphiné, &c., 299
Eiger, the, 30
Enfer, glacière de l', description of, 95

Epidemic insanity at Morzine, 292
Erratic blocks, signs of ice action, 79; examples of, near Monthey, 79; on the slopes of the Jura, 80

F.

Falcon, the, 193
Fariolo, granite quarries of, 112
Faulberg grotto, the, 101
Faust, Walter, the Swiss patriot, 309, 310
Fedaia pass, the, perforation in the cliff of, 103
Fées, Grotte aux, 100, 101; Temple des, 100
Fer à Cheval, the cirque of, example of a limestone precipice, 20
Ferns in the Alpine regions, 223
Feuds of the Chamois hunters, 183; of the keepers and poachers, 185
Finster Aarhorn, the, 29
Firs, the spruce, 211; silver, 213; Scotch, ib.; arolla or arve, ib.
Fish in the Alpine regions, 197; price of, in the fourteenth century, 198
Fleas and glacier fleas, 206
Floods, accounts of, 134
Flowers of the Alps, beauty and profusion of, 219; various kinds of, 220; highest levels at which they flourish, 222; works on the, 337
Föhn, the, effects of, 142
Forbes' theory of glacier motion, 75
Forests, Alpine, use and value of, 233; laws respecting, ib.
Fortresses defending the Alpine passes, 300
Fox, the, 167
Frescoes in the Italian Alps, 302
Frogs and toads, 198
Fruit-bearing shrubs, 218
Fuel, scarcity of, 338
Funerals, curious customs at, 294
Furka pass, 270
Furniture of an Alpine cottage, 239

INDEX. 345

G.

Garda, Lago di, 52
Gaudenzio Ferrari, the artist, 302
Geiselstein, the, perforation in the cliff of, 103
Gemmi pass, the south face of, a limestone precipice, 20
Geneva, lake of, 41
Gentians of the Alps, 222
Geology of the Alps, 329
Gessler, Hermann, his connexion with the story of Tell, 309
Giessbach waterfall, the, 54
Glacières or ice-caves, 88; visit to the Grand Anu, 91; to L'Enfer, 95; to Chappet-sur-Villaz, 97; probable cause of them, 99
Glaciers, their erosive power over-estimated, 7; nature and formation of, 70; structure of the ice of, 63; theories regarding their motion, 74; their previous extension marked by moraines, 77; by erratic blocks, 79; by rounded and striated rocks, 81; theories of their action in the formation of valleys and lakes, 84; epoch of their greatest extension, 85; modern changes in their extent, 86; the hyperbolic dirt-bands and white-ice seams in, 334
Glacier fleas, 206
Glacier tables, cause of their formation, 61
Glacier, the Gorner, account of an expedition to, 55
Glissade, descent by a, 73
Goats, numbers of, in Switzerland, 258; the three classes of, 259
Gorner glacier, the, account of an expedition to, 55
Graian Alps, the, scenery of, 23; the mineral springs in, 107
Grand Anu, a visit to the ice-cave of, 91
Grand Paradis, the, height of, 23
Grande Casse, the, height of, 23
Grande Combin, the, height, &c. of, 27
Grande Jorasses, the, shape of the peak of, 19
Granite, distribution of, 11; its influence on scenery, 12; form of summits composed of, 18; the quarries of, at Fariolo, 112
Gravel, beds of, washed down from the Alps, 8
Gressoney, tradition at, 290
Grimsel Hospice, avalanches at, 125
Grindelwald, scenery of the valley of, 30
Grivola, the, shape of summit of, 19; the height of, 23
Gross Glockner, the position and height of, 34
Grotte aux Fées, 100, 101
Ground avalanches, accounts of, 117
Guilestre (Dauphiné), marble quarry near, 112

H.

Hannibal's passage, supposed scenes of, 265; various theories of, 338
Hare, the, two species of, 172
Harvest in the Alpine regions, 229
Haut-de-Cry, fatal avalanche on, 122
Hawk, the, 193
Heiligenblut, the story of, 291
Heiterloch, the, 103
Herdsmen, their duties at the châlets, 251
Hills, action of water upon, 7
Hints for the Alpine tourist, 321
Historical events, the principal, in the Alpine regions, 303
Historical legends of the Alps, 290
Hofer, the fate of, 319
Hollenstein-thal, the pass through, 274
Holly-fern, abundance of, in the higher Alps, 223
Horns, the, of the chamois, 179; of the bouquetin, 187

Horses, sensitive of an approaching avalanche, 124
Houses, construction and appearance of, in the northern Alpine regions, 241; on the southern slopes, 302

I.

Ice, its agency in the sculpture of the Alps, 7; structure of, in glaciers, 63; marks of, on rocks, 77, 82; prismatic structure of, 94, 334
Ice avalanches, accounts of, 114
Ice caverns at the termination of glaciers, 56
Ice caves, v. Glacières
Insects of the Alpine regions, 205
Invertebrata in the Alpine regions, numbers of, 201
Iseo, lago d', 52
Italian Tyrol, the, scenery of, 34

J.

Julian Alps, the, 35
Julier pass, the, 268; pre-historic columns on, 297
Jungfrau, the: the north cliff a limestone precipice, 20; the position of, 30
Junipers of the Alps, 215
Jura, the, erratic blocks on the slopes of, 80; explanation of this, 81; the glacières in, 88; caverns in, 100

K.

Keepers and poachers in the Bavarian Alps, hatred between, 185
Kestrel, the, 193
Kite, the, 193
Knapsack, the, requisite contents of, 322

L.

La Balma, deposits of nickel at, 111
La Grave, silver mines at, 111; curious funeral custom at, 294
Lakes in the Alpine regions, 41; theories of their formation by glacier action, 84
Lake settlements, description of, 297
Lämmergeier, the, v. Vulture
Larch, the, 210
Larius lacus, v. Como
La Saxe, mineral springs at, 107
Lauterbrunnen, scenery of the valley of, 30
Lecco, lago di, 51
Legends current in the Alpine regions, 285
Léman, lac, v. Geneva
Lepidoptera, the, of the Alps, 202
Lepontine Alps, scenery of, 30
Le Prese, baths of, 111
Leuk, mineral springs of, 107
Leukerbad, destruction at, from an avalanche, 117
Levanna, the, peak of, 19
Lichens of the Alps, 225
Limestone, distribution of, 14; form of peaks of, 20; grandeur of precipices of, ib.
Lizards of the Alpine regions, 199
Locarno, storm and flood at, 136
Lombard Alps, scenery of, 33; the campaniles of the district, 302
Lucerne, lake of, 47; the dragon-stone in the museum of, 288
Lugano, lake of, 51
Lunatics, the, of Morzine, 293
Lynx, the, of the Alps, 169
Lys-joch, the, ascent of, 69
Lyskamm cliffs, the, 68

M.

Macdonald, General, sufferings of his

army from avalanches, 117, 318; his passage of the Splügen, 317
Maggiore, lago, 49, 50
Maloya pass, 267
Matterhorn, the, shape of summit, 19; position of, 27; cause of the fearful accident on, 325
Marmot, the, habits of, 172; its hybernation, 174
Martens, beech and pine, 171
Martinsloch, the, 103
Melchthal, Arnold von, the Swiss patriot, 309, 310
Mezzola, lago di, 51
Migiandone, deposits of nickel at, **111**
Mines in the Alpine regions, **111**; their effect on the forests near, 233
Mollusca, the, of the Alps, 202
Mönch, the, position of, 30
Mondloch, the, 100
Monêtier, the baths of, 106
Mont Blanc, geological formation of, **13**; form of summit, 20; scenery of the range of, 25; avalanches on, 119; storm in the corridor of, 141; thunderstorms on, **144**; sunset on, described by M. Necker, 152
Mont Cenis, pass and tunnel of, 262
Mont de Lans, Roman arch at, 299
Mont Iséran, deception respecting, 307
Mont Vélan, height and position of, 26
Monte della Disgrazia, position and height of, 32
Monte Rosa, peaks of, 20; position and height of, **27, 28**; tradition regarding, 290
Monte Sacro, the, at Varallo and Orta, 303
Monte Viso, shape of summit of, 19; height of peak, 21
Monthey, erratic blocks near, 79; explanation of this, 81
Moraines, the formation of, 57, 61; signs of the former presence of glaciers, 77; examples of, 78
Morat, lake of, 44

Morzine, epidemic insanity at, 292
Mosses of the Alps, 225
Moulins, **manner** of their formation, 62
Mountaineer, the, character of, 295
Mountains, causes affecting **the** forms of, 17; crystalline, 18; limestone, **20**
Mountain sickness, 336
Moutiers Tarentaise, salt-springs at, 105
Mower, the, of the Alps, 229
Mystery play, the, of Ammergau, 296

N.

Napoleon I., his passage of the St Bernard, **316**; his execution of Hofer, 319
Necker, M., his description of sunset on Mont Blanc, **152**
Neff Felix, the pastor of the Vaudois, 304
Neuchâtel, lake of, **43**
Noric chain, the, **33**
Notre Dame de Sex; chapel of, in a cavern, 101
Nutcracker, the, 195

O.

Oberalp Joch, the, 271
Oberland, the, scenery of, 28; picturesqueness of cottages in, 240
Oetztbaler Alps, the, 33
Ornavasso, marble quarry at, 112
Orta, lago d', 49; the Monte Sacro at, 303
Orteler group, the, scenery of, 33
Ossuaries, the, of Switzerland, 294
Otter, the, 171
Owls, various species of, 193

P.

Partridge, the Greek, or bartavelle, wide range of, 197
Passes in the Alpine regions, 261; table of the altitudes of, 340

348   INDEX.

Peasants of the Alps, their hard life and food, 237
Pedestrian's outfit for Alpine travelling, 322
Pennine Alps, the, scenery of, 24; account of a two days' journey in, 277—284
Perched blocks, signs of ice-action, 79; examples near Monthey, 79; on the Jura, 80
Perforations in the face of cliffs, instances of, 103; legends of St Martin connected with these, ib.
Pestarena, gold mines at, 111
Pfäfers, mineral springs and gorge of, 108
Phosphorescence of the snow, 149
Pic de Tenneverges, the, 29
Piedmont, the way-side crosses of, 294; the Campaniles of, 302
Pilatus, mont, legend of, 290
Pile buildings, the, of the lakes, 297
Pine, the dwarf, 214
Pinewood scenery in mountain districts, 211
Piz Mortaratsch, the, avalanches on, 121
Plants, note on the distribution of, in the Alpine regions, 337
Pleurs, destruction of, by a landslip, 131
Po, its source derived from the Alps, 2
Poachers and keepers in the Bavarian Alps, hatred between, 185
Pointe des Ecrins, the, shape of summit of, 19; height of, 22
Population, pre-historic, the, of the Alps, discoveries concerning, 297
Porphyry, bed of, in neighbourhood of Botzen, 13, 32
Portmanteau, its use in Alpine travelling, 322
Pourri, the, shape of summit of, 19; height of, 23
Precipices, grandeur of, in limestone districts, 20
Pré St Didier, mineral springs at, 107
Presanella, the, height and position of, 33

Primiero, silver mines at, 111
Ptarmigan, the, 195; its preference for cold and solitude, ib.
Puster-thal, the, road-side crosses in, 294

Q.

Quadrupeds, Alpine, 160

R.

Rabbit, the, rare in the Alps, 172
Randa, village of, fearful damage to, from avalanches, 115
Ranz des vaches, or pastoral tunes, 254
Rarefaction of air, effects of, 336
Raven, the, 193; anecdote of a tame one, ib.
Reichenbach, the, fall of, 54
Reptiles, Alpine, 198
Reschen-scheideck pass, 269
Rhætian Alps, scenery of, 31
Rhine, the, source of, in the Alps, 2; its effect on the lake of Constance, 45; falls of, 54
Rhododendrons of the Alps, 216; exquisite beauty of, 217
Rhone, the, source of, in the Alps, 2; its course in the lake of Geneva, 41
Riffelhorn, the, 77
Rivers fed from the Alpine regions, 2; their origin in glaciers, 56
Roads, bridle-paths and byways, 277
Roches moutonnées, occasioned by glaciers, 82
Rocks, classification of, 10; their distribution, 12; effects of erosive action on, 15; ice-marks on, 77, 82; striated, caused by glaciers, 82; singular perforations in, attributed to St Martin, 103
Roe, the, 189
Roman antiquities in the Alpine regions, 299, 301
Rossberg, the, fatal landslip from, 129
Ruäras, destruction at, from an avalanche, 117
Ruskin, Mr, on pinewood scenery, 211; on mosses and lichens, 225

INDEX. 349

S.

St Bernard, Great, the dogs of, 260; the convent of, 275; Napoleon's passage of, 316
St Bernard, Little, the carriage-road over, 264; pre-Roman antiquities on, 297
St Gothard pass, 266
St Martin, the giant, legends of, connected with the perforation of rocks, &c., 103, 291
St Maurice, historical legend of, 291; abbey church of, 301
St Michael, chapel of, in the cavern at Appenzell, 101
St Moritz, the baths of, 110
St Ours, the church of, 302
St Théodule, pass of, 277
St Vincent, mineral springs of, 107
Sta Catherina, baths of, 111
Sallenche, the, waterfall of, 54
Sandstones, distribution of, 14
Savoy Alps, the, scenery of, 23; lakes of, 41
Schaffhausen, the Rhine-fall near, 54
Scorpion, the, in the Italian Alps, 205
Season, the, for Alpine travelling, 320
Sempach, lake of, 44
Septimer pass, 268
Séracs, description of, 68
Sheep, Alpine, management of, 256; different varieties of, 257
Shepherds on the Alps, life of, 255, 257
Shreckhorn, the, shape of peak of, 19
Sickness in going down mountains, 336
Sieben Brunnen, the, 104
Simplon, the, pass of, 265
Skeletons, the practice of exhuming in Switzerland, 294
Sky, glorious colouring of, in the Alpine regions, 150
Slaty crystallines, distribution of, 13; effect of erosive action on, 15; the forms of crests of, 18

Snakes, Alpine, 201
Snow, its influence on the skin and eyes, 146; varied colours of, 147; its phosphorescence, 149; red snow and its cause, ib.; danger of, in Alpine travel, 326
Songs, pastoral, of the Alps, 254
Sphyngidæ, Alpine, 204
Splügen Pass, the, 266; General Macdonald's passage of, 317
Springs, subterranean and salt, 104
Spruce fir, the, 211
Squirrel, the, 177
Stachelberg, mineral springs of, 108
Staubbach, the, waterfall of, 54
Stauffacher, Werner, the Swiss patriot, 309, 310
Steinbock, v. Bouquetin
Stelvio Pass, 267, 271
Stoat, the, 171
Storms in the Alps, notices of, 135
Stubayer Alps, the, 34
Subterranean springs, 104
Sunset on Mont Blanc, 152
Suwarroff, his exploits in the campaign of 1799, 314—318
Swiss Alps, the, mineral springs in, 107
Switzerland, lakes of, 41; statistics of, 227; curious local customs of, 294; pre-historic antiquities of, 297; struggles for liberty in, 309—312

T.

Tannes de Corgeon, the, 100
Taschhorn, the, height and position of, 28
Tauern Group, the, scenery of, 34
Taurentunum, fall of the mountain of, 131
Tell, the story of, 309
Temple des Fées, the, 100
Terglou *massif*, the, its position and height, 35

Theban legion, the, site of the martyrdom of, 291
Thunderstorms among the mountains, 144
Thun, lake of, 46
Timber, laws respecting, 233; trade and statistics of, 234; modes of its conveyance, *ib.*; construction of slides for, 235
Toblach-plateau pass, 269
Tödi, the, position of, 30
Tosa, the, waterfall, 54
Tourists, Alpine, various hints to, 321
Tourmente, the, description of, 138
Trees in the Alpine regions, 209; heights and temperatures at which they flourish, 210
Trient, gorge of the, 38
Tyndall, Dr, on the veined structure of glacial ice, 66; results of his experiments on ice, 74, 75; on the colour of snow, 148, 159; on the hyperbolic dirtbands, &c. of glaciers, 334
Tyrol, the, (Austrian), mountains of, devoid of lakes, 49; (Italian) singular forms of the dolomitic rocks, 18; grandeur of the scenery of the dolomite districts, 34; scenery in the valleys of, 37; the waterfalls in, 54; curious courtship customs of, 294; ruined castles in, 300; picturesque streets in, 302; the insurrection of, under Hofer, 318

U.

Upheaval, signs of, in the Alpine regions, 4; probable cause of this, 10
Uriage, mineral springs at, 106
Uri, the bay of, its connexion with the story of Tell, 309

V.

Val d'Aoste, its richness in Roman remains, 301
Val de Blegno, the inundation of, 134

Valleys, Alpine, classification of, 3; questions as to their formation, 5; distinguishing features of, 36; valleys of depression and outcrop, 40, 334; theories of their formation by glacier action, 84
Varallo, the Monte Sacro at, 303
Vaudois, Beaume des, massacre of the Waldenses in, 101, *v.* **Waldenses**
Vegetables, Alpine, 228
Verbanus lacus, *v.* Maggiore
Vertebrate animals in the Alpine regions, numbers of, 201, 337
Vevay, inundation at, 136; the vintage festival of, 296
Vine, the, on the Alps, highest level of, 209; cultivation of, 231
Vintschgau, the, road-side crosses in, 294; ruined castles in, 300
Viscous theory of glacier motion, 75
Visp-thal, the, earthquake in, 137
Vulture, the bearded, or lämmergeier, 190; its habits, 191; instances of its carrying off children, 192

W.

Waldenses, or Vaudois, the, massacre of, in the Beaume des Vaudois, 101; the persecutions of, and their struggles for liberty, 303—306; their remarkable Alpine journey under Henri Arnaud, 306—309; MSS. relating to, in Cambridge University Library, 339
Walking, Alpine, advice upon, 323
Wallenstadt, lake of, 48
Water, denudation caused by the action of, 6
Waterfalls, Alpine, 53
Weisshorn, the, shape of the summit of, 19; position of, 27
Weisskogel, the, position and height of, 34
Wetterhorn, the, north cliff of, a limestone precipice, 20
Wild cat, the, 169

Wildhorn, the, 29
Wildstrubel, the, 29
Windlochs or Blow-holes, the cause and examples of, 102
Wines, manufacture of, 231
Witchcraft, belief in, among the Alps, 222
Wolf, the, in the Alps, habits of, 165
Wood, the use of, in the construction of houses, 240
Woodman, dangers of his occupation, 234

Worther See, the, 49

Z.

Ziller-thaler Alps, the, 34
Zmutt glacier, the, difficulties in crossing, 279
Zug, Canton, the churchyard crosses of, 294
Zug, lake **of, 44**
Zurich, lake of, 44

By the same Author.

Jerusalem Explored. Being a Description of the Ancient and Modern City. By Dr Ermete Pierotti. Translated and Edited by T. G. Bonney, M.A. 2 Vols. Imp. 4to. £5. 5s.

The Customs and Traditions of Palestine. Compared with the Bible from observations made during a residence of eight years. By Dr Ermete Pierotti. Translated and Edited by T. G. Bonney, M.A. 8vo. 9s.

Outline Sketches in the High Alps of Dauphiné. 4to. 16s.

Peaks and Valleys of the Alps; a descriptive text to Twenty-one Chromo-Lithographs from Drawings by Elijah Walton. Folio. £8. 8s.

Death and Life in Nations and Men; Four Sermons Preached before the University of Cambridge. 8vo. 3s. 6d.

www.ingramcontent.com/pod-product-compliance
Lightning Source LLC
Chambersburg PA
CBHW030402230426
43664CB00007BB/707